THE DO-IT-YOURSELF GUIDE TO INVESTMENT INFORMATION

WHERE TO FIND
WHAT YOU NEED TO KNOW

INCLUDING
NEWSLETTERS
RATING SERVICES
CHARTING SERVICES
AUTOMATED QUOTATIONS
BOOKS
PERIODICALS
AUDIOTAPES

SPENCER McGOWAN

PROBUS PUBLISHING COMPANY
Chicago, Illinois
Cambridge, England

CREDITS

Spencer D. McGowan
Editor

Dean McGowan
Technical Advisor

Ruth Bison
Publishing Consultant

Susan M. Batista
Production Manager

Laura Hooper
Research Coordinator

Cathy Harrison
Research Assistant

This publication is designed to provide accurate and authoritative information in regard to the subject matter covered. It is sold with the understanding that the publisher is not engaged in rendering legal, accounting or other professional service.

ISBN 1-55738-453-3

Printed in the United States of America

BB

2   3   4   5   6   7   8   9   0

TABLE OF CONTENTS

Introduction

Congratulations on selecting *The Do-It-Yourself Guide to Investment Information,* the most comprehensive guide to sources of financial information and advice.

This guide can literally save you hours of research and thousands of dollars in your search for the best possible sources of information and advice. Because investment decisions are usually made through a combination of information and advice, improved access to market data and recommendations means a corresponding improvement to investment performance. Over a lifetime, improved access to information can make a difference of millions of dollars to most investors.

As investors and brokers, we noticed several years ago that a search for quality information can be time consuming and frustrating. Individual and institutional investors need a quick reference guide to find out where to go for information. Too often good investment ideas are abandoned because the right information cannot easily be located.

This guide is a solution to the need for a comprehensive menu of investment information sources. Because the quality and presentation of the information used in investing is so important, the guide is formatted so sources of information relevant to each type of investment can easily be found by using the cross reference.

The cross reference is organized by investment topic:

Stocks	Mutual Funds
Bonds	Futures and Commodities
Options	Investment Planning

Each chapter represents a type of information source:

Newsletters and Chart Services	Brochures and Pamphlets on Investing
Computer and Quote Services	Magazines, Newspapers, and Periodicals
Performance Rating Services	Financial Television Programs
Stock and Bond Research Services	Books and Tapes on Investing
Brokerage Research Publications	General Reference

By using the cross reference and referring to the chapters that provide the type of data source wanted, an investor can quickly find the relevant sources of information and advice.

For example, if an investor is searching for information on bonds, specifically mortgage-backed securities, the bond section of the cross reference includes all relevant entries listed by chapter. Each entry provides the name and address of the publication or source, a brief description of information provided, and approximate pricing information.

This guide has attempted to verify that each entry is accurate and legitimate. However, the complete accuracy and reliability of the individual publications listed, of course, cannot be guaranteed.

For computer use, this guide provides a feast of listings for information sources, specially designed software packages, chart services, and on-line quote/retrieval services.

Portfolio managers will be excited to see that almost all major newsletters are listed and that the major brokerage research pieces are described with some detail.

Individual investors will enjoy the chapter listing brochures and pamphlets on investing, many of them available at no charge through brokerage houses.

All investors will enjoy the expansive listings of current books, newsletters, and periodicals that focus on investing and market information.

The *Do-It-Yourself Guide to Investment Information* offers a unique reference tool. We hope you find this guide indispensable in improving your knowledge of the markets and, of course, increasing the performance of your portfolio.

Comments and suggestions are encouraged.

How to Use This Guide

This guide is designed to provide a reader with almost all potential sources of information on a given investment topic. The sections are organized by type of information source:

Newsletters and Chart Services
Computer and Quote Services
Performance Rating Services
Stock and Bond Research Services
Brokerage Research Publications
Brochures and Pamphlets on Investing
Magazines, Newspapers, and Periodicals
Financial Television Programs
Books and Tapes on Investing
General Reference

The Cross Reference chapter lists all sources of information for a given investment topic:

Stocks
Bonds
Options
Mutual Funds
Futures and Commodities
Investment Planning

For example, a reader seeking to find information on government bonds can find a list of all sources of information by turning to the cross reference section on bonds. The reader must then decide what source of information is to be used. If the reader is seeking a book on government bonds, all books on bonds are listed alphabetically by title. The reader will find approximately two pages of books on bonds. After reviewing the list, if *The Complete Bond Book* is selected as a potential source, its page number is listed to the side. Turning to the entry for *The Complete Bond Book* a brief description of the book along with cost and ordering information can be found.

If the reader is searching for a free guide to investing in government bonds, the bond section of the cross reference lists Brochures and Pamphlets on Investing that focus on bonds, the page number for each entry is listed, and on that page the reader will find how to order that brochure or pamphlet for its publisher along with a brief description of the contents. All potential sources of information for a given investment topic are listed by type of source in the cross reference.

If an investor is seeking to improve a computer system and wants to focus on trading stocks, the cross reference section on stocks has a breakdown of over 100 computer software and on-line quote systems that focus on stocks. Furthermore, time and money are saved because each entry has a brief description of the service with pricing information. Each potential service can be easily called for further information without wasting time on computer services that do not relate to stocks.

Finally, this guide can be used as a starting place for improved access to information on any investment category simply because almost every major information source is contained in one easy-to-use book. By starting with the chapter listing the source of information, or the cross reference of an investment subject, new ways to improve investment information and performance can easily be found.

Newsletters and Chart Services

Selecting a newsletter or chart service is time consuming. We have attempted to include all newsletters and chart services available in the United States, and therefore can save investors hours of research and days of waiting for information in the mail. This chapter is organized alphabetically. The cost of subscription and first issue date are listed along with a brief description of the publication.

Obviously, we do not recommend the listed publications or guarantee the accuracy of the information and advice included in the publications listed. If you are selecting a source of investing or trading advice, it is best to test the advice on paper before committing your own money to someone else's opinions.

Research of existing newsletters revealed that some have been published successfully for decades and at the other end of experience others were established by a sole proprietor less than a year ago. Most newsletters will send you a complimentary sample of their work. Investors are wise to take advantage of sampling a newsletter before subscribing.

There are services that rank the performance of the advice given by different newsletters. These rating services are listed in the Performance Rating Services chapter. One of these listings could be the best place to start a selection process for a good newsletter.

In the cross reference section, all the publications are listed according to their specialties: Stocks, option, and futures traders should enjoy the ability to compare services without having to pour over daily advertisements to find new sources of information.

With the advent of toll numbers or "900" numbers that automatically bill a caller, a new investment advice industry has emerged. This chapter lists these services as "telephone newsletters." As with every new industry there have been a few less than reputable services enter the telephone investment advice field. Many listings are by subscription only and others charge by the call and minute. Most services are designed to provide frequently updated trading and investing recommendations. Obviously the advantage to using a recorded message is the speed with which new recommendations can be acted upon. A good service can provide timely advice and more successful investment results.

Investors are urged to use caution before implementing investment strategies using the advice of others. We do not recommend or guarantee the accuracy and advice of any service listed. However, for daily and more frequent sources of trading and investment recommendations, telephone newsletters can be an outstanding tool.

Each year many new newsletters are launched and many disappear. We have included a return page for suggestions and any publishers that have been inadvertently left out.

TABLE OF CONTENTS

1-900-HOT-WIRE

Dow Jones & Company, Inc.
P.O. Box 300
Princeton, NJ 08543-0300

PH: (900) HOTWIRE
Cost: $2.00 for the first minute, $1.00 thereafter
Started in 1990

TELEPHONE NEWSLETTER
Rumors, recommendations, buyouts, buybacks....the hottest news on companies experiencing unusual trading, from the Dow Jones Professional Investor Report.

AAII Journal

American Association of Individual Investors
625 N. Michigan Avenue
Chicago, IL 60611-3110

PH: (312) 280-0170
Cost: $45.00 (free to members of American Association of Individual Investors
Frequency: 10 times a year
Date of first issue: 1978

Covers: stocks, bonds, treasuries.
Provides a continuing stream of information on investment theory and practice. Includes practical explanations of investment mathematics, interviews with leading professional money managers, and examines their approaches to managing investments and warns of investment traps. AAII Quoteline is free to members to obtain real-time quotes on stocks, options, and mutual funds. You may make 2 calls per day—just pay normal long distance phone charges. Many other benefits available to members also.

Abbey Equity and Option Letter

Abbey Investment Group, Inc.
P.O. Box 412
Crete, IL 60417

PH: (900) 740-9300 for update line at $2.00 per minute.
Cost: $99.00 annually
Frequency: monthly

Includes: technical analysis. Covers: options.
Concise market analysis and predictions—contrarian by nature. Specific OEX and equity put & call recommendations, and portfolio to follow.

Abbey Option Trader - Update Line

Abbey Investment Group, Inc.
P.O. Box 412
Crete, IL 60417

PH: (900) 740-9300
(212) 416-2000
Cost: per minute $2.00
24 Hour service
Frequency of update: Sun-M-W-TH-or several times daily when they have a long position.

Covers: options.
Specific buy/sell recommendations for OEX and equity put and call options. Also market commentary and analysis.
COMMENTS: Newsletter available for $99.00 per year.

The Acquisition - Divestiture Weekly Report

Quality Services Company
5290 Overpass Road
Santa Barbara, CA 93111

PH: (805) 964-7841
Cost: $695.00 per year
Frequency: weekly
Date of first issue: 7/80

Includes: Technical analysis. Covers: stocks, chart tables, graphs. "Reports merger, acquisition, and divestiture activity, including in-depth analysis of major transactions. Publishes statistics on seller's and buyer's sales, profits, net worth, book value and earnings per share, and multiples of earnings, sales, and net worth compared with purchase price."

The Addison Report

Andrew L. Addison
P.O. Box 402
Franklin, MA 02038

PH: (508) 528-8678
Cost: $185.00 annually
Frequency: 17 issues every 3 wks
Date of first issue: 1980

Includes: technical and fundamental analysis. Covers: stocks, commodities, mutual funds, municipal, corporate, and government bonds. Stock, bond, and commodity market overview. 30-40 stock recommendations per issue. Mutual fund switch advice, conservative and speculative monitored lists and special quarterly reports focusing on technical analysis of the Dow Industrials and Dow Utilities, and various stock groups.

Adrian Day's Investment Analyst

Investment Consultants International,
1990 & Agora, Inc.
824 E. Baltimore Street
Baltimore, MD 21202

PH: (800) 787-0138 (301) 234-0515
Cost: $87.00 annually
Frequency: monthly
Date of first issue: 1981

Covers: stocks, mutual funds, bond(municipal, corporate, and government), and precious metals. Gives economic and market commentary and forecasts, along with specific recommendations, investment, and financial planning advice. Includes hotline.

Advisor Line

Investor Link

PH: (900) 446-1111 to bill calls to your phone; #(800) 395-4400 to bill calls to a major credit card
Cost: per minute 95 cents

Today's investment recommendations. Martin J. Pring, Pring's Market Review; Al Frank, The Prudent Speculator; Andy Addison, The Addison Report. example of what was covered on Feb 27th 1991.

AIC Investment Bulletin

AIC Investment Advisors, Inc.
7 North Street
Pittsfield, MA 01201

PH: (413) 499-1111
Cost: $48.00 per year
Frequency: semi-monthly
Date of first issue: 1963

Includes: Fundamental analysis. Covers: stocks, charts and graphs, bonds, precious metals. "Serves investors by covering current business conditions, gold, silver, and the Tax Reform Act. Also covers securities markets, South African socio-economic conditions, interest rates, bonds, and domestic common stocks. Analyzes industries and individual securities on an approved list, and discusses general economic conditions and special factors that influence security values.

AIQ Expert Signals to Go

AIQ
916 Southwood Blvd, Suite 2-C
P.O. Drawer 7530
Incline Village, Nevada 89450

PH: (900) 776-7600
Cost: per minute $2.50
24 Hour service
Frequency of update: daily M-F

Covers: stocks, market timing, and options. Phone for proven buy/sell signals for market timing, stocks, and options recommendations. Gives you access to the kind of unemotional, intelligent trading information that only the power of a computer can provide.

AIQ Fax Advisory

AIQ
916 Southwood Blvd, Suite 2-C
P.O. Drawer 7530
Incline Village, Nevada 89450

PH: (800) 332-2999
Cost: $175.00 per month
Frequency of update: daily M-F

Covers: stocks, market timing, and options. Receive complete advisory via fax by 11 PM Eastern Time. Expert computer systems generate market timing information, stock & option buy/sell recommendations and "Best of Signals Stock Portfolio."

American Abroad

AMAB
PF249 A-9500
Villach, Austria

PH: 43-4254-3985
FAX: 43-4254-3985
Cost: $195.00
Frequency: 12-18 times per year

Includes: Fundamental analysis. Covers: European stocks and mutual funds. "Investment advice for Americans working and investing abroad. European stock market review and forecast." Includes a model portfolio and recommendations.

America's Fastest Growing Companies

Financial Data Systems, Inc.,
Jonathan Steinberg-Editor
38 East 29th Street
New York, NY 10016

PH: (212) 689-2777
ORDERS (800) 346-8800
Cost: $245.00 annually
Frequency: monthly
Date of first issue: 1958

Includes: fundamental analysis. Covers: stocks.
The original growth stock investment survey. Features all relevant data and analysis for each company that are required for sensible common stock investing. Simple, easy format presented in a way a novice investor can understand.

Argus Research

Argus Research Corporation
17 Battery Place
New York, NY 10004

PH: (212) 425-7500
Cost: $390.00 annually
Frequency: weekly
Date of first issue: 1934

Includes: fundamental analysis. Covers: stocks.
Weekly staff report covering overview of market, individual company analysis and news updates.

Argus Viewpoint 91

Argus Research Corporation
17 Battery Place
New York, NY 10004

PH: (212) 425-7500
Cost: $390.00
Frequency: monthly
Date of first issue: 1934

Includes: fundamental analysis. Covers: stocks. "Defines Argus' investment policy and it's relationship to economic, political and market developments. The report discusses investment strategies for the stock and bond markets and also incorporates a tabular update of the stock recommendations in the Portfolio Selector."
Also includes a subscription to Portfolio Selector.

Asian Markets Monitor

240 Valley Drive
Brisbane, CA 94005

PH: (852) 832-8338 Hong Kong
FAX: (852) 572-2436 Hong Kong
Cost: $599.00 per year
Frequency: weekly
Date of first issue:

Covers: stocks and Asian markets and news.
Keeps you abreast of market developments with a stable of reporters and specialists "on the ground" in every rising Asian nation. Every issue includes inside market news and analysis, timely previews of government financial policies, the latest rumors driving the markets and their correspondents' unbiased weekly individual stock picks.

The Astute Investor

Charles E. Cardwell, Ph.D
Rt. 3 Box 310-D
Kingston, TN 37763

PH: (615) 376-2732
Cost: $30.00 annually
Frequency: monthly
Date of first issue: 1982

Covers: stocks. A monthly summary of 4-6 pages, plus reference lists of addresses and phone numbers of all the companies mentioned, discussions of investing philosophies and approaches, and reviews of other people's systems and writing on the subject. Includes 3 stock lists: stocks trading below book value, stocks trading at least 30% below net current assets (NCA) , and top 10 profitable companies whose stocks sell below (NCA) .

Babson United Investment Report

United & Babson Investment Advisors
101 Prescott Street
Wellesley Hills, MA 02181

PH: (617) 235-0900
FAX: (617) 235-9450
Cost: $215.00
Frequency: weekly
Date of first issue: 1916

Includes: fundamental analysis. Covers: stocks, municipal and corporate bonds, and market timing.
Ten page report including market commentary, forecasts of business, financial and economic conditions, and stock recommendations.

Baxter

William J. Baxter/Baxter World Economic Service
1300 E. Putnam Avenue
Greenwich, CT 06830

PH: (203) 637-4559
Cost: $175.00 annually
Frequency: monthly
Date of first issue: 1924

Includes: fundamental analysis.
Covers: stocks and treasuries.
Comprehensive review of significant business and economic developments, continuing study of monetary conditions, domestic and abroad, specific stock recommendations, special situations, continuous follow-up of all previous recommendations, regular analysis of U.S. Treasury securities and more.

The Bears Hotline

PH: (900) 230-ABCD
(914) 365-6074 of blocked from 900's
Cost: per minute $2.00
Frequency of update: every evening at 9PM

Covers: stocks, commodities, and bonds (municipal, corporate, government, foreign).
Comprehensive review of all negative rumors, dividend cuts, OTC shorts, underwritings & underwriters in trouble, puts & scalp shorts. Management long 5000 shares recommended position.
COMMENTS: traders speak very fast - difficult to take it all in - there is a menu at the beginning to tell you how to access the different categories.

Bert Dohmen's 900#

Wellington Financial Corporation
6600 Kalanianaole Highway #114C
Honolulu, HI 96825

PH: (900) 776-4400
(808) 396-2220
FAX: (900) 329-9355 - $5.00 per call
Cost: $2.00 per minute
24 Hour service
Frequency of update: daily

TELEPHONE NEWSLETTER
Phone and Fax service. Covers: stocks, mutual funds, futures. The latest fundamental and technical analysis of market conditions along with specific buy/sell recommendations.

Bi Research

Thomas C. Bishop, Editor
Bi Research, Inc.
P.O. Box 301
South Salem, NY 10590

PH: (203) 938-9170
Cost: $80.00 per year
Frequency: every 6 weeks
Date of first issue: 2/81

Covers: stocks, mutual funds. "Contains 5 - 8 in-depth investment recommendations per year, featuring common stocks judged likely to at least double over the next 1 - 3 years. Updates each open recommendation in detail approximately every 6 weeks."

The Blue Book of CBS Stock Reports

Marpep Publishing Limited
133 Richmond Street West
Suite 700
Toronto, Ontario M5H3M8

PH: (416) 869-1177
Cost: $279.00
Frequency: every two weeks
Date of first issue: 1941

Includes: fundamental analysis and technical analysis. Covers: Canadian stocks, charts. Statistical financial analysis on Canadian stocks. Provides buy, sell, hold recommendations as well as five year performance data and company description.

Blue Chip Barometer

P.O. Box 42023
Philadelphia, PA 19101

Cost: $195.00
Frequency: twice monthly

Includes: Technical analysis. Covers: stocks, market timing. "...uses a highly accurate econometric model to generate statistically reliable forecast of the Dow and 26 key industry groups over the next 6 months. Also pinpoints which stocks in each industry group should perform best over the next 6 months."

Board Watch

Thomas E. Aspray
P.O. Box 2141
Spokane, WA 99210-2141

PH: (509) 838-0434
Cost: $240.00 annually
 $440.00 annually with hotline
Frequency: semi-monthly
Date of first issue: 1986

Covers: commodities. Includes: technical analysis. Twelve page newsletter of unique technical analysis with charts of many CompuTrac derived technical indicators for most markets. Hotline includes specific recommendations.

Bob Brinker's Marketimer

Robert J. Brinker
P.O. Box 7005
Princeton, NJ 08543

PH: (908) 359-8838
Cost: $165.00 annually
Frequency: monthly

Covers: mutual funds, stocks, treasuries, gold, interest rates, and market timing. Designed to help you make the most of your investment potential. Includes: no-load mutual fund recommendation list, model portfolios, analysis of the Fed's monetary policy, business cycle, supply/demand & technical market condition, individual stock selections, interest rate and gold updates, asset allocation, U.S. Treasury note offering details.

Bob Nurock's Advisory

Bob Nurock
Box 988-B
Paoli, PA 19301

PH: (800) 227-8883
 (215) 296-2411
Cost: $247.00 annually
Frequency: every three weeks
Date of first issue: Early 80's

Includes: technical analysis. Covers: stocks, mutual funds, bonds and gold comments.
Includes thought provoking comments on the economy, rates, stocks, sectors/groups, funds, binds & gold. All with specific buy/sell ideas.
COMMENTS: Includes twice weekly hotline - update.

Bond Fund Survey

Survey Publications
P.O. Box 4180
Grand Central Station, NY 10163

PH: (212) 988 2498
Cost: $450.00 annually
Frequency: monthly
Date of first issue: 1981

Includes: fundamental analysis. Covers: bond funds and unit investment trusts. The most comprehensive and authoritative source of information on bond funds ever assembled. Includes fund vs fund performance report on over 300 funds, updated every month. Fund Reports on each fund continually with updated facts, performance charts, and tables. A complete directory shows each fund's strategy, address, toll-free #, investment advisor, portfolio manager, and more.

Bondweek

Institutional Investor Systems
488 Madison Avenue
New York, NY 10022

PH: (212) 303-3300
Cost: $1,150.00 annually
Frequency: weekly
Date of first issue 1975

Covers: corporate, government, and foreign bonds. Bondweek covers the major taxable debt markets — treasuries and foreign sovereigns, mortgages, and investment-grade and high-yield corporates. Its chief function is to provide institutional fixed-income investors with information about economic, regulatory, business, and market developments that could affect the performance of these securities, and to inform sell-side firms about the investment demands of buy-side institutions. It also keeps both sides of the market up to date on key personnel moves and new technological developments in the industry.

The Bowser Report

R. Max Bowser
Box 6278
Newport News, VA 23606

PH: (804) 877-5979
Cost: $48.00 annually
Frequency: monthly

Includes: fundamental analysis, covers: stocks. Ten page report specializes in analyzing stocks that sell for $3.00 per share or less. Each month they highlight a "Company of the Month" The Bowser Report follows its recommendations very closely.

Breakout Alert! & Trend Letter

Joel Rensink
P.O. Box 267
Balaton, MN 56115

PH: (507) 734-2052
Cost: $150.00
Frequency: monthly
Date of first issue:

Covers: commodities. Primarily focuses on the needs of the professional commodities trader. Gives recommendations with stop-losses.

Broadcast Investor

Paul Kagan Associates, Inc.
126 Clock Tower Place
Carmel, CA 93923-8734

PH: (408) 624-1536
FAX: (408) 625-3225
Cost: $625.00 annually
Frequency: monthly
Date of first issue: 1969

Includes: fundamental and technical analysis, and uses charts. Covers: investments in private radio, TV stations, and public broadcast companies. Newsletter on investments in private radio and TV stations plus public broadcast companies. Analysis of cash flow multiple, valuations of stations and companies.

Broadcast Investor Charts

Paul Kagan Associates, Inc.
126 Clock Tower Place
Carmel, CA 93923-8734

PH: (408) 624-1536
FAX: (408) 625-3225
Cost: $395.00 annually
Frequency: monthly
Date of first issue: 1983

Includes: technical analysis and charts. Covers: stocks. A monthly chart service showing stock price movements of 41 publicly held broadcast companies for the past two years.

BSMA: Bill Staton's Money Advisory

Bill Staton Enterprises
300 East Blvd. #B4
Charlotte, NC 28203

PH: (704) 335-0276
 (800) 345-0096
Cost: $87.00
Frequency: monthly
Date of first issue: 1985

Includes: fundamental analysis. Covers: stocks, mutual funds, municipal bonds, corporate bonds, and government bonds. "The smart guide for you and your money." A general financial newsletter. Covers investing, insurance matters and taxation and provides minimal recommendations.

The Bullish Consensus

Hadady Corporation
Earl Hadady
1111 S. Arroyo Parkway, Suite. 410
P.O. Box 90490
Pasadena CA 91109-0490

PH: (818) 441-3457
Cost: $395.00 with weekly hotline
 $695.00 with daily hotline
 Annually
Frequency: weekly
Date of first issue: 1964

Includes: sentiment analysis. Covers: commodities. The Bullish Consensus is a unique tool for trading stocks, bonds, mutual funds, indexes, foreign currencies, precious metals, options and futures based on the degree of bullish sentiment on a particular market. The newsletter gives you market commentary, recommendations, bullish consensus data, fundamental and open interest evaluation of 31 markets and a two-page supplement "Cogent Comments" from other sources.

The Bullish Consensus

Hadady Corp - Earl Hadady
1111 S. Arroyo Parkway, Suite 410
P.O. Box 90490
Pasadena, CA 91109-0490

PH: (900) 234-7777
(818) 441-3457
Cost: per minute $2.00
Frequency of update: daily Monday through Friday at
9:00 PM EST

Covers: commodities, stocks, interest rates, currencies,
and precious metals.
Includes: sentiment analysis.

A unique tool based on the degree of bullish sentiment
on a particular market. Daily 1 minute updates and
recommendations. Avoid paying for information you
don't need because each investment category has its
own extension to request. Newsletter in existence since
1964 - this is fairly new

The Burning Match

J.F. (Jim) Straw
301 Plymouth Drive N.E.
Dalton, GA 30721-9983

PH: (404) 259-6035
Cost: $48.00 per year
Frequency: monthly
Date of first issue:

Each issue explains in detail how to use The Burning
Match principle to make money. Gives inside information about the "hot" investment opportunities you should
buy and those to avoid and why. Learn how to quit being
a victim of unscrupulous brokers, promoters, research
advisors and phony investment opportunities.

The Cabot Market Letter

Carlton Lutts, editor
Cabot Heritage Corp. publisher
P.O. Box 3044
Salem, MA 01970

PH: (800)777-2658 (508) 745-5532
FAX: (508) 744-3109
Cost: $235.00
Frequency: bi-monthly
Date of first issue: 1970

Includes: technical analysis (sells) , and fundamental
analysis. Covers: stocks, market timing.
Follows growth stocks in America. Gives specific recommendations and model a portfolio. Buys based on
fundamental analysis primarily and sells are based on
technical analysis. The Cabot Market Letter looks closely
at stock selection and market timing. Cabot's model
portfolio on page 2 of each letter is made up of as many
as twelve (but never more than twelve) dynamic growth
stocks. They are selected and monitored by Cabot's
unique Momentum Analysis, which is based on relative
strength. It helps you buy stocks that are under intense
investor accumulation, with rapidly rising prices. Momentum Analysis also tells you when to sell a stock. On
page six of every letter is Growth and Income Portfolio
of solidly growing, dividend-paying stocks.

Cabot's Mutual Fund Navigator

Timothy Lutts - editor
Cabot Heritage Corp.
P.O. Box 3044
Salem MA 01970

PH: (800) 777-2658
Cost: $125.00 annually
Frequency: monthly
Date of first issue: 1987

Includes: fundamental and technical analysis. Covers: mutual funds and market timing.
This is a 3 portfolio newsletter with 3 different groups of funds. The three portfolios are: Growth Portfolio - this represents actual money invested in the very best no-load mutual funds; Growth & Income Portfolio - these funds pay regular dividend; Income Portfolio. There are five funds in each portfolio. They also provide a list of 100 funds which they feel are best.

California Technology Stock Letter

Michael Murphy
P.O. Box 308
Half Moon Bay, CA 94019

PH: (415)726-8495
Cost: $270.00 annually
Frequency: bi-weekly
Date of first issue: 1982

Includes: fundamental analysis. Covers: stocks.
Concentrates on the computer and electronics industries. Each letter contains specific stock recommendations. Subscriptions include a hotline service.

CDA Mutual Fund Charts

CDA Investment Technologies, Inc.
1355 Piccard Drive
Rockville, MD 20850

PH: (800) 232-2285
(301) 975-9600
FAX: (301) 590-1350
Cost: $260.00 annually
Frequency: quarterly

CHART SERVICE
Covers: mutual funds. A quarterly chart service that covers over 1500 funds. Each chart portrays the total return over a 10 year period based on a $1000 initial investment. The Chart Book contains 1, 5, & 10 year return as well as yields computed by the funds themselves. Acetate overlays allow the user to compare each fund with several popular market indices. Mailed 7 days after quartered.

The CFA Newsletter

Institute of Chartered Financial Analysts
P.O. Box 3668
Charlottesville, VA 22903

PH: (804) 977-6600
Cost: $25.00 per year
Frequency: 6 per year
Date of first issue: 11/64

Includes: Fundamental analysis. Covers: educational programs. "Offers articles about the ongoing activities and educational programs of the Institute. Recurring features include news of upcoming educational opportunities for members and the investment community, examination, information, and announcements of recent publications by the Institute.

Charles N. Chen, Ph.D. Math

PH: (900) 226-5430 or call
(818) 501-7307 from blocked numbers
Cost: $2.25 per minute
24 Hour service
Frequency of update: Three times daily

TELEPHONE NEWSLETTER
Covers: market forecast. Two time winner in the U. S.
Investing Championship - Options Division offers his
market forecast.

Chartcraft, Inc.

The publisher: Chartcraft, Inc.
30 Church Street
P.O. Box 2046
New Rochelle, NY 10801

PH: (914) 632-0422
FAX: (914) 632-0335
Cost: $360.00 annually
Frequency: monthly
Date of first issue: 1983

CHART SERVICE.
Includes: technical analysis. Covers: stocks. 50 technical indicator charts, 88 industry charts, 20 x 60, 10x30,
5x15, DJIA Technical Chart, 200 NYSE/ASE stocks
with top/bottom Relative Momentum, Fidelity Fund
Charts, Option Indexes, world markets, Technical Indicator Review, Introduction to Charting. Includes toll-
free hotline.

Chartcraft Hot Line

Chartcraft, Inc.
30 Church Street
P.O. Box 2046
New Rochelle, NY 10801

PH: (900) 990-0909 ext 31
(914) 632-0422
Cost: per minute $2.00
24 Hour service
Frequency of update: daily

Covers: stocks.
Technical figures are Wednesdays at 11AM, other days
there is a "Chart of the Day" featured at 11AM except
Mondays which is at 9AM.

Chartcraft O-T-C Point and Figure Chart Book

Chartcraft, Inc.
30 Church Street
P.O. Box 2046
New Rochelle, NY 10801

PH: (914) 632-0422
FAX: (914) 632-0335
Cost: $100.00 annually
Frequency: quarterly

CHART SERVICE
Includes: technical analysis. Covers: stocks and chart
service. More than 1350 OTC stocks, NASDAQ composite chart and introduction to P&F charting. Each
large grid chart is 2" x 3" with 9 charts to the page.

Chartcraft Technical Indicator Review

Chartcraft, Inc.
30 Church Street
P.O. Box 2046
New Rochelle, NY 10801

PH: (914) 632-0422
 (914) 632-0335
Cost: $90.00 per year
Frequency: Bi-weekly
Date of first issue: 1961

CHART SERVICE
Includes: Technical analysis. Covers: stocks, graphics. "Provides a concise review of the stock market. Each stock in the Dow Jones Industrial Averages is listed and marked bullish or bearish. Discusses industry group trends, relative strength, and bullish percentage."

Chartcraft Weekly Service

Chartcraft, Inc.
30 Church Street
P.O. Box 2046
New Rochelle, NY 10801

PH: (914) 632-0422
(914) 632-0335
Cost: $224.00 per year
Frequency: weekly
Date of first issue: 1949

Includes: Fundamental analysis. Covers: stocks, charts and graphs. "Offers recommendations to investors in New York and American Stock Exchange securities, including buy and sell signals and relative strength. Discusses industry groups and option indexes. Lists more than 1,400 stocks, and includes point and figure of each stock covered."

The Chartist

Dan Sullivan
P.O. Box 758
Seal Beach, CA 90740

PH: (213) 596-2385
(213) 493-5906
Cost: $150.00 annually
Frequency: twice a month
Date of first issue: 1969

Includes: technical analysis. Covers: stocks.
Stock advisory service, publishes an actual "Trader's Portfolio with current results and mental stop recommendations for more speculative traders and an "Actual Cash Account" which mirrors his own personal portfolio.

The Chartist Mutual Fund Timer

Dan Sullivan
P.O. Box 758
Seal Beach, CA 90740

PH: (213) 596-2385
(213) 493-5906
Cost: $100.00 annually
Frequency: monthly
Date of first issue: 1988

Includes: technical analysis. Covers: mutual funds and market timing. Publishes an "Actual Cash Account" which mirrors Dan Sullivan's own fund portfolio. Question and Answer section for subscribers. Includes Hotline - hotline includes daily updates of "actual cash account" recommendations.

The Cheap Investor

Bill Mathews
Mathews & Associates, Inc.
2549 W. Golf Road
Hoffman Estates, IL 60194

PH: (708) 830-5666
Cost: $87.00 annually
Frequency: monthly

Includes: fundamental analysis. Covers: stocks. Each issue includes 3 or 4 buy recommendations on quality, low-priced stocks along with updates on previous recommendations. The Cheap Investor searches for and finds small, quality stocks under $5.00 on the OTC, ASE, and NYSE and new issues with growth potential for a 50-100 % stock price move.

CIS Cattle Hotline

Commodity Information Systems, Inc.
P.O. Box 690652
Houston, TX 77269-0652

PH: (713) 890-2700
(800) 231-0477
(Credit card orders only)
Cost: $600.00 a year
Frequency of update: daily

TELEPHONE NEWSLETTER
Covers: cattle
A service designed specifically for the professional cattle trader that keeps you up-to-date with the latest trade information, statistics, and all other major aspects of the cattle market. It covers direct trade volume and prices, packer break-even levels, what the feedlot sources expect, closing beef prices, closing cutout values and boxed beef volume, special analysis of government reports the day of release, daily analysis of the market, both near and long-term, and more.

The Clean Yield

Clean Yield Publications Ltd.
P.O. Box 1880
Greensboro Bend, VT 05842

PH: (802) 533-7178
Cost: $85.00 annually
Frequency: monthly (11 issues)
Date of first issue: 3/1/85

Includes: fundamental and technical analysis. Covers: stocks and market timing. Specializes in socially responsible companies providing unhedged advice and recommendations on when and at what price to buy and sell their stocks.

CODA Smartline

Committee on Data Analysis, Inc.
100 Easy Street
Suite 6
Carefree, AZ 85377

PH: (800) 545-5751
(602) 488-1107
Cost: $290.00
Frequency: monthly
Date of first issue:

Includes: fundamental analysis. Covers: stocks and chart service. Large, easy to read charts on almost 600 stocks. Also includes a model portfolio, performance graphs, 18 different ranking tables from percentage change to relative strength data.

Commodex Daily Signals

Equidex, Inc.
7000 Blvd. East
Guttenberg, NJ 07093-4808

PH: (800) 336-1818
(201) 868-2600
Online through Data America (800)876-0045
Cost: $495.00 year
Frequency: daily immediately after the close
Date of first issue: 1959

Includes: technical analysis. Covers: commodities. The oldest and most consistently profitable daily futures trading system publication in the world. Each bulletin includes more than 45 commodity and financial futures with up to 100 contract months. Easy to use signal codes tell you exactly what to trade.

Commodex Daily Signals

Equidex, Inc.
7000 Blvd East
Guttenberg, NJ 07093-4808

PH: (900) 234-7777
Cost: per minute $2.00
24 Hour service
Frequency of update: twice daily

Covers: commodities.
Follow the commodity on financial futures contracts you need - up to 45 different futures with as many as 100 contract months. Your complete daily self management system.

Commodex Signals

Eqidex, Inc.
7000 Blvd. East
Guttenberg, NJ 07093-4808

PH: (800) 336-1818
(201) 868-2600
Cost: $1695.00 annually
Frequency of update: twice daily

FAX SERVICE
Covers: commodities.
Each bulletin includes more than 45 commodity and financial futures with up to 100 contract months. The easy to use signal codes tell you exactly what to trade. Special "Turbo-Fax" sends latest bulletin in less than two minutes.

Commodity Closeup

Glen Ring - Editor
Oster Communications Inc., - Publisher
219 Parkade
Cedar Falls, IA 50613

PH: (800) 221-4352 ext. 434
(319) 277-1271
Cost: $199.00 annually
Frequency: weekly
Date of first issue: 1978

Includes: technical analysis. Covers: commodities. Provides you with complete technical data, educational market information, and low risk profit recommendations in 27 of the most popular and widely traded markets.

Includes free hotline updated three times daily.

Commodity Futures Forecast

Equidex, Inc. - Philip Gotthelf
7000 Blvd. East
Guttenberg, NJ 07093-4808

PH: (800) 336-1818
(201) 868-2600
Cost: $350.00 annually
Frequency: weekly
Date of first issue: 1956

Includes: fundamental analysis, technical analysis used for timing. Provides complete trading details for carefully selected commodity, financial, and energy futures. Incorporates latest charts, weather-fax, government reports and confidential information Recommendations are clear, concise, and easy to use. Subscriber also receives periodic special reports providing fundamental and technical background data. Available via fax or mail. If you have Commodex you may also receive C.F.F. online through Data America.

Commodity Information Systems

Bill Gary
Commodity Information Systems, INc.
P.O. Box 690652
Houston, TX 77269-9974

PH: (800) 231-0477
(713) 890-2700
FAX: (713) 890-4938
Cost: $360.00 annually
Frequency: bi-monthly

Includes: fundamental analysis. Coveres: commodities Fundamental analysis of all major commodity and financial markets. Also includes special reports on outstanding developing trades, situation analysis of major economic changes, specific long-term trading strategies, graphics and commentary that make fundamental factors easy to understand and editorials on feature topics as they relate to commodity and financial markets.
Includes daily hotline.

Commodity Price Charts

Oster Communications
219 Parkade
Cedar Falls, IA 50613

PH: 800-221-4352 ext 750
FAX: (319) 277-7896
Price: $415.00 /year
Frequency: weekly
Date of first issue: 1975

CHART SERVICE
Includes: technical analysis. Covers: commodities. In addition to weekly charts, 6 times a year receive long term historical charts, 10 & 20 year charts. 49 commodities covered, 255 charts in each issue. Large charts - 14 1/2 x 22 3/4 give you up to fifteen months of price history on each major commodity - 49 commodities. Comments: shipped Friday with Friday's close for Monday delivery . $315 for new customers, may cancel at any time for refund.

Commodity Timing

Larry Williams
140 Marine View Drive #102T
Solana Beach, CA 92075

PH: (800) 800-8333
Cost: $200.00 annually
Frequency: annually
Date of first issue: 1969

Includes: technical analysis. Covers: commodities. You'll receive a monthly market letter following all trades and teaching you what Larry's learned about markets during the last 25 years. Plus you'll have free access to Williams during market hours for questions or comments. You'll also be given reports and analyses of other commodity products, services, software, etc. as they become available on the market. Includes daily hotline.

The Complete Strategist

Howard Young, Editor
Wall Street On-Line Publishing
P.O. Box 6
Riverdale, NY 10471

PH: (212) 884-5408
Cost: $50.00 per year
Frequency: monthly
Date of first issue: 1991

Includes: Fundamental and Technical analysis. Covers: stocks, futures and commodities, mutual funds, options, interest rates, precious metals, municipal bonds, corporate bonds, government bonds. "Monthly advisory newsletter. Predicts market direction. Illustrates and explains indicators. Includes Model Portfolio, with buy/sell range for stocks. Future portfolios will list mutual funds, bonds and futures."

Computerized Investing

American Association of Individual Investors
625 N. Michigan Avenue
Chicago, IL 60611-3110

PH: (312) 280-0170
Cost: $60.00 annually
($30.00 for members of American Association of Individual Investors)
Frequency: 6 times a year
Date of first Issue: 1978

Covers: computerized investing. Keeps investors abreast of the latest investment related computer developments. Includes comprehensive investment software reviews, news of developments in software and database services, as well as how-to-do-it articles on using computers to assist in investment analysis and valuation.

The Contrary Investor

Fraser Management Associates, Inc.
P.O. Box 494
309 S, Willard Street
Burlington, VT 05402

PH: (802) 658-0322
Cost: $95.00 annually
Frequency: 26 issues annually

Includes: fundamental analysis. Covers: stocks. "Ponders the stock market passing on brain work in the field of investment and speculation. Lists specific securities with contrary speculative possibilities most likely to succeed." Concentrates on value versus fashion, discovering unusual situations with superior profit potential. Investigates market areas away from the "mob-minded" investor. Market success based on contrary values. Comments: Follow-up letter available for $65.00 a year. Analysis and regular reports on all Contrary Investor selections until they are all closed out with a definite selling prices.

Corporate Financing Week

Institutional Investor Systems
488 Madison Avenue
New York, NY 10022

PH: (212) 303-3300
Cost: $1,150.00 annually
Frequency: weekly
Date of first issue 1975

Includes: fundamental analysis. Covers: stocks and bonds. The mission of CFW is to inform all finance officials at corporations on innovations, trends, and ways to save money on new debt and equity issues, private placements, mergers, and acquisitions, leveraged buyouts, venture capital, and tax and accounting issues. Also covers new regulations and legislation, political skirmishes between investment banks, and corporate finance personnel moves.

Crawford Perspectives

Arch Crawford
205 E. 78th Street
New York, NY 10021

PH: (212) 628-1156
Cost: $250.00 annually
Frequency: monthly
First issue 1977

Includes: technical analysis. Covers: market timing General stock market timing with astronomical cycles and technical analysis. Also includes short summary on gold and bond markets.

CTCR Commodity Traders Consumer Report

Bruce Babcock
1731 Howe Avenue, Suite 149
Sacramento, CA 95825

PH: (916) 677-7562 or
(800) 999-CTCR
FAX: (916) 672-0425
Cost: $168.00 annually
Frequency: every two weeks
Date of first issue: 4/83

Covers: commodities. Monitors major commodity trading advisory services - both their letters and hotline and summarizes the results of their recommendations. Designed to make you a smarter consumer and better trader in the exciting world of commodity trading.

The Cummings K.I.$.$.

Charles C. Cummings, Jr.
R. R. 6
Guelph, Ontario Canada N1H6J3

Cost: $69.00
Frequency: monthly
Date of first issue: 1988

Includes: Fundamental and technical analysis. Covers: stocks. Focused on "Profitable Preservation of Capital." Provides market commentary and forecasts, stock advisory and guest columns written by editors of other major newsletters.

Current Yield

Ostrander Asset Management
711 N. E. Windrose Ct.
Suite A
Kansas City, MO 64155

PH: (816) 468-7521
Cost: $79.95
Frequency: Monthly
Date of first issue:

Includes: fundamental analysis. Covers: municipal bonds and corporate bonds. Focuses on fixed income investing. Each issue contains a rate forecast, bond valuations, money market fund list showing the highest yields and which ones to purchase or avoid, short-term global asset allocation and much more; including bond funds, annuities, GNMA's and others.

Cycles Research

Advertising and Marketing Strategies
1314 Alps Drive
McLean, VA 22102

PH: (703) 448-3358
FAX: (703) 448-0814
Cost: $200.00
Frequency: approximately every month
Date of first issue:

Includes: technical analysis. Covers: stocks, municipal bonds, corporate bonds and gold. Identifies and interprets financial market cycles providing valuable recommendations to keep investors ahead of the pack. Service includes 10 reports and interim news flashes. Hotline available for $144.00 for subscribers or $233.00 for non-subscribers.

Cyclewatch

Walter Bressert
6987 North Oracle Road
Tucson, AR 85704

PH: (800) 677-0120
Cost: $179.00 per year
Frequency: monthly
Date of first issue: 7/91

Includes: Technical analysis and Oscillator/Cycle Charts with commentary. Covers: stocks, market timing, charts, government bonds. Cyclewatch uses cycles to forecast time and price moves in the S&P Index, Bonds, Gold and DJIA, plus Oscillator/Cycle Combinations to mechanically identify cycle tops and bottoms as they appear.
Comments: Also daily or weekly Cyclewatch Hotline for $2.00 for the first minute and $1.50 for each additional minute.

Czeschin's Mutual Fund Outlook and Recommendations

Walter Bonner, Publisher
Robert W. Czeschin, Editor
Agora, Inc.
824 E. Baltimore Street
Baltimore, MD 21202

PH: (301) 234-0691
Cost: $147.00 per year
Frequency: monthly
Date of first issue: 1987

Includes: Fundamental analysis. Covers: stocks. "Includes commentary on the stock market outlook and specific recommendations for one or more of three model portfolios: the income, the long-term growth, and the jaguar portfolios."

The Daily Bankruptcy Review

Federal Filings, Inc. (a Dow Jones Company)
P.O. Box 300
Princeton, NJ 08543-0300

PH: (800) 522-3567 ext. 3301
(609) 520-8349 ext. 3301 in New Jersey
Cost: $100.00 per month
Frequency: 20 issues a month
Date of first issue: 1991

Includes: Fundamental analysis. Covers: Daily bankruptcy. Provides detailed coverage of major Chapter 11 and Chapter 7 proceedings nationwide. Coverage includes: Interim Monthly and Quarterly financial statements; Disclosures affecting continuing operations and cash flow; Reorganization Plans; Court Proceedings and decisions; Interviews with key participants; Filing dates and deadlines; Asset Dispositions; Local newspaper stories.

Daily Graphs

William O'Neil & Co. Inc
Box 24933
Los Angeles, CA 90024-0933

PH: (213) 820-2583
(213) 820-7011
Date of first issue: 1974
Costs and frequencies:

CHART SERVICE. Includes: fundamental and technical analysis. Covers 2500 NYSE, AMEX & OTC Companies arranged by industry groups. Includes 41 fundamental and 26 technical factors in every chart.

	Weekly	Bi-weekly	Monthly
NYSE	$429.00	$305.00	$203.00
AMEX	$399.00	$280.00	$189.00
NY/			
AMEX/			
OTC	$719.00	$549.00	$345.00

Daily Graphs Option Guide

William O'Neill and Company, Inc.
P.O. Box 24933
Los Angeles, CA 90024

PH: (213) 820-2583
Cost: $229.00 per year
Frequency: Weekly
Date of first issue:

Covers: chart service and options. The guide gives graphic and statistical data on active CBOE, AMEX, PSE, PHIL, NYSE options and underlying issues. It also includes a weekly listing of quarterly earnings due, stocks going x-dividend, short term technical indicators, computer selected call writes, yearly graphs of market averages with 50 and 200-day moving averages, options expiration information and more.

The Daily Market Comment - Market Fax

Market Mani, Inc.
P.O. Box 1234
Pacifica, CA 94044

PH: (415) 952-8853
FAX: (415) 952-0844
Cost: $150.00 a month per fax location
Frequency of update: daily - one page format

Types of investments: Stocks and chart service. Since late 1987, Glenn Cutler has written the Market Fax, a one-page analysis of the day's happenings in the markets, including comments and ideas for the coming day. Each night prior to trading days, it is faxed directly to your office, usually by 3:00 AM] time, so that it will be available for use and review by your office well before any of the markets open.

Daily Market Report

Coffee, Sugar and Cocoa Exchange, Inc.
Four World Trade Center
New York, NY 10048

PH: (212) 938-2800
Cost: $110.00
Frequency: daily
Date of first issue:

Includes: Technical analysis. Covers: commodities. Trading prices, open interest and volume for all four commodities, spot prices for sugar, warehouse stocks for coffee and cocoa, opening and closing prices for London coffee and sugar, and Paris cocoa.

The Dallas Morning News Stock/Business Hotline

PH: (900) 990-9900 (then enter 195)
(214) 977-8809
Cost: $.95 per minute
24 Hour service
Frequency of update: every 15 minutes

TELEPHONE NEWSLETTER
Includes: stocks. Covers: business news. Use your touch-tone phone to get timely stock quotes (15 minute delayed) on more than 9000 publicly traded issues and concise hourly business news updates prepared by business experts from the Associated Press.

Dessauer's Journal of Financial Markets

John P. Dessauer
P.O. Box 1718
Orleans, MA 02653

PH: (508) 255-1651
(800) 272-7550
FAX: (508) 255-9243
Cost: $195.00 annually
Frequency: twice a month
Date of first issue: Fall 1980

Includes: fundamental analysis. Covers: stocks and the world financial markets. Dessaur's Journal provides analysis and advice on world trade trends. Mr. Dessaur believes it is futile to determine investment strategies while watching only the U.S. financial markets. He feels the 'secret' of the success of European investors had always been their global view of economies and financial markets. He learned to respect gold and silver, and he developed the skill needed to implement an international investment strategy.

Includes twice weekly hotline and quarterly special reports (also available by fax or computer) .

Dick Davis Digest

Dick Davis Publishing Company / Steven Halpern
P.O. Box 9547
Ft. Lauderdale, FL 33310-9547

PH: (305) 771-7111
FAX: (305) 771-1756
Price: $140.00 annually
Frequency: bi-monthly
Date of first issue: 1982

Includes: fundamental analysis. Covers: stocks, and mutual funds. Investment ideas from the best minds on Wall street. Presents news and information to convey helpful, factual information which may include the views, opinions, and recommendations of individuals or organizations whose thoughts are deemed of interest.

The Dines Letter

James Dines
P.O. Box 22
Belvedere, CA 94920

PH: (800) 84-LUCKY
Cost: $195.00
Frequency: twice monthly
Date of first issue: 1960

Includes: Technical analysis. Covers: stocks, precious metals. Explicit buy/sell advice, information on precious metals markets and hedging strategies, futuristic predications for long term investors, market analysis and commentary.

Comments: Fax interim warning bulletins available to subscribers only for $195.00 per year.

Doane's Agricultural Report

Doane's Information Services / Paul Justis
11701 Borman Dr.
St. Louis, MO 63146

PH: (314) 569-2700
(800) 535-2342
FAX: (314) 569-1083
Cost: $84.00 per year
Frequency: Weekly
Date of first issue: 1938

Includes: fundamental analysis. Covers: commodities. Marketing and management information for the agricultural market. Gives world news relevant to the agricultural market. "When to Sell and Buy" section gives investment recommendations on individual commodities. Last page titled "From Washington" brings you the latest government information, pending legislation, etc., which could affect the agricultural markets.

Donoghue's Moneyletter

The Donoghue Organization, Inc.
P.O. Box 8008
360 Woodland Street
Holliston, MA 01746-8008

PH: (800) 343-5413
 (508) 429-5930
FAX: (508) 429-2452
Cost: $109.00 per year
Frequency: Bi-monthly
Date of first issue: 3/80

Includes: Fundamental analysis. Covers: mutual funds. "Explains high-interest money market investment options and strategies in clear, easy-to-read terms. Offers investment advice and options for the do-it-yourself investor. Lists top-performing money market funds and includes coverage of no-load mutual fund switch families. Features updates on economic events and legislation, and explains what influence they will have on investments."

Donoghue's Money Fund Report

The Donoghue Organization, Inc.
P.O. Box 8008
360 Woodland Street
Holliston, MA 01746-8008

PH: (800) 343-5413
 (508) 429-5930
FAX: (508) 429-2452
Cost: $845.00 per year
Frequency: weekly
Date of first issue: 10/75

Includes: Fundamental analysis. Covers: mutual funds, tables. "Publishes weekly and monthly statistics on 351 taxable and tax-free money funds. Provides information and commentary on net assets; 7- and 30-day yields, average maturity, valuation method, number of share holdings, and sales and redemptions."

Don Wolanchuk

PH: (900) 999-1900
(313) 776-7555
Cost: $2.35 first minute then $2.25 per minute
24 Hour service
Frequency of update: consistently updated

TELEPHONE NEWLESLETTER
Covers: market timing, treasury bond futures, gold futures, and financial futures.
Market commentary and analysis with recommendations. Timer Digests 1990 Timer of the Year.

Dowbeaters

Peter Diangeles
P.O. Box 284
Ionia, NJ 07845

PH: (201) 543-4860
Cost: $100.00 annually

Frequency: monthly
Includes: fundamental analysis. Covers: stocks.
Looks for obscure, overlooked situations and emerging growth stocks of low price with good fundamentals. Each issue has 1 or 2 specific recommendations and market evaluations.

Dowphone

Dow Jones & Co., Inc.
P.O. Box 300
Princeton, NJ 08543-0300

PH: (800)345-NEWS
Cost: Peak hours 9-6 EST - .95 cents /minute—off Peak
hours .75 cents/minute
$15.00 sign up fee refunded in the form of a usage credit.
24 Hour service
Frequency of update: constantly

Covers: stocks.
A voice information service providing alerts to company news, market updates and the day's top stories. Real time stock and investment opinions.

Dow Theory Forecasts

Chuck Carlson
7412 Calumet Avenue
Hammond, IN   46324

PH: (219) 931-6480
FAX: (219) 931-6487
Cost: $212.00 annually
Frequency: weekly
Date of first issue: 1946

Includes: technical analysis. Covers: stocks and market timing. Information and analysis of stocks; uses Dow Theory as primary investment tool, Dow & transportation index, most subscribers in 50's & 60's - conservative approach to investing in equities.

Dow Theory Letters

Richard Russell
P.O. Box 1759
La Jolla, CA 92038

PH: (619) 454-0481
Cost: $225.00 per year
Frequency: every two weeks
Date of first issue: 1958

Includes: technical analysis. Covers: stocks, mutual funds, charts, precious metals. Primarily an investment theory/trend letter. Focuses on the Primary Trend Index. Provides some general investment recommendations.

The Economy at a Glance

Argus Research Corporation
17 Battery Place
New York, NY 10004

PH: (212) 425-7500
Cost: $160.00
Frequency: monthly
Date of first issue:

Includes: Fundamental analysis. Covers: economic analysis. Economic analysis portrayed by charts and bar graphs showing various economic trends with commentary for each graph or chart. Also includes a calendar of release dates for important economic indicators.

The Ehrenkrantz and King Report

Ladenburg, Thalmann and Company, Inc.
540 Madison Avenue
New York, NY 10022

PH: (212) 872-1706
(212) 872-1711
(800) LAD-THAL
Cost: $120.00
Frequency: Monthly
Date of first issue: approximately 8 years

Includes: fundamental analysis. Covers: stocks. Each issue highlights a specific stock as well as giving performance results on the model portfolio. Hotline available for $2.00 per minute - (900) 726-5566.

Electric Utility Rankings

Argus Research Corporation
17 Battery Place
New York, NY 10004

PH: (212) 425-7500
Cost: $225.00
Frequency: monthly
Date of first issue: 1934

Includes: Fundamental analysis. Covers: stocks. "...ranks 50 utility companies according to five 'quality' categories ranging from 'highest' to 'lowest' within the respective quality groups, each company's stock is then rated 'Buy,' 'Hold,' or 'Sell.'" Includes a subscription to Electric Utility Spotlight."

Electric Utility Spotlight

Argus Research Corporation
17 Battery Place
New York, NY 10004

PH: (212) 425-7500
Cost: $225.00
Frequency: monthly
Date of first issue: 1934

Includes: Fundamental analysis. Covers: stocks. Focuses on subjects of interest to electric utility stock investors. Generally contains extensive tabulations supporting the points made. Includes a subscription to Electric Utility Rankings.

The Elliott Wave Currency and Commodity Forecast

Peter Desario and James P. Chorek/ New Classics Library, Inc.
P.O. Box 1618
Gainesville, GA 30503

PH: (404) 536-0309
(800) 336-1618 ORDERS
Cost: $249.00 annually
Frequency: monthly
Date of first issue: 1987

Includes: technical analysis. Covers: commodities, market timing, currencies. Designed for speculator wishing to recognize tradable turning points in the physical commodities and currencies. Sifts through charts of over 25 commodities, currencies, and indexes using the Wave principle, Fibonacci calculations and supporting methods to identify the key emerging markets. Comments: use of hotline with subscription - 30 cents per minute.

The Elliott Wave Theorist

Robert R. Prechter, Jr./New Classics Library, Inc.
P.O. Box 1618
Gainesville, GA 30503

PH: (404) 536-0309
(800) 336-1618 ORDERS
Cost: $233.00 annually
Frequency: monthly
Date of first issue: 1976

Includes: technical analysis. Covers: stocks, market timing, chart service, bonds: municipal, corporate, government, and gold and silver. Each issue thoroughly analyzes Elliott Wave, Fibonacci relationships, fixed time cycles, momentum, sentiment, and supply-demand factors in a comprehensive approach covering stocks, precious metals, interest rates and the economy. Use of hotline with subscription 30 cents per minute.

Emerging and Special Situations Standard & Poor's

25 Broadway
New York, NY 10004

PH: (800) 777-4858
(212) 208-8768
Cost : $210.00 year
First issue: 1982

Regular features: stock choices and new issues. Points out lesser known stocks which S&P's analysts deem to be overlooked and undervalued. Alerts investors to the growth situations that have appreciation potential. Also providesll regarded analysis of new issues before they go public

Emerging Profit Newsletter

Ron Cram
26127 Edgemont Drive
Highland, CA 92346

PH: (714)
Cost: $120.00
Frequency: Monthly
Date of first issue:

Includes: fundamental analysis. Covers: stocks. Focuses on emerging profit stocks in the high tech and mid tech areas. Has a model portfolio and provides specific recommendations.

Environmental Investing News

Robert Mitchell Associates
2 Cannon Street
Newton, MA 02161-9923

PH: (617) 244-7819
Cost: $108.00
Frequency: monthly
Date of first issue: 1989

Includes: Fundamental analysis. Covers: stocks. Focuses on environmental industries and provides news and information to assist subscribers in making their own sound investment decisions. Profiles several companies each issue and gives news on the most recent developments in environmental regulations and enforcement.

Executive Stock Report

Media General Financial Services
301 E. Grace Street
Richmond, VA 23219

PH: (800) 446-7922
FAX: (804) 649-6097
Cost: $205.00 for 15 stocks per year
Frequency: monthly
Date of first issue: 10 - 15 years

Includes: fundamental analysis. Covers: stocks. Provides fundamental data and performance analysis on the companies of your choice. 6200 publicly held companies to choose from.

Executive Wealth Advisory

National Institute of Business Management, Inc.
1328 Broadway
New York, NY 10001

PH: (800) 543-2054
(703) 548-2400
(212) 971-3300 in VA
Cost: $72.00 annually
Frequency: twice a month
Date of first issue: 1978

Covers: stocks, mutual funds, market timing, municipal bonds, economy, taxes, financial planning. A personal financial guide to increasing wealth.

Fabian's Telephone: Switch Newsletter

Richard J. Fabian -
Fabian Companies
2100 Main Street, Suite. 300
Huntington Beach, CA 92648

PH: (714) 898-2588
(800) 950-8765
(714) 536-1931
Cost: $137.00 annually
Frequency: monthly
Date of first issue 1977

Includes: technical analysis. Covers: mutual funds, market timing. Monitors 250 mutual funds including U.S., International, gold asset allocation, and money market funds - all with telephone: switching privileges. The "Getting Started" guidebook teaches you how to use the Fabian Compounding Plan to accumulate and protect your wealth. Includes hotline updated weekly.

"Fament" Stock Advisory Service

Gordon D. Mors
9157 Trujillo Way
Sacramento, CA 95826

PH:
Cost: $168.00
Frequency: Bi-monthly
Date of first issue:

Covers: stocks. General market commentary with specific buy/sell/hold recommendations.

Feuilleton for Sophisticated Investors

Bradley K. Ingram and Associates
2146 Alameda Diablo
Box 380
Diablo, CA 94528

PH: (415) 743-9765
FAX: (415) 743-0244
Cost: $500.00 per year (negotiable)
Frequency: Bi-weekly or daily
Date of first issue: 30 years (privately) , 2 years (publicly)

Includes: statistical analysis. Covers: commodities. The newsletter is devoted entirely to commodity futures arbitrage and spread trading. Advises subscribers on recommended spread trades sponsored by their firm. Each issue includes a "Report Card" representing trading results year-to-date on the recommended trades. Trading philosophy keys on speculation, risk taking and risk management.

Fidelity Monitor

Jack Bowers
P.O. Box 1294
Rocklin, CA 95677-7294

PH: (916) 624-0191
Cost: $96.00 annually
Frequency: monthly
Date of first issue: 1988

Includes: fundamental and technical analysis. Covers: mutual funds. As an independent newsletter, we have no business connections with Fidelity Investments. This frees us to give you unbiased recommendations on all of Fidelity's funds. Here's a summary of what you will find in each issue: feature articles; growth model - our portfolio aims to outperform the market by holding 2 or 3 of Fidelity's best performing stock funds; select model - our system is based on a technical moving average approach; buy/hold/sell ratings for all of Fidelity's funds; extensive past performance data; graphs.

Fidelity Profit Alert

Mutual Fund Investors Association
20 William Street G-70
Wellesley Hills, MA 02181-9135

PH: (800) 638-1987
FAX: (617) 235-5467
Cost: $149.00
Frequency: monthly
Date of first issue: 1985

Includes: Fundamental analysis. Covers: mutual funds. "Your independent guide to making more money - with less risk on your Fidelity Mutual funds."

Finance Over 50

The Ron Jackson Company
661 Calmar Avenue
Suite 1002
Oakland, CA 94610

PH: (415)
Cost: $79.00
Frequency: monthly
Date of first issue:

Includes: Fundamental analysis. Gives conservative advice on investing over 50. Includes specific, low-risk recommendations, tax and real estate advice and more.

Financial Analysts Journal

Association for Investment Management Research
P.O. Box 7947
Charlottesville, VA 22906

PH: (804) 977-5724
Cost: $150.00 annually
Frequency: 6 issues per year
Date of first issue: 1945

Includes: technical analysis. Covers all investments. A technical academic journal covering the entire investment industry. Contains informative articles written by experts in the investment industry. Also discussed investment procedures, how investment decisions are made, different formulas, how to calculate risk, etc.

Financial Planning Strategies

Liberty Publishing, Inc.
42 Cherry Hill Drive
Danvers, MA 01923

PH: (508) 777-8200
(800) 722-7270 ext 128
(800) 322-4237
Cost: $600.00 annually for 100 copies @ .50 cents each (minimum
Frequency: monthly
Date of first issue: Nov 1990

Includes: fundamental analysis. Covers: mutual funds, bonds (municipal and government), financial planning. A personally imprinted client and prospect newsletter available exclusively to Certified Financial Planner professionals and at a discount to members of the Institute of Certified Financial Planners. A very effective marketing tool discusses recent updates in estate taxation, retirement planning, insurance, annuities, mutual funds, the economy, and investments.

Forbes Special Situation Survey

Forbes Investors Advisory Institute, Inc.
60 Fifth Avenue
New York, NY 10011

PH: (212) 620-2210
Cost: $495.00 per year
Frequency: monthly
Date of first issue: 1954

Includes: Fundamental analysis. Covers: securities. "Covers investment in unusual equity securities...for sophisticated investors seeking potential above-average capital gains and able to take a degree of risk. Recommends the individual speculative equity securities."

Ford Value Report

Ford Investor Services, Inc.
11722 Sorrento Valley Road
Suite 1
San Diego, CA 92121

PH: (619) 755-1327
Cost: $120.00
Frequency: monthly
Date of first issue: 1970

Includes: Fundamental analysis. Covers: stocks. Provides financial data on 2000 leading common stocks, investment value analysis to determine if over or under valued, analysis of current earning trends and stock market commentary on fundamentals and recommendations.

Forecaster

Forecaster Publishing Company
19623 Ventura Blvd.
Tarzana, CA 91356

PH: (818) 345-4421
Cost: $120.00 annually
Frequency: weekly - 40 issues a year
Date of first issue: 1962

Includes: fundamental analysis. Covers: gold, silver, and wholesale coin market. A weekly money letter for speculators. Provides exclusive information on the gold, silver, and wholesale coin market, business trends, predictions and forecasts.

Forecasts & Strategies

Phillips Publishing, Inc.
7811 Montrose Road
Potomac, MD 20854

PH: (800) 777-5005
(301) 340-2100
Cost: $139.00 annually
Frequency: monthly
Date of first issue: 1980

Includes: fundamental analysis. Covers: stocks, mutual funds, bonds (municipal, corporate, government) and currencies. Concentrates on low-risk investments, protection of capital. Gives general investment advice with a few specific recommendations

Fortucast Propicks Hotline

Barry Rosen
P.O. Box 2066
Fairfield, IA 52556

PH: (900) 988-3342
Cost: $2.00 per minute
Frequency of update: daily - Sunday thru Thursday

TELEPHONE NEWSLETTER
Covers: stocks, commodities, municipal bonds, corporate bonds, government bonds, currencies, gold, silver, crude. The call begins with all the new trades, followed by commentary on financials, grains, then metals.

Fortucast Regular Hotline

Barry Rosen
P.O. Box 2066
Fairfield, IA 52556

PH: (800) 247-3678 to subscribe
Cost: $500.00 per year
Frequency of update: 3 times per week
24 Hour Service

TELEPHONE NEWSLETTER
Covers: Futures and commodities. "Trades, stops and detailed commentary including support and resistance, breakouts, breakdowns, direction and velocity of the markets over the next few days on 16-20 markets covered in the Fortucast Newsletter."

The Fractal Behavior of Markets

LJH Investments
18484 Preston Road
Suite 102-LB-160
Dallas, TX 75252-5474

Covers: stocks, market timing, treasury bonds, gold, OEX and DJA. Get advance notice of market reversals which are precise, accurate and consistent.

PH: (214) 985-7571
(900) 226-1618 - $2.25 per minute
Cost: $233.00
Frequency: monthly
Date of first issue: 1991

The Fractal Behavior of Markets

LJH Investments
18484 Preston Road
Suite 102 LB-160
Dallas, TX 75252-5474

TELEPHONE NEWSLETTER
Covers: stocks, Treasury Bonds, gold and market timing. Market timing to give advance warning of market reversals.

PH: (900) 226-1618 (214) 985-7571
Cost: $2.25 per minute
Frequency of update: daily

The Fractal Behavior of Markets

LJH Investments
18484 Preston Road., Suite #102-160
Dallas, TX 75252

Covers: Market timing
When the time arrives for the market to reverse, it doesn't care what the price is. Knowing the time well in advance can prepare you to take proper action. Pinpointing the time for you is what this service is all about by using a technique called FRACTALS.

PH: (900) 226-1618 (hotline)
Cost: per minute $2.25

Franklin's Insight

Franklin Research & Development
711 Atlantic Avenue
Boston, MA 02111

Includes: fundamental analysis. Covers: stocks. Investment newsletter specializing in socially responsible investing. Social profiles on 3-4 companies each month. Includes monthly letter "Investing for a Better World" for the socially responsible investor, gives recommendations and commentary. Also includes "Equity Briefs" - profiles of the social and financial performance of selected companies, "Quarterly Reports" & Big Cap Social Profile" - which provide social information on widely followed high capitalization companies. Fundamental data is taken into consideration but recommendations are primarily made on social responsibility of company.

PH: (617) 423-6655
Cost: $195.00 annually
Frequency: monthly
Date of first issue: 1983

FSA Market Outlook

G. Jules Csaszi, Editor
FSA, Inc.
P.O. Box 6547
Lake Worth, FL 33466

Cost: $250.00 per year
Frequency: 24 times a year
Date of first issue: 1980

Includes: Technical analysis. Covers: stocks, commodities, charts. Advisory service features cycles, sesonals, supports and resistances, specific signals and profitable trades. With the exclusive JC System 34, Market Outlook is #1 in profits.
Comments: Bonus - subscription for one year or longer will include Trading Tips booklet. Also available - JC System 34 Manual for $245.00.

The Fund Exchange Report

Paul A. Merriman and Associates, Inc.
1200 Westlake Avenue N. Suite 700
Seattle, WA 98109-3530

PH: (206) 285-8877
FAX: (206) 286-2079
OTHER: (800) 423-4893
Cost: $125.00 annually
Frequency: monthly

Includes: fundamental analysis. Covers: mutual funds and market timing. Offers for the do-it-yourself investor timing signals for equity, bond, gold, and international mutual funds. Includes 10 model portfolios, feature articles on investing in no-load funds and tips for the market timing investor. Shows you how to profit with no-load mutual funds that offer tele
PH: switching privileges and provide nine different model portfolios - updated monthly - that fit your personal investment needs and preferences. Also shows you how to double your gains by buying funds on margin. Includes 24 hour "Switch Alert" hotline.

Fundline

David H. Menashe & Company
P.O. Box 663
Woodland Hills, CA 91365

PH: (818) 346-5637
(717) 497-5437
Cost: $127.00 per year - includes telephone hotline
Frequency: monthly

Includes: technical analysis. Covers: mutual funds and market timing. Specializes exclusively in the Fidelity Selects funds - including the gold and silver funds. Uses a 2-fold system based on theory exclusive "39-week Momentum" formula and proprietary "Trading Oscillator and Long Term Indicator." Includes investment strategies and recommendations.

Fund Performance Chartbook

Bert Dohmen
Wellington Financial Corporation
6600 Kalanianole Highway
Suite 114C
Honolulu, HI 96825-1299

PH: (800) 992-9989
(808) 396-2220
FAX: (808) 396-8640
Cost: $25.00 per issue
Frequency: quarterly
Date of first issue: 1991

Covers: mutual funds. Over 100 charts showing relative performance versus S&P 500. The charts cover the last 5 1/2 years.

Futures and Options Factor

Russell R. Wasendorf
Wasendorf and Associates, Inc.
P.O. Box 849
Cedar Falls, IA 50613

PH: (319) 277-5240
Cost: $228.00 annually
Frequency: 50 times per year
Date of first issue: 1990

Includes: Technical analysis. Covers: futures. "The Futures Portfolio Advisor." Contains graphs and charts and specific recommendations and market commentary.

Comments: the subscription is free if you open an account with Wasendorf and Associates.

Futures Charts

Joe Van Nice
Commodity Trend Service
P.O. Box 32309
Palm Beach Gardens, FL 33410

PH: (800) 331-1069
(407) 694-0960
FAX: (407) 622-7623
Frequency: weekly
Cost: $450.00   annually
        $145.00   quarterly
        $250.00   six months
        $275.00   1/yr bi-monthly
        $180.00   1/yr monthly
Date of first issue: 1973

CHART SERVICE
Includes: technical analysis. Covers: commodities, financial and agricultural markets. The industry's most comprehensive charts. In addition to covering all key markets, futures charts also provides: daily bar charts with this Friday's close; stochastics on daily, weekly, and monthly charts; stochastics and RSI plotted on every market and updated through Friday's close; 4,9,18, & 40 day moving averages, weekly charts with stochastics; ADX, net trader position charts and market sentiment, volume and open interest; 30 & 60 minute bar charts and point & figure charts, "market Reflections" a valuable overview from the staff of the weekly commodity market, spreads, cycles and much more.

Futures Factors: The Futures Portfolio Advisor

Wasendorf and Associates, Inc.
802 Main Street
P.O. Box 849
Cedar Falls, IA 50613

PH: (319) 268-0441
Cost: $228.00 per year
Frequency: weekly
Date of first issue: 1980

Includes: Fundamental analysis, graphs. Covers: Commodities. "Analyzes actively traded commodity futures markets in the U.S. based on commodity index analysis in various market groupings, including grains, meats, metals, food/fiber, and financial/currencies."

F.X.C. Report

F.X.C. Investors Corporation
62-19 Cooper Avenue
Glendale, NY 11385

PH: (718) 417-1330
Cost: $290.00 per year
Frequency: 2 - 4 times a month
Date of first issue: 1971

Includes: Fundamental analysis. Covers: securities. Reports on the securities of companies that have the potential for extreme capital appreciation. Offers news of research for investors with risk capital, investment recommendations, and performance reports. Each recommendation is backed by in-depth analysis.

The Garside Forecast

Garside and Co.
P.O. Box 1812
Santa Ana, CA 92702

PH: (714) 259-1670
Cost: $125.00 annually
Frequency: twice a month
Date of first issue: 1970

Includes: technical analysis. Covers: stocks and market timing. Market commentary and outlook. Indicator summaries and buy and short recommendations.

Global Market Perspective

Robert Prechter
P.O. Box 1618-B
Gainesville, GA 30503

PH: (800) 472-9283
(404) 534-6680
Cost: $599.00 per year
Frequency: Monthly
Date of first issue:

Includes: technical analysis. Covers: stocks, commodities, charts. Each issue gives you over 100 pages (with more than 50 charts) covering: more than 20 world equity markets, over a dozen global fixed-income markets, international currency and cross rate relationships, gold, energy and a "spotlight" commodity, social and economic trends.

The Global Market Strategist

Dan Ascani
Supercyle Research, Inc.
P.O. Box 5309 H
Gainesville, GA 30504

PH: (800) 633-1332
(404) 967-1332
Cost: $297.00 year
Frequency: monthly
Date of first issue: 1991

Includes: technical analysis and chart services. Covers: stocks, commodities, market timing, world stock markets, interest rates, currencies and commodities. Get Mr. Ascani's eye-opening technical and Elliott Wave analysis. COMMENTS: He built the Elliott Wave Currency and Commodity Forecast into one of the most highly regarded market letters.

The Global Market Strategist 900 Update

Supercycle Research, Inc.
P.O. Box 5309-H
Gainesville, GA 30504

PH: (900) USA-2200
(303) 440-3344 if 900 number is blocked.
Cost: per minute $2.00
24 Hour service
Frequency of update: daily 10AM & 2PM

TELEPHONE NEWSLETTER
Covers: stocks, commodities, municipal, corporate, government bonds, and currencies.
"The ultimate intraday telephone hotline!"

Global Research

Nelson Publications
1 Gateway Plaza
Port Chester, NY 10573

PH: (800) 333-6357
FAX: (914) 937-8908
Cost: $95.00 annually
Frequency: 10 issues per year
Date of first issue: 1985

Includes: Fundamental analysis. Covers: research reports. Global Research provides investment and financial professionals with a complete catalog of research reports - over 50,000 reports a year. Four easy-to-use sections: Section 1 - Research reports by company - U.S.; Section 2 - Research reports by company - International; Section 3 - Research reports by originating firm; Section 4 - Industry reports arranged by industry group.

Goerlich/van Brunt Newsletter

Mr. Goerlich and Bob van Brunt
604 S. Washington Square, Suite 2715
Philadelphia, PA 19106

PH: (215) 923-8870
Cost: $160.00 annually
Frequency: bi-monthly
Date of first issue: 1989

Includes: technical analysis. Covers: stocks and market timing. Stock market updates, twice a month Bullish list of 50-75 stocks, bearish also.

Gold Investment Review

James R. Blakely
3 Riverside Road, Drawer A
Sandy Hook, CT 06482-0845

PH: (203) 426-7790
Cost: $120.00 annually
Frequency: 24 issues a year
Date of first issue 1989

Fundamental and technical analysis. Covers: precious metals. Provides coverage of all precious metals and their markets. Also monitors affairs relating to futures, options, stocks and precious metals which influence prices. Includes a top-notch report and analysis of what has come to pass on the precious metals stage since the last issue, includes charts and graphs as well as important data from U.S. Bureau of Mines, Canadian Government Department of Energy, Reuters Metal Reports Satellite.

Gold Mining Stock Report

Target, Inc.
Box 1217
Lafayette, CA 94549-1217

PH: (510) 283-4848
Cost: $119.00 per year
Frequency: monthly
Date of first issue: 10/83

Includes: Fundamental analysis. Covers: stocks. "Offers analysis and specific recommendations for investors interested in penny mining stocks, particularly shares traded in Spokane and Vancouver."

Gold Newsletter

James U. Blanchard, III
Jefferson Financial, Inc.
2400 Jefferson Highway, Suite 600
Jefferson, LA 70121

PH: (504)837-3033
(800) 877-8847
Cost : $95.00 annually
Frequency: monthly
Date of first issue: 1970

Covers: gold. Economic commentary on news affecting gold.

Gold Standard News

Conrad J. Braun
Gold Standard Corp
1805 Grand Avenue
Kansas City, MO 64108

PH: (800) VIA-GOLD
(816) VIA-GOLD
Cost: $139.00 annually
Frequency: monthly
Date of first issue: 1977

Articles, commentary and insights on gold and metals.

Gold Stocks Advisory

Paul Sarnoff
Box 1437
Burnsville, MN 55337

Cost: 96.00 per year
Frequency: monthly
Date of first issue: 1988

Includes: Fundamental analysis. Covers: stocks, gold shares. Commentary on news affecting gold shares. The editor, Paul Sarnoff, has two goals: in bad markets his goal is to help subscribers preserve their capital; in the good markets to help subscribers be among the beneficiaries. Bonus offer with subscription.

Good Money

Good Money Publications
Ritchie P. Lowry
P.O. Box 363
Worcester, VT 05682

PH: (800) 535-3551
(802) 223-3911
FAX: (802) 223-8949
Cost: $75.00 annually
Frequency: bi-monthly
Date of first issue: 1982

Includes: fundamental analysis. Covers: stocks, bonds, and mutual funds. The first issue for socially concerned investors. Profiles 13 major socially screened funds, 9 environmental sector funds, 9 funds with limited social screens & includes social funds for institutional investors. Includes performance comparisons, social analysis of fund investment consumer charts, telephone : numbers, where to buy, minimum investments sales charges and more. Includes NETBACK - a companion newsletter which is a subscriber forum and bulletin board for the social investing community.

Grant's Interest Rate Observer

Patricia Kavanagh
233 Broadway
New York, NY 10279

PH: (212) 608-7994
FAX: (212) 608-5925
Cost: $450.00 per year
Frequency: every other Friday
Date of first issue: 11/83

Includes: Fundamental analysis. Covers: stocks, bonds, securities. Grant's emphasizes the fundamentals of interest rate movement and the credit markets but includes an extraordinary range of subjects.

The Granville Market Letter

Joseph E. Granville
P.O. Box 413006
Kansas City, MO 64141

PH: (816) 474-5353
(800)-7876-LETTER
Cost: $800.00 year for 46 issues faxed Thursday morning

FAX SERVICE
Covers: stocks and market timing, technical analysis. Text of the newsletter by the same name. Includes market commentary and analysis, review of indicators and 3 extensive model portfolios - common stocks, options and low-priced stock for speculators.
Comments: Mr. Granville is available for telephone consultation for $900.00 per half hour with a minimum of one half hour.

The Granville Market Letters

Joseph E. Granville
P.O. Drawer 413006
Kansas City, MO 64141

PH: (816) 474-5353
(800) 876-LETTER
Cost: $250.00 annually
Frequency: 46 issues annually
Date of first issue: 1963

Includes: technical analysis. Covers: stocks and market timing. Includes market commentary and analysis, review of indicators, and 3 extensive model portfolios one for common stocks and one for options and one for low-priced stocks. Mr. Granville is available for telephone consultations for $900/ half hour (1/2 hour minimum)

Graphic Fund Forecaster

Fred Hohn - editor
P.O. Box 673
Andover, MA 01810

PH: (508) 470-3511
Cost: $145.00 annually
Frequency: 26 issues - every other week
Date of first issue 1984

CHART SERVICE
Includes: technical analysis. Covers: mutual funds. The Graphic Fund Forecaster attempts to forecast the market and apply this to mutual funds. There are approximately 54 charts and a small section which ranks the funds and highlights the best.

Growth Fund Guide

Growth Fund Research, Inc.
Box 6600
Rapid City, SD 57709

PH: (800) 621-8322
(605) 341-1971
Cost: $89.00
Frequency: Monthly
Date of first issue: 1968

Includes: fundamental and technical analysis. Covers: mutual funds. "The nation's oldest and most sophisticated no-load fund publication." Several model portfolios and market information included.

Growth Stock Outlook

Charles Allmon - Editor
Growth Stock Outlook, Inc.
P.O. Box 15381
Chevy Chase, MD 20825

PH: (301) 654-5205
Cost: $195.00 annually
Frequency: twice a month
Date of first issue: 1964

Includes fundamental analysis. Covers: stocks. Designed for brokers, institutions, sophisticated private investors who recognize the risks and possible rewards of investing in vigorously growing companies. Includes model portfolio, insider trading information, charts and periodic new company recommendations mailed at anytime. Extensive stock selection guide and performance record presented 12 times a year. Supplements include Junior Growth Stocks, New Issue Digest, Utility Analyst and Bank Stock Analyst. Includes weekly hotline billed as a regular long distance call.

Guardian Research Report

Guardian Financial Corporation
2207 Third Street
Livermore, CA 94550

PH: (510) 443-7010
Cost: $180.00
Frequency: monthly
Date of first issue: 1985

Includes: Fundamental analysis. Covers: stocks. Market perspective and commentary with recommendations and 2 model portfolios (speculative and conservative).

Guru Review

Jeff Bower
Suite 209
1740 44th Street SW
Wyoming, MI 49509

PH: (616)
Cost: $233.00
Frequency: 17 issues per year
Date of first issue:

Includes: Technical analysis. Covers: stocks, mutual funds, market timing. Get Jeff Bower's market and mutual fund timing as well as stock recommendations, "Sentiment Survey" and more.

Halco Trading Strategies

P.O. Box 795429
Dallas, TX 75379

PH: (214) 385-2570
(214) 385-2511 HOTLINE
Cost: $495.00 annually
Frequency: bi-monthly
Date of first issue: 1974

CHART SERVICE
Includes: technical analysis and chart service with every other issue. Covers: commodities. Leaders in cyclic and technical analysis of the financial and agricultural markets since 1974. Each issue contains specific recommendation with bull and bear scenarios and trading strategies.

Harmonic Research

Mason Sexton - Harmonic Research, Inc.
650 Fifth Avenue
New York, NY 10019

PH: (212) 484-2065
Cost: $360.00 annually or $960.00 including daily hotline with specific recommendations
Frequency: monthly
Date of first issue 1983

Includes: technical analysis. Covers: stocks and commodities. Ten page letter covering futures and stock markets from a unique cycle and Gann perspectives. Editor Mason Sexton also uses solar and lunar phases, eclipses, and sunspot activity in his analysis.

Harry Browne's Special Reports

Harry Browne
P.O. Box 5586
Austin, TX 78763

PH: (512) 453-7313
(800) 531-5142
Cost: $225.00 for 10 issues
Frequency: approx 8-10 issues a year
Date of first issue: 1974

Includes: fundamental analysis. Covers: stocks; commodities; municipal, corporate, and government bonds; market timing. Financial advisory newsletter. Has specific recommendations for 2 portfolios. The Fundamental portfolio is the safe, conservative recommendations. The Variable portfolio consists of speculative recommendations. Series of reports detailing economic conditions, foreign currencies, world news and prices, investment outlook with recommendations, model portfolio and market commentary.

Heim Investment Letter

Heim Investment Services, Inc.
Lawrence H. Heim - Editor
P.O. Box 19435
Portland, OR 97219

PH: (503) 228-9553
(503) 624-4816
(503) 244-2223
Cost: $150.00 year
Frequency: every 2 weeks
Date of first issue: 1974

Includes: fundamental and technical analysis. Covers: stocks, currencies, gold & silver. The letter is a comprehensive investment service for the professional and private investor. Includes technical and fundamental studies on national and international developments affecting stocks, bonds, gold, silver and coins.

The Holt Advisory

Weiss Research
P.O. Box 2923
West Palm Beach, FL 33402

PH: (800) 289-9222
(215) 527-8030
Cost: $160.00 annually
Frequency: twice a month
Date of first issue: 1977

Covers: stocks, mutual funds, bonds (municipal, government and corporate), and gold. An executive investment newsletter. Has 3 different portfolios - Primary, Balanced Hedge, and Guaranteed Gold and Treasury Strategy. Includes specific recommendations and positions with buy and sell limits, and a Q&A section. Also discusses economic data and outlooks relating to muni's, treasuries, and banking.

Hotline

TLM, Inc.
420 Westchester Avenue
Port Chester, NY 10573

PH: (800) 451-1392
Cost: $69.00 annually
Updated daily after 6PM EST

FAX SERVICE
Covers: index futures and options.
TLM's proprietary trading model uses the high, low, and close of the index daily and generates two to four trading signals per month for options and two signals per month for futures trading. The simple manual explains how to make your trade and manage it with stops and limits.

Hot Wire

PH: (900) 468-9473 (hotline)
Cost: $2.00 first minute + $1.00 each additional minute

TELEPHONE NEWSLETTER
Covers: buyouts, buybacks, recommendations and rumors.
The hottest news on companies experiencing unusual trading, from the Dow Jones Professional Investor Re-

Hulbert Financial Digest

Mark Hulbert
316 Commerce Street
Alexandria, VA 22314

PH: (703) 683-5905
Cost: $135.00 annually
Frequency: monthly
Date of first issue: 6/80

Tracks the performance of 125 financial newsletters. Gives a percentage rating on each based on following their recommendations. In January issue, he rates the performance of each newsletter going back to 1980.

The Hume MoneyLetter

Hume Publishing, Inc.
835 Franklin Ct.
Marietta, GA 30067

PH: (800) 222-4863
(404) 426-1920
Cost: $95.00 annually
Frequency: Bi-monthly
Date of first issue: 1976

Includes: fundamental analysis. Covers: securities.
The Hume MoneyLetter features several authors who write articles and give recommendations on various investments. Each letter ends with an investment update on previously recommended investments.

The Hummer Market Letter

Wayne Hummer & Company
175 West Jackson Blvd.
Chicago, IL 60690

PH: (312) 431-1700
(800) 621-4477
FAX: (312) 431-0704
Cost: free
Frequency: monthly
First published Jan 1932

Includes: fundamental analysis. Covers: stocks and bonds.
Written by experienced professionals of Wayne Hummer & Co., gives timely investment advice and comments on the stock and bond markets. Gives several recommendations per issue.

IBC's Money Market Insight

The Donoghue Organization, Inc.
P.O. Box 8008
360 Woodland Street
Holliston, MA 01746-8008

PH: (800) 343-5413
(508) 429-5930
FAX: (508) 429-2452
Cost: $445.00 annually
Frequency: monthly
Date of first issue: 1983

Includes: Fundamental analysis. Covers: money markets. This publication will provide: insight into the challenges facing the money market industry today; expert analysis and commentary on important issues affecting the $2-Trillion money market industry; trends in short-term investing, interest rates and yields; developments in the international arena...and the effects these events have on worldwide money markets.

Income and Safety - The Consumer's Guide to High Yields

The Institute for Econometric Research
3471 N. Federal Highway
Ft. Lauderdale, Fl. 33306

PH: (800) 327-6720
(305) 563-9000
Cost: $100.00 annually
Frequency: monthly
Date of first issue: 1981

Includes: fundamental and technical analysis. Covers: mutual funds, government securities, and charts. Every issue contains "Best Buys" Income Investment Directory, interest rate forecasts, recommendations on new funds, "avoid" warnings, tax strategies and continuous follow-ups on all income investments.Income & Safety is devoted exclusively to income investments. It is a comprehensive and objective guide to earning the highest returns on income mutual funds, money market investments, bank deposit, and government securities. Includes free hotline updated every Friday evening

Individual Investor Special Situations Report

Financial Data Systems, Inc.
38 E. 29th street, 4th floor
New York, NY 10016

PH: (800) 321-5200
FAX: (609) 858-2007
OTHER: (212) 689-2777
Cost: $150.00 annually
Frequency: monthly
Date of first issue: 12/15/89

Includes: fundamental analysis. Covers: stocks.
Monthly in-depth confidential report on the single most
promising stock Individual Investor sees in the market.
Their unqualified #1 buy recommendation, updates on
already featured stocks included each month.

Industry Forecasts

Levy Economic Forecasts
P.O. Box 26
Chappaqua, NY 10514

PH: (914) 238-8470
(914) 238-3665
Cost: $250.00 annually
Frequency: monthly
Date of first issue: 1949

Descriptions, analysis, and forecasts on the economy.
Also includes four quality reports relating economic
conditions to the markets.

The Inger Letter

Gene Inger
100 E. Thousand Oaks Blvd.
Suite 227
Thousand Oaks, CA 91360

PH: (900) 933-GENE
(800) 966-9965
Cost: $2.00 for the first minute, $.95 thereafter
24 Hour service
Frequency of update: hourly from 10:00 am - 6:00 pm

TELEPHONE NEWSLETTER
Covers: stocks and market timing. Includes specific
S&P, stock and option targets, gold, oil and bond calls.

Insider Report

Larry Abraham
P.O. Box 84903
Phoenix, AZ 85071

PH: (602) 252-4477   (800) 528-0559
Cost: $124.00 per year special rate
$199.00 per year regular rate
Frequency: monthly
Date of first issue: 5/83

Includes: Fundamental analysis. Covers: stocks. Every
issue is based on an understanding of who the key
Insiders are and what they are doing now. Each investment recommendation is based on the same question -
What are the Insiders up to?

The Insiders

The Institute for Econometric Research
3471 N. Federal Highway
Ft. Lauderdale, Fl. 33306

PH: (800) 327-6720
(305) 563-9000
Cost: $100.00 annually
Frequency: bi-monthly
Date of first issue: 12 years

Includes technical analysis. Covers: stocks. Designed to be a complete stock selection and investment program. Contains insider ratings on thousands of stocks, specific buy and sell recommendations, market timing, advice, the "Nifty Fifty" list of industry rankings and recommendation follow-ups. Includes weekly hotline free.

Interinvest Review and Outlook

Interinvest Corporation
294 Washington Street
Suite 754
Boston, MA 02108

PH: (617) 423-1166
Cost: $125.00 per year
Frequency: monthly
Date of first issue: 1/77

Includes: Fundamental analysis. Covers: stocks, charts. "Provides a review of domestic and international markets. Includes information on the U.S. stock market and currency exchange rates. Comments on relevant geopolitical issues. Issues a portfolio review."

The International Fund Monitor

Research International, Inc.
P.O. Box 5754
Washington, D.C. 20016

PH: (202) 363-3097
Cost: $84.00 annually
Frequency: monthly

Includes: fundamental analysis. Covers: mutual funds. Regular features include: monthly wrap-up covering economic trends; currency fluctuations and stock market performance; summary of performance of leading international funds and categories (global, foreign, country, sector); insights into the best markets at present and those likely to excel in the future; Country Focus - an extensive analysis of a specific market; Guest Expert; Fundamentals; News & Views, & tables.

In-Touch

PH: (900) 468-6824 (hotline)
Cost: per minute $2.99
24 hour service
Frequency of update: daily

Covers: stocks
Predicts short term stock market direction, tops & bottoms.

InvesTech Market Analyst

James B. Stack - Investech
2472 Birch Glen
Whitefish, MT 59937

PH: (800) 955-8500
(406) 862-7777 OTHER
Cost: $165.00 annually
Frequency: every three weeks
Date of first issue: 1979

Includes: technical analysis. Covers: stocks and market timing, bond market analysis. Technical and monetary investment analysis. Model portfolio and position review in each issue. Includes twice weekly hotline. Subscribe to Investech Mutual Fund Advisor also for only $235.00 for both letters.

InvesTech Mutual Fund Advisor

James B. Stack - Investech
2472 Birch Glen
Whitefish, MT 59937

PH: (800) 955-8500
(406) 862-7777 OTHER
Cost: $165.00 annually
Frequency: every 3 weeks
Date of first issue: 1985

Includes: technical analysis. Covers: mutual funds and market timing. Model portfolio and recommendations based on an objective, technical approach. Also includes the Top Rated Funds from Lipper Analytical Services, Inc. Includes twice weekly hotline. Subscribe to Investech Market Analyst also for only $235.00 for both letters.

Investment Counselors, Inc.

Patrick Donelan
1010 Market Street, Suite 1540
St. Louis, MO 63101

PH: (314) 421-3080
FAX: (314) 421-5287
Cost: FREE
Frequency: quarterly
Date of first issue: 1976

Includes: technical analysis. Covers: stocks, market timing. Newsletter contains topics of interest to their firm, general market information, and a list of their current holdings.

Investment Quality Trends

Geraldine Weiss
7440 Girard Avenue, #4
La Jolla, California, 92037

PH: (619) 459-3818
FAX: (619) 459-3819
Cost: $250.00
Frequency: bi-monthly
Date of first issue: 4/66

Includes: technical and fundamental analysis
Covers: stocks, market timing and charts.
Follows 350 blue chips. Recommendations made in each issue as well as investment outlooks and editorial comments on market.

Investment Reporter

Marpep Publishing Limited - Patrick McKeough
133 Richmond Street West
Toronto, Ontario M5H3M8

PH: (416) 869-0456
FAX: (416) 869-0456
Cost: $257.00
Frequency: weekly
Date of first issue: 1941

Includes: fundamental analysis. Covers: stocks. Canadian stock market investment advisory newsletter. You will know "What to Buy," "When to Switch," "When to Sell" and get opinions and recommendations that are clear and specific.
Comments: hotline available for $75.00.

Investor Advisory Service

National Association of Investors Corp.
1515 East Eleven Mile Road
Royal Oak, MI 48067

PH: (313) 543-0612
Cost: $125.00 - Club $108.00 - Individual
Frequency: monthly
Date of first issue 195'

Includes: fundamental and technical analysis. Covers: stocks and includes charts. A report on three stocks which are judged to be in the buy range. With the report of the three companies, you will receive a completed stock selection guide on each company so that you can see the record yourself and check the conclusions of the investment advisors. Also, for each company, you will receive a brief statement of the Advisors' conclusions concerning the prospects of the stock. On occasion the advisors will put NAIC's Challenge Tree Approach to work and suggest a switch from one stock to another judged to have better prospects.

Investor Forecasts

Sy Harding / Asset Management Research Corp.
P.O. Box 352016
4440 N. Oceanshore Blvd.
Palm Coast, FL 32135

PH: (904) 446-0823
Cost: $195.00 per year
Frequency: every 3 weeks
Date of first issue: 1987

Includes: technical analysis. Covers: market timing, stocks, bonds, gold, mutual funds. Searches out undervalued, relatively undiscovered stocks, then monitors them until technical analysis tells them they're ready to move. Then they are bought for the portfolios. Each issue has specific recommendations, model portfolios and follow-ups. Hotline available for $2.00 per minute.

Investor's Digest

Norman King Fosback - Editor
The Institute for Econometric Research
3471 N. Federal Highway
Ft. Lauderdale, Fl. 33306

PH: (800) 327-6720
(305) 563-9000
Cost: $58.00 annually
Frequency: monthly
Date of first issue: May 1990

Includes: fundamental and technical analysis.
Covers: stocks, mutual funds, and market timing.
Every issue includes stock recommendations and market timing advice, mutual fund selections, stock of the month, market timers index, short sales, portfolio strategies and advisory sentiment index. Includes free daily hotline .

Investors Fax Weekly

12335 Santa Monica Blvd.
Suite 128
Los Angeles, CA 90025

PH: (213) 479-0645
Cost: $150.00 per year
Frequency: weekly
Date of first issue: 06/15/91

Covers: stocks, technical and fundamental analysis. Each letter contains 6 - 10 recommended issues and gives a specific buypoint recommendation representing a chart breakout. Newsletter is faxed on Sunday for Monday's opening. Hotline available for $2.00 per minute - (900) 535-9800 extension 627.

Investor's Fax Weekly

12335 Santa Monica Blvd.
Suite 128
Los Angeles, CA 90025

PH: (900) 535-9800 extension 627
(213) 479-0645
FAX: (213) 394-0220
Cost: $2.00 per minute
Frequency of update: daily

TELEPHONE NEWSLETTER
Covers: stocks. Computer based analysis performs a weekly review of all NYSE, AMEX and OTC issues. Criteria used to select stocks include: current and annual earnings, new highs, shares outstanding, industry leaders, institutional sponsorship and market movement.

Investor's Fortucast

Barry Rosen
P.O. Box 2066
Fairfield, IA 52556

PH: (515) 472-6866
(800) 247-3678
Cost: $249.00
Frequency: monthly
Date of first issue: 1988

Includes: Technical analysis. Covers: market timing, futures and commodities. A futures market timing newsletter providing precise entry and exit dates, usable 3, 6, 18 plus month forecasts, 5000 year old ancient Indian trading secrets, and hidden Gann, Timed Elliott Waves and Fibonacci secrets.
Comments: several different Hotlines available at a discount to subscribers.

Investor's Intelligence

Chartcraft, Inc.
Michael L. Burke - Editor
30 Church Street
P.O. Box 2046
New Rochelle, NY 10801

PH: (914) 632-00422
FAX: (914) 632-0335
Cost: $124.00 annually
Frequency: bi-weekly
Date of first issue: 33 years

Includes: fundamental and technical analysis. Covers: stocks, mutual funds, and market timing. General market newsletter by Contrarians. Have model portfolios on mutual funds and stocks. Also surveys other leading newsletters and analyzes their sentiments on the market. Includes toll-free hotline .

Investor's Intelligence

PH: (900) 990-0909 ext 31 (hotline)
Cost: per minute $2.00
Frequency of update: daily at 11:00 AM except Monday at 9:30 AM.
Portfolio changes on Monday and Wednesday.
Mike Burke's mutual switch fund portfolio.

Investors Hotline

PH: (900) 420-8606
Cost: $10.00 per call - about 30 seconds

24 Hour service
Frequency of update: daily

Buy and sell recommendations from Wall Street's most successful traders. Key call and put option recommendations. Gold and Oil strategy. Includes general information on market and current news and its affect on the market.

Investor's Update

525 W. Manchester Blvd.
Inglewood, CA 90301

PH: (213) 674-3330
Cost: $50.00
Frequency: monthly
Date of first issue:

Includes: Fundamental analysis. Covers: commodities, precious metals. "Provides investment information for rare coins and the precious metals market, as well as oil and commodity futures markets. Carries economic statistics and news of world events affecting investors. Reviews previous investment recommendations."

It's Your Money/The Jorgensen Report

Jorgensen & Associates, Inc.
810 Idyllberry Road
San Rafael, CA 94903

PH: (800) 359-6267
(415) 472—6265
Cost: $38.00 annually
Frequency: monthly
Date of first issue 1983

Includes: fundamental analysis. Covers: stocks, mutual funds and bonds. A 12 page letter on financial planning and money management. Covers stocks and bonds trends, tax-free and tax-deferred investments and mutual funds. Shows how to protect your credit, plan for college, what to avoid, etc.

Jag Notes

125 Half Mile Road
Red Bank, NJ 07701

PH: (908) 747-6938
Cost: $1,850.00 per year or $500.00 per quarter
Frequency of update: three times daily

TELEPHONE NEWSLETTER
Covers: stocks. Have all the latest market information and recommendations on your desk at 9:00 sharp (EST) each morning. Daily summary of over 25 brokerage firms and market timers early each morning. Comments and recommendations.

Japanese Candlestick Charts

Joe Van Nice, Publisher
Commodity Trend Service
P.O. Box 32309
Palm Beach Gardens, FL 33420

PH: (800) 331-1069
FAX: (407) 622-7623
Cost: $250.00 per year
Frequency: weekly
Date of first issue: 10/90

CHART SERVICE
Includes: Technical analysis. Covers: stocks, charts. Candlesticks can spot technical strengths and or weaknesses by highlighting the relationship between the open and close. The candlestick method gives you deeper insight into market conditions by creating a visual aid for each trading period. The candlestick method is purely price dependent. Candlesticks can be hand updated daily.
Comments: Offer includes extra bonuses.

J & J's Hedged Option Trader

J & J Market Letters
1112 Bering Drive
Suite 65
Houston, TX 77057

PH: (800) 992-6123
Cost: $175.00 plus online charges
Frequency: daily
Date of first issue: 2/90

Includes: Fundamental analysis. Covers: market timing, options. Focuses on short-term, speculative, aggressive capital growth through option trading.
Comments: Delivered by computer only via IBM-PC or compatible with modem.

J & J's Undervalued Growth Stocks Letter

J & J Market Letters
1112 Bering Drive
Suite 65
Houston, TX 77057

PH: (800) 992-6123
Cost: $135.00 plus online charges
Frequency: weekly
Date of first issue: 2/90

Includes: Fundamental analysis. Covers: stocks, market timing. Seeks aggressive capital growth via growth stocks trading at a discount to their true value. Includes recommendations and portfolio and performance information.
Comments: Delivered by computer only via IBM-PC or compatible with modem.

John Bollinger's Capital Growth Letter

John Bollinger
P.O. Box 3358
Manhattan Beach, CA 90266

PH: (800) 888-8400   (213) 545-0610
Cost: $169.00
Frequency: monthly
Date of first issue:

Includes: Technical analysis. Covers: stocks, municipal bonds, corporate bonds, government bonds, and gold. Each issue contains specific stock and mutual fund selections, current trends in gold, energy and the dollar, and technical analysis basis to support the recommendations. Includes a weekly hotline.

Journal Phone

Dow Jones Information Services Group
World Financial Center
200 Liberty Street
New York, NY 10281

PH: (900) JOURNAL   (212) 416-2000
Cost: per minute 95 cents
24 Hour service
Frequency of update: continual

Offers Journal and other Dow Jones news, stock quotes, business news via tough tone phone. Codes and information printed daily in The Wall Street Journal.

Junk Bond Reporter

American Banker - Bond Buyer
A Division of The Thomson Publishing Corporation
P.O. Box 30240
Bethesda, MD 20824

PH: (212) 943-2210   (800) 733-4371
(301) 654-5580
Cost: $645.00
Frequency: weekly
Date of first issue: 1990

Includes: Fundamental analysis. Covers: junk bonds. Gives a brief bond market commentary and highlights specific issues which have been in the news and gives other news relevant to this market. Also includes latest price, yield, ratings, call date and other information on the "Bellwether Group" of actively traded high yield issues.

Kelly 900 Hotline

PH: (900) 226-2466
(303) 476-9731
Cost: $2.45 per minute
Frequency of update:

TELEPHONE NEWSLETTER
Covers: S&P futures. An S&P Futures Day Trading System. "Specific, Unambiguous Buy, Sell and Exit Recommendations."

Kenneth J. Gerbino Investment Letter

Ken Gerbino and Co.
9595 Wilshire Blvd., Suite. 200
Beverly Hills, CA 90212

PH: (213) 550-6304
FAX: (213) 550-0814
Cost: $78.00 annually
Frequency: monthly
Date of first issue: 6/84

Includes: fundamental analysis. Covers: stocks and gold.
Stock market strategy, stock follow-ups, market updates, the Gold Report, The Economy, and Ken's editorial and analysis.

The Kiplinger Washington Letter

Austin Kiplinger
1729 H. Street NW
Washington, DC 20077-2733

PH: (202) 887-6400
(800) 544-0155
Cost: $63.00
Frequency: weekly
Date of first issue: over 65 years old

Covers: Business and investment news. Provides insightful business and investment forecasts to subscribers before the trends ever hit the news. Consists of four easy to read pages packed with concise, to the point forecasts on the outlook for business and investment growth.

Knight-Ridder Commodity Perspective

Knight-Ridder Financial Publishing
P.O. Box 94513
Chicago, IL 60690

PH: (800) 621-5271
(312) 454-1801
FAX: (312) 454-0239
Cost: $455.00
Frequency: Weekly
Date of first issue: 21 years

Chart service. Covers: commodities. Commodity charts showing: daily prices, moving averages, stochastics, weekly ranges, spreads, cash markets, RSI's, volume/open interest, Bullish consensus, technical comments, option volatilities and more.

Kondratieff Wave Analyst

Donald J. Hoppe
Investment Services, Inc.
P.O. Box 977
Crystal Lake, IL 60014

PH: (815) 459-2477
Cost: $125.00 per year
Frequency: monthly
Date of first issue: 1986

Includes: Fundamental analysis. Covers: stocks, precious metals. Provides a comprehensive cyclo-historical analysis of current economic, financial and market trends, based on the long-wave theory orginated by Nicolai D. Kondratieff in 1925. The emphasis is on long-term investment opportunities, trends, gold and silver. Offers continous coverage of the precious metals and the leading gold and silver mining stocks.

The Kon-Lin Letter

Kon-Lin Research and Analysis Corporation
5 Water Road
Rocky Point, NY 11778

PH: (516) 744-8536
Cost: $95.00
Frequency: Monthly
Date of first issue: about 10 years old

Includes: fundamental and technical analysis. Covers: stocks and market timing. "Reviews 30-35 different stocks on a monthly basis and monitors a broad range of technical indicators for the best possible Market Timing Device. Specializes in low priced stocks under $10 with an emphasis on emerging growth and special situations poised for explosive price appreciation." Special Service - free annual reports for most companies.

La Loggia's Special Situation Report and Stock Market Forecast

Charles M. LaLoggia
P.O. Box 167
Rochester, NY 14601

PH: (800) 836-4330
Cost: $230.00 annually
Frequency: every 3 weeks
Date of first issue: 1974

Covers: stocks and bonds (municipal, corporate, government). An 8 page newsletter covers takeover candidates, short sell recommendations, stock and bond market analysis, and economic outlook.

The Lancz Letter

Alan B. Lancz and Associates, inc.
3930 Sunforest Court #110
Toledo, OH 43623

PH: (419) 474-6733
FAX: (419) 474-6482
Cost: $250.00 annually
Frequency: monthly
Date of first issue: 1981

Includes: fundamental analysis. Covers: stocks. Market commentary and opinions. Has specific stock recommendations and several model portfolios to follow depending on objectives, i.e. high income, blue-chip, aggressive growth. Also gives portfolio allocation recommendations.

Lead Contract

Data Lab Publications
7333 N. Oak Park Avenue
Niles, IL 60648

PH: (800) 422-1599
 (708) 647-6678
Cost: $295.00 per year
Frequency: Weekly
Date of first issue: 15 years old

Chart service. Covers: commodities. Commodity futures charting service which includes: high, low, open, close, RSI and Stochastic Indicators, stacked 'Back Contracts' for hedging analysis, intra and inter commodity spreads and more.

Long Term Values

William O'Neil & Co./Daily Graphs
11915 La Grange Avenue
Los Angeles, Ca 90025
P.O. Box 24933
Los Angeles, Ca 90024-0933

PH: (213) 820-2583
(213) 820-7011
Cost: $219.00 annually
Frequency: every 6 weeks

CHART SERVICE
Includes: technical analysis. Covers: stocks.
15 year graphs on over 4000 stocks. Information includes description of company, quarterly earnings, EPS, sales performance, percentages, volume, earnings, beta & more.

Louis Rukeyser's Wall Street

Louis Rukeyser
1101 King St. Suite 400
Alexandria VA 22314

PH: (800) 892-9702
Cost: $39.50 annually
$79.00 2 years
Frequency: monthly
Date of first issue: March, 1992

Includes: analysis from Wall Street's top analysts, economists, and market experts. Each page features a different analyst with ideas, recommendations, and economic forecasts.

The Low Priced Stock Survey

Dow Theory Forecasts, Inc.
7412 Calumet Avenue
Hammond, IN 46324-2692

PH: (219) 931-6480
Cost: $48.00 every 6 months
Frequency: Bi-weekly
Date of first issue: 1946

Includes: Fundamental analysis. Covers: stocks. Stocks in the survey come from many industry groups and most trade under $25.00. Each issue includes a 2 page analysis of a new stock and also includes a Recommended List of low-priced stocks with our "Best Value" selections clearly highlighted for you. Nearly 90% of the recommended stocks are under $15.00 per share. Bonus offer with subscription.

Major Moves

Bruce Babcock
1731 Howe Avenue, Suite 149

PH: (916) 677-7562
Cost: $195.00 annually
Frequency: every 2 weeks
Date of first issue: 4/85

Includes: technical analysis and chart service.. Covers: commodities. Searches for special situations designed for long-term commodity traders. Gives specific recommendations illustrated with charts. Free with subscription to CTCR.

The Managed Account Advisor

Zin Investment Services
7 Switchbud Place #192-312
The Woodlands, TX 77380

PH: (713) 363-1000
Cost: $144.00
Frequency: monthly
Date of first issue:

Includes: Technical analysis. Covers: mutual funds. A mutual funds advisory letter with specific buy/sell recommendations. Includes a free hotline.

Managed Account Reports

MAR, Inc.
220 Fifth Avenue, Tenth Floor
New York, NY 10001

PH: (212) 213-6202
Cost: $225.00 annually
Frequency: monthly

Includes: technical analysis. Covers mutual funds. The publication provides in-depth reports on trading advisors, monthly performance data on over 100 private pools and all publicly held offered futures funds, as well as important educational research and current development material to help you better understand what to look for in determining the true performance of account managers.

Mansfield Stock Chart Service

Mansfield Investments
2173 Kennedy Blvd
Jersey City, NJ 07306

PH: (201) 795-0629
Date of first issue: 1971

CHART SERVICE- Costs and frequencies: annually

	weekly	bi-weekly	monthly
1 exchange	$688.00	$422.00	$217.00
2 exchanges	$1208.00	$770.00	$398.00
3 exchanges	$1706.00	$1081.00	$559.00

Includes: technical analysis. Covers: stocks. Weekly plotted charts on all stocks on NYSE, America, & OTC exchanges. Charts updated each Friday after the close and leave printer at 10:30 PM for delivery.

Margo's Market Monitor

Minuteman Publishing Co.
P.O. Box 642
Lexington, MA 02173

PH: (617) 861-1489
Cost: $125.00 annually
Frequency: twice a month

Includes: fundamental analysis. Covers stocks, mutual funds, and includes charts. Margo's primary aim is ling-term capital appreciation. Margo prefers to concentrate on stocks that seem to be out-of-favor yet possess identifiable price characteristics that have historically represented limited risk and above average potential. The Market Monitor also tracks only the sector funds offered by the Fidelity family of mutual funds.

Market Action

New Era Trading Company
6205 S. Mirror Lake Drive
Sebastian, FL 32958

PH:
Cost: $69.00 per year
Frequency: approximately every 2 weeks
Date of first issue:

Covers: market timing. "The letter's objective is to find 'Action Levels' where buying or selling can be done with minimum risk, whether you are trading stocks, futures, options or switching mutual funds."

Market Advisory

PH: (900) TEK-MOVE
Cost: $2.25 per minute
24 Hour service
Frequency of update: daily and sporadically throughout the day

TELEPHONE NEWSLETTER
Covers: stocks, commodities, municipal bonds, corporate bonds, and government bonds. Provides current market trends/actions, entry/exit points, resistance/support levels and target prices for specific issues.

Market Analytics

KRS Investment Services
Kenneth Stewart
P.O. Box 1368
Rockville, MD 20849-1368

PH: (602) 488-1586 - residence
Cost: $69.00 annually for monthly
$295.00 annually for weekly
Date of first issue: 1-7-91

Includes: technical analysis. Covers: stocks and charts. Each gives: price, volume, relative strength, high and low, risk, earnings, dividend, P/E, and Yield. Semilog charts covering S&P 500. A technical analysis using analytical methods to improve investment performance. Features include: model strategy, market condition, portfolio condition, and asset allocation. Includes free hotline updated every Friday evening.

Market Beat

Market Beat, Inc.
1436 Granada
Ann Arbor, MI 48103

PH: (313) 426-2146
Cost: $150.00 annually
Frequency: monthly
Date of first issue: 1987

Includes: technical analysis. Covers stocks and includes charts. The newsletter offers you: A mechanical trading signal that has outperformed the Dow; predicted dates of future highs and lows in the stock market given up to one year in advance; interest rate barometers given weekly on the hotline and forecasts for the high and low dates; DJI 30 component stock rankings and Fidelity Select Fund rankings; hourly DJI price projections given before each trading day, background indicators of market condition.

Market Charts

Market Charts, Inc.
20 Exchange Place 13th floor
New York, NY 10005

PH: (212) 509-0944
Cost: $550.00 annually twice a month
$330.00 annually for monthly
Date of first issue 1971

CHART SERVICE
Includes: technical analysis. Covers: stocks and includes charts. Market Charts is the only P&F service that brings you both short-term and long-term charts. The 1-point (short-term) chartbook is available on semi-monthly or monthly, while the long-term chartbook is published on a quarterly basis. Both books contain all common listed stocks on the NYSE & the ASE, plus selected South African Gold Stocks (ADRs) and Toronto listed gold stocks. The chartbooks are arranged by industry group rather than alphabetically, thus enabling you to study an entire group on one or two pages. You will also find a table of the S&P groups, showing how they rank against each other.

Market Cycle Investing

R. Earl Andrews, Editor
Andrews Publications
995 Oak Park Drive
Morgan Hill, CA 95037

PH: (408) 778-2925
Cost: $140.00 per year
Frequency: 17 per year
Date of first issue: 1974

Incluldes: Fundamental analysis. Covers: stocks, bonds. "Advises investors of economic and business trends, including the cycle phase of the investment market, interest rates, stocks, bonds, and real estate."
Comment: Looseleaf format; back issues available

Market Express

Strategic Communications
3443 Parkway Center Court
Orlando, FL 32808

PH: (407) 290-9600
(800) 333-5697
Cost: $49.00 annually
Frequency: monthly
Date of first issue 1974

Includes: fundamental analysis.Covers stocks.
This publication enables the reader to 'jump' on unique opportunities. The purpose of Market Express bring you fast, accurate information requiring immediate action so you can maximize your profits, i.e. stock recommendations.

Market Fax

DMC Market Fax - Glenn Cutler

PH: (415) 952-8853
Cost: $99.00 introductory offer / 2 months
regularly $150.00 a month
Frequency of update: nightly

FAX SERVICE
Covers: stocks, bonds, gold, and currencies.
Market Fax arrives on you fax just hours before the stock market opened. And in just 5 minutes, you'll know what the nation's #1 Stock Market TImer is thinking. and which stocks to buy and sell. By Glenn Cutler.

Market Line

Phone Express, Inc
4961 N. 106th Street
P.O. Box 25342
Milwaukee, WI 53225

PH: (900) USA-4444
Cost: per minute $1.99 not available in all areas
Frequency of update: 6AM EDT Every market day

Covers: futures, and stocks.
The top five U.S. market advisors. Specific buy and sell recommendations given daily. Low cap stocks with Glenn Cutler, Hot Stocks with Mark Leibovit, and OEX Futures with Jordan Goodman.

Market Logic

The Institute for Econometric Research
3471 N. Federal Highway
Ft. Lauderdale, Fl. 33306

PH: (800) 327-6720
(305) 563-9000
Cost: $200.00 annually
Frequency: bi-weekly
Date of first issue: 1975

Includes: fundamental and technical analysis. Covers: stocks, mutual funds, options, gold, stock index futures, and income securities. Every issue features stock recommendations, market advice, continuous follow-ups, gold forecast, option portfolio, strongest stocks advisory survey, Dow Theory, chart folio, the economy, and much more.

Market Mania

Market Mania, Inc.
P.O. Box 1234
Pacifica, CA 94044

PH: (415) 952-8853
Cost: $119.00 annually
Frequency: monthly
Date of first issue: 1983

Includes: fundamental analysis. Covers: stocks. The newsletter generally follows growth stocks and under-valued stocks. Most of the recommendations are OTC and AMEX stocks trading under $20.00 per share. It looks for insider buying and 13D filings for potential takeovers and special situations. Market Mania's hotline service is offered 3 days a week at no additional cost.

Market Momentum

Thomas D. Kienlen Corporation
P.O. Box 2245
Jasper, OR 97438

PH: (800) 999-3303
(900) 988-1838 ext. 819 - $2.00 per minute for updates
Cost: $175.00
Frequency: monthly
Date of first issue: 1991

Includes: Technical analysis. Covers: market timing. Uses technical analysis to "determine the market's direction, distance and duration." Gives specific buy/sell/hold recommendations and an in-depth report on a technical factor each month.

Market Momentum

Thomas D. Kienlen Corporation
P.O. Box 2245
Jasper, OR 97438

PH: (900) 988-1838 ext. 819
(800) 999-3303
Cost: $2.00 per minute
Frequency of update:

TELEPHONE NEWSLETTER
Covers: market timing. Uses technical analysis to "determine the markets' direction, distance and duration." Gives specific buy/sell and hold recommendations.

Market Month

Standard and Poor's Corporation
25 Broadway
New York, NY 10004

PH: (212) 208-8000
Cost: $53.00 per year
Frequency: monthly
Date of first issue: 1984

Includes: Fundamental analysis. Covers: stocks, tables, graphs. "Supplies individual investors with current market information in order to stimulate new business opportunities. Discusses market trends and offers specific stock recommendations and advice on pruning protfolios."

Market Trend Analysis

Lowry
631 US HWY 1
N. Palm Beach, FL 33408

PH: (800) 345-0186
Cost: $260.00 annually
$410.00 for both Power & Velocity and Market Trend
Analysis,
See Market Trend Analysis.
Frequency: weekly
Date of first issue: 1960

Includes: technical analysis. Covers: stocks. Provides
concise, factual commentary, graphics and a wealth of
statistical market information. Reports on the market as
a whole.

Market Viewpoint

Mike Chalek

PH: (900) 420-4246
Cost: $2.99 per minute
Frequency of update:

TELEPHONE NEWSLETTER
Offers market forecasting in the financials and energies
markets.

Marketarian, Inc.

Marketarian, Inc.
P.O. Box 1283
Grand Island, NE 68802

PH: (900) 226-6699
(800) 279-7751
Cost: $2.00 per minute
Frequency of update: 10:00 a.m., 3:00 p.m., and 7:00
p.m. EST

TELEPHONE NEWSLETTER
Covers: S & P Futures. Message is approximately 1 to
2 minutes in length.

The Marketarian Letter

Marketarian, Inc.
P.O. Box 1283
Grand Island, NE 68802-1283

PH: (800) 658-4325
(308) 381-2121
Cost: $225.00 per year
Frequency: every 3 weeks
Date of first issue: 1977

Covers: stocks, bonds, options and futures, and market
timing. Each issue provides stock recommendations,
industry group analysis, bond timing advice, up-to-date
analysis of current market activity, mutual fund switching, model portfolio review and model portfolios. Hotline
available for $2.00 per minute - (900) 226-6699.

Marples Business Newsletter

911 Western Avenue, Suite 509
Seattle, WA 98104

PH: (206) 622-0155
Cost: $64.00 annually
$35.00 6 months
Frequency: Every other Wednesday
Date of first issue 1949

Includes: fundamental analysis. Covers: stocks, and includes company reviews. The letter keeps busy executives and business people up to date in important developments in the Pacific Northwest. In addition to covering important economic trends, companies in the Pacific Northwest are regularly profiled that may be of interest to investors. The newsletter also covers stock trading by corporate insiders, earnings in banking and manufacturing, and salary trends. Supplement four times a year covers stock market action of more than 140 Pacific Northwest companies.

McAlvany Intelligence Advisor

Research Publications
P.O. Box 84904
Phoenix, AZ 85071

PH: (800) 528-0559
(800) 525-9556 Colorado
Cost: $95.00 annually
Frequency: monthly
Date of first issue 1978.

Includes: fundamental and technical analysis. Covers: precious metals and stocks. Uses charts.
Global economic review of in-depth monetary and geopolitical trends that impact the gold and precious metals markets.

Medical Technology Stock Letter

Jim McCamant
Piedmont Venture Group
P.O. Box 40460
Berkeley, CA 94704

PH: (415) 843-1857
Cost: $260.00 annually
Frequency: twice a month
Date of first issue: 12/83

Includes: fundamental analysis. Covers: stocks, market timing. An 8 page newsletter written in layman's language discussing current developments in medical technology. Gives specific buy price limits on recommended stocks and updated target prices until a sale is advised. MTSL is committed to helping subscribers make money from the changes taking place in the area of medical technology. Biotechnology promises to be the technology of the 1990's Breakthroughs are expected in treatments for cancer, AIDS, and arthritis. MTSL covers these developments and show how they will impact individual companies. Includes hotline access - 2 page company profiles on recommended stocks.

Mega-Trades

Taurus Corporation
P.O. Box 767
Winchester, VA 22601

PH: (703) 667-4827
Cost: $425.00 per year
Frequency: monthly
Date of first issue: 1983

Includes: Fundamental analysis. Covers: commodities, graphs. "Provides specific recommendations in the commodities investment field. Covers feeds and grains; livestock; foodstuffs; metals; cotton; heating oil and wood products; British, Canadian, German, Swiss, and Japanese currencies; Value Line, Standart & Poor's 500, and Treasury bills and bonds. Provides market analysis and buy/sell recommendations with stop-loss points."

Merrill Lynch Market Letter

Merrill Lynch
World Financial Center - North Tower
New York, NY 10281

PH: (212) 236-1000
(212) 449-8076
Price $49.00
Frequency: bi-monthly
Date of first issue: 1974

Includes: fundamental analysis. Market and economic commentary, investment ideas, earnings reports on recommended stocks, calendar with news to watch for.

Merriman Market Analyst Cycles Report

P.O. Box 1074
Birmingham, MI 48012

PH: (313) 626-3034
(800) 96204613
Cost: $195.00 annual or
$75.00 3 month trial
Frequency: every 3 weeks
Date of first issue: 1985

Includes: fundamental and technical analysis. Covers: gold, stocks, commodities, bonds, and includes graphs and charts. The main focus point of the newsletter is gold and other commodities. Features include: Review and Preview, Precious Metals, Trader's Recommendations, Stocks, T-Bonds and Foreign Currencies, Grains and more. Recommendations by Raymond A. Merriman - Account Vice President, Retail Futures of PaineWebber.

Middle/Fixed Income Letter

MASTCA Publishing Corp.
P.O. Box 55
Loch Sheldrake, NY 12759

PH: (914) 794-5792
Cost: $45.00 annually
Frequency: monthly
Date of first issue: 1981

Educational perspective. Covers all types of investment instruments. Uses an educational perspective to teach the functions of various financial instruments.

Momentum

7516 Castlebar Road
P.O. Box 470146
Charlotte, NC 28226

PH: (704) 365-4070
Cost: $88.00
Frequency: monthly
Date of first issue: 1985

Includes: Fundamental analysis. Covers: stocks, mutual funds, market timing, convertible bonds. Market commentary. Stock analysis divided into industry groups and including buy/sell/hold advice and stops. Same information provided for mutual funds. Also includes 6 model portfolios.

Monetary Digest

Certified Mint
2873 Sky Harbor Blvd.
Phoenix, AZ 85034

PH: (800) 528-1380
Cost: $36.00 per year
Frequency: Quarterly
Date of first issue: 1974

Includes: Fundamental analysis. Covers: precious metals. "Published as a service to customers of Certified Mint, a broker of precious metals. Reviews economic, monetary, and political developments affecting the prices of gold and silver. Lists current gold and silver prices and makes recommendations."

Monetary & Economic Review

FAMC, Inc.
3500 JFK Parkway, United Bank Building
Fort Collins, CO 80525

PH: (800) 325-0919
(800) 528-0559
FAX: (303) 223-4996
Cost: $150.00
Frequency: monthly
Date of first issue: 1984

Includes: fundamental analysis.
Covers options, stocks, commodities/futures, and precious metals. Table of Contents: Investments at a Glance; Taxes; U.S. & World Update; Inflation Watch; Financial Education; Book Review; Financial Insights; Inside Washington; Opinion of the Month; Letter. The focus of the letter is on economic and market forecasting, which includes information and analysis of world and domestic political events and their resultant impact on markets and business cycles.

Money and Markets

Weiss Research, Inc.
2200 N. Florida Mango Road
West Palm Beach, FL 33409

PH: (407) 684-8100
(800) 289-9222
Cost: $125.00
Frequency: monthly
Date of first issue: 1971

Includes: Fundamental analysis. Covers: stocks, municipal bonds, corporate bonds, government bonds, foreign bonds, interest rates, insurance. Features articles on important news and developments relating to T-Bills, banks, interest rates, insurance companies and more. Investment advice for the conservative and speculative investor.

Money and Markets Newsletter

Weiss Research, Inc.
P.O. Box 2923
West Palm Beach, FL 33402

PH: (407) 684-8100
(800) 289-2222
Cost: $125.00 annually
frequency: monthly
Date of first issue 1971

Includes: fundamental analysis. Overview of economy and stocks. Money & Markets is a newsletter for long-term investors and savers who demand outstanding total returns and maximum liquidity with minimum risk. Each issue features: main articles, conservative strategies, speculative strategies, the bank safety monitor, the money fund report, the metals detector, the delta strategy and high yields.

Money Management Letter

Institutional Investor Systems
488 Madison Avenue
New York, NY 10022

PH: (212) 303-3300
Cost: $1,150.00 annually
Frequency weekly
fundamental analysis
Date of first issue 1975

Covers pension fund investments (domestic stocks, bonds, and international securities) . Money Management Letter is a bi-weekly newsletter which covers the business of U.S. pension fund investment management. MML reports on which pension funds are hiring new money managers and why, what new strategies and products are being utilized and developed, and personnel changes that shift market power. MML follows the performance of all investment sectors popular among pension funds, including domestic stocks and bonds, international securities and real estate. Its goal is to provide marketing information to money managers and help plan sponsors act as more knowledgeable and effective fiduciaries.

Money Manager Verified Ratings

Norman Zadeh
P.O. Box 7634
Beverly Hills, CA 90212

PH: (213) 305-9300
FAX: (213) 273-7941
Cost: $200.00 per year
Frequency: monthly
Date of first issue: 1984

Covers: Money Manager Ratings. Requires money managers to specify a $1,000,000+ account at the beginning of each year and then send copies of brokerage statements to verify performance. Rates the best managers in several different categories: traditional buy and hold, mutual fund timers, small accounts, short selling and more.

Money Reporter

Marpep Publishing
133 Richmond Street West
Toronto, Ontario M5H 3M8, Canada

PH: (416) 869-1177
Cost: $197.00 annually
Frequency: weekly
Date of first issue: 1971

Covers: stocks, mutual funds, convertible securities and annuities. The Money Reporter covers various income producing investments, personal tax planning and financial planning, bonds and preferred share convertible securities, annuities, and mutual funds.

Money Reporter

MPL Communications and Marpep Publishing Limited
133 Richmond Street West
Toronto, Ontario M5H3M8

PH: (416) 869-1177
(416) 869-3021 Hotline for updates
Cost: $103.79
Frequency: weekly
Date of first issue: over 25 years old

Includes: fundamental analysis. Covers: Canadian stocks. A Canadian financial advisory newsletter providing recommendations, investment and tax tips, money rates and more.

The Money Strategy Letter

James McKeever
P.O. Box 4130
Medford, OR 97501

PH: (503) 826-9279
Cost: $195.00 per year
Frequency: monthly
Date of first issue: 1974

Includes: Fundamental analysis. Covers: stocks, commodities. "Provides investment advice and analyses of the stock market, including gold and silver, currencies, and energy futures. Also discusses interest rates, compound interest, the economy, insurance, and commodities."

Moneyline

USA Today
1000 Wilson Blvd.
Arlington, VA 22229

PH: (900) 555-5555
(800) USA-0001
Cost: $.95 per minute
24 Hour service

TELEPHONE NEWSLETTER
Covers: stocks. Use your touch tone phone to access stock quotes, CD rates, interest calculations, updates on your personal investments and used car prices. Quotes are delayed 15 minutes during trading hours.

The Moneypaper

Temper of the Times Communications, Inc.
1010 Mamroneck Avenue
Mamroneck, NY 10543
ISSN# 0745-9858

PH: (914) 381-5400
Cost: $72.00 annually
$108.00 for 2 years
Frequency: monthly
Date of first issue: 1981

Includes: fundamental analysis. Covers stocks and bonds. The contents of this newsletter are: Market Outlook, Portfolio Follow-up, Smarts - The ideas and information for this section are those of the editors or as a result of their research, Stocktrack - recommended stocks, Summing Up - Reaction to or restatement of items of interest read elsewhere, Direct Stock Purchase Plan.

Moody's Bond Survey

Moody's Investors Service
99 Church Street
New York, NY 10007

PH: (212) 553-0383
(212) 553-0437 - subscriptions
Cost: $1,175.00
Frequency: weekly
Date of first issue: 1909

Includes: Technical analysis. Covers: municipal bonds, corporate bonds, government bonds. "Presents statistical information and analysis of corporate, municipal, government, federal agency, and international bonds, preferred stock, and commercial paper. Includes ratings changes and withdrawals, calendars of recent and prospective bond offerings, and Moody's bond and preferred and preferred stock yield averages."

Motion Picture Investor

Paul Kagan Associates, Inc.
126 Clock Tower Place
Carmel, CA 93923-8734

PH: (408) 624-1536
Cost: $550.00
Frequency: monthly
Date of first issue: 1984

Includes: Fundamental analysis. Covers: stocks, tables, graphs. "Concerned with motion picture investment, financing and limited partnerships. Analyzes trends in motion picture stocks of publicly held companies, makes projections, and reports industry news."

MPT Review

Navellier & Associates, Inc.
P.O. Box 6349
Incline Village, NV 89450

PH: (702) 831-7800
Cost: $225.00
Frequency: monthly
Date of first issue: 1987

Includes: technical analysis. Covers: stocks.
Louis Navellier's MPT Review specializes in modern portfolio theory. Features include: Buy List, Investment Outlook & Strategy, Stocks to Watch, Q&A, Personal Picks, the qualified collective trust, MPT fund review, model portfolios, money management, and custom stock and portfolio analysis.

Muni Week

American Banker - Bond Buyer
One State Street
New York, NY

PH: (212) 943-8200
(800) 367-3989
(214) 741-1210 Dallas
Cost: $525.00 annually
Frequency: weekly
Date of first issue: 1988

Includes: fundamental analysis. Covers municipal bonds. Muni Week is news for tax-exempt issuers, lawyers and finance professionals. Contents include: market review, investing, state budgets, public finance, law, issuers, opinion, editor's comments, and Washington Watch.

Municipal Market Developments

Public Securities Association
1 World Trade Center
Suite 5271
New York, NY 10048

PH: (212) 809-7000
Cost: $125.00 per year
Frequency: Quarterly
Date of first issue: 1977

Includes: Technical analysis. Covers: tables, municipal bonds. "Provides new issue information on municipal securities. Analyzes financing trends and volume; statistical information on long- and short-term volume; volume by types of issues and issuers; type of offering; uses of proceeds of the bond issues; volume by state; average net interest costs; and underwriter ranking in various categories."

Mutual Fund Forecaster

The Institute for Econometric Research
3471 N. Federal Highway
Ft. Lauderdale, Fl. 33306

PH: (800) 327-6720
(305) 563-9000
Cost: $100.00 annually
Frequency: monthly
Date of first issue: 1979

Includes: fundamental analysis and charts. Covers: mutual funds. Each issue is filled with specific recommendations, market advice, money making ideas, performance ratings, follow-ups of prior recommendations, and a mutual fund directory. Includes free hotline updated every Friday evening.

Mutual Fund Forecaster

Institute for Econometric Research
3471 N. Federal Highway
Fort Lauderdale, FL 33306

PH: (800) 327-6720 ext. 351
(305) 563-9000
Cost: $100.00 per year
Frequency: monthly
Date of first issue: 2/85

Includes: Fundamental analysis. Covers: tables, graphs, mutual funds. "Forecasts performance for more than 300 mutual funds and rates best buys. Recurring features include a Directory of Mutual Funds, listing performance data, one-year profit projections, and risk rating."
Comments: Offers a weekly hotline to give current recommendations.

Mutual Funds Guide

Commerce Clearing House, INc.
4025 West Peterson, Avenue
Chicago, IL 60646

PH: (312) 583-8500
Cost: $570.00 annually
Frequency: every other week
Date of first issue: 1969

Includes: fundamental analysis. Covers: mutual funds. The Mutual Fund Guide combines federal and state regulatory requirements. The guide discusses initial planning strategies and formation of funds to the effective day-to-day operational details. Comments: 2 looseleaf volumes updated every other week.

Mutual Fund Investing

Phillips Publishing, Inc.
7811 Montrose Road
Potomac, MD 20854

PH: (800) 722-9000
Cost: $179.00 per year
Frequency: monthly
Date of first issue: 3/85

Includes: Fundamental analysis. Covers: mutual funds. "Offers analysis and advice concerning the mutual fund market. Makes specific recommendations and discusses related financial management issues."

The Mutual Fund Letter

Investment Information Services, Inc.
680 N. Lake Shore Drive, Tower Suite 2038
Chicago, IL 60611

PH: (312) 649-6940
FAX: (312) 649-5537
Date of first issue: 1983

Covers: mutual funds. Includes: fundamental analysis. Each issue contains investment outlook and strategy, model portfolios for five different investment objectives, investment ideas and portfolio management strategies, buy/hold/sell advice for specific funds, funds family reports and much more. This 12 page newsletter begins with a section on Current Outlook and Strategy.

Mutual Fund Marketing Newsletter

Investment Company Institute
1600 M street, N.W. suite 600
Washington, D.C. 20036

PH: (202) 293-7700
Cost: $25.00 annually
Frequency: quarterly
Date of first issue: 1988

Includes: fundamental analysis. Covers mutual funds. A quarterly newsletter that addresses issues of interest to those involved in mutual funds marketing and communications. It contains articles of interest by member mutual fund organization marketers, outside experts, and Institute staff.

Mutual Fund Strategist

Progressive Investments
Charlie Hooper - Editor
P.O Box 446
Burlington, VT 05402

PH: (802) 658-3513
Cost: $149.00 a year
Frequency: monthly
Date of first issue: 1982

Includes fundamental and technical analysis. Covers: mutual funds and market timing. Features short to intermediate and long term timing indicators for switching between growth and money market funds. Each issue also features a review of 25 other fund advisories and selected excerpts from mutual fund and stock market newsletters, buy/sell recommendations and model portfolios.Includes daily free hotline.

Myers Finance and Energy

P.O. Box 3082
Spokane, WA 99220

PH: (509) 534-7132
Cost: $149.00 annually
$240.00 2 years
Frequency: monthly

Includes: fundamental analysis. Covers: stocks, precious metals. Overview of worldwide economic situation recommendations on where to safely invest your money.

National Association of Small Business Investment Company News

1156 15th Street N.W.
Washington, DC 20005

PH: (202) 833-8230
Cost: $100.00 annually
Frequency: monthly
Date of first issue 1961

Includes: fundamental analysis. Covers: small business investment companies.NASBIC News is a letter for small business investment companies. Features include: Regulatory Issues, Industry Briefs, Meeting Calendar, and more.

Nelson's Earnings Outlook

Nelson Publications
1 Gateway Plaza
Port Chester, NY 10573

PH: (800) 333-6357
FAX: (914) 937-8908
Cost: $240.00 annually
Frequency: monthly
Date of first issue: 1990

Includes: Fundamental analysis. Covers: stocks. Earnings outlook gives investors instant access to Wall Street's latest earnings estimates on 3000 stocks - NYSE, AMEX, NASDAQ. Every month you will get a list of the stocks with the most significant change in earnings estimate from the previous month. "Up" and "Downs." For every company Earnings Outlook provides EPS for latest fiscal year, consensus earnings estimate for current and next fiscal year, change in estimate from the previous month, consensus rating, P/E using current year's estimate and number of analysts reporting estimates.

New Issues

The Institute for Econometric Research
3471 N. Federal Highway
Ft. Lauderdale, Fl. 33306

PH: (800) 327-6720
(305) 563-9000
Cost: $200.00 year
Frequency: monthly
Date of first issue: 1979

Includes: fundamental analysis. Covers: stocks - new issues. An authoritative source of information on the exciting new issues market. Each issue contains comprehensive analysis of the #1 new issue recommendations, other buy recommendations, avoid warnings, IPO calendar, follow-ups and more. Includes free hotline weekly hotline.

Ney Report

Richard Ney & Associates Asset Management
P.O. Box 9
Pasadena, CA 91109

PH: (818) 441-2222
(800) 444-2044
Cost: $81.25 10 week regular rate
$39.95 5 issue trial offer
Frequency twice an month
Date of first issue: 1976

Fundamental and technical analysis. Covers stocks and includes charts. The newsletter tracks stock exchange specialists - buying what they buy and selling what they sell. Mr. Ney starts by tracking the activity of 500 high-quality stocks on the ticker tape every day. The trade-by-trade data is fed into his computer which is programmed to record and reorganize big block transactions. He then coordinates this data with charting techniques. Then, by analyzing price movement and volume statistics, he is able to find patterns that reveal specialist buying and selling. On a daily basis he also monitors the movements of the Dow Average, interest rates, arranged openings and closings of the Dow and individual stocks, corporate announcements, and financial headlines for clues to specialist intent. Free telephone hotline with subscription - updated three times a week.

Nielsen's International Investment Letter

Thor Nielsen
P.O. Box 7532
Olympia, WA 98507
Cost: $125.00 annually
Frequency: 10 issues per year
Date of first issue: 1982

Includes: Fundamental analysis. Covers: stocks, currencies, commodities, gold and silver. An international investment advisory letter concentrating on capital appreciation. Includes specific recommendations for "super speculators" to the conservative investor, gives trading activity, stock comments and earnings reports and market comments.

The No Load Fund Investor

Sheldon Jacobs
P.O. Box 283
Hastings-on-Hudson, NY 10706

PH: (800) 252-2042
(914) 693-7420
Cost: $95.00
Frequency: monthly
Date of first issue: 10 years old

Includes: fundamental analysis. Covers: mutual funds. "Gives concrete practical advice and sound strategies for creating an investment portfolio that will grow steadily and safely." "Each issue tracks 644 no load funds and gives you comparative reports of their performance based on original research." Also provides specific recommendations and model portfolios.

No Load Fund X

DAL Investment Co.
Burton Berry
235 Montgomery Street #662
San Francisco, CA 94101

PH: (415) 986-7979
(800) 323-1510
FAX: (415) 986-1595
Cost: $109.00 annually
Frequency: monthly
Date of first issue: 1976

CHART SERVICE Includes: fundamental analysis. Covers: mutual funds and market timing. Highlights the 5 best funds by risk categories. A unique monitoring system designed to provide fund investors with the key information they need to know which funds to be in and when.

North American Gold Mining Stocks

Taylor Hard Money Advisors, Inc.
P.O. Box 1065
Jackson Heights, NY 11372

PH: (718) 457-1426
Cost: $60.00 annually
Frequency: monthly

Includes: fundamental and technical analysis. Includes gold, stocks, and charts. North American Gold Mining Stocks newsletter covers Junior Gold Stocks, and special situation. Features include: Industry Review, Portfolio and Performance Summary and more.

The Oberweis Report

Hamilton Investments, Inc.
841 N. Lake Street
Aurora, IL 60506

PH: (800) 323-6166
Cost: $95.00 or $145.00 by FAX
Frequency: monthly
Date of first issue: 1976

Includes: Fundamental analysis. Covers: stocks. Each issue highlights several current stocks of interest, gives extensive data on current portfolio including performance figures, lists closed out positions by year showing gain/loss and number of months held.

O.I.L.: Oil Income Letter

Securities Investigations, Inc.
Mill Hill Road
P.O. Box 888
Woodstock, NY 12498

PH: (914) 679-2300
Cost: $145.00 per year
Frequency: monthly
Date of first issue: 11/83

Includes: Fundamental analysis. Covers: oil and gas investments. "Presents information and analysis of current developments in the oil income industry. Provides advice concerning oil and gas funds as investments and as tax shelters. Also reviews legislation and governmental regulation affecting the industry."

On The Wires

Dow Jones News Services
Dow Jones and Company, Inc.
P.O. Box 300
Princeton, NJ 08543-0300

PH: (800) 223-2274
Cost: Free
Frequency: Monthly
Date of first issue:

Highlights from the prior broad tape news.

Opportunities in Options

David L. Caplan
P.O. Box 2126
Malibu, CA 90265

PH: (800) 255-3199
OTHER: (213) 457-3199 CA
Cost: $450.00 annually
Frequency: monthly
Date of first issue: 1983

Includes: technical analysis and option volatility. Covers: commodities and options. Includes actual trades. Professional option strategy - newsletter and "Hands On" trading manual. Includes twice a week hotline, and "Ask a Trader" personalized advice and weekly update on Hotline with recommendations.

The Option Advisor

Investment Research Institute
110 Boggs Lane, Suite 365
Cincinnati, OH 45246

PH: (800) 922-4869
Cost: $99.00 annually
Frequency: monthly
Date of first issue: 1981

Includes: technical analysis. Covers: options.
Easy to follow advice tells you exactly what to buy and when to sell. Speculative and aggressive portfolios.

Option Traders Hotline

Charles M. LaLoggia

PH: (900) 988-8080
INFO: (800) 836-4330
Cost: $2.00 per minute or any portion thereof
24 Hour service
Frequency of update: Daily M-F at NOON EST

Covers: options.
Daily option trading recommendations, US market commentary, and Tokyo market commentary for Nikkeii put traders. Each message includes: general market commentary, optionable stocks for call option buyers with specific break out levels to watch for, optionable stocks for put option buyers with specific break down levels to watch for, optionable stocks with unusual trading activity - potential takeover targets.

The Ord Oracle

7275#D South Xenia Circle
Englewood, CO 80112

PH: (900) 446-8899
(303) 440-3344
Cost: $2.25 per minute
Frequency of update: 5 times daily

TELEPHONE NEWSLETTER
Covers: options. "Nationally ranked trader reveals trading secrets. Picks tops and bottoms, predicts the big moves."

OTC Growth Stock Watch

OTC Research Corp.
P.O. Box 305
Brookline, MA 02146

PH: (617) 327-8420
Cost:
$75.00 w/o advisory hotline
$125.00 w/ unlimited advisory line
Frequency: monthly
Date of first issue: 1979

Includes: fundamental analysis. Covers: stocks.
The newsletter concentrates on providing a detailed report on little-known companies in the five to one hundred million dollar sales range that are growing at a rate consistently higher than most larger corporation. The reports are broken down into four specific areas: Market Commentary; Our Stock Recommendation of the Month; Corporate News Updates; Update List - stocks previously recommended.

The Outlook

Standard & Poor's
25 Broadway
New York, NY 10004

PH: (800) 777-4858
(212) 208-8768
Cost: $280.00 annually
Frequency: weekly

Regular features: stock choice and market update. Analyzes and projects business and stock market trends. Brief data on individual securities with buy recommendations. Also includes current S&P market indexes.

The Outside Analyst

The Outside Analyst N. V.
114 E. 32nd Street
Suite 602
New York, NY 10016-5583

PH: (212) 685-6900
FAX: (212) 685-8566
Cost: $320.00
Frequency: Monthly
Date of first issue: 6 years

Covers: stocks. Analyzes and summarizes the economic and financial reports from over 30 countries and offers specific advice on which stocks to buy or sell and which to keep watch on for the future.

Outstanding Investor Digest

Portfolio Reports
14 East 4th Street, Suite 501
New York, NY 10012

PH: (212) 777-3330
Cost: $175.00 annually
Frequency: monthly
Date of first issue 1985

Includes: fundamental analysis. Covers interviews of equity money managers. Outstanding Investor Digest brings you the most important ideas and insights of the money managers with the best long-term records in the business. Each issue provides you with a clear window on their personalities, investment philosophies, strategies, and approaches. Each is filled with exclusive conversations, in-depth interviews and substantive excerpts from their most recent letters to shareholders, partners, and private clients.

Overpriced Stock Service

Michael Murphy
P.O. Box 308
Half Moon Bay, CA 94019

PH: (415) 726-8495
FAX: (415) 398-7865
Cost: $495.00 annually
Frequency: monthly
Date of first issue: 1973

Includes: fundamental analysis. Covers: stocks and bonds (municipal, government, and corporate). Approximately 45 issues covered, industry coverage, general market trends and economy information. Subscription includes in house Hot Line recording updated twice a week.

Partnership Watch

Robert Stanger & Co.
1129 Broad Street
Shrewsbury, NJ 07701

PH: (800) 631-2291
(201) 389-3600
Cost: $147.00 annually
Frequency: monthly
Date of first issue: 1978

CHART SERVICE. Covers: partnerships.
Tracks all current and open partnerships. Lists and ranks each partnership, gives description, minimum purchase, all other pertinent details including telephone numbers. COMMENTS: For $395.00 total, also receive Stanger Report on all closed partnerships.

Pearson Investment Letter

1628 White Arrow
Dover, FL 33527

PH: (813) 659-2560
Cost: $150.00 annually
Frequency: monthly
Date of first issue: 1986

Includes: fundamental analysis. Covers stocks The newsletter addresses current economic occurrences throughout the country. Each letter lists 6 or more stocks with recommendations on what are good buys. Subscribing to this service will enable you to use a discount broker.

The Penny Stock Analyst

Joseph K. Cohen / The Penny Stock Analyst
P.O. Box 333
Woodstock, MD 21163-0333

PH:
Cost: $45.00 per year
Frequency: Monthly
Date of first issue:

Covers: penny stocks. "An investor's guide to low priced stocks." Provides specific recommendations on several issues each month.

Personal Advantage/Finance

Boardroom Reports, Inc.
P.O. Box 5371
Boulder, CO 80322

PH: (212) 239-9000
(800) 365-0939
Cost: $49.00 annually
Frequency: twice a month
Date of first issue: 1988

Covers: stocks and bonds. The purpose of this newsletter is to bring business people the most useful and timely advice from knowledgeable experts on all facets of personal finance. Features include: Fresh Thinking, Tax Advantage, Portfolio Strategy, Income Improvement, Recession Advantage, Bargains, Tax Traps, and Capital Preservation.

Personal Finance

Stephen Leeb -Editor
KCI Communications, Inc.
1101 King Street, Ste 400
Alexandria, VA 22314

PH: (800) 832-2330
Cost: $78.00 annually
Frequency: bi-monthly
Date of first issue: 1973

Includes: technical analysis. Covers: stocks and mutual funds. America's most popular full coverage investment advisory. Follow growth stocks, mutual funds, income investments with a model portfolio in each. Also has a money wise column dealing with topics of interest such as: taxes, insurance, divorce, etc. Includes free hotline with daily updates and recommendations.

The Peter Dag Investment Letter

Peter Dag & Associates, Inc.
65 Lake Front Drive
Akron, OH 44319

PH: (216) 644-2782
Cost: $250.00 per year
Frequency: 29 times a year
Date of first issue: 10/77

Includes: Fundamental analysis. Covers: stocks, bonds, precious metals. "Describes how to develop an investment strategy that will allow one to take advantage of emerging opportunities. Offers forecasts of short- and long-term stock market trends, short-term interest rates, bond prices, gold and silver, the economy, and overall business conditions. Also provides advice for managing retirement/pension funds."

The Philadelphia Advisor

Cardwell Nieves, Inc.
Andrew Cardwell
P.O. Box 1369
Woodstock, GA 30188

PH: (404) 591-7030
FAX: (404) 591-0672
Cost: $595.00 annually
Frequency: bi-monthly
Date of first issue: 1985

Includes: technical analysis. Covers: stocks, futures, and market timing. A trade service focusing on intermediate and long-term moves in commodity futures, stocks, and Dow timing. It has a totally technical trading program based on the RSI and designed to identify those few low-risk, high-profit opportunities that occur each month. The telephone update service issues the buy points.

PivotPlus Signals

PH: (900) 329-7001
(312) 989-7151
Cost: $2.00 per minute
24 Hour service
Frequency of update: 3 to 5 times daily

TELEPHONE NEWSLETTER
Covers: S & P Futures, Bonds, OEX, NYFE, Gold, Crude, and Currencies.

Plain Talk Investor

Plain Talk Investor, Inc.
Fred Gordon, Author
1500 Skokie Blvd., Suite 203
Northbrook, IL 60062

PH: (708) 564-1955
Cost: $115.00 annually
Frequency: every 3 weeks (17 times a year)
Date of first issue: 1983

Covers: stocks. Includes: fundamental and technical analysis. The newsletter includes: Portfolio Notes - a follow-up and news on recommended stocks, pro or con; Portfolio Reviews - every issue, every recommended stock is listed: date purchased, cost, current price, percent of gain or loss, and the price at which you should sell; Personal Best Portfolio - Mr. Gordon's top choice of earnings - powered quality growth stocks; High Risk/High Reward Portfolio - under-followed and often undiscovered stocks; Market Insight - the market's technical and fundamental signs; Opening Commentary; Reading the Signs - a menu of the technical indicators used; Odd Lots - snippets of market wisdom; Stock Recommendations.

Portfolio Letter

Institutional Investor Systems
488 Madison Avenue
New York, NY 10022

PH: (212) 303-3300
Cost: $1,150.00 annually
Frequency: weekly
Date of first issue: 1975

Includes: fundamental analysis. Covers: stocks. Portfolio Letter covers the equity markets world-wide by breaking down news on issues that affect the broad market and its industry groups, and by covering developments in specific stocks. Portfolio Letter speaks to money managers, analysts, institutional salesmen, traders, and arbitragers, among others, to get its leads, and also interviews corporate officials. The newsletter covers a wide range of industries and also includes coverage of developments in Washington, D.C. that can affect stocks and industry groups.

Portfolio Reports

Portfolio Reports
14 East 4th Street
New York, NY 10012

PH: (212) 777-3330
Cost: $475.00 annual (12 reports)
$195.00 annual (4 reports)
Frequency: monthly or quarterly
Date of first issue: 1985

Includes: fundamental analysis. Covers: common stock purchases. Portfolio Reports brings you the most important and latest common stock purchases of the money managers with the best long-term records in the business. Each report the 10 stocks most purchased recently by more than 80 top managers in well over 100 of their portfolios. For each stock, they highlight the number of shares purchased and total shares owned, the dollar value of each and recent market price or cost per share. Portfolio Reports comes in two versions: By money manager or by security.

Portfolio Selector

Argus Research Corporation
17 Battery Place
New York, NY 10004

PH: (212) 425-7500
Cost: $390.00
Frequency: monthly
Date of first issue: 1934

Includes: Fundamental analysis. Covers: stocks. Represents Argus' best buy ideas. Stocks are arranged by investment objectives such as Capital Gains and Income, Long-Term Growth, Businessman's Risk and Emerging growth Fundamental data and commentary included on the recommended stocks. Includes subscription to Viewpoint.

Powell Monetary Analyst

Reserve Research
P.O. Box 4135
Portland, ME 04101

PH: (207) 774-4971
Cost: $285.00 annually
$150.00 6 months
$85.00 3 months
Frequency: bi-weekly
Date of first issue: 1971

Includes: fundamental analysis. Covers: stocks, gold, silver, platinum. Focuses on fundamental trends in the economy. A large portion of the letter addresses the trends and demands on gold, silver, and platinum. Usually one company is reviewed. There are also sections on foreign currency and gold coin.

Power and Velocity Ratings

Lowry
631 US HWY 1
N. Palm Beach, FL 33408

PH: (800) 345-0186
Cost: $260.00 annually
$410.00 for both Power & Velocity and Market Trend Analysis.
See Market Trend Analysis.
Frequency: weekly
Date of first issue: 1960

CHART SERVICE
Includes: technical analysis. Covers: stocks. Provides unique relative strength rankings on 700+ institutional quality NYSE issues.

P.Q.'s Real Time Market Comments

P.Q. Wall
P.O. Box 480601
Denver, CO 80248-0601

PH: (900) 234-7777 ext 77
(303) 440-3344
Cost: $2.00 per minute
24 Hour service
Frequency of update: 4 times daily EST 10:10, 12:30, 3:00, 5:00

Covers: commodities, and market timing.
Tries to keep recordings under one minute. Market commentary with recommendations to buy/sell based on level of Dow.

PQ Wall Forecast, Inc.

P.Q. Wall
P.O. Box 480601
Denver, CO 80248-0601

PH: (303) 458-8720
OTHER (800) 748-2136
FAX: (303) 455-1523
Cost: $198.00 annually
Frequency: monthly
Date of first issue: 1981/ 1/1/88 as PQ Wall

Includes: fundamental analysis. Covers: stocks and market timing. Stock market letter with specific recommendations, market commentary and his theories.
For additional $300/year - receive daily telephone update. Available 1 and a half hours after the market closes.

Precision Timing

Don Vodopich
P.O. Box 11722
Atlanta, GA 30355

PH: (404) 355-0447
Price $205.00 year
Frequency: weekly
Date of first issue 1974

Covers: commodities and futures. The letter focuses on the futures market including an overall look at all major markets.

The Primary Trend

James R. Arnold
Arnold Investment Counsel, Inc.
First Financial Center
700 N. Water Street
Milwaukee, WI 53202

PH: (800) 443-6544
(414) 271-2726
Cost: $180.00 per year
Frequency: every 3 weeks
Date of first issue: 4/79

Includes: Fundamental analysis. Covers: stocks, mutual funds, government bonds, tables, graphs. "Comments on general market conditions and makes recommendations to buy, sell or hold specific stocks based on the investment philosophy of Arnold Investment Counsel." And it is the same advice that is used to guide The Primary Trend Fund, a no-load growth and income fund managed by Arnold Investment Counsel. Intended for: "Investors whose strategy is to structure their portfolios in harmony with the primary (long-term) trend of the various markets."
Comments: Registered with the Securities and Exchange Commission as an investment adviser.

Pring Market Review

International Institute for Economic Research
P.O. Box 329
Washington Depot, CT 06794

PH: (800) 221-7514
(203) 868-7772
FAX: (203) 868-2683
Cost: $395.00 annually
Frequency: monthly
Date of first issue: 1984

Includes: technical analysis. Covers: stocks, commodities, market timing, chart service, municipal and government bonds. Designed and written for the resourceful and sophisticated investor who is willing to learn the art of cyclical investing through a study of technical analysis.

Professional Tape Reader

Stan Weinstein
P.O. Box 2407
Hollywood, FL 33022

PH: (800) -868-7857
Cost: $295.00 annually
Frequency: bi-monthly
Date of first issue: 1976

Includes: technical analysis.
Covers: stocks, mutual funds, options, and market-timing. Technical advisory newsletter.

The Professional Tape Reader

RADCAP, Inc.
P.O. Box 2407
Hollywood, FL 22033

PH: (900) 872-4787 (Hotline)
Cost: per minute $2.00
Frequency of update: daily at 8PM EST
Covers: stocks, bonds, gold

It covers the market's short term outlook, stock index futures, most promising and most vulnerable stocks and trading outlook for bonds and gold.

Professional Timing Service

Curtis Hesler - Publisher
P.O. Box 7483
Missoula, MT 59807

PH: (800) 348-2729 ext 13
(Orders) (406) 543-4131
Cost: $185.00 for 14 months
Frequency: monthly
Date of first issue: 1987

Includes: fundamental and technical analysis.
Covers stocks, bonds, mutual funds, and market timing. The model is based on monitoring money flow - if money is flowing into the market at sufficient intensity, the model tells us to buy. At that time, we switch managed accounts into equity funds and announce on our hotline that subscribers should do likewise. When the money flow dries up, the model will tell us to move back to money markets. Subscription includes monthly market letter and hotline three times a week.

The Profit Letter

Profit Letter, Inc.
908-4390 Grange Street
Burnaby, BC Canada V5H1P6

PH: (604) 436-3751
FAX: (604) 436-3751
Cost: $125.00
Frequency: Bi-monthly
Date of first issue: 1987

Includes: Fundamental analysis. Covers: stocks. Concentrates on capital gain stocks and gives specific recommendations and updates on previous recommendations.

The Prudent Speculator

Al Frank Asset Management, Inc.
P.O. Box 1767
Santa Monica, CA 90406-1767

PH: (213) 395-5275
Cost: $60.00 trial offer 4 issues
$225.00 yearly 17 issues
Frequency: every three weeks
Date of first issue: 1977

Includes: fundamental and technical analysis Covers: stocks, charts, market timing. The Prudent Speculator recommends under-valued stock selling at 50% of value which will at a minimum double in 3-5 years. Includes strategies for investing in common stocks using fundamental analysis for stock selection and technical analysis for market timing.

The Psychic Forecaster

Roberto Veitia/Strategic Communications USA, Inc.
3443 Parkway Center Court
Orlando, FL 32808

PH: (800) 333-5697
Cost: $58.00 annually
Frequency: monthly
Date of first issue 1989

Includes: fundamental analysis. Covers: stocks and charts.
The psychic Forecaster provides a solar horoscope(used only as a general indicator) , and financial predictions.

Quarterly Performance Report

LJB/Communications, Inc.
200 Joseph Square
Columbia, MD 21004

PH: (301) 730-5365
Cost: $265.00 per year
Frequency: Quarterly
Date of first issue: 10/81

Includes: Fundamental analysis. Covers: commodities. "Contains statistical information about commodity trading advisors and commodity pool operators mentioned in Managed Accounts Reports (see separate listing) . Each individual trading advisor is rated by performance and operating statistics in the areas of Net Asset Value (NAV) per unit, MAR performance index, rate of return, profits/losses, largest drawdown, and number of individual accounts managed. Covers up to a 3 year period for each advisor."

Rate Watch

Bauer Communications, Inc.
P.O. Drawer 145510
Coral Gables, FL 33114

PH: (305) 441-2062
Cost: $99.00 annually
or $59.00 for 6 months
Frequency: monthly
Date of first issue 1983

Covers: money market accounts and CD's. The news-letter tracks current rate Money Market Accounts and CD's with a minimum deposit of $100-50,000 with credit-worthy institutions. They provide you with a contact person,
PH: number, safety rating, rate and yield and penalty. The terms are 3-months to ten years.

Rational Investment Outlook

Arie Vilner
Vilner Enterprises, Inc.
Bowling Green Station
P.O. Box 1605
New York, NY 10274-1132
Cost: $139.00
Frequency: monthly
Date of first issue: 1990

Includes: Technical analysis. Covers: stocks, mutual funds, market timing, gold. Uses a proprietary method of market trend forecasting - not the typical technical analysis. Provides stock and mutual fund selections, company report, investment strategies, new technologies, world investment environment and more.

The Reaper

A.N., Inc.
P.O. Box 39026
Phoenix, AZ 85069

PH: (800) 528-0559
Cost: $195.00 per year
Frequency: 36 issues a year
Date of first issue: 6/77

Includes: Fundamental analysis. Covers: commodities. "Provides investors with an analysis of the international and domestic economic, political and financial environment. Offers projections particularly in the area of commodities, specific buy and sell recommendations in the commodity futures markets, and instructions on how to analyze the market."

REIT Watch

National Association of Real Estate Investment Trusts, Inc.
1129 20th Street, N.W. Suite 705
Washington, D.C. 20036

PH: (202) 785-8717
Cost: $145.00 annually
Frequency: quarterly
Date of first issue: fall 1990

Includes: fundamental analysis. Covers: REIT's.
Investment publication detailing REIT industry performance including; a concise review of industry activities, comparative investment return scorecard, total return, dividend yield and other stats for all publicly traded REITs, REIT article reference list and discussion of issues relevant to REITs. Subscription also includes Directory of Members and REIT Sourcebook, and is restricted to retail stock brokers and financial planners.

Retirement Letter

Phillips Publishing
7811 Montrose Road
Potomac, MD 20854

PH: (800) 722-9000
Cost: $49.00 per year
Frequency: monthly
Date of first issue: 1981

Includes: Fundamental analysis. Covers: stocks, mutual funds. "Provides analysis of the performance of 83 mutual funds and of the economic and market outlook. Also carries stock and gold market forecasts and two model portfolios."

The Richland Report

Kennedy Gammage
P.O. Box 222
La Jolla, California 92038

PH: (619) 459-2611
Cost: $197.00 annually
Frequency: every 2 weeks
Date of first issue: 1976

Covers: stocks, mutual funds, and market timing. General overview of the market, concentrating on market timing, McClellan Oscillator, occasional market recommendations.

The Richland Report

The Richland Company
P.O. Box 222
La Jolla, CA 92038

PH: (619) 459-2611
Cost: $177.00 per year
Frequency: Semi-monthly
Date of first issue: 1976

Covers: stocks, bonds, precious metals. "Reports on the investment outlook for markets in stocks, bonds, gold, silver, interest rate, money instrument, and others. Analyzes political, social, and economic events of interest to investors."

The Risk Report

Richard Schmidt
3479 N. High Street
Columbus, OH 43214

PH: (800) 466-RISK
Cost: $199.00
Frequency: every 3 weeks
Date of first issue: 1991

Includes: Technical analysis. Covers: stocks, mutual funds, municipal bonds, corporate bonds, government bonds. An investment advisory newsletter with a common sense approach. Information is delivered in plain english and includes very specific investment recommendations. Also available via fax for an additional $129.00.

The Risk Report

Richard Schmidt
3479 N. High Street
Columbus, OH 43214

PH: (800) 466-RISK
Cost: $328.00 annually
Frequency of update: every 3 weeks

TELEPHONE NEWSLETTER
Fax service. Covers: stocks, mutual funds and bonds.
An investment advisory service with a common sense
approach delivered in plain English. Gives very specific
recommendations.

The Roesch Market Memo

Larry Roesch
P.O. Box 4242
Shawnee Mission, KS 66204

PH: (913) 381-0857
Cost: $42.00 annually
Frequency: monthly
Date of first issue: 1980

Includes: fundamental and technical analysis.
Covers: stocks. The memo recommends stocks using
both fundamental and technical analysis. The author
also gives political comments related to the market, buy
and sell recommendations, and major market turns.

The Ron Paul Investment Newsletter and Political Report

Ron Paul & Associates, Inc.
1120 NASA Blvd., Suite 104
Houston, TX 77058

PH: (713) 333-4888
Date of first issue: 1985
Cost: $99.00 annually
Frequency: monthly
new subscribers can access financial hotline every
Monday

Includes: fundamental analysis. Covers: stocks, commodities, mutual funds, and bonds. Each month Ron
Paul gives the facts and analysis and specific recommendations that you need to protect yourself, and dra-
matically increase your wealth, in the spastic economy
of the 1990's.

The Ruff Times

Main Street Alliance
4457 Willow Road
Pleasanton, CA 94566

PH: (415) 463-2200
ISSN# 0891-5547
Cost: $149.00 annually
Frequency: twice a month (26 issues)
Date of first issue: 1976

Includes: fundamental analysis. Covers stocks, mutual
funds, and bonds (municipal, corporate, government).
The newsletter focuses on the general market - strong vs
weak areas. The author, Howard Ruff, looks closely at
long-term trends before making his recommendations.
Some of the features include: Ruff Goofs, Ask Howard,
Good News/Bad News, Truth in Lending and more.

Ruta Financial Services Newsletter

Phillip Ruta
P.O. Box 952
Bronxville, NY 10708

PH: (914) 779-1983
(800) 832-1891
Cost: $90.00 annually
Frequency: monthly
Date of first issue: 1984

Includes: fundamental analysis. Covers: stocks, commodities, and market timing; municipal, government, and corporate bonds. Issues 24 in depth stock recommendations per year/ 2 each month plus periodic investor alerts on issues that can't wait until the next printing. Gives conservative recommendations, and has a very good track record.

Sarcoh Report

Sarcoh Report, Inc.
48 Park Terrace
Spring Valley, NY 10977

PH: (914) 354-0030
(914) 354-2114
Cost: $165.00 annually
Frequency: 20-24 issues per year
Date of first issue: 1991

Includes: Fundamental and technical analysis. Covers: stocks, bonds, futures, options, market timing, mutual funds. A conservative investment advisory letter focused on risk avoidance. Includes charts and several recommendations. Also includes daily telephone updates.

The Seasonal Trader Report

SJS, Inc.
889 Ridge Lake Blvd., Suite 350
Memphis, TX 38119-9947

PH: (800) 526-4612
(901) 766-4510 (outside U.S.)
Frequency: weekly
Cost: $349.00 annually
Date of first issue: 1981

Includes: fundamental analysis. Covers commodities, precious metals, and financials. A 4-page weekly letter with one specific short-term recommendation based on computer research. Detailed historical performance data on each recommendation is provided.

SEC Docket

Commerce Clearing House, Inc.
4025 West Peterson Avenue
Chicago, IL 60646

PH: (312) 583-8500
Cost: $230.00 annually
Frequency: weekly
Date of first issue: Nov 1981

Includes: fundamental analysis. Covers: SEC Dockets Every week you receive new releases of SEC Dockets. An updated index is included every 20 issues.

SEC Today

Washington Service Bureau
655 15th Street N.W., Suite 270
Washington, D.C. 20005

PH: (202) 833-9200
(800) 828-5354
Cost: $525.00 annually
Frequency daily
Date of first issue: 1983

Includes: fundamental analysis. Covers: SEC releases. The newsletter begins with a letter from the editor addressing a current news item. It also lists various filings such as, 8K filings, Williams Act filings, and new registered securities, This is followed by comments from SEC News Digest. On a weekly basis, Supreme Court SEC related cases and No Action letters are covered.

Sector Fund Connection

Mannie Webb
8949 La Riviera Drive
Sacramento, CA 95826

PH: (916) 363-2055
Cost: $35.00 annually
Frequency: quarterly
Date of first issue: 1981

Includes: fundamental analysis. Covers mutual funds. The newsletter covers a variety of mutual fund trading methods.

Securities Industry Trends

Research Department - Securities Industry Association
120 Broadway
35th Floor
New York, NY 10271

PH: (212) 608-1500
Cost: $60.00 for members
$90.00 for nonmembers
Frequency: 8 per year
Date of first issue:

Includes: Fundamental analysis. Covers: securities. "Examines economic developments affecting securities firms, including tax policy, the changing composition of the securities industry, and major trends in the industry. Supplies a series of security industry statistics tables and a reading list."

Securities Week

McGraw-Hill Publications
1221 Avenue of the Americas
Nw York, NY 10020

PH: (212) 512-3144
(800) 445-9786
Cost: $1310.00 annually
Frequency: weekly
Date of first issue: 1972

Includes: fundamental analysis. Covers: stocks and commodities/futures. Securities Week is a report on the securities industry and financial futures markets. The four areas of security firms covered are: exchange, institutional investment banking firms, futures and options, regulatory and legislative.

Sentinel Investment Letter

Hanover Investment Management Corp.
P.O. Box 189
52 South main Street
New Hope, PA 18938

PH: (215) 862-5454
Cost: $150.00 annually
Frequency: monthly
Date of first issue: 1986

Includes: fundamental analysis. Covers: stocks and bonds.
The newsletter focuses in unique things that affect the stock market, such as interest rates and inflation. The author also discusses opportunities of when to buy and sell.

Shelburne Securities Forecast

Robert Shelburne
P.O. Box 5566
Arlington, VA 22205

PH: (703) 532-4416
Cost: $49.00 annually
Frequency: twice a month
Date of first issue: 1976

Includes: fundamental analysis. Covers: utilities stocks.
This 6-8 page newsletter covers stocks and utilities.
Spoke with Robert Shelburne.

Short Term Consensus Hotline

Dr. Harry B. Schiller

PH: (900) 860-9990
(415) 956-3766
Cost: $2.00 for the first minute - $1.00 thereafter
Frequency of update:

TELEPHONE NEWSLETTER
Covers: market timing. Rating service for short-term timers.

Shortex

6669 Security Blvd. #201 Dept. S.
Baltimore, MD 21207-4024

PH: (800) 877-6555
Cost: $249.00 per year
Frequency: bi-weekly
Date of first issue: 1 and 1/2 years

Includes: fundamental analysis and technical analysis.
Covers: stocks. Chart selected short sales. New trades in each issue with stop loss, profit objective and price to cover. Also includes a special advisory on long positions.

Silver and Gold Report

Dan Rosenthal
Weiss Research Publications, Inc.
P.O. Box 2923
West Palm Beach, FL 33402

PH: (800) 289-8100
Cost: $96.00 annually
Frequency: monthly
Date of first issue: 1981

Includes: fundamental analysis. Covers silver and gold. The author, Dan Rosenthal, surveys 23 leading firms in the bullion industry. He explains where and what to buy is as important as when to buy. He also lists dealers with the best prices.

Small + Tomorrow's Commodities

Techno-Fundamental Investments, Inc.
Robert Jubb
P.O. Box 6216
Scottsdale, AZ 85261

PH: (602) 996-2908
Cost: $295.00 annually
Frequency: twice monthly
Date of first issue: 1974

Includes: fundamental and technical analysis. Covers: commodities. Detailed analysis of only a few recommendations using proprietary technical and fundamental research tools. Includes charts and follow-up discussion of previous recommendations.

Small + Tomorrow's Stocks

Techno-Fundamental Investments, Inc.
Robert Jubb
P.O. Box 6216
Scottsdale, AZ 85261

PH: (602) 996-2908
Cost: $145.00 annually
Frequency: twice monthly
Date of first issue: 1974

Includes: fundamental and technical analysis. Covers: stocks. Detailed analysis of a few recommendations using proprietary technical and fundamental research tools. Includes charts and updates on previous recommendations.

Smart Money

The Hirsch Organization
6 Deer Trail
Old Tappan, NJ 07675

PH: (201) 664-3400
Cost: $98.00 annually
Frequency: monthly
Date of first issue: 1972

Includes: fundamental analysis. Covers: company reviews and stocks. Smart Money focuses on America's most undiscovered companies.

SMR Commodity Service

Security Market Research, Inc.
Box 7476
Boulder, CO 80306-7476

PH: (303) 781-6005
(303) 442-4121
Cost: $500.00 annually for SMR commodities only
$750.00 annually for SMR commodities and stocks
Frequency: weekly
Date of first issue: 1967

Includes: Technical analysis. Covers: commodities, chart service. Each chart covers 155 - Trading Days; with commodities having open, high, low, close; total volume, and open interest. Commodity charts have the 49-day moving average; and the SMR Trading Oscillator; with all prices and indicators updated through Friday's close. Two charting styles are offered: Standard Bar or Japanese Candlestick. Also available via Daily Hotline Fax Service - $490.00 for one service, stocks or commodities - $790.00 for both services, stocks and commodities.

SMR Stock Service

Security Market Research, Inc.
Box 7476
Boulder, CO 80306-7476

PH: (303) 781-6005
(303) 442-4121
Cost: $500.00 annually for SMR stocks only
$750.00 annually for SMR stocks and commodities
Frequency: weekly
Date of first issue: 1967

Includes: Technical analysis. Covers: stocks, chart service. Each chart covers 155 - Trading Days; with stocks having open, high, low, close, and volume. Stock charts have the 49-day moving average; and the SMR Trading Oscillator; with all prices and indicators updated through Friday's close. Two charting styles are offered: Standard Bar or Japanese Candlestick. Also available via Daily Hotline Fax Service - $490.00 for one service, stocks or commodities - $790.00 for both services, stocks and commodities.

Sound Advice

Gray Emerson Cardiff
191 North Hartz Avenue, Suite 6
Dunville, CA 94526

PH: (800) 423-8423
Cost: $125.00 annually
Frequency: monthly
Date of first issue: 1981

Includes: fundamental and technical analysis. Covers: precious metals, stocks, and includes charts. Sound Advice is the advisory letter for panic-proof investing. Features which may be included: Business Cycle Signals, The Stock Market Risk Indicator, Precious Metals and Portfolio Update.

Southeast Business Alert

Word Merchants, Inc.
2000 Riveredge Parkway
Atlanta, GA 30328

PH: (404) 984-0151
Cost: $198.00
Frequency: monthly
Date of first issue: 1989

Includes: fundamental analysis. Covers: Southeast businesses stocks, and provides some charts. This 8 page newsletter focuses on businesses in the Southeast. A few regular features are: Insider Trading Report, Six month Activity Summary and Business Brief.

Special Situation Report

Charles LaLoggia
P.O. Box 167
Rochester, NY 14601

PH: (716) 232-1240
Cost: $230.00 annually
Frequency: every 3 weeks
Date of first issue: 1974

Includes: fundamental and technical analysis. Covers: stocks, and provides some charts. The report gives a general market commentary and what to look for in regards to takeover targets. The author also recommends other stocks with an emphasis on insider buying or selling.

Special Situations

Argus Research Corporation
17 Battery Place
New York, NY 10004

PH: (212) 425-7500
Cost: $390.00
Frequency: monthly
Date of first issue: 1934

Includes: Fundamental analysis. Covers: stocks. A new stock pick is introduced every other issue and updates on previous recommendations are included. Each issue contains EPS, price/earnings ratio, return on equity and performance record on all recommendations.

Special Situations Newsletter

Charles H. Kaplan
150 Nassau Street
Room 1926
New York, NY 10038

PH: (212) 908-4168
Cost: $50.00 per year
Frequency: monthly

Date of first issue:

Includes: Fundamental analysis. Covers: stocks. "Examines companies by providing a corporate profile and analysis of investment rating, financial condition, earnings per share growth for the year, and takeover potential, then suggests an investment stratgey."

The Speculator

Growth In Funds, Inc.
77 South Palm Avenue
Sarasota, FL 34236

PH: (813) 954-0330
Cost: $95.00 for six months
$175.00 annually
Frequency: every 3 weeks
Date of first issue: 1968

Includes: fundamental and technical analysis.
Covers: stocks and uses charts. The Speculator includes: buying ideas, including low-prices OTC choices; trading suggestions; insider buying details; "What to Do About" the most active low-priced stocks; "Stock of the Week" feature and follow-ups.

Spread Scope Commodity Charts

Spread Scope, Inc.
P.O. Box 5841
Mission Hills, CA 91345

PH: (800) 232-7285
Cost: weekly $325.00 annually bi-weekly
$205.00 annually monthly $205.00 annually
agricultural only... $205.00 annually   f i n a n c i a l
only....... $205.00 annually
Frequency: weekly, bi-weekly, or monthly.
Date of first issue: 1976

Includes: technical analysis. Covers: commodities.
Spread Scope Commodity Spread Charts offers both agricultural and financial charts.

Spread Scope Commodity Spread Letter

Spread Scope, Inc.
P.O. Box 5841
Mission Hills, CA 91345

PH: (800) 232-7285
Cost: $195.00 annually
Frequency: weekly
Date of first issue: 1976

Includes: Technical analysis. Covers: commodities. The Spread Letter includes current open positions, recommendations, and comments.

Spread Scope Long Term Charts

Spread Scope, Inc.
P.O. Box 5841
Mission Hills, CA 91345

PH: (800) 232-7285
Cost: $35.00 for all 80 charts
$20.00 for 40 bar charts
$20.00 for 40 spread charts
Frequency: monthly
Date of first issue: 1976

Includes: Technical analysis. Covers: commodities, chart service. Spread Scope Long Term Charts offers both agricultural and financial charts. Weekly high-low close published monthly.

SRC Blue Book of 5 Trend Cyclic - Graphs

Babson-United Investment
 Advisors Inc.
101 Prescott Street
Wellesley Hills, MA 02181

PH: (800) 343-4300
(617) 235-0900
Cost: $25.00 ea or $89.00 annually
Frequency: quarterly
Date of first issue: 1935

Includes: fundamental analysis. Covers: stocks and chart service. 12 year coverage of 1108 listed stocks. Set each stock's extended history of monthly price ranges, relative market action, volume, earnings, and dividends. Semi-logarithmic grids present this wealth of information in a clear, visually accurate format suited to easy measurement and immediate performance comparisons.

SRC Brown Book of 1012 Active OTC Stocks

Babson-United Investment
Advisors Inc.
101 Prescott Street
Wellesley Hills, MA 02181

PH: (800) 343-4300
(617) 235-0900
Cost: $15.00 each or $139.00 annually
Frequency: monthly
Date of first issue: 1935

Includes: fundamental analysis. Covers: stocks and chart service. 256 pages chart the 20 month trends in earnings and dividends of 1012 active OTC stocks. Prices, volume, and relative performance are charted week by week, plus 13 & 39 week moving averages.

SRC Red Book of 1108 Security Charts (Securities Research Co.)

Babson-United Investment Advisors Inc.
101 Prescott Street
Wellesley Hills, MA 02181

PH: (800) 343-4300
(617) 235-0900
Cost: $14.00 each or $109 annually
Frequency: monthly
Date of first issue: 1935

CHART SERVICE. Includes: technical analysis. Covers: stocks, chart servic . 288 pages of charted data, fully adjusted for stock dividends and splits. Unabridged 21 months graphics feature weekly price ranges, volumes, relative performance, 13 & 39 week moving averages and quarterly earnings and dividends.

Standard & Poor's Credit Week

Standard & Poor's
25 Broadway
New York, NY 10004

PH: (800) 777-4858
(212) 208-8768
Cost: $1695.00 year

Regular features: bond analysis. Focuses on trends and outlooks for fixed income securities including corporate and government bonds and money market instruments. Offers the latest info on S&P's new and changed ratings for corporate, municipal and structured issuers.

Standard and Poor's The Edge

Hank Riehl
P.O. Box 7588
San Francisco, CA 94120

PH: (800) 845-3498
Cost: $360.00 per year
Frequency: twice monthly
Date of first issue: late 1990

Includes: fundamental analysis. Covers: stocks. The only advisory service that considers input from 2500 security analysts at 140 brokerage firms. Combines proven stock selection strategies that focus on capital appreciation with price and earnings data resulting in winning ideas. Includes portfolio and economic overview, industry and company reviews, model portfolio and recommendations.

Standard and Poor's Trendline Chart Guide

Standard and Poors
25 Broadway
New York, NY 10004

PH: (800) 777-4858
Cost: $108.00 per year
Frequency: Monthly
Date of first issue: 1991

Includes: fundamental analysis. Covers: stocks, chart service. Details on over 4400 NYSE, AMEX, and NASDAQ issues in a format similar to Standard and Poor's Stock Guide. Information includes: price performance data for past 52 weeks including high, low, close and volume, 30 week moving average, exclusive relative strength values, industry group, number of shares outstanding, primary exchange where traded and last 12 months earnings per share, dividend rate and more.

Stanger Report

Robert Stanger & Co.
1129 Broad Street
Shrewsbury, NJ 07701

PH: (800) 631-2291
(201) 389-3600
Cost: from $350.00 annually
Frequency: monthly
Date of first issue: 1978

CHART SERVICE
Covers: partnerships. A guide to partnership investing. Follows closed partnership and the secondary market. Tracks all closed partnerships and gives evaluations, total performance, distributions, tax benefits, and other pertinent information.
COMMENTS: For an additional $45.00 subscribe to Partnership Watch - their newsletter on current partnerships.

S.T.A.R. Futures Daily

John J. Kosar
S.T.A.R. Futures, Inc.
P.O. Box 88510
Carol Stream, IL 60188-8510

PH: (708) 830-0800
Cost: $150.00 to 300.00 per month (available via delivery, fax or modem)
Frequency: daily
Date of first issue: 1982

Includes: technical analysis. Covers: commodities. A daily traders report on 14 futures markets including grains, stock indices, interest rates and foreign currencies. Their daily support and resistance levels included in each day's report have been used by Chicago floor traders and the arbitrage and trading desks of many major trading firms since 1982 to enter and exit intraday positions at the most profitable levels. Also included are daily in-depth market commentaries and specific trading recommendations.

S.T.A.R. Futures Hotline

S.T.A.R. Futures, Inc.
John D. Kosar
P.O. Box 88510
Carol Stream, IL 60188-8510

PH: (900) 990-0909 ext 194
(708) 830-0800
Cost: per minute $2.00 (average message is 3-4- minutes long)
24 Hour service
Frequency of update: daily

Covers: commodities.
Includes S.T.A.R. Futures, Inc.'s current open positions in the markets and stop loss placement, previous day's settlement, daily market commentary, Key Daily Support, and Key Daily Resistance areas. Covers 14 futures markets including grains, stock indices, interest rates and foreign currencies.

S.T.A.R. Futures Weekly

John J. Kosar
S.T.A.R. Futures, Inc.
P.O. Box 88510
Carol Stream, IL 60188-8510

PH: (708) 830-0800
Cost: $250.00 annually
Frequency: weekly
Date of first issue: 1990

Includes: fundamental analysis. Covers: commodities, currencies, financial markets. Weekly four page letter complete with detailed technical analysis of 14 markets. Grains, stock indices, interest rates, and foreign currencies. Includes charts and specific recommendations.

Staton's Stock Market Advisory

Author - Bill Staton; Publisher Bill Staton Enterprises
300 East Blvd., Suite B-4
Charlotte, NC 28203

PH: (704) 335-0276
Cost: $87.00 annually
Frequency: monthly
Date of first issue: 1986

Includes: fundamental analysis. Covers: stocks.
Bill Staton advises individuals, corporations, and associations on a wide variety of money and investment topics including: How to Easily Manage Your Personal Finances; The Three Smartest Places to Invest Your Money Today; Getting Financially Fit for Life After Work; Understanding Today's Economy & making it Work for You; How to Get Your Employees Excited About Their Benefits.

Stock Market Cycles

P.O. Box 6873
Santa Rosa, CA 95406-0873

PH: (707) 579-8444
Cost: $480.00 annually w/hotline
$198.00 annually w/o hotline
Frequency: every 3 weeks
Date of first issue: 1975

Covers stock index futures, bills, bonds, gold, and market timing. This newsletter is a stock market timing advisory service covering stock index futures, bills, bonds, and gold.

The Stock of the Month Club

Erie Hamilton
8 Park Plaza
Suite 417
Boston, MA 02117

PH: (800) 237-8400 ext. 722
Cost: $119.00 annually
Frequency: monthly
Date of first issue: 1988

Includes: Fundamental and technical analysis. Covers: stocks. Each month they screen over 6500 stocks to find the best performers. Then the issue tells you why a stock was chosen, gives information about the stock and price graphs for recent past. Portfolio performance is also tracked each issue.

Stock Option Trading Form

K. L. Kardly
P.O. Box 24242
Fort Lauderdale, FL 33307

PH: (305) 566-4500
Cost: $96.00 per year
Frequency: monthly
Date of first issue: 1974

Includes: Fundamental analysis. Covers: stocks. "Provides information for persons interested in buying and selling stock options. Publishes a 30-day stock market forecast and news on the market's technical position, special spreads, straddles, and combination strategies. Underlying stock and option ratings include: insider buying; P/E ratios; technical action; volatility and liquidity."
Comments: Teletape Hotline $72.00 per year toll free.

Stocks, Bonds, Bills and Inflation

Ibbotson & Associates, Inc.
8 South Michigan Avenue, 7th floor
Chicago, IL 60603

PH: (312) 263-3435
FAX: (312) 263-1398
Cost: $35.00 annually

Shows the growth of a dollar invested in common stocks, small stocks, government bonds, treasury bills, and inflation from 1926, to the most recent year-end. Key historical events are highlighted, adding perspective to the markets performance. Charts are in full color, high resolution posters suitable for framing. Also available as prints, slides, or transparencies for $20.00. Four other charts available: Stocks, Bonds, Bills, & Inflation, with Real Estate & Gold; Mutual Fund Styles of Investing; Wealth of the World and of the U.S.; Wealth Indices of Investments After Taxes and Transaction Costs.

Stock Tips @ Your Fingertips

UniBridge - The Anytime, Anyplace, Investment Advisor

PH: (900) 820-STOCK
Cost: per minute $1.50 first
.75 each additional
24 Hour service
Frequency of update: continual

Covers: stocks and market timing.
Comprehensive reference library covering real time quotes on over 50,000 securities, market alerts, insider trading tips, ratings on over 3000 stocks, expert buy-sell recommendations. Obtained by using touch tone phone and extensive menu choices.

Strategic Investment

James Davidson & Lord William Rees-Mogg
Agora, Inc.
824 E. Baltimore Street
Baltimore, MD 21202

PH: (800) 787-0138
(301) 234-0515
Cost: $109.00 annually
Frequency: monthly
Date of first issue: 1980

Includes: technical analysis. Covers: stocks, currencies, treasuries, options, and futures. An 8-page monthly letter covering the entire political and investment universe. Emphasis on inside information and anticipating trends. Various investment portfolios are handled by individual experts.

Strategies

Box 9E
245 East 93rd Street
New York, NY 10028

PH: (900) 446-6555 Strategies Marketline
Cost: $1.00 per minute
OTHER: (900) 226-7952 Strategies Market Commentary
Cost: $2.00 per minute
24 Hour service

TELEPHONE NEWSLETTER
Strategies Marketline gives the latest stockmarket data and business news. Also available is a monthly newsletter for sophisticated investors. Call (900) 246-3200 to order - $9.95 per issue.

Street Smart Investing

Street Smart, Inc.
2000 Maple Hill Street
Yorktown Heights, NY 10598

PH: (914) 278-6500
Cost: $350.00 per year
Frequency: Bi-weekly
Date of first issue:

Includes: Fundamental analysis. Covers: stocks. "Provides investment recommendations. Focuses on a particular corporation in each issue, providing investment history and predictions. Updates previous recommendations."

Switch Fund Timing

Dave Davis (editor and publisher)
P.O. Box 25430
Rochester, NY 14625

PH: (716) 385—3122
Cost: $89.00 annually
Frequency: monthly
Date of first issue: 1983

Covers: stocks, mutual funds, market timing.
This newsletter is directed towards long-term investors offering strategies on market timing.

Sy Harding

Sy Harding Investor Forecasts
Palm Coast, FL 32135

PH: (900) 776-7427 (hotline)
Cost:per minute $2.00
Frequency of update: 7PM Mon-Fri and Monday 9AM

Covers: options, stocks, and market timing.
Daily message includes: latest market timing, plus "best stocks, options and short sales of the week".

Systems and Forecasts

Signalert Corporation
Gerald Appel
150 Great Neck Road
Great Neck, NY 11021

PH: (516) 829-6444
Cost: $195.00
Frequency: Bi-weekly
Date of first issue: 17 years old

Includes: Technical analysis. Covers: stocks, mutual funds, market timing. A stock and bond market timing service. Includes rankings of top 60 of more than 200 mutual funds tracked for relative strength with 3 model portfolios. Also includes book reviews and advisory service information and a free hotline.

Taipan

Agora, Inc.
824 E. Baltimore Street
Baltimore, MD 21202-4799

PH: (301) 234-0515
(800) 787-0138
FAX: (301) 837-3879
Cost: $87.00 annually
Frequency: monthly
Date of first issue:1981

Covers: foreign stocks and bonds.
Foreign market commentary, recommendations, forecasts, and analysis. Based on foreign technologies.

Taking Stock

Harvey Research Organization, Inc.
1400 Temple Building
Rochester, NY 14604

PH: (716) 425-7880
Cost: $128.00 per year
Frequency: monthly
Date of first issue:

Includes: Fundamental analysis. Covers: stocks. "Acts as an in-depth research report on undervalued stocks. Offers the "inside story" on specific stocks and on those companies exhibiting substantial insider buying activity. Discusses inflationary trends in relation to unit sales and dollar sales through a continuing survey of nine core industries."

Taurus

Taurus Corporation
P.O. Box 767
Winchester, VA 22601

PH: (703) 667-4827
Cost: $1,325.00 per year
Frequency: weekly
Date of first issue: 1/76

Includes: Fundamental analysis. Covers: commodities. "Makes specific recommendations on 30 commodities including buy-sell points and stop-loss points. Includes news items, book reviews, editorials, and seminar notices."

T-Bond & Eurodollar/ T-Bill Futures Update

Optima Futures Analysis
327 S. LaSalle Street, Suite 612
Chicago, IL 60604

PH: (212) 427-3616
Cost: $180.00 a month
Published daily

Covers: stock indexes, currencies, and precious metals. Includes: fundamental and technical analysis.
A newsletter for professional investors covering all markets. Fundamental and technical analysis with no recommendations.

Technical Alert Letter

Howard V. Prenzel Research Association
P.O. Box 893
Floral City, FL 32636

PH: (904) 726-1339
Cost: $75.00
Frequency: monthly
Date of first issue:

Includes: technical analysis. Covers: stocks. Includes two model portfolios: the aggressive account and the investment management account. Also gives market commentary and general investment advice.

Technical Analysis of Stocks & Commodities

Jack Hudson
3517 S.W. Alaska Street
Seattle, WA 98126

PH: (800) 832-4642
(206) 938-0570
FAX: (206) 938-1307
Frequency: monthly
Cost: $64.95 annually
First issue: 10/82

Regular features: market update, mutual fund review, and bond analysis. Teaches serious investors how to better trade stocks, bonds, options, mutual funds & futures. Includes charting techniques, computer programs for trading, profit taking and trade timing, risk management and avoidance, computerized trading applications and more.

Technical Traders Bulletin

Island View Financial Group
Charles LaBeau - Editor
25550 Hawthorne Blvd. #100
Torrance, CA 90505

PH: (213) 791-2182
Cost: $195.00 annually
Frequency: monthly
Date of first issue: 7/89

Includes: technical analysis. Covers: commodities. The newsletter for technical analysts. Includes valuable tips and advice, readers idea exchange, informative interviews, day trading tactics, stochastics - parabolic, moving averages - %r, momentum - ADX/DMI, MACD - relative strength.

Technical Trends

P.O. Box 792
Wilton, CT 06897

PH: (203) 762-0229
Cost: $147.00 annually
Frequency: weekly
Date of first issue: 1959

Includes: technical analysis. Covers: stocks and provides chartsThis stock market newsletter provides a commentary on the most accurate indicators used in technical analysis.

Tech Street Journal

TFS, Inc.
238 Littleton, Road
Westford, MA 01886

PH: (508) 692-2290
FAX: (508) 692-4760
Cost: $325.00 annually
Frequency: monthly
Date of first issue: 1983

Includes: fundamental analysis. Covers high-tech businesses and stocks. Tech Street Journal is a high-tech business and stock market performance newsletter. Features include: company profiles and industry trends.

TeloFund Investment Funds

David C. Joel
1355 Peachtree Street N.E.
Suite 1280
Atlanta, GA 30309

PH: (404) 881-6221
(800) 828-2219
Cost: $250.00
Frequency: monthly
Date of first issue: 10/22/90

Includes: fundamental analysis and technical analysis. Covers: mutual funds. A telephone switch advisory based on an extensively researched computer model. Currently offers three hotline systems: The Vanguard family of funds and two involving the Fidelity Family of Funds.

13D Small Cap Opportunities Report

13-D Research Services
100 Executive Drive, Southeast Executive Park
Brewster, NY 10509

PH: (914) 278-6500
FAX: (914) 278-6797
Prices: $6500.00 annually
Frequency: every 2 weeks
Date of first issue: 1983

Includes: fundamental analysis. Covers: stocks. Screens 13D filings to discover the investment opportunities in the small cap universe. You will receive 50-55 investment ideas per year along with timely updates on previous company reports and a complete listing of all 13D filings that have occurred during the preceding 2 week period. Several other services available.

Tiger on Spreads

Phillip E. Tiger
P.O. Box 1414
McLean, VA 22101

PH: (202) 463-8608
Cost: $200.00 per year
Frequency: Semi-monthly
Date of first issue: 8/81

Includes: Fundamental analysis. Covers: commodities. "Discusses spread relationships in commodity futures, including agricultural commodities, metals, financial futures and currencies, and international commodities. Surveys the market with attention to overall price movement and the state of the economy."

Timer Digest

Jim Schmidt
P.O. Box 1688
Greenwich Village, CT 06836

PH: (800) 356-2527
Cost: $225.00 annually
Frequency: every 3 weeks
Date of first issue: 1982

Includes: fundamental and technical analysis. Covers: stocks and market timing. Monitors 90-100 market timers and rates their performance against the S&P 500. Each issue publishes the top 10 timers, a model portfolio plan with strategy and stock recommendations.
COMMENTS: Includes free hotline - updated Wed & Sat evenings.

The Timing Device

Kelly Angle & Company
1020 E. English
Wichita, KS 67211

PH: (316) 685-6034
FAX: (316) 685-6945
Cost: $195.00 annually
Frequency: monthly
Date of first issue: 1985

Includes: technical analysis. Covers: options, futures, and market timing. An 8-12 page letter concentrating on the highest volatility markets. Ranks 32 markets by volatility and gives recommendations. Specializes in long-term trading with low risk. Includes daily hotline.

Timing Market Letter

Timing Financial Services, LTD
10410 North 31st Avenue, Suite 404
Phoenix AZ 85051

PH: (602) 942-3111
Cost: $144.00 annually
Frequency: twice a month
Date of first issue: 1980

Includes: fundamental and technical analysis.
Covers: commodities.futures, market timing and uses charts. This newsletter normally contains a lead article as well as a weather article by Timing Climatologist, Cliff Harris. This letter attempts to be medium to long-term oriented in its views and recommendations. Also, the letter gives projected turn dates, support and resistance points, which can give investor's an edge in entering or exiting the markets.

Today's Options

Techno-Fundamental Investments, Inc.
Robert Jubb
P.O. Box 6216
Scottsdale, AZ 85261

PH: (602) 996-2908
Cost: $195.00 annually
Frequency: twice monthly
Date of first issue: 1974

Includes: fundamental and technical analysis.
Covers: options. Detailed analysis of a few recommendations using proprietary technical and fundamental research tools. Includes charts and updates on previous recommendations.

Tradecenter Market Letter

Knight - Ridder Financial Information
55 Broadway
New York, NY 10006

PH: (212) 269-1110
Cost: $400.00 annually
Frequency: weekly
Date of first issue: 1988

Includes: technical analysis. Covers: stocks commodities/futures, bonds, dollar, cross currencies, and precious metals. The Tradecenter Market Letter makes recommendation on actively traded futures markets and stocks based exclusively on technical analysis. Views of futures markets are typically for one week while the investment horizon for stocks is usually no longer than three months.

Trade Plans

Futures and Options Daily Trading Group, Inc.
1220 S.W. Morrison, Suite 815
Portland, OR 97205

PH: (800) 444-3684
FAX: (503) 241-1015
OTHER: (503) 241-0107
Cost: $180.00 annually
Frequency: weekly (42 issues)
Date of first issue: 1/90

Includes: technical analysis. Covers: commodities, options
A weekly market analysis newsletter designed to give speculators possible futures trades to concentrate on during the following trade week. Features a "Trade of the Week" and "Trades to consider this Week" and a "Weekly Strength and Trend Analysis." Also available via FAX for additional $40.00

The Trader's and Timers Hotline

Teleshare, Inc.
6684 Gunpark Drive East
Boulder, CO 80301

PH: (800) 777-4273
(303) 292-3362
Cost: per minute: $1.50 + .50 cents on 800 number or .20 cents on 303 number plus long distance charges
24 Hour service
Frequency of update: daily except Sunday

Covers: mutual funds.
Mutual fund switch instructions for two different programs: long term investors and aggressive investors.

The Trader's Edge

McFarland Commodities, Inc.
601 St. Charles Avenue
New Orleans, LA 70130

PH: (900) 988-4455
(800) 264-2160
Cost: per minute $3.00
24 Hour service
Frequency of update: continual

Covers: commodities.
A total recommendation service. Up to the minute recommendations for S&P 500, currencies, crude and metals. Opening and closing comments, precise entry/exit signal, tight stops and track record available. Over 45 years trading experience between two brokers who give recommendations. Also available on 1-800-subs service. 800 service is not a recording, but the information is the same. 1 year subscription $420.00. Fax service is the same. Two times per day, 7:15 AM and 11:00 AM. 1 year subscription is $485.00.

Trader's Hotline

Commodity Information Systems, Inc.
P.O. Box 690652
Houston, TX 77269-0652

PH: (900) 990-0909
(713) 890-2700
Cost: $2.00 per minute or
$120.00 for FAX service
Frequency of update: daily

Covers: commodities.
Daily recording providing "short-term" recommendations based on a technical trading system.
COMMENT: This service is free to subscribers of Trade Selection Program (see Newsletter section).

Trader Vic's Market Views

Victor Sperandeo - Rand Management Corporation
1 Chapel Hill Road
Short Hills, NJ 07078

PH: (900) 933-0933
Cost: $1.65 per minute
24 Hour Service
Frequency of update: daily

TELEPHONE NEWSLETTER
Covers: stocks, commodities. Different topics scheduled throughout the day such as: Today's Trading Views, Stock and Commodity Picks, Closing Out the Day, Reasons for the Future, The "Why's" of the past week and the "How's" of the coming week.

Trading Advisor

Richard Luna
1737 Central Street
Denver, CO 80211

PH: (303) 433-3202
 (800) 950-9339
FAX: (303) 433-2731
Cost: $295.00 per year
Date of first issue: 1986

Includes: fundamental analysis. Covers: Commodity Trading Advisors. The leading source of Commodity Trading Advisor information in the nation with both an extensive data base and a large number of accounts traded with Commodity Trading Advisors. Newsletter profiles specific Trading Advisors and includes their performance. Rates the top Commodity Trading Advisors for the past three years and gives pertinent data and key statistics on them. (Follows over 75 advisors.)

Trading Cycles

Andrews Publications
995 Oak Park Drive
Morgan Hill, CA 95037

PH: (408) 778-2925
Cost: $140.00 annually
Frequency: 17 times per year
Date of first issue: 1973

Includes: Technical analysis. Covers: market timing, S&P Futures, T-Bonds, currencies, gold, indices. A technical timing newsletter which "interprets technical price volume, momentum data and evaluates the extremes of investor reactions to the market." "It then projects the next minor and major lows or highs."

Trading Trends

Minneapolis Grain Exchange
150 Grain Exchange Building
400 S. Fourth Street
Minneapolis, MN 55415

PH: (612) 338-6212
Cost:
Frequency: weekly
Date of first issue:

Includes: Technical analysis. Covers: commodities. "Monitors grain and oil seed trading. Compiles analysis and statistics on specific commodities."

Trendline Chart Guide

Standard and Poor's Corporation
25 Broadway
New York, NY 10004

PH: (212) 208-8792
 (800) 221-5277
Cost: $135.00 annually
Frequency: monthly
Date of first issue: 1962

Covers: stocks and chart service. Includes over 4400 stock charts from NYSE, AMEX and OTC exchanges. Each chart covers one year of market activity and shows the weekly high/low, close and volume, and 30 week moving averages. Also shows industry grouping, exchange traded on, 12 month earnings data, dividend rate, and more.

Trendline Current Market Prospectus

Standard & Poors
25 Broadway
New York, NY 10004

PH: (800) 777-4858
(212) 208-8768
Cost: $195.00 annually + 24.60 postage
Frequency: monthly
Date of first issue: 1970

CHART SERVICE. Includes: technical analysis. Covers: stocks. Gives weekly price volume charts on over 1400 widely traded stocks for a period of up to 4 years. Alternate issues include an Industry Group Relative Strength Line to provide comparisons of stocks vs industry group performance and vs S&P 500. Also includes 3 year data on sales, earnings, dividends and yields.

Trendline Daily Action Stock Charts

Standard & Poors
25 Broadway
New York, NY 10004

PH: (800) 777-4858
(212) 208-8768
Cost: $520.00 annually + 75.40 postage
Frequency: weekly
Date of first issue: 1970

CHART SERVICE. Includes: fundamental and technical analysis. Shows daily trends for the past 12 months on 728 active NYSE and ASE stocks. Charts are plotted daily and issued every Friday after the markets close. Also includes most actively traded options.

Trendline OTC Chart Manual

Standard & Poors
25 Broadway
New York, NY 10004

PH: (800) 777-4858
(212) 208-8768
Cost: $160.00 annually +14.40 postage
Frequency: bi-monthly
Date of first issue: 1970

Includes: fundamental and technical analysis. Covers: stocks. Charts on over 800 actively traded OTC Stocks. Each chart presents the weekly bid price range, closing bid and volume for a period up to 4 years. Also includes sales data, dividends, yields, profit margins, cash flow and more.

Trend-Setter

Commodity Trend Service/
Joe Van Nice
P.O. Box 32309
Palm Beach Gardens, FL 33420

PH: (800) 331-1069
(407) 694-0960
FAX: (407) 622-7623
Cost: $495.00 a year
$995.00 a year for FAX
$995.00 a year for IBM with Modem
Frequency of update: daily

Covers: futures
Provides a comprehensive daily coverage of over 40 top futures markets. A complete trading program incorporating five different trading rules: Trade with the Trend, Have a Plan, Limit Losses and Allow Profits to Grow, Use Stops, and Do Not Overtrade. You get daily entry and exit signals and stops for each position, summary of all trades in progress. For chart traders, they give daily stochastics, RSI and projected range for the next day.

The Turnaround Letter

New Generations, Inc.
225 Friend Street, Suite 801
Boston, MA 02114

PH: (617) 573-9550
Cost: $195.00 annually
Frequency: monthly
Date of first issue: 1987

Includes: fundamental analysis. Covers: stocks. The newsletter tracks bankrupt companies and gives recommendations on associated stocks.

Turning Point

P.O. Box 12176
Scottsdale, AZ 85267

PH: (900) 234-7777 ext 50
Per minute $2.00
Frequency of update: several times a day

FAX SERVICE
Can receive free sample
Fibonacci/Gann projections. Specific recommendations by Walter Studnicki, Editor of Turning Point.

Turning Point

C.E.R. Institute, Inc.
P.O. Box 12176
Scottsdale, AZ 85267

PH: (602) 991-3410
Cost: $144.00 annually
Frequency: monthly
Date of first issue: Jan 1985

Covers: stocks, commodities, government bonds, gold, Eurodollars, Swiss Franc. The newsletter pinpoints, well in advance, the most probable tops and bottoms. Turning Point is also a teaching letter. In addition to showing you how to project turning points well in advance, it teaches Fibonacci/Gann technique, Elliott Wave Theory, Dow Theory, cyclic concepts, and other technical tools.

Tuxworth Stock Advisory

Robert Buffington, Ph.D.
P.O. Box 33794
Decatur, GA 30033-0794

PH: (404) 325-8348
Cost: $180.00 annually
Frequency: monthly
Date of first issue: 1987

Includes: Fundamental and technical analysis. Covers: stocks, market timing. Market commentary and forecasting, performance tracking of proprietary Market Direction Indicator, current portfolio and performance data. Also includes free hotline with updates and recommendations three times a week.

United Mutual Fund Selector

Babson United Investment Advisors, Inc
101 Prescott Street
Wellesley Hills, MA 02181

PH: (617) 235-0900
FAX: (617) 235-9450
Cost: $130.00 annually - 1st class
$125.99 annually 2nd class
Frequency: bi-monthly

Includes: fundamental analysis. Covers: mutual funds. Short newsletter giving performance comparisons and other information including data on specific recommended funds.

U.S. Investment Report

25 Fifth Avenue 4-C
New York, NY 10003

PH: (212) 995-2963
FAX: (212) 477-6070
Cost: $228.00
Frequency: every 2 weeks
Date of first issue: 1985

Includes: Fundamental analysis. Covers: stocks. A stock recommendation newsletter with both a conservative and aggressive model portfolio. Sticks to established stocks with no new issues or "hot" issues.

Value Investing Letters

Charlie Davis
41 Sutter Street #1355
San Francisco, CA 94104

PH: (415) 776-5622
Cost: $55.00
Frequency: 8 times per year
Date of first issue: 1990

Covers: stocks. Market commentary strategy for stock picking and specific recommendations and lists the editor's current portfolio with a summary.

Value Line Convertibles

Value Line, Inc.
711 Third Avenue
New York, NY 10017

PH: (212) 687-3965
(800) 633-2252 (subscriptions)
Cost: $475.00 per year
Frequency: weekly
Date of first issue: 9/70

Includes: Fundamental analysis. Covers: stocks. "Shows the investor how to build and maintain a convertible portfolio, how to decide upon the appropriate amount of risk, and how to select issues that fall within those risk limitations. Provides weekly evaluations of 585 convertibles, investment strategies, and market news." Comments: Online through Interactive Data Corporation, 486 Totten Pond Road, Waltham, MA 02154.

The Value Line Investment Survey

Value Line, Inc.
711 Third Avenue
New York, NY 10017-4064

PH: (800) 833-0046 ext. 2964 - credit card orders only
(212) 687-3965
Cost: $525.00 annually
Frequency: weekly
Date of first issue: 1943

Includes: Fundamental and Technical analysis. Covers: stocks. "Presents specific investment advice, including year-ahead and 3-5 year performance evaluations, projections of key financial measures, and concise, objective commentary on current operations and future prospects for over 1700 stocks. Also offers analysis of the economy and stock market overall."

Value Line Options

Value Line, Inc.
711 Third Avenue
New York, NY 10017

PH: (212) 687-3965
(800) 633-2252 (subscriptions)

Cost: $445.00 per year
Frequency: weekly
Date of first issue: 5/75

Includes: Fundamental analysis. Covers: stocks. "Designed to show the investor how to build and maintain an option portfolio, how to decide on the appropriate amount of risk, and how to select issues that fall within those risk limitations. Provides weekly evaluations of over 8,000 options, investment strategies, and market news."

Vancouver Stockwatch

John Woods - Canjex Publishing
P.O. Box 10371
Pacific Centre
700 W. Georgia Street
Vancouver, British Columbia

PH: (604) 687-1500
(800) 267-7400
Cost: $395.00
Frequency: Weekly
Date of first issue: 1984

Weekly magazine. Covers: stock choices. An informa-tion service which provides valuable information on every company (over 1500) listed on the Vancouver Stock Exchange.

The Venture Capital Portfolio

Zin Investment Services
7 Switchbud Place #192-312
The Woodlands, TX 77380

PH: (713) 363-1000
Cost: $195.00 - includes a free hotline
Frequency: monthly
Date of first issue:

Includes: technical analysis. Covers: stocks. "...a stock advisory service which specializes in analyses of the publicly traded companies that have previously been financed by professional venture capitalists." Provides recommendations and a model portfolio. A Hot Line is also available for $2.00 per minute - (900) 226-5463.

Venture Returns

KD & Associates
1855 N.W. Tyler Avenue
Corvallis, OR 97330

PH: (503)
Cost: $75.00 per year
Frequency: every 2 weeks
Date of first issue:

Covers: stocks. Each issue recommends one stock in particular and follow ups on prior recommendations. The newsletter's goal is to build a risk-averse portfolio, keep yields high and still have outstanding capital gains and to adjust portfolios to the financial climate.

The Volume Reversal Survey

Mark Leibovit
Almarco Trading Corp.
P.O. Box 1451
Sedonia, AZ 86336

PH: (602) 282-1275
(800)554-5551
Cost: $360.00 annually
Frequency: every 3 weeks - 17 issues a year
Date of first issue: 1979

Includes: technical analysis. Covers: stock, treasuries, currencies, precious metals and futures.Every issue contains: volume analysis of all major markets; clear and specific instructions on whether to buy, sell, or hold stocks, bonds, precious metals and select futures mar-kets; proprietary Volume Reversal technique gives you information about what knowledgeable buyers and sell-ers are doing in the marketplace. Includes hotline, updates, instruction booklet, and annual forecast.

Wall Street Letter

Institutional Investor Systems
488 Madison Avenue
New York, NY 10022

PH: (212) 303-3300
Cost: $1,295.00 annually
Frequency: weekly
fundamental analysis
Date of first issue: 1975

Covers: institutional and retail brokerage business. The Wall Street Letter focuses primarily on the institutional and retail brokerage business. Coverage includes the big firms as well as a number of smaller regional brokerages, mutual fund companies, and companies that provide services to the brokerage industry. Also covers the regulators in Washington and the products, personalities, and regulations of the exchanges (including NYSE, ASE, and the National Association of Securities Dealers) whose decisions and pronouncements have an impact on the brokerage industry.

Wall Street Micro Investor

Howard Young
P.O. Box 6
Riverdale, NY 10471

PH: (212) 884-5408
Cost: $30.00 annually
Frequency: bi-monthly
Date of first issue: Jan 1982

Includes: technical analysis. Covers stocks and computer investing. Wall Street Micro Investor: key indicators; create an expert system - generate buy/sell signals; options and technical indicators; new indicators - directional index, point and figure charting, Elliott Wave Theory,; anatomy of a stock; identifying trading patterns.

Washington Bond & Money Market Report

David A. Alecock
1545 New York Avenue, N.E.
Washington, D.C. 20002

PH: (800) 345-2611
(202) 526-9664
FAX: (202) 636-3992
Cost: $325.00 annually
Frequency: bi-weekly
Date of first issue: 1946

Includes: fundamental analysis. Covers: municipal and government bonds, and treasuries. Sound, on-the-money analyses of the thinking in official Washington and in the market in New York. Subjects include the interest rate outlook, where the economy and the money supply are heading, how the Federal Reserve is reacting to current trends, and the impact of developments abroad.

Washington International Business Report

IBC, Inc.
818 Connecticut Avenue N.W., Suite 1200
Washington, D.C. 20006
ISSN 0049-691X

PH: (202) 872-8181
Cost: $288.00 annually
Frequency: monthly
Date of first issue: 1972

Includes: fundamental analysis.
The report is an analytical review and outlook on major government developments impacting international trade and investment.

Water Investment Newsletter

U.S. Water News, Inc.
230 Main Street
Halstead, KS 67056

PH: (800) 251-0046
Cost: $140.00
Frequency: monthly
Date of first issue: 1987

Includes: Fundamental analysis. Covers: stocks. "A newsletter on Water Stocks and Investments." Provides a stock profile, model portfolio with performance data and news relevant to water investments each month.

Weber's Fund Advisor

Ken Weber
P.O. Box 3490
New Hyde Park, NY 11040

PH: (516) 466-1252
Cost: $135.00 annually
Frequency: monthly
Date of first issue: 1983

Includes: fundamental and technical analysis. Covers: mutual funds.Each month you'll see Ken Weber's analysis of the stock market in general and commentary about developments affecting the mutual fund investor. Uses a "Go-with-the-winner" strategy which finds the hottest mutual funds and stays with them till they cool off. Over 115 funds are tracked and all are no-load or low-load. Includes toll-free hotline .

Weekly Report of the Market

Coffee, Sugar and Cocoa Exchange, Inc.
Four World Trade Center
New York, NY 10048

PH: (212) 938-2800
Cost: $20.00
Frequency: weekly
Date of first issue:

Includes: Technical analysis. Covers: commodities. Synopsis of market activity in each commodity traded on our exchange.

Weekly Technical Letter

W. D. Gann Research, Inc.
P.O. Box 8508
St. Louis, MO 63126

PH: (314) 843-1810
Cost: $200.00
Frequency: weekly
Date of first issue: 1919

Includes: Technical analysis. Covers: stocks, commodities. Strictly a technical trading newsletter based on proven chart principles with preservation of capital as a prime concern. Gives specific recommendations with stops.

Whitfield's Utility Letter

J. Charles Whitfield
2472 Bolsover
Suite 240
Houston, TX 77005

PH: (713) 521-2536
Cost: $
Frequency:
Date of first issue: 1984

Includes: Fundamental analysis. Covers: stocks. Market commentary and specific buy/sell recommendations on utility stocks.

World Investment Strategic Edge

Courtney D. Smith, Editor
Pinnacle Capital Management, Publisher
P.O. Box 135
Cooper Station
New York, NY 10276-0135

PH: (212) 254-6613
FAX: (212) 995-0158
Cost: $395.00 per year
Frequency: 20 times per year
Date of first issue: 1991

Covers: stocks, bonds, currencies, gold. Searches the globe for investments with the potential for superior returns and limited risk. Includes specific recommendations and market commentary.

World Market Perspective

WMP Enterprises, Inc.
P.O. Box 2289
2211 Lee Road, Suite 103
Winter Park, FL 32790

PH: (407) 290-9600
Cost: $49.00 annually
Frequency: monthly
Date of first issue: 1959

Includes: technical and fundamental analysis.
Covers: gold and currencies, includes charts.Research in economic science and world markets aimed at discovery and dissemination of significant ideas and information.

World Money Analyst

Newstar Orient, Ltd.
45 Lyndhurst Terrace
Hong Kong

PH: 541-6110
FAX: (852) 854-1695
Cost: $189.00
Frequency: 10 times per year plus 2 special reports
Date of first issue:

Includes: Fundamental and Technical analysis. International news relevant to investing, currency and interest rate trend charts, broad investment recommendations.
Comments: Includes hotline updated weekly.

World 100 Report

Gene Walden
Walden Communications
5805 Dale Avenue, Suite 1000
P.O. Box 39373
Minneapolis, MN 55439-9780

PH: (800) 736-2970
(612) 926-1079
Cost: $89.00
Frequency: monthly
Date of first issue: 1990

Includes: Fundamental analysis. Covers: stocks, mutual funds. Reports on the fastest growing foreign markets, the changing U.S. Market, the best global mutual funds and the top performing stocks.

Worldwide Investment News

Offshore Banking News Service
301 Plymouth Drive N.E.
Dalton, GA 30721-9983

PH: (404) 259-6035
Cost: $90.00
Frequency: monthly
Date of first issue: 1983

Includes: Fundamental analysis. Covers: mutual funds, international investments. "The world's first and foremost sentinel of offshore banking and investment opportunities." Covers a wide array of international investments and gives an international resource directory as well as a brief opportunities classified section.

Wright Bankers' Service: Investment Advice and Analysis

Wright Investors' Service
10 Middle Street
Bridgeport, CT 06604

PH: (203) 333-6666
Cost:
Frequency: weekly
Date of first issue:

Includes: Technical analysis. Covers: stocks. "Carries economic and stock market analyses and forecasts. Provides specific recommendations for investment, and updates previous recommendations."

The Zweig Forecast

Dr. Martin E. Zweig
P.O. Box 360
Bellmore, NY 11710

PH: 800-633-2252 ext 9000
FAX: (516) 785-0537
Cost: $265.00 annually
Frequency: every 3 weeks
Date of first issue: 1971

Includes: technical analysis. Covers: stocks.
Model portfolio, gives specific stock recommendations, when to buy and when to sell. 24 hour hotline access free with subscription. 3 times per week gives latest readings of his key indicators and specific strategy recommendations.

Michael Murphy

PH: (900) 321-4321
Cost : per minute $2.00
Frequency of update: daily

Covers: stocks.

Gives market commentary, easy to understand - not technical - for novice/average investor. Different categories accessed by touch-tone phone, longs or shorts.

Computer and Quote Services

This section could be the most valuable for sophisticated investors. Computer Services range from hand-held quote machines to online chart services automatically updated by satellite. Software services may range from a single disk on financial planning to online interactive data services utilizing stochastic analysis.

Tailoring a computer system to an investor's needs requires time, money, and a knowledge of what is available. As an investor's computer system evolves, access to what products and services are available can save hours of time and thousands of dollars. This section can provide a tremendous advantage by allowing investors to shop for services without being pressured.

We have attempted to include descriptions of services including online, software, and hardware requirements, and costs of services are briefly described. Some services are relatively inexpensive while major data services annual charges are justified only by portfolio values over $10 million.

Better information means better investment results and portfolio managers who are not constantly updating their information sources are falling behind. This section could be the most valuable tool to building a superior computer system for investing.

TABLE OF CONTENTS

ABI/Inform

Thomson Financial Networks
11 Farnsworth Street
Boston, MA 02210

PH: (617) 345-2000
(800) 662-7878
FAX: (617) 330-1986

ONLINE
Compatibility : IBM/DOS, Macintosh, any PC with modem or call (800) 662-7878
Online charges per hour $105.00
Provides concise 150 word summaries of more than 100,000 management-oriented articles from over 800 of the world's leading professional publications, trade magazines and academic journals.

Accuron

National Computer Network Corp.
223 W. Jackson Blvd., Suite 1202
Chicago, IL 60606

PH: (302) 427-5125

Cost of service: $129.00 (includes $30.00 initiation fee + $99.95 initial cost) includes 1 free hour of usage of Nite-Line service for end of the day information, and test data disk to ensure compatibility with your software, 3 years of daily historical data. Online charges:from $13.00 per hour (depending on Baud network and time of day used) .Stock quote service with end of day quotes at .04 cents per issue day. Compatibility: IBM and compatibles with modem.

Historical data at .03 cents per issue day - quantitative discounts on over 20,000 issue days/month. An easy to use daily pricing service that helps you create computerized files for tracking security histories. Provides information on over 70,000 current daily issues and on corporate and government bonds, mutual funds, indexes, financial and commodity futures, plus all US listed stock, index, and futures options. Designed for the novice PC user. You can simply set a timer and your PC will call the Nite-Line database, get the prices, hang up the phone, and automatically update you files off-line while you sleep!

Ace T-Bonds

Essex Trading Co., Ltd
300 W. Adams, Suite 319
Chicago, IL 60606

PH: (800) 726-2140
(708) 416-3530

SOFTWARE
Cost: $995.00 + $25.00 shipping and handling
Compatibility : IBM/DOS

Covers: treasury bond futures. Advanced trading system for Treasury Bond futures featuring a fully researched ready to trade program along with comprehensive back-testing routines. Charts - graphics at not additional cost. Automatic updates through CSI and FNN Signal. COMMENTS: Offers unlimited free technical support on all trading programs via telephone.

Advanced G.E.T.

Trading Techniques, Inc.
677 W. Turkeyfoot Lake Road
Akron, OH 44319

PH: (216) 753-7676
(216) 645-0077
FAX: (216) 645-1230

SOFTWARE
Cost - $2750.00 - 33 markets or $3250.00 includes
additional 14 international markets.
Compatibility: IBM/DOS

Covers: futures. Futures market technical analysis software. Uses complex forms of analysis that are based on theories and historical analysis. Capabilities include: Elliott Wave, graphics, Gann, 2 unique proprietary cycles, pattern matching and more. Data must be provided through another source.

AIQ Index Expert

AIQ Systems, Inc.
916 Southwood Blvd, Suite 2C
P.O. Drawer 7530
Incline Village, NE 89450

PH: (800) 332-2999
(702) 831-2999
FAX: (702) 831-6784

SOFTWARE
Cost: $1588.00 for software package. Data must be
supplied through and outside vendor, communications
software is included.
Compatibility : IBM

Cover: index options, market timing, and charts. The complete index option trading system that includes market timing. Uses Black-Scholes model for option analysis, signals short-term market moves and based on the status of the market, recommends a strategy and the positions to take and advises you when to clear a position. A valuable asset to option traders.

AIQ Market Expert

AIQ Systems, Inc.
916 Southwood Blvd, Suite 2C
P.O. Drawer 7530
Incline Village, NE 89450

PH: (800) 332-2999
(702) 831-2999

SOFTWARE
Cost: $488.00 for software package. Data must be
supplied through and outside vendor, communications
software is included.
Compatibility : IBM

Cover: market timing and charts. A valuable system for any trader which signals near-term changes in the direction of the market signaled both the 1987 and 1989 October crashes. This technical analysis system does not forecast, it generates signals for market timing based on a knowledge base of facts and rules. Programmed with a knowledge base of expert timing rules and the most reliable technical indicators, the system analyzes daily market data and computes Expert Ratings that signal changes in the direction of the market.

AIQ Option Expert

AIQ Systems Inc.
P.O. Drawer 7530
Incline Village, NV 89450

PH: (800) 332-2999
Costs:
AIQ Stock Expert $988 The Stock Trading System
AIQ Market Expert $488 The Market Timing System
AIQ Data Transfer Utility $188

Covers: options, stocks, and market timing. Developed specifically for use on desktop personal computers, AIQ software utilizes that same expert system technology previously limited to mainframe computers and accessible only to large, high tech investment firms. The systems sort through large amounts of data and make quick and emotionless buy and sell selections.

AIQ Option Expert

AIQ Systems, Inc.
916 Southwood Blvd, Suite 2C
P.O. Drawer 7530
Incline Village, NE 89450

PH: (800) 332-2999
(702) 831-2999
FAX: (702) 831-6784

SOFTWARE
Cost: $1588.00 for software package. Data must be supplied through and outside vendor, communications software is included.
Compatibility : IBM

Cover: options, market timing, and charts. "An option trader's wish come true." Expert equity option system with capability to signal short-term stock moves. Analyzes daily price and volume data for all stocks in your data base and recommends the best strategy or positions to take and when to clear positions.

AIQ Stock Expert

AIQ Systems, Inc.
916 Southwood Blvd, Suite 2C
P.O. Drawer 7530
Incline Village, NE 89450

PH: (800) 332-2999
(702) 831-2999
FAX: (702) 831-6784

SOFTWARE
Cost: $988.00 for software package. Data must be supplied through and outside vendor, communications software is included.
Compatibility : IBM

Cover: stocks, market timing, and charts. An expert system that does technical analysis for you. It is capable of sorting through huge amounts of data and signaling buy and sell recommendations. Through connecting with communications networks, it analyzes daily price and volume movements and computes and Expert Rating for every stock you follow. The system then prints a daily Expert Analysis Report and an Action List that select which stocks you should consider for trading. Once you take a position, the StockExpert Profit Management function takes over to protect your principle and your profits, advising you to hold, sell or cover based on your own risk parameters.

Analyst

Tech Hackers, Inc.
50 Broad Street
New York, NY 10004

PH: (212) 344-9500

SOFTWARE
Cost: Financial Analyst $195.00
      Stats Analyst $195.00
      Bond Analyst $495.00
      Options Analyst $495.00
      MBS Analyst $495.00
$50.00 discount for each additional library when purchasing more that one library.
Compatibility: IBM

Covers: options, bonds (municipal, agency, corporate, and government).Analyst is a series of five mathematical and financial function add-in libraries for Lotus 1-2-3 and Symphony. Each library is comprehensive and offers sophisticated analytics for use in an array of financial and investment areas. Five libraries for the Financial Professional: Financial analyst, Stats Analyst, Bond Analyst, Options Analyst, and MBS Analyst.

APEX-BCI

N-Squared Computing
5318 Forest Ridge Road
Silverton, OR 97381

PH: (503) 873-4420
(800) 446-4950
FAX: (214) 680-680-1435

SOFTWARE
Cost: $390.00 includes 12 monthly updates
Compatibility: IBM/DOS

Graphic time series analysis software. APEX-BCI stands for Access, Plot, & Export - Business Cycle Indicators. The BCI database provides you with over 225 Economic and Business Cycle Indicators (those published monthly by the U.S. Dept of Commerce) . APEX software lets you update any indicators as soon as the data is released, and to export any part of the database to other popular formats for use with other software programs. You can produce charts that will enable you to establish where you are in the business cycle, identify economic turnarounds, make meaningful forecasts of future trends in the economy and determine cause and effect relationships between indicators.

Argus On-Line

Argus Research Corporation
17 Battery Place
New York, NY 10004

PH: (212) 425-7500

ONLINE
Cost: $50.00 annually $1.00 per minute online
Covers: stocks.
Compatibility: any PC with modem.

Information contained in the online service: market comments, stock analysis and rating by symbol, Argus stock screens, portfolio selections, utility scope, latest updates, and market tactics.

Asset Mix Optimizer

CDA Investment Technologies, Inc.
1355 Piccard Drive
Rockville, MD. 20850

PH: (300) 975-9600
(800) 232-2285
FAX: (301) 590-1350

SOFTWARE
Cost: $700.00 a year

Covers: Stocks, mutual funds, and bonds (municipal, corporate, government and foreign) .
A semi-annual PC compatible software package with graphics that determines how much of a portfolio should be invested in various asset classes such as common stocks, bonds, money market instruments, real estate, precious metals, and others. The program considers four variables: forecasted rate of return for each asset, expected risk of each asset, relationship between each asset, and every other asset in terms of market behavior i.e. the extent to which a particular investor is willing to incur risk.

AVA

Market Maker
55 Sutter Street
Suite 26
San Francisco, CA 94104

PH: (415) 943-1945

SOFTWARE
Cost:
Compatibility: IBM/DOS

Covers: stocks, mutual funds, municipal bonds, corporate bonds, government bonds. A portfolio management package for investors for tracking stocks, bonds, mutual funds, options, futures and other investments. Prices can be updated manually or via modem with Dow Jones News/Retrieval, Warner Computer Services, Compuserve, The Source, or Merlin Dial/Data.

Bond Buyer Full Text

Dialog Information Services, Inc.
3460 Hillview Avenue
Palo Alto, CA 94304

PH: (800) 334-2564
(415) 858-3785
FAX: (415) 858-7069

ONLINE
Cost: Standard Service Plan - $45.00 for the first password $25.00 each additional password
Annual Service Fee - $35.00 per password
Online charges $2.50 per minute or $150.00 per hour
Compatibility: IBM/DOS, MacIntosh

Covers: corporate bonds, government bonds. Online database containing daily coverage of government and Treasury securities, financial futures, corporate bonds, and mortgage securities. Corresponds to publications, The Bond Buyer and Credit Markets.

Bonds

Emerging Market Technologies, Inc.
1230 Johnson Ferry Road
Suite F-1
Marietta, GA 30068

PH: (404) 973-2300
FAX: (404) 973-3003

SOFTWARE
Cost: $395.00
Compatibility: IBM/DOS

Bond portfolio system that includes duration calculations.

Bonds and Interest Rates

Programmed Press
599 Arnold Road
W. Hempstead, NY 11552

PH: (516) 599-6527

SOFTWARE
Cost: Contact Vendor
Compatibility: IBM/DOS, MacIntosh, TRS, Commodore

Covers: bonds. Bonds and interest rates evaluation package.
Evaluates price, risk and return on fixed income securities and annuities.

Bond Sheet

Emerging Market Technologies, Inc.
1230 Johnson Ferry Road
Suite F-1
Marietta, GA 30068

PH: (404) 973-2300
FAX: (404) 973-3003

SOFTWARE
Cost: $149.00
Compatibility: IBM/DOS

Bond calculator including bond swap module.

Bond Smart

Wall Street Consulting Group
89 Millburn Avenue
Millburn, NJ 07041

PH: (201) 762-4300

SOFTWARE
Cost: Basic monthly charge $175.00
Compatibility: IBM/DOS, Xenix

Covers: municipal bonds, corporate bonds, government bonds, foreign bonds. System for managing, accounting, reporting and tracking bonds in single or multi portfolios. Includes general ledger accounting, bond calculator, mortgage calculator and over 70 standard reports. Also has ten types of trades, four methods of paydowns, three methods of pricing, fourteen types of securities and nine types of amortization.

Bond Value

Resource Software International, Inc.
330 New Brunswick Avenue
Fords, NJ 08863

PH: (201) 738-8500

SOFTWARE
Cost: Hook-up charges $65.00
Compatibility: IBM/DOS

Covers: municipal bonds, corporate bonds, government bonds, foreign bonds. Calculates the present value of available bonds. By comparing the calculated value of the bond to a pre-established minimum return on investments, the user can determine if the bond can be purchased at a price that meets or exceeds requirements. Also calculates accrued interest.

BondWare

Davidge Data Systems Corp.
20 Exchange Place
New York, NY 10005

PH: (212) 269-0901

Cost: Complete BondWare Package $450.00
       Pop-up Yield Calculator $89.95
       Up-grade new version $35.00
Compatibility: IBM/DOS compatibles

Covers municipal, government, and corporate bonds and agencies. The integrated solution to Fixed Income Security Yield Calculation, Portfolio Analysis and Swap Analysis including the Revolutionary Bond Swap Modeler. Bondware provides an integrated collection of functions to calculate yields on all types of fixed income securities, to create and maintain bond portfolios, to produce reports on portfolios and to model and analyze bond swaps.

Bond Yielder II

Decision Programming Corporation
807 Georgia Avenue
Suite 607
Silver Spring, MD 20910

PH: (301) 585-7121

SOFTWARE
Compatibility: IBM/DOS

Covers: municipal bonds, government bonds. Handles five major types of fixed-income investments: Munis, Treasuries, Notes, Certificates and Discounts. Fully compatible with zero coupon securities including Accretion Schedules or Amortization Schedules suitable for client distribution for tax purposes.

Bonneville Market Information

19 West South Temple
Salt Lake City, UT 84101-1503

PH: (800) 255-7374
FAX: (801) 532-3202

QUOTE SERVICE
Cost: For all quote systems in Texas would need satellite $597.00 plus installation: if you install $100.00, if they install $395.00.

Covers: stocks, futures, also chart service. Bonneville delivers futures, stocks, and option quotes - with news, weather and private mail via satellite and FM radio stations throughout the United States. Monitors are available for display only; however, by using your computer with a variety of available software, you may display quotes, news, charts, and technical analysis.

Boras

First Data Services, Inc.
38 Park Avenue
Rutherford, NJ 07070

PH: (201) 507-5910

SOFTWARE
Cost: $1,000.00 per year
Compatibility: IBM/DOS

Covers: corporate, government, and convertible bonds. A bond research and analysis system that provides a complete database of over 8,000 corporate, convertible and government bonds, fully footnoted with cash call and sinking fund schedules. The software also enables you to obtain Moody's and S&P ratings, do Swap analysis, and has a built in bond calculator.

BrokerMagic

Emerging Market Technologies, Inc.
1230 Johnson Ferry Road
Suite F-1
Marietta, GA 30068

PH: (404) 973-2300
FAX: (404) 973-3003

SOFTWARE
Cost: $695.00 with TeleMagic
 $295.00 upgrade to TeleMagic
Compatibility: IBM/DOS

Broker specific upgrade to TeleMagic package from Emerging Market Technologies.

Broker's Notebook

Quotron Systems, Inc.
17 Haverford Station Road
Haverford, PA 19041

PH: (215) 896-8780

Cost: from $695.00, $210.00 per year maintenance,
Network module $700.00 with $150.00 per year maintenance.
Compatibility: IBM/DOSA PC based portfolio management and prospecting software system.

The features include: custom report capabilities,
pre-designed reports such as holdings summary, annual
income statements, realized gains/losses, and more,
automatically posts dividends, interest and reinvest-
ments, tickler lists, generates correspondence, mail/
merge data and labels for mass mailings and much,
much more.

BTC-64

Bonneville Market Information
19 West South Temple, UT 84101-1503

PH: (800) 255-7374
FAX: (801) 532-3202

QUOTE SERVICE
Cost: BTC-64 $287.00 one time fee. plus monthly
subscriber fee of $197.00. Compatibility: Hardware
provided

Covers: futures. Features: 64 pages of tick-by-tick information, three news pages, specialty news, one page
of opening calls, financial update page, two programmable pages, options, spread page, crawl line, news
annunciators, high, low, last, net, volume, bid/ask, opening range, closing range, open interest, seven months of
futures prices, and print capabilities. Futures Quote
System offering all U.S. and selected foreign exchanges
and related options.

Business Dateline

Dialog Information Services, Inc.
3460 Hillview Avenue
Palo Alto, CA 94304

PH: (800) 334-2564
 (415) 858-3785
FAX: (415) 858-7069

ONLINE
Cost: Standard Service Plan - $45.00 for the first pass-
word
$25.00 for each additional password
$35.00 annual fee for each password
 Online charges $2.10 per minute or $126.00 per hour
Compatibility: IBM/DOS, MacIntosh

Online database containing full text articles from re-
gional business publications from the U.S. and Canada.
Also, Crain News Service, nine daily newspapers and
Business Wire are included. Updated weekly.

Business Wire

Dialog Information Services, Inc.
3460 Hillview Avenue
Palo Alto, CA 94304

PH: (800) 334-2564
 (415) 858-3785
FAX: (415) 858-7069

ONLINE
Cost: Standard Service Plan - $45.00 for the first password
$25.00 for each additional password
$35.00 annual fee for each password
 Online charges $1.60 per minute or $96.00 per hour
Compatibility: IBM/DOS, MacIntosh

Online database containing unedited text of news releases from over 10,000 sources including companies, public relations firms, government agencies, political organizations, colleges and universities, and research institutes. Updated continuously.

Candle Power 2.1

N-Squared Computing
5318 Forest Ridge Road
Silverton, OR 97381

PH: (503) 873-4420
 (214) 680-1445
FAX: (214) 680-1435

SOFTWARE
Compatibility with IBM/DOS.
Cost: $295.00 includes chart service.

Japanese Candlestick charting, ARM's equivolume charting, standard bar charting & the new CandlePower charting — all in one software program. A new and upcoming analysis technique that combines the best of Japanese candlesticks with the equivolume principles. Includes 10 of the most popular indicators and is complete with database management and downloading capabilities for Warner Computer Systems. Automatic recognition of pattern signals.

Capital Investment System

Portfolio Dynamics
53 West Jackson
Suite 562
Chicago, IL 60604

PH: (312) 461-9760
FAX: (312) 461-0380

SOFTWARE
Cost: Contact Vendor
Compatibility: IBM/DOS

Capabilities include option writing (puts, calls, expirations, exercises and assignments.) Satisfies total Schedule D reporting requirement. Cash report ties in with either general ledger and/or bank statements. Interfaces to Lotus 1-2-3, dBase III and Chartmaster.

CAPTOOL

Techserve, Inc.
Box 70056
Bellevue, WA 98007

PH: (206) 747-5598
(800) 826-8082

SOFTWARE
Cost: $99.00
Compatibility : IBM/DOS

Covers: Stocks, commodities, mutual funds, options, and bonds (municipal, corporate, and government) . Integrates portfolio management security evaluation, data acquisition, and client management into a single powerful package for individual investors and investment professionals. Enables users to track return on investment while managing multiple portfolios.

CDA Asset Mix Optimizer for Financial Planners

CDA Investment Technologies, Inc.
1355 Piccard Drive
Rockville, MD 20850

PH: (800) 232-2285

SOFTWARE
Cost: $700.00
Compatibility: IBM compatibles

Covers: stocks and bonds. A semi-annual PC compatible software package with graphics, that determines how much of a portfolio should be invested in various asset classes such as common stocks, bonds, money market instruments, real estate, precious metals, and others. CDA' Optimizer includes 32 asset classes. Optimization is a process of systematically selecting assets so that the combined portfolio represents the most efficient trade-off between rate of return and risk.

CDA Mutual Fund Hypotheticals

CDA Investment Technologies, Inc.
1355 Piccard Drive
Rockville, MD 20850

PH: (800) 232-2285

SOFTWARE
Cost: $600.00.
Compatibility: IBM compatibles

Covers: mutual funds. This quarterly PC-compatible software package, including graphs, enables the user to take into account and analyze: any pattern of investments and withdrawals; reinvest options for all types of distributors; tax rates on income and capital gains; load and redemption fees; and more for over 1,500 funds.

CDA Mutual Fund Hypotheticals with Reallocations

CDA Investment Technologies, Inc.
1355 Piccard Drive
Rockville, MD 20850

PH: (800) 232-2285

SOFTWARE
Cost: $200.00.
Compatibility: IBM compatibles.

Covers: mutual funds. We've added an optional function to our Hypotheticals software. You choose a composite of funds from over 1,500 in our database. The program provides hypothetical illustrations - both tables and charts - of the past performance of each fund, along with results for the composite, based on your strategy of timing investments and withdrawals. You can reallocate capital between funds as often as monthly, and compare your composite's results to several indices.

Client Asset Management System (dbCAMS)

Financial Computer Support, Inc.
Route 4 Box 527
Deer Park, MD 21550

PH: (301) 387-4445

SOFTWARE
Cost: Contact Vendor
Compatibility: IBM/DOS

Covers: mutual funds. Data management system for tracking insurance, assets, portfolios, gain/loss, mutual funds and money market funds for either consolidated family or individual reporting. A client Billing and Time Management module and a Dow Jones Pricing Link module are also available. Interfaces to MPLAN, financial Profiles, Sawheny's Exec Plan, Leonard, ProPlan and other financial planning packages.

Commodex Signals

Equidex, Inc.
7000 Blvd East
Guttenberg, NJ 07093-4808

PH: (800) 336-1818
(201) 868-2600

Cost: $1695.00 per year must have a built in or external modem.

Covers: futures. Receive instant 24 hour access through computer telephone network to commodex signals. New signals processed twice daily. Intra-day bulletin available at approximately 12:30 PM EST.

Commodities and Futures Software

Programmed Press
599 Arnold Road
W. Hempstead, NY 11552

PH: (516) 599-6527

SOFTWARE
Cost: Hook-up charges $120.00
Compatibility: IBM/DOS, MacIntosh, TRS

Covers: commodities. Package provides forecasting capabilities concerning the evaluation of price, risk and return on commodities and futures.

Company Intelligence

Dialog Information Services, Inc.
3460 Hillview Avenue
Palo Alto, CA 94304

PH: (800) 334-2564
 (415) 858-3785
FAX: (415) 858-7069

ONLINE
Cost: Standard Service Plan - $45.00 for the first pass-
word
$25.00 for each additional password
 $35.00 per year for each password
 Online charges $1.75 per minute or $105.00 per hour
Compatibility: IBM/DOS, MacIntosh

Online database containing a combined directory and
company news file published by Information Access
Company. Contains current address, financial and marketing information on approximately 10,000 U.S. private and public companies. Updated daily.

Complete Bond Analyzer

Larry Rosen Company
7008 Springdale Road
Louisville, KY 40241

PH: (502) 228-4343

SOFTWARE
Cost: Hook-up charges $89.00
Compatibility: IBM/DOS, MacIntosh

Covers: bonds. Supports many bond related calculations. Purchase price given yield to maturity; yield to
maturity (pre and after-tax) given purchase price, yield
to call; results for precise time periods; accrued interest
at purchase or sale, duration and revised duration;
theoretical spot rates; results for taxables or tax-exempts;
and results for governments, agencies, conventional or
zero coupon bonds.

Compu / Chart EGA

New Tek Industries
P.O. Box 46116
Los Angeles, CA 90046

PH: (213) 874-6669

SOFTWARE
Cost: Hook-up charges $299.95 - $359.95 with 1200
baud modem
Compatibility: IBM/DOS

Includes: Chart service. Automatic data retrieval and
technical analysis program using high-resolution color
graphics. Many chart screens include Moving Averages
/ Bar Chart, The Portfolio Scanner, Oscillator - Scan,
Comparisons, Point and Figure Chart. Includes built in
communications module called 'The Retriever.'

Compu / Chart 3 with The Retriever

New Tek Industries
P.O. Box 46116
Los Angeles, CA 90046

PH: (213) 874-6669

SOFTWARE
Cost: Hook-up charges $299.95 - $398.95 with 2400 baud modem
Compatibility: IBM/DOS

Covers: stocks, commodities, mutual funds, chart service. Trend analyzer that goes online via modem with TrackData Dial/Data Service and retrieves price and volume information in its own format, automatically. Charting modules plot moving averages, oscillation, price/volume indicators, comparisons, point and figure, and more for non-graphics computers.

CompuServe Information Service

(An H&R Block company)
5000 Arlington Centre Blvd.
Columbus, OH 43220

PH: (800) 848-8199
(614) 457-0802

Cost: membership fee - $39.95 (includes $25.00 usage credit)
monthly fee - $1.50
online charges - from $6.00 per hour
communications surcharge - .30 cents per hour
Compatibility: any PC/modem.

Includes: stocks, commodities, charts, mutual funds, options, and currencies. The ultimate guidance system for personal investing. Services include Quote, Snapshot (quotes relative to market) , historical trading, range-review, up to 12 years of daily, weekly, and monthly pricing statistics, issue characteristics (P/E ratio, dividend data, earnings projections & Value Line Forecasts, S&P online, disclosure menu to check for any lawsuits, Business News and Other Opinions lets you talk shop with other investors, from novice to the most experienced.

CompuTrac

Telerate, Inc.
1017 Pleasant Street
New Orleans, LA 70115

PH: (800) 535-7990
(504) 895-1474
(800) 274-4028
FAX: (504) 895-3416

SOFTWARE
Hook-up charges $1900.00 includes chart services. Optional maintenance program for $300.00 per year, provides program updates and telephone assistance line. Stock quote service provided through outside vendor of your choice. For specific costs, speak with a CompuTrac representative.

Covers: stocks, commodities, chart service, market timing, options. A data service gathers price information for thousands of items into a mainframe computer. It will provide the proper communications software to allow your personal computer to access their mainframe through a telephone modem. This communications software will collect and store data in a special directory called CT-DATA which is later read by CompuTrac. Superior technical analysis software can take the gray out of your trading decisions and give you more time to judge the buy and sell signals. The most complete library of price forecasting techniques available anywhere.

Comstock

Standard & Poor's Information Group
670 White Plains Road
Scarsdale, NY 10583

PH: (800) 431-5019
(914) 725-3477 (NY & Canada)
FAX: (914) 725-4271

Cost: Hook-up charges $750.00
Basic monthly charge $420.00
Online chgs per min   n/a
Security deposit $500.00
Immediate stock quote service at no additional cost.
Chart Service available if you provide software.
Compatibility : IBM/DOS   MacIntosh

Covers: stocks, bonds(municipal, government, corporate, foreign) , commodities, mutual funds, market timing, and charts. Provides global market data coverage and extensive news service through a dictionary size controller. Provides professional, real-time market quotes at an affordable price.

Continuous Contractor

Technical Tools
334 State Street, Suite 201
Los Altos, CA 94022

PH: (415) 948-6124

SOFTWARE
Cost: $150.00.
Compatibility :IBM

Software which synthesizes long, continuous contracts from the individual contract data. Allows you to set up data files into a number of different popular formats such as CSI, CompuTrac, Lotus, Symphony, MetaStock, etc.

Convertible Bond Analyst

Analytical Service Association
21 Hollis Road
Lynn, MA 01904

PH: (617) 593-2404

SOFTWARE
Cost: Hook-up charges $99.95
Compatibility: IBM/DOS

Covers: bonds. Finds undervalued convertible bonds. Evaluates convertible bonds giving premium over investment value in points and percent, conversion parity price, premium over conversion in percent, current yield, pay back in years, break-even time in years, yield to maturity, undervaluation factor and the convertible price and percent gained or lost for a 50 percent stock price and gain loss.

The Convertible Securities Arbitrager (CSA)

Micro Code Technologies, Inc.
501 5th Avenue, 22nd Floor
New York, NY 10017

PH: (800) 442-9111
Cost: $99.95 for package
Compatibility : IBM/DOS or equivalent

Covers: convertible securities. The program allows you to: enter your daily trading sums; perform fast 'what-if' analysis; delete old convertibles from the database; change the prices, hedge ration, and interest rates; do an end-of-day mark-to-market; add new convertibles to your CSA database; edit the contents of any file in the CSA database; print arbitrage/portfolio reports.

CQG System One

CQG, Inc.
P.O. Box 758
Glenwood Springs, CO 81602-0758

PH: (800) 525-7082
(303) 945-8686 Hdqts

Cost: Basic monthly charge $390.00 + exchange fees includes immediate futures quote service at no additional cost. Chart services at $50.00 and up per month.
Compatibility : CQG hardware

Covers: commodities, chart service, news - Futures World News. Turn-key system - hardware and data link, comprehensive market quotation service that is ready when you need it for quotes, charts, news, market and technical information.

D & B - Duns Financial Records Plus

Dialog Information Services, Inc.
3460 Hillview Avenue
Palo Alto, CA 94304

PH: (800) 334-2564
 (415) 858-3810
FAX: (415) 858-7069

ONLINE
Cost: Standard Service Plan: $45.00 for the first password
$25.00 for each additional password
$35.00 annual fee for each password
 Online charges $2.45 per minute or $147.00 per hour
Compatibility: IBM/DOS and MacIntosh

Provides up to three years of financial statements for over 650,000 private and public companies. Information provided by Dun & Bradstreet Credit Services. Updated quarterly.

The Dallas Morning News Stock/Business Hotline

PH: (900) 990-9900 (then enter 195)
 (214) 977-8809

Cost: $.95 per minute
Frequency of update: every 15 minutes

QUOTE SERVICE
Includes: stocks. Covers: business news. Use your touch-tone phone to get timely stock quotes (15 minute delayed) on more than 9000 publicly traded issues and concise hourly business news updates prepared by business experts from the Associated Press.

Data Mover (CompuTrac)

Automated data collection
Winning Strategies, Inc.
761 Covington Road
Los Altos, CA 94022-4906

PH: (415) 969-8576

Cost: $139.00 for Data Mover and users manual
Compatibility: IBM compatibles

Covers: options, stocks, commodities, and indexes. Features: update CompuTrac daily files from Telemet, Signal, PC-Quote files; fully menu driven and self-prompting; up to 600 files may be updated at once; multiple passes may be made; program automatically selects appropriate stock or commodity data files for file updating; checks file before updating to ensure it hasn't already been updated; optionally can overwrite last data; low cost and user friendly.

DataTimes

14000 Quail Springs Parkway
Suite 450
Oklahoma City, OK 73134

PH: (800) 642-2525
 (405) 751-6400

Cost: $85.00 hook-up charges, $75.00 basic monthly charge, online charges from $.35 per minute. Immediate stock quote service available from $.25 per minute.
Compatibility: any PC with modem.

Covers: News. "Provides access to over 800 regional, national and international news sources including newspaper, newswire, magazine and financial databases." Also provides access to quotes, company and industry information (including Standard and Poors) and personal services.

DBC/LINK2

Computer Investing Consultants
9002 Swinburne Ct.
San Antonio, TX 78240

PH: (512) 681-0491

Cost: $98.00
Compatibility: IBM compatibles.

Covers: stocks. For use with CompuTrac. DBC/LINK2, a program for interfacing FNN/Marketwatch data to MetaStock, CompuTrac or N2 (stocks and indexes) and spreadsheet programs is also available. This program can save up to 255 stocks to your database in about 2 minutes, identify major price and volume moves and give you a spreadsheet/database readable file in a single operation. A special feature will let you run the screen on intra-day data so that you can have this information before the market closes.

DCA

Emerging Market Technologies, Inc.
1230 Johnson Ferry Road
Suite F-1
Marietta, GA 30068

PH: (404) 973-2300
FAX: (404) 973-3003

SOFTWARE
Cost: $95.00
Compatibility: IBM/DOS

Modelling software for dollar cost averaging for bond and stock investments.

Dial Data

Track Data Corp.
61 Broadway
New York, NY 10006

PH: (718) 522-6886

Cost: Hook-up charges $25.00
Basic monthly charge $15.00 minimum..
stock quote service (15 minute delayed) from .01 cents per issue per day, and .50 cents per data retrieval session. A more detailed pricing list is available through the vendor.
Compatibility: IBM/DOS

Covers: stocks, commodities, mutual funds, options, and bonds (municipal, corporate and government)
You can track daily, weekly, and monthly prices for securities. Intra-day prices are available for securities, options, commodity futures and commodity future options. Provides historical information also. The Dial Data service provides a program for IBM-PC users with the following capabilities: symbol list and data file maintenance on your computer; automatic dial-up through Autonet or Telenet public networks; automatic data retrieval in daily, weekly, or monthly series; dynamic data files in CompuTrac format.

DIALOG

Dialog Information Services, Inc.
3460 Hillview avenue
Palo Alto, CA 94304

PH: (800) 334-2564

Costs: $45.00 start-up fee (separate) then pick from several starter packages ranging from $125.00 to $230.00, then you pay online charges per minute.
Compatibility: IBM/DOS compatibles, Macintosh and others (need modem)

The DIALOG service lets you search through thousands - even millions - of documents in seconds. DIALOG draws from more sources than any other online service in the world. You'll have access to over 320 databases covering thousands of journals and publications, i.e. locate financial data on over 2.5 million public and private companies, research and analyze industry trends and development etc.

Dialog Quotes and Trading

Dialog Information Services, Inc.
3460 Hillview Avenue
Palo Alto, CA 94304

PH: (800) 334-2564
 (415) 858-3810
FAX: (415) 858-7069

ONLINE
Cost: Standard Service Plan: $45.00 for the first password
$25.00 for each additional password
$35.00 annual fee for each password
 Online charges $.60 per minute or $36.00 per hour
Compatibility: IBM/DOS, MacIntosh

Covers: stocks. Stocks and options quotes delayed at least 20 minutes from the New York and American Stock Exchanges, NASDAQ, and the four major options exchanges. Order entry allows purchase or sale of any stock or option listed in the Wall Street Journal. Updated daily (20 minute delay) .

Disclosure Database

Dialog Information Services, Inc.
3460 Hillview Avenue
Palo Alto, CA 94304

PH: (800) 334-2564
 (415) 858-3810
FAX: (415) 858-7069

ONLINE
Cost: Standard Service Plan: $45.00 for the first password
$25.00 for each additional password
$35.00 annual fee for each password
Online charges $.75 per minute or $45.00 per hour
Compatibility: IBM/DOS, MacIntosh

Financial information on over 12,500 companies. Derived from reports filed with the U.S. Securities and Exchange Commission by publicly owned companies. Information provided by Disclosure, Inc. Bethesda, MD. Updated weekly.

Dow Jones News Retrieval

Dow Jones and Company, Inc.
P.O. Box 300
Princeton, NJ 08543-0300

PH: (609) 520-4000
(609) 520-4641
FAX: (609) 520-4660

Cost: Hook-up charges $29.95
Online charges per minute - from .40 cents per minute
Immediate stock quote service from .50 cents per minute
additional cost

Covers: stocks, mutual funds, corporate bonds, foreign bonds, treasury issues, and options. Users have stock quotes and detailed financial data on thousands of companies at their fingertips, along with the historical information that provides a solid foundation for action, You get exclusive online access to The Wall Street Journal, the strengths of Dow Jones & Company, Inc., the complete text of selected articles from national business publications (Barron's Business Week, Fortune, Money, Inc. and the Washington Post) , and articles from regional newspapers and business publications. Also includes the Professional Investor Report which keeps you on top of unusual trading stories behind trading patterns. PIR gives immediate notification of SEC filings and follow-up detail with selected Federal Filings news wires online.

DTN Wall Street

Data Transmission Network Corp.
9110 W. Dodge Road, Suite 200
Omaha, NE 68114

PH: (800) 755-7503

Cost: $295.00 Monitor, receiver, and dish $34.95 basic monthly charge, stock quote service(delayed) at no additional cost.
Compatibility : IBM Apple

Covers: stocks, commodities, mutual funds, municipal, corporate, and government bonds, petroleum, metals, currencies, and interest rates. Brings you delayed quotes on stocks, bonds, funds, government issues, interest rates, currencies, metals, petroleum, and commodities, plus fast-breaking news. Needs no phone, modem, TV or computer. accessible 24 hours a day.

Encore

Telemet America, Inc.
325 First Street
Alexandria, VA 22314

PH: (800) 368-2078
(703) 548-2042

Cost: Basic monthly charge $169.00 + Delayed Stock quote service and chart services at no additional charge, immediate charges are:
$27.50/mo - NYSE,AMEX $16.00/mo - NASDAQ
$80.00/mo - CBOT $12.00/mo - options
$25.00/mo - HEADLINE NEWS
Compatibility : IBM/DOS

Covers: stocks, commodities,chart service, News - McGraw Hill. A sophisticated market quotation and news system which gives you instant stock, option, futures quotes, and business news 24 hours a day.

Ensign III

Ensign (manufacturer) Bonneville Market Information
19th West S. Temple
Salt Lake City, Utah 84101

PH: (800) 255-7374

QUOTE SERVICE
Cost: Basic monthly charge $227.00 + exchange fees :
deposit for dish $597.00 installation fee for dish $395.00,
software - $1195.00, + $10/mo maintenance for updates. Includes stock quote service, and chart services.

Financial trading software featuring real-time commodity, stock and option quotes, technical studies,
charts, and news. Portfolio: 16 user-defined pages with
20 entries per page, various column layouts including
bid and ask; Charts: 320 intraday, daily, weekly, and
monthly, diverse technical tools and studies; News:
retrieve 500 stories by headline search, weather maps;
Quotes: display last and net on 10,000 items, automatically created and alphabetized; Equity: 20 portfolios of
open positions, shows profit/loss and margin.

EPIC

Ford Investor Services, Inc.
11722 Sorrento Valley Road, Suite 1
San Diego, CA 92121

PH: (619) 755-1327
FAX: (619) 455-6316

ONLINE AND SOFTWARE
Cost: annual charges $3600.00 with monthly updates,
$7200.00 with weekly updates, online service add $24.00
per hour of connect time. Compatibility with IBM/
DOS.

Covers: stocks. Equity Portfolio and Investment Computing (EPIC) has the capability to screen and rank
stocks, perform sector and industry analysis, compute
portfolio data averages, and S&P 500 averages, maintain a portfolio of companies, add, delete, or modify data
base records, generate reports, and import data to spreadsheet software.

The Equalizer

Charles Schwab and Co., Inc
101 Montgomery Street
San Francisco, CA 94101

PH: (800) 648-4248

SOFTWARE
Cost: Basic monthly charge - $110.00 for exchange fees
Online charges per minute vary with database
Immediate stock quote service available for $1.45 per
minute. Software $99.00 with modem $199.00

Covers: stocks, commodities, mutual funds, options,
news(Dow Jones) , and bonds (municipal, corporate,
government and foreign) . Lets you access the information used by many professional investors so you can
make your own investment decisions. Enter your own
trades and take advantage of Schwab's discount commissions.

Equities

Bridge Information Systems, Inc.
717 Office Parkway
St. Louis, MO 63141

PH: (800) 325-3282
(314) 567-8100
FAX: (314) 432-5391

Cost: Basic monthly charge $2000.00 minimum + exchange fees. Includes immediate stock quote service and interactive stock data at no additional charge. Compatibility: IBM compatible.

Covers: stocks, commodities, money market instruments, listed bonds, currencies, options, futures, indexes, and includes charts. Provides market professionals with a wide range of investment information on more than 100,000 financial instruments from around the world. Includes over 75 different displays and hundreds of modifying parameters. Delivers its classic service via a PC workstation providing user friendly access, programmable function keys, high resolution color graphics, single-screen, multiple window displays and automatic page printing capabilities. This service requires retail or institutional use for cost-effectiveness.

Euro Equities

Detroyat & Associates, Inc.
535 Madison Avenue, 37th floor
New York, NY 10022

PH: (212) 759-0160
FAX: (212) 759-0109

SOFTWARE
Compatibility with IBM/DOS, and Macintosh
Cost: $12,000 updated twice monthly.

Covers: European equities. A micro-computer database on European listed companies designed for investment professional, research analysts an traders. Includes 1500 companies in 15 European countries, 8 years of historical data, 2 years of estimates, 12 months price charts and company profiles.

Exchange Access

Warner Computer Systems, Inc.
17-01 Pollitt Drive
Fair Lawn, NJ 07410

PH: (201) 797-4633
(800) 336-5376

Cost: Hook-up charges $60.00
Online charges per minute varies from .08 cents per minute.
Stock quote service at close from .0295 cents per minute.
** Costs very greatly depending on software you choose
- be it technical or portfolio management.

Covers: stocks, mutual funds, market indices & indicators, options, futures, and bonds (municipal and corporate). A data service designed to meet the needs of the serious investor. Exchange Access is your gateway to a single comprehensive source of investment information created and maintained by Warner's staff of professionals. Gives you both end of the day and historical securities information.

Fabozzi's Fixed Income Calculator

Frank J. Fabozzi
Probus Publishing Co.
1925 North Clybourn Avenue
Chicago, IL 60614

PH: (800) PROBUS-1
FAX: (312) 868-6250

SOFTWARE
Cost: $149.95
Compatibility: IBMs, Compaqs and compatible PCs and SUN workstations.

Covers: bond analysis, discount securities analysis, CDs and options. A comprehensive system for analyzing a broad spectrum of fixed income, money market, options and related financial markets. All calculations are based on both industry standard and "street" adopted conventions. The calculator is a page oriented system. Each page covers a specific set of analyses. Additional pages cover bond swaps, total return and sensitivity analyses, yield curve analysis, foreign exchange cross rates, generalized cash flow analysis, finance functions, and a calendar calculator.

Fast Track

Investors Fast Track
11752 C S. Harrell's Ferry
Baton Rouge, LA 70812

PH: (800) 749-1348

Compatibility: IBM with graphics monitor and modem
Cost: $19.95 one month access to database; introductory offer complete product then pay $69.00 for manual and software, (includes anther 30 days. Then pay $30.00 monthly, $75.00 quarterly or $240.00 annually.

Covers 395 mutual funds, and provides a chart service, plus 9 market indexes. Fast Track helps you take advantage of "telephone switching" offered by the fund companies. Fast Track shows how your current fund compares to the market and other funds in its family. Fast Track will tell you when other funds or families have better potential. You can switch between funds at any time at little or no cost, even funds bought from a broker.

Financial System One

Automatic Data Processing
2 Journal Square Plaza
Jersey City, NJ 07306-0817

PH: (201) 714-3000

ONLINE
Cost: Basic monthly charge $650.00, $85.00 for each desk unit. Includes monitor, keyboard, maintenance, Executive summary, Market Minder, Market Monitor, Snap Quote. Dow Jones News available at additional charge.

Covers: stocks, commodities, option, and bonds (municipal, corporate, and government). A dedicated online stock market information system that delivers up to the second quotes on over 35,000 stocks, bonds, commodities, and options at the touch of a button. Designed for investment professional, it is used and trusted by registered representatives in leading brokerage firms.

FINIS: Financial Industry Information Service

Dialog Information Services, Inc.
3460 Hillview Avenue
Palo Alto, CA 94304

PH: (800) 334-2564
 (415) 858-3810
FAX: (415) 858-7069

ONLINE
Cost: Standard Service Plan: $45.00 for the first password
$25.00 for each additional password
$35.00 annual fee for each password
 Online charges $1.30 per minute or $78.00 per hour
Compatibility: IBM/DOS, MacIntosh

Marketing information on organizations that comprise the financial services industry and on products and services offered to corporate and retail customers. Information provided by Bank Marketing Association (BMA), Chicago, IL. Updated every two weeks.

Fixed Asset System

Best Programs
2700 S. Quincy Street
Arlington, VA 22206

PH: (800) 368-2405
(703) 820-9300

SOFTWARE
Cost: $795.00

Covers: fixed assets. Software to automate fixed asset management and depreciation. It maintains precise, auditable record, calculates depreciation, generates reports and backup documentation currently required by law, generates tax worksheets for filing with the IRS, provides customized management reports and projections to support your business decision, meets FASB 96 projection requirements automatically and handles short years automatically with a complete audit trail. Many enhancement features available at additional costs.

Fixed Income Pricing Services

Street Software Technology
230 Park Avenue, Suite 857
New York, NY 10169

PH: (212) 922-0500
FAX: (212) 922-0058

SOFTWARE
Cost: DAILY PRICES -
Hookup charges $300.00, basic monthly charge
$450.00, online charges per hour from $25.00
INTRA-DAY PRICES -
Hookup charges $300.00, dial-in service
first 25 calls $4.00 each next 25 - $3.00 each
LEASED LINE -
Hookup charges $1500.00, basic monthly charge
$500.00 a month + lease line charges

A fixed-income pricing service that has been supplying prices to Wall Street Banking Community since 1975. Daily prices are ready at 4:30 EST and include CUSIP # for easy identification. Intraday prices are updated every 15 minutes between 9AM and 3PM - EST. Available via dial-in service or transmitted over a leased line.

Fixed Income Securities Calculations (FISCAL)

Vertisoft, Inc.
2402 Route 9 South
Howell, NJ 07731

PH: (201) 780-8641

SOFTWARE
Cost: Contact Vendor
Compatibility:

Covers: government bonds. Computes price, yield and accrued interest for more than forty types of securities. Includes U.S. Treasury Bills, U.S. Treasury Bonds, Certificates of Deposit, Bankers' Acceptance and Commercial Paper. All calculations meet standards from Securities Industry Association.

Ford Investor Services, Inc.

Ford Investor Services, Inc.
11722 Sorrento Valley Road
Suite 1
San Diego, CA 92121

PH: (619) 755-1327
FAX: (619) 455-6316

See Epic

Ford Value Report

Ford Investor Services, Inc.
11722 Sorrento Valley Road
Suite 1
San Diego, CA 92121

PH: (619) 755-1327

ONLINE
Cost: Online charges $96.00 per hour
Compatibility:

Covers: stocks. Provides fundamental financial data on 2000 leading stocks. Also provides investment value analysis to determine if over or under valued, analysis of current earnings trends, stock market commentary on fundamentals, recommendations and more.

FTI Banc Investor: Securities Accounting System

Financial Technology, Inc.
70 East Lake Street
Suite 1200
Chicago, IL 60601

PH: (800) 541-9537
 (312) 606-1500

SOFTWARE
Cost: $3,300.00 to $8,500.00
Compatibility: IBM/DOS, NCR, Unisys

Securities management in four parts, Bond Accounting System, Portfolio Analysis, Multi-Bond Swapper and Bond Calculator. Permits in-house securities analysis, accounting and pricing on a PC. Optional modules include Bond Swapper Module, Bond Calculator Module, Graphics/Spreadsheet Interface and Telecommunications Pricing Module.

The Fundamental Investor

Savant Corp
11211 Katy Freeway, Suite 250
Houston, TX 77079

PH: (800) 231-9900
(713) 973-2400

SOFTWARE
Cost: $395.00
Compatibility: IBM/DOS

Covers: Stocks, mutual funds. A fundamental screening and ranking program covering more than 10,000 companies and 1800 mutual funds. Comes with over 50 predefined financial equations with capacity to change them and add up to 150 more. COMMENTS: Includes communications to retrieve price and fundamental information from Ford Investor Services and Warner Computer Systems.

Fundwatch Plus

Hamilton Software, Inc.
6432 East Mineral Place
Englewood, CO 80112

PH: (303) 795-5572
 (303) 770-9607

SOFTWARE
Cost: Hook-up charges $29.00
Compatibility: IBM/DOS

Covers: mutual funds. Evaluates and compares common investments including mutual funds, stocks, many commodities and market averages like the Dow Jones. Allows home investors to evaluate investments inexpensively without a modem or online data subscription.

Future Link

Oster Communications
219 Parkade
Cedar Falls, Iowa 50613

PH: (800) 553-2910 ext 224

Cost: Hook-up charges	$199.95
Basic monthly charge	$79.95
Online charges per minute	n/a
** Need Satellite Dish	$699.00
*** Future Source	$420.00 a month + exchange fees - immediate quotes

Compatibility: IBM/DOS

Covers: stocks, bonds (municipal, corporate, government, foreign) , commodities, mutual funds, market timing, and charts. 10 minute snap-shot quotes, world wide online market news, complete futures and options prices, floor commentary, technical commentary and studies, bar charts, automatic position and spread tracking, and more.

Futures Margin System (FMS)

Software Options, Inc.
210 Sylvan Avenue
Englewood Cliffs, NJ 07632

PH: (201) 568-6664

SOFTWARE
Cost: $24,000.00
Compatibility: IBM/DOS

A futures margin accounting system designed for a futures Commission Merchant or large institutional client, keeps futures and options positions, daily mark-to-market P/L, client margin requirements and daily trade confirmations, open position statements, and monthly statements to clients and/or clearing brokers.

Future Source

Oster Communications
955 Parkview Blvd.
Lombard, IL 60148

PH: (800) 621-2628
(708) 620-8444 (other)
FAX: (708) 620-4315

Cost: If you have access to a satellite dish: 500 deposit + 150.00 shipping & handling, or they can provide a dish for about $900.00 + installation. Basic monthly service is $150.00 + 50.00 transmission fee. No online charges per minute. Provides chart services at an additional cost of $100 -$200 depending on how technical you want to get.
Compatibility: IBM/DOS

Covers: commodities, options, chart service, news, futures, & world news. Gives you real time futures and options quotes on every contract traded on all major worldwide exchanges. Chart database includes tick data, daily bar charts, continuation charts, spread charts, & archive data.

Future Update

Oster Communications, Inc.
219 Parkade
Cedar Falls, IA 50613

PH: (800) 553-2910
(800) 221-4352
FAX: (319) 277-7896

Cost: $48.00 hook-up charges, $19.00 basic monthly charge, per minute charge at ling distance rates, includes 10 minute snapshot quotes and stock quote service for futures and options only.
Compatibility: IBM, Macintosh, virtually any computer.

Covers: futures, options, and news. A dial-up market service that lets you display current futures and options prices, market news and other critical trading data right on your computer - anytime - day or night. Also have access to technical and historical data including moving averages, stochastics, relative strength index, and more. You can download this information and use it with software programs such as CompuTrac, CSI, Lotus 1-2-3, and more. You pay only for the information you use.

Genesis Data Service

P.O. Box 49578
Colorado Springs, CO 80949

PH: (719) 260-6111

Cost: prices are too variable to list - too many variables.
Compatibility: IBM/DOS

Covers: stocks, commodities, and mutual funds. Historical data software to update your Metastock, CompuTrac, AIQ and CSI format files for all your favorite stocks, options and commodities.

Global Information for Executive Decisions

DRI/McGraw-Hill
24 Hartwell Avenue
Lexington, MA 02173

PH: (617) 863-5100
(800) 541-9914
FAX: (617) 8600-6332

Cost: minimum Cost: $2500.00 annually. Online charges - $1.00 per minute plus additional charge per report or request (charge amount varies with type of information requested). IBM compatible.

Covers: world markets. Provides comprehensive coverage of key financial markets, industry trends, and economic conditions, along with in-depth analysis of events as they affect your organization. The core services cover world markets, United States, Regional U.S. markets, Europe, Canada, Energy & Chemical, Cost & Inflation Information. DRI has the historical data and forecasts you need to understand today's markets and better plan for tomorrow's.

Graph-in-the-Box Executive

New England Software, Inc.
Greenwich Office Park #3
Greenwich, CT 06831

PH: (203) 625-0062
FAX: (203) 625-0718

SOFTWARE
Cost $299.95 suggested retail price (stores) available in store much cheaper than ordering direct from company)
Compatibility: IBM/DOS

Chart service. A complete professional business graphics program that makes 15 different chart types, including text and organization charts.

Hi-Portfolio

CCF Group, PLC.
Eldon House
203 Eldon Street
London, England EC2M7LS

PH: 01-377-9755

SOFTWARE
Cost: Contact Vendor
Compatibility: IBM/DOS

Facilities for managing portfolios and securities. Transactions, reporting and inquires are available at both the individual client level and consolidated fund level. Handles ordinary shares, convertible notes, fixed interest investments, call and put options, right issues, discounted securities and futures.

Historical Data Services

Historical Data Services
205 S. M-291 Highway
Suite 195
Lee's Summit, MO 64063

PH: (800) 873-8861
(816) 633-7593

ONLINE OR DISKETTE
Cost: Consult company for pricing per your individual
needs.

Covers: stocks, commodities, mutual funds. Responsive efficient and highly accurate reporting of historical financial information including historical data on more than 15,000 stocks; 1,500 mutual funds; 100 commodities/futures, all major markets, nearly every index, fundamental and technical data, major market statistics back over 70 years, government statistics and interest rates back decades and more.

ICC British Company Financial Datasheets

Dialog Information Services, Inc.
3460 Hillview Avenue
Palo Alto, CA 94304

PH: (800) 334-2564
(415) 858-3810
FAX: (415) 858-7069

ONLINE
Cost: Standard Service Plan: $45.00 for the first password
$25.00 for each additional password
$35.00 annual fee for each password
Online charges $1.60 per minute or $96.00 per hour
Compatibility: IBM/DOS, MacIntosh

Financial information for over 100,000 British companies including up to 100 leading companies in 140 selected industry sectors. Information provided by ICC Information Group Ltd, London England. Updated weekly.

IDCPRICE

Interactive Data
95 Hayden Avenue
Lexington, MA 02173-9144

PH: (617) 863-8100

Cost: initial set up fee $25.00, no monthly minimum. Daily current or historical data per security or commodity per day $.03. Weekly current or historical data for indices reported on a weekly basis, per index per week$.03. Weekly current or historical data, calculated from daily data, per security or commodity per week $.06. Daily current or historical data per specified daily indicator per day $.06.
Compatible with IBM/DOS and Macintosh.

Includes: options, stocks, and commodities.For use with CompuTrac.System features: IDCPRICE is menu-driven, making it easy to use; IDCPRICE lets you retrieve and store data; you can create, delete, copy, and modify your data files; you can retrieve for a single security for a single date or for a range of dates, or multiple securities for a single date via your portfolio; you can price your portfolios whenever you like; you can convert the data files that you have created either manually in CompuTrac or through selected vendor's data services.

IFS Securities History Data

Iverson Financial Systems, Inc.
1020 Foster City Blvd. Suite 290
Foster City, CA 94404

PH: (415) 349-4767

Costs are figured on a per item/per record fee
Additional fees: setup and processing, per job minimum
of $20.00, diskette, mailer and mailing per tape $5.00,
magnetic tape, mailer and mailing, per tape $30.00,
transmission per job $5.00.
Compatibility:IBM, Macintosh, Apple

Data service on stocks, mutual funds. Features: Buy
only needed data, example: only closing prices; any
periodicity; special formats and processing request welcomed; regular transmission customers welcomed -
example: weekly highest high; ad hoc requests welcomed - example: daily closing prices.

Infomart Online

Southam Business Information and Communications
1450 Don Mills Road
Don Mills, Ontario M3B2X7

PH: (800) 668-9215
 (416) 445-6641
FAX: (416) 445-3508

Cost: $175.00 hook-up charges, basic monthly charge
from $10.00, online charges from $2.73 per minute.
Compatibility: any terminal with a modem and dedicated phone lines.

Covers: Canadian stocks, news. An electronic information source that offers cross-Canada scope, depth and
breadth of information. It has over 600 news and business sources (including Dow Jones News/Retrieval)
which provide: access to Canadian stock quotes, current
and historical; directory and financial data on more than
7,000 Canadian companies; daily newspapers from
across the country; the Financial Post and Financial Post
Corporate Survey and more.

Information Globe

444 Front Street West
Toronto, Ontario, Canada M5V2S9

PH: (416) 585-5438
FAX: (416) 585-5249

Cost: Hook-up charges $99.00, online charges
$3.60 per minute prime time, $ .65 per minute non-
prime + .02 cents per data line. Includes delayed stock
quote service (at close) .

Types of investments covered: stocks, commodities,
bonds, options, indexes, and Canadian mutual funds. A
historical data service. Provides five years of hi/low,
close, volume, earnings and dividend data. Also includes extensive databases for Canadian companies,
Canada News-Wire, access to relevant articles from The
Globe and Mail (Canada's national newspaper) & Dow
Jones News Retrieval.

Insider Trading Monitor

Dialog Information Services, Inc.
3460 Hillview Avenue
Palo Alto, CA 94304

PH: (800) 334-2564
 (415) 858-3810
FAX: (415) 858-7069

ONLINE
Cost: Standard Service Plan: $45.00 for the first pass-
word
$25.00 for each additional password
$35.00 annual fee for each password
 Online charges $1.40 per minute or $84.00 per hour
Compatibility: IBM/DOS, MacIntosh

The transaction details of all insider trader filings (ownership changes) received by the U.S. Securities and
Exchange Commission since January 1984. Updated
daily. Information provided by Invest/Net, Inc., North
Miami, FL.

Intex Bond Amortization Program

Intex Solutions, Inc.
161 Highland Avenue
Needham, MA 02194

PH: (617) 449-6222
FAX: (617) 444-2318

SOFTWARE
Cost: $295.00
Compatibility:

Covers: bonds. Produces a bond amortization schedule
and calculates bond yield for tax and accounting purposes. Supports the straight-line method and the scientific method.

Intex Bond Calculations

Intex Solutions, Inc.
161 Highland Avenue
Needham, MA 02194

PH: (617) 449-6222
FAX: (617) 444-2318

SOFTWARE
Cost: Contact Vendor
Compatibility:

Covers: bonds. Does the following bond calculations:
yield, price, duration, Macaulay duration, bond equivalent yield of a T-bill, accrued interest, price and yield on
discount securities and other functions. Advanced and
international versions available. Versions available for
Excel, Paradox, Lotus 1-2-3, Symphony, mini, mainframe and workstations.

Intex Mortgage-Backed Calculations

Intex Solutions, Inc.
161 Highland Avenue
Needham, MA 02194

PH: (617) 449-6222
FAX: (617) 444-2318

SOFTWARE
Cost: Contact Vendor
Compatibility: IBM/DOS

Covers: bonds. Automates complex mortgage-backed bond calculations. Includes quoted and cashflow yield and price, balance, principal, interest, duration and life. Advanced version available. Also available for Lotus 1-2-3, Symphony and Paradox.

Intex Option Adjusted Spread

Intex Solutions, Inc.
161 Highland Avenue
Needham, MA 02194

PH: (617) 449-6222
FAX: (617) 444-2318

SOFTWARE
Cost: $8,000.00 for a single user
Compatibility: IBM/DOS

Covers: bonds, mortgage-backed securities. Values callable bonds and mortgage-backed securities including pools and whole loans. Accepts several prepayment models to take into account effects of future interest rate volatility. Projects cash flows and other factors such as stable yield and bond equivalent yield.

Intex Option Price Calculations

Intex Solutions, Inc.
161 Highland Avenue
Needham, MA 02194

PH: (617) 449-6222
FAX: (617) 444-2318

SOFTWARE
Cost: Contact Vendor
Compatibility: IBM/DOS

Covers: stocks, commodities, short-term options. Ready-to-use functions for options buyers and sellers. Included are theoretical value, implied volatility, historical volatility, Greek sensitivity values (delta, gamma, vega, theta, phi and rho) and data functions to determine appropriate option expiration date. Choice of a modified Black-Scholes or binomial pricing model.

Intex Solutions

161 Highland Avenue
Needham, MA 02194

PH: (617) 449-6222
FAX: (617) 444-2318

SOFTWARE
Cost: Bond $395.00 basic $695.00 advanced
$895.00 International (Add $100.00 for Release 3)
Mortgage backed is same as above but $895.00 is called
advanced version with excess servicing.Options $395.00
(add $100.00 for release 3) .
Compatible with IBM.

Types of investments covered: options and bonds, municipal, corporate, government and agencies. Expand the analytical capabilities of Lotus 1-2-3 and Symphony. Attach one or more of the add-in function programs listed below, then perform your calculations in any available spreadsheet cell. Intex functions: Intex Bond Calculations, Intex Mortgage Backed Calculations, Intex Option Price Calculations, etc.

Investext

Thomson Financial Networks
11 Farnsworth Street
Boston, MA 02210

PH: (617) 345-2000
(800) 662-7878
FAX: (617) 330-1986

ONLINE
Cost: Hookup charges $75.00 - Online charges per hour
$95.00.
Compatibility: IBM/DOS, Macintosh, any PC with a
modem or call (800) 662-7878

A full-text online database comprised of company and industry reports from 123 of the world's leading investment banks and research firms. Contains over 170,000 research reports on more than 14,000 domestic and international public companies in 53 industries. An average of 1200 new reports are added each week. The reports provide competitor profiles, market share data, forecasts, new product and technology data, recent operating results, sales/earnings analysis, and critical assessments of industry trends.

Investment Analysis For Stocks, Bonds, and Real Estate

Larry Rosen Company
7008 Springdale Road
Louisville, KY 40241

PH: (502) 228-4343

SOFTWARE
Cost: $89.00 for a single user
Compatibility: IBM/DOS, MacIntosh

Covers: stocks, real estate, bonds. Evaluates existing and proposed real estate, stock and bond investments by internal rate of return analysis after taxes. Cashflow analysis.

Investment Manager I

Integrated Decision Systems, Inc.
1950 Sawtelle, Suite 255
Los Angeles, CA 90025

PH: (213) 478-4015

SOFTWARE
Cost: $4000.00 for complete package + 60.00 a year for maintenance.
Compatibility: all makes of XT, 286 or 386 desktop computers

A comprehensive single-user portfolio management system for small to mid-size investment firms. They system tracks positions in all investment vehicles, continually updates entire portfolios as new information is entered and produces over 30 internal and client reports for measuring, analyzing, and recording investment risk and performance.

Invest Now! Personal

Emerging Market Technologies, Inc.
1230 Johnson Ferry Road
Suite F-1
Marietta, GA 30068

PH: (404) 973-2300
FAX: (404) 973-3003

SOFTWARE
Cost: $79.00
Compatibility: IBM/DOS

Personal version of stock/option calculator.

Invest Now! Professional Version 2.0

Emerging Market Technologies, Inc.
1230 Johnson Ferry Road Suite F-1
Marietta, GA 30068

PH: (404) 973-2300
FAX: (404) 973-3003

SOFTWARE
Cost: $129.00
Compatibility: IBM/DOS

Covers equity investment scenarios: buy calls, buy puts, combinations, stock yield, dividend roll, short sales, spreads, covered calls, naked calls and naked puts. Many calculations for stock and option investments. "What-if" capability.

INVESTigator +

INVESTment TECHnology
5104 Utah
Greenville, TX 75401

PH: (800) 833-0269
(903) 455-3255

Cost: $199.00.
Compatibility: IBM/DOS

Covers: stocks, commodities, mutual funds, indices, and options. Provides chart service. A powerful, modestly priced and easy to use. Charting, technical analysis, and data management program for stocks, options, indices, mutual funds, or commodities. Maintains up to 300 data files, each with up to 900 days or 900 weeks of data. Automatic or manual data file updating via Warner Computer Systems or your own keyboard.

Investor's Accountant

Hamilton Software, Inc.
6432 East Mineral Place
Englewood, CO 80112

PH: (303) 795-5572
 (303) 770-9607

-SOFTWARE
Cost: $395.00
Compatibility: IBM/DOS

Investment portfolio accounting and analysis system. Tracks performance of investments individually and by type. Includes fully integrated version of Fundwatch Plus for tracking, evaluating and graphing securities. Demo-trainer version available for $20.00 (applies toward purchase) .

Investor's Guide to Online Databases

Kenneth M. Landis & J. Thomas Monk
Business One Irwin
1818 Ridge Road
Homewood, IL 60430

PH: (800) 634-3966

Published 1988
Cost: $60.50

BOOK
Subjects addressed: online investment information services. This book established guidelines for determining what information is needed, how to get it, and how to use it. The book takes a detailed look at online investment information services and focuses on the information needs of investors.

The Investor's Portfolio

Savant Corporation
11211 Katy Freeway
Suite 250
Houston, TX 77079

PH: (800) 231-9900   (713) 973-2400

SOFTWARE
Cost: $495.00 for a single user
 $695.00 for the international version
Compatibility: IBM/DOS

Portfolio management, analysis, report and communications programs. Tracks almost any security and transaction, including spreads, shorts, open orders, zero coupon bonds, etc. Calculates return on investment and prints Schedule B and D and over 30 standard reports. Includes automatic updating of security prices by modem.

IPS Investment Portfolio Accounting

Interactive Planning Systems, Inc.
1800 Century Boulevard N.E.
Suite 800
Atlanta, GA 30345

PH: (800) 241-3246

SOFTWARE
Cost: $3,500.00 for a single user
 $5,000.00 for the network version
Compatibility: IBM/DOS

Automates interest accruals and amortization/accretion calculations, providing full management and accounting information. Multiple portfolio version available. Interfaces with Lotus and other software. Automatic pricing update via modem.

Klatu Software

Nirvana Systems, Inc.
3415 Greystone Drive, Suite 205
Austin, TX 78731

PH: (512) 345-2545

Cost: $595.00 for software package, $1295.00 for speech hardware by Texas Instruments which allows KLATU to say anything using the SAY command and recognize up to 50 phrases.
Compatibility: AT compatibles

Covers: stocks and mutual funds. A combination batch file and macro programs that works inside your favorite programs. You can collect data late at night when it is less expensive, convert and transport data between programs, run analysis on hundreds of issues nightly, track intraday issues without watching the screen yourself, have your computer call you on any condition, do "what if" scenarios using the programs you have now and much more. Named 1989 "Product of the Year" by Commodity Trader's Almanac.

Knight-Ridder Financial News

Dialog Information Services, Inc.
3460 Hillview Avenue
Palo Alto, CA 94304

PH: (800) 334-2564
(415) 858-3810
FAX: (415) 858-7069

ONLINE
Cost: Standard Service Plan: $45.00 for the first
password
$25.00 for each additional password
$35.00 annual fee for each password
Online charges: $1.60 per minute or $96.00 per hour
Compatibility: IBM/DOS, MacIntosh

Has complete text of news stories on worldwide financial and commodity markets and the events that move them. Information provided by Knight-Ridder Financial Information, Inc., New York, NY. Updated continuously.

LaPorte Asset Allocation System

Burlington Hall Asset Management Inc.
126 Petersburg Road
Hackettstown, NJ 07840

PH: (201) 852-1694

SOFTWARE
Cost: $1975.00 a year with all updates.

Covers: stocks, commodities, mutual funds, and charts. Provides you with all the tools you need to optimize combinations of investments or investment managers, plus much more. LaPorte is also a database management system for storing performance data on an unlimited number of investments. You can prepare performance graphs, transfer spreadsheet, prepare a variety of reports, prepare pie charts of asset allocations, project a range of future performance, compare managers against a universe and much, much more.

Lexis/Nexis

Mead Data
P.O. Box 933-NR
Dayton, OH 45401

PH: (800) 543-6862
(800) 227-4908

Cost: Basic monthly charge from $1,000.00. Online charges vary for unlimited usage with many options available.
Compatibility: almost any kind of PC with a modem.

Covers: stocks, news. A comprehensive electronic information source which provides: real time quotes, two major newswires updated every fifteen minutes from 8 am - 8 pm each business day, wire services from more than 650 worldwide news bureaus updated four times daily, major international, national and regional newspapers and financial sources are online within 24 hours and an extensive legal research service which includes corporation information.

Live-Line

National Computer Network Corporation
1929 N. Harlem Avenue
Chicago, IL 60635

PH: (800) 942-NCNC

ONLINE
Cost: Basic monthly charge from $400.00 or
 Online charges from $6.00 per hour
Immediate stock quote service at no additional cost.
Compatibility: Any PC with modem

Covers: stocks, options, futures, indexes and futures options. "An affordable real-time quote display system which monitors all U.S. equities, options, indexes, futures and future options."

Live Wire

CableSoft, Inc.
8207 Melrose Drive, Suite 111
Lenexa, KS 66214

PH: (913) 888-4449

COMPUTER SERVICES
Cost : Personal Investor: $29.50 Tracks up to 500 issues
Professional:$595.00 tracks 1000 + issues; Historical
Data Retriever $49.95.
Compatibility: IBM DOS and compatibles

Covers: general securities. Includes charts. The Live Wire software automates every step of the investment process. In real-time Live Wire lets you: monitor quotes, graph and analyze price movements, compare investments, set alarms, enter transaction, measure profit and loss. Provides technical analysis. COMMENTS: Also offers Historical Data Retriever. collects data from dial-up service and integrates data into Live Wire Historical data files.

Lotus Realtime

Lotus Development Corp
55 Cambridge Parkway
Cambridge, MA 02142

PH: (800) 343-5414

Lotus Realtime Engine $350.00 - $1000.00
Kit $25,000.00.
Compatibility: IBM/DOS compatibles.

Covers: securities. Lotus 1-2-3 Release 3 is an ideal analysis, display, and modeling environment for securities traders and analysts. Lotus Realtime enables you to perform realtime analytics on data from any digital data source, directly within Lotus 1-2-3 Release 3.

Market Analyzer

N-Squared Computing
5318 Forest Ridge Road
Silverton, OR 97381

PH: (503) 873-4420
(214) 680-1445
FAX: (214) 680-1435

SOFTWARE
Cost: $395.00.
Compatibility: IBM/DOS.

Sophisticated data manipulation and charting. This program will let you manipulate any type of data, create spreads, chart interest rates, overlay any 2 data items and much, much, more. It is an excellent program for general market breadth indicators and mutual funds. Complete database management and downloading of data from Warner Computer Systems and/or Track Data is included. Also is a database of market information from Barron's Market Laboratory pages.

Market Analyzer 2.0

Dow Jones & Co. Inc
P.O. Box 300
Princeton, NJ 08543-0300

PH: (609) 520-4641
(609) 520-4000
FAX: (609) 520-4660

SOFTWARE
Cost: IBM/DOS $349.00 Macintosh $299.00
Compatibility: IBM/DOS, Macintosh

Covers: stocks, mutual funds, bonds (corporate, government, and foreign), options and stock indexes. Helps you spot issues that are driving the market and identify underlying market trends. With the program's charting power, you can create technical analysis charts to help you make informed, confident trading decisions. It automatically collects current day prices, and daily, weekly, and monthly price histories. You get up to 15 years of historical price and volume data on more than 120,000 issues.

Market Analyzer Plus

Dow Jones & Co. Inc
P.O. Box 300
Princeton, NJ 08543-0300

PH: (609) 520-4641
(609) 520-4000
FAX: (609) 520-4660

SOFTWARE
Compatibility: IBM/DOS $499.00

Covers: stocks, commodities, mutual funds, bonds (corporate, government, and foreign), options and treasuries. A complete investment program with sophisticated charting, flexible technical screening and detailed portfolio management. Builds on Market Analyzer 2.0 software and adds historical pricing data for commodities dating back to 1970, more power and more flexibility in data handling and storage.

Market Base

MP Inc.
P.O. Box 37
388 Hillside Avenue
Needham Heights, MA 02194

PH: (800) 735-0700
(617) 449-8460

SOFTWARE
Cost: Basic annual charge - $345.00 with quarterly updates; $695.00 with monthly updates; $2300. with weekly updates.

Covers: stocks. An advanced analysis and database system which finds stocks you believe offer the best investment opportunity. Provides data of unsurpassed accuracy directly from annual reports and the latest company SEC filings on about 4600 stocks. Over 100 data items for each company, interim and five year history of financial data, trend graphs showing latest 60 months and 52 week closing prices, institutional and closely held stock positions, SIC code for industry breakdowns, numerous financial ratios and more.

Market Center

Bonneville Market Information
19 West South Temple
Salt Lake City, UT 84101-1503

PH: (800) 255-7374
FAX: (801) 532-3202

QUOTE SERVICE
Cost: $297.00 for software, plus monthly subscriber fee of $227.00 for both stocks and commodities or $197.00 for one.

Covers: options, stocks, commodities. Features: real-time or delayed quotes on commodities, real-time quotes on stocks and options, follow up to 6,000 quotes with added memory, automatic option chaining, trend for last eight ticks, spread quotes, snap quotes, indices, two page formats to use, additional fields, up/down stop alerts, news, save news stories for later retrieval, print, portfolio management, ASCII transfer, modem interface for dial-up services. Real-time commodity stock and option quote system.

The Market Forecaster

Dynacomp, Inc.
The Dynacomp Office Building
178 Phillips Road
Webster, NY 14580

PH: (716) 265-4040

-SOFTWARE
Cost: $299.95
Compatibility: IBM/DOS

Predicts the magnitude and direction of stock market movements over the next two to four months. Updated version of Finnegan econometric model. Includes "what-if" capability.

Market Maker

Inmark Development Corporation
139 Fulton Street
Suite 810
New York, NY 10038

PH: (212) 406-2299

SOFTWARE
Cost: Contact Vendor
Compatibility: IBM/DOS

Charting package to create classical and customized technical studies for stocks, commodities and options. Includes the Inmark Strength Indicator which tracks the movement of money. Has communications package.

Market Manager Plus (version 2.0)

Dow Jones and Co., Inc.
P.O. Box 300
Princeton, NJ 08543-0300

PH: (609) 520-4641
(609) 520-4000
FAX: (609) 520-4660

SOFTWARE
Cost: $299.00 version 3.0 for IBM - $299.00
Professional version $499.00 for high level management.
Compatibility: Macintosh

Portfolio management software to track, buy, sell, short sell and buy to cover transactions, collect automatically from News/Retrieval prices for stocks, bonds, options, mutual funds, and treasury notes and bonds. It will also selectively update your portfolio, save collected security prices in SYLK format for further analysis in your spreadsheet, set up hypothetical portfolios. Market Manager Plus has a built in financial calendar, graphics, and capacity to enter up to 256 portfolios with 1800 holdings.

MarketMaster

Dancotec
2835 Sierra Rd.
San Jose, CA 951132

PH: (800) 344-2545
FAX: (408) 923-7061

SOFTWARE
Compatibility: IBM/DOS
Cost: MarketMaster with end-of-day analysis only (2 indicators) $399.00; MarketMaster with end-of-day analysis only (4 indicators) $499.00; MarketMaster with Intra-day analysis + end-of-day analysis (4 indicators) $699.00; File converter - $50.00.

Covers stocks and provides chart service. MarketMaster uses new algorithm technology. The spreadsheet employs a spreadsheet-like command menu. Only high, low, close, and possibly volume are required for input. Both end-of-day and intra-day analysis are supported. Data files are in dBase file format. Manual input is easy or data may be downloaded in METASTOCK or CSI format and converted to dBase format with our file converter. Also offer MarketMaster Hotline forecasts FREE (408) 733-9341 or (408) 746-0477.

Market Max

TriStar Market Data, Inc.
600 Montgomery Street
San Francisco, CA 94111

PH: (415) 627-2345

SOFTWARE
Compatibility: Macintosh

Covers: futures options, stocks, commodities. Market Max is a Macintosh-based dynamic trader workstation. It provides real-time quotes, analysis, fundamental and historical data on U.S. stocks, options, futures, futures options and listed corporate bonds on Canadian and London securities. Uses Telekurs Ticker IV.

Market Monitor

Bonneville Market Information
19 West South Temple
Salt Lake City, UT 84101-1503

PH: (800) 255-7374
FAX: (801) 532-3202

QUOTE SERVICE
Cost: Market Monitor $197.00 one time fee plus monthly subscriber fee of $197.00. Hardware provided.

Covers: commodities. Features: 46 pages of real-time tick-by-tick information, one page of financial and industrial averages, three news pages, two fully programmable pages, price alerts, high, low, net, last trade, volume, opening range, bid/ask, open interest,options - three or six months, seven months of futures prices, print feature, one page of opening calls. Real time commodity quote system offering U.S. and selected foreign exchanges and related options.

Market Quote

Market Quote, Inc.
P.O. Box 8585
Deerfield Beach, FL 33443

PH: (305) 782-9511

QUOTE SYSTEM
Cost: $10.00 software. Monthly charge - $29 00 for 180 contracts per day, $39.00 for 275 contracts per day. Includes futures quote service at close.
Compatibility:IBM compatibles

Covers: futures. Historical and daily data futures quote software. Downloads information to your PC daily. Information available after 5:15 PM. Gives open, high, low, close, volume and open interest.

Market Screen

Market Guide, Inc.
49 Glen Head Road
Glen Head, NY 11545

PH: (516) 759-1253

SOFTWARE
Cost: $7500.00 a year updated on a weekly basis via diskette. Compatibility: IBM compatible.

Covers: company profiles. The Market Guide Database contains vital financial and textual information on over 6800 US and foreign public companies traded on the New York and American Stock exchanges as well as the NASDAQ and OTC markets. The database covers a wide spectrum of companies spanning every industry and size.

Market Statistics Data Base

(MARSTAT)
CSI Data Retrieval Service
200 W. Palmetto Park Road
Boca Raton, FL 33432

PH: (800) 327-0175
(407) 392-8663
FAX: (407) 392-1379

SOFTWARE
Cost: 20 cents per stock or mutual fund per month, 29
cents per commodity or option contract per month.
Compatibility : IBM Apple

Covers: stocks, commodities,and mutual funds. Historical data base. Holds a multitude of financial data
which supports the specific interests of commodity and
stock traders. Includes Perpetual Contracts and Perpetual Indices which were developed to overcome price
discontinuities that occur when attempting to concat-
enate several futures contracts.

Market Watch

FNN Data Broadcasting Corp
1900 S. Norfolk Street
San Mateo, CA 94403

PH: (800) 367-4670

ONLINE
Cost: Hook-up charges - $99.00. Basic monthly charge
$30.00 for receiver leasing plus services you want (real
time quotes, commodities, etc.)
Stock & option: $180.00 real time, $90.00 delayed
Futures & comm: $150.00 CBOT - other futures ex-
changes are extra.

Covers: stocks, commodities, and options. Works off
existing TV cable giving a choice of real-time or 15
minute delayed quotes that are second to none in accuracy and reliability. Up to 25,000 stocks, options, futures & commodities from all the major exchanges.
Comments: 15% discount for annual subscription paid
in advance

Market Window

F.B.S. Systems
P.O. Drawer 248
Aledo, IL 61231

PH: (309) 582-5628

SOFTWARE
Cost: Contact Vendor
Compatibility: IBM/DOS

Features include automatic file update and chart generation, chart file and directory, price interrogation, 200M,
frame, trendlines, channels, percentage mode, moving
averages, volume open interest and cycle finder.

Market-By-Price

The Toronto Stock Exchange
The Exchange Tower, Z
1st Canadian Place
Toronto, Canada M5X1J2

PH: (800) 387-1010
(416) 941-0843
FAX: (416) 947-4727

Cost: Basic monthly charge from $750.00.

Covers: Canadian stocks. Real time transmission of the central orderbook of the TSE. Delivers all committed, tradeable limit orders at the market and up to four price levels away for all stocks traded on the TSE (Toronto Stock Exchange).

Master Chartist

Robert Slade, Inc.
750 N. Freedom Blvd., Suite 301-B
Provo, UT 84601

PH: (800) 433-4276 ext. 250
(801) 375-6847 ext. 250(UT)
FAX: (801) 375-6847

Cost: Hook-up charges $295.00
Basic monthly charge $295.00 per year
Compatibility: IBM/DOS and MacIntosh for additional cost

Covers: stocks, bonds (municipal, government, corporate, and foreign), mutual funds, commodities, and charts. A technical analysis service. Tracks stocks, commodities, options, cash & news.

MBS Analysis System

Financial Publishing Company
82 Brookline Avenue
Boston, MA 02215

PH: (617) 262-4040

SOFTWARE
Cost: Contact Vendor
Compatibility: IBM/DOS

Analyzes yields, prices and cash flows of agency mortgage-backed securities. Includes a database of all agency pools and is updated monthly. Available in three versions, GNMA-only, FNMA/FHLMC data and a complete version.

Media General Plus

Dialog Information Services, Inc.
3460 Hillview Avenue
Palo Alto, CA 94304

PH: (800) 334-2564
 (415) 858-3810
FAX: (415) 858-7069

ONLINE
Cost: Standard Service Plan: $45.00 for the first password
$25.00 for each additional password
$35.00 annual fee for each password
 Online charges: $1.40 per minute or $84.00 per hour
Compatibility: IBM/DOS, MacIntosh

Provides detailed financial and stock price information on approximately 5,100 public companies. Covers all New York Stock Exchange and American Stock Exchange companies, plus all NASDAQ National Market System companies and selected OTC companies. Information provided by Media General Financial Services, Inc., Richmond, VA. Updated weekly.

MetaStock Professional Software

Equis International
P.O. Box 26743
Salt Lake City, UT 84126

PH: (800) 882-3040
(801) 974-5115
FAX: (801) 974-5130

Cost: $349.00
Compatibility:IBM/DOS

Includes: chart service.Covers: stocks, commodities, mutual funds, market timing, and bonds, (municipal, government, corporate, foreign) .
This is strictly a software package that allows you to chart. Technical analysis charting program. It's easy to use, profitability tester generates buy/sell signals insuring greater success in trading.

MF Analysis

Spreadware
P.O. Box 4552
Palm Desert, CA 92261-4552

PH: (619) 347-2365

SOFTWARE
Cos: $14.95 for software
Compatibility: IBM/DOS compatible if requested, Macintosh

Covers: mutual funds. Analyze your mutual fund to determine the return on investment (ROI) and gain/loss you would experience if the position were to be liquidated. The MF Analysis model allows the user to keep a running analysis on a mutual fund investment, including tax basis cost, funds withdrawn, etc.

Money Center

Knight-Ridder
Dept. A One Exchange Plaza
55 Broadway
New York, NY 10008

PH: (800) 433-8430
(212) 269-1110

QUOTE SERVICE
Cost: Hookup charges $880.00, Basic monthly charge $475.00,includes AT&T, WGS PC & satellite dish. Immediate stock quote service at an additional cost of $50.00 on positions you trade, others are last trade prices. Chart service at an additional $150.00 a month. Futures quotes for $100.00 a month, news available for $200.00 a month.

Covers stocks, commodities, and bonds (municipal and corporate). PC based service gives real time quotes plus financial news on all the securities you buy, sell or hedge. Create your own dynamic yield or price charts and spreads, download to Lotus spreadsheets and much more.

Moneyline

USA Today
1000 Wilson Blvd.
Arlington, VA 22229

PH: (900) 555-5555
 (800) USA-0001

Cost: $.95 per minute 24 Hour service

Covers: stocks. Use your touch tone phone to access stock quotes, CD rates, interest calculations, updates on your personal investments and used car prics. Quotes are delayed 15 minutes during trading hours.

Moody's Bond Information Database Service (BIDS)

Moody's Investor Service
99 Church Street
New York, NY 10007

PH: (800) 342-5647 ext 0435
(212) 553-0435
FAX: (212) 553-4700

Cost: $5000.00/year with weekly updates
$1895.00/year with monthly updates
$ 995.00/year with quarterly updates
Compatibility : IBM/DOS

Covers: corporate bonds. Accurate and authoritative information on over 10,000 US corporate bond issues updated monthly. Includes bond ratings, coupon rates, maturity dates and more. Gives you immediate access to a world of comprehensive up-to-date information in a way that lets you sort, screen, and analyze debt issues by CUSIP, company name, issue name, Moody's ratings, coupon rate, maturity, interest dates or bond issue features. A vital source for any financial professional who need immediate access to information about the corporate bond market.

M-Search

Emerging Market Technologies, Inc.
1230 Johnson Ferry Road
Suite F-1
Marietta, GA 30068

PH: (404) 973-2300
FAX: (404) 973-3003

SOFTWARE
Cost: $3,000.00 annually
Compatibility: IBM/DOS

Search through hundreds of money managers located all over the U.S.

Mutual Fund Edge

Emerging Market Technologies, Inc.
1230 Johnson Ferry Road
Suite F-1
Marietta, GA 30068

PH: (404) 973-2300
FAX: (404) 973-3003

SOFTWARE
Cost: $265.00
Compatibility: IBM/DOS

Add on product to Telescan Analyzer/Edge from Emerging Market Technologies. Allows searches on mutual funds.

"National Quotation Service"

National Quotation Service
National Quotation Bureau, Inc.
The Harborside Financial Center
600 Plaza Three
Jersey City, NJ 07311

PH: (201) 435-9000
(201) 435-0713
FAX: (201) 435-9000

NOT AVAILABLE ONLINE. NO SOFTWARE
AVAILABLE
PRINTED DAILY HARDCOPY
Cost: $744 annually

The most complete quotation service of non-exchange traded stocks and bonds available. For daily information and pricing, bonds are printed on "yellow sheets" and stocks are printed on "pink sheets." Quotation service contains indicated Bid, Ask, Market Maker with phone numbers, Symbol, and Security Description. Contains over 10,000 stocks and 3,000 bonds.

NewsNet

945 Haverford Road
Bryn Mawr, PA 19010

PH: (800) 345-1301
(215) 527-8030
FAX: (215) 527-0338

ONLINE
Cost: Basic monthly charge $15.00, 20 minute delayed stock quote service available for $108.00 an hour, real-time on Dow Jones Industrial average.

Covers: stocks, commodities, and bonds(municipal, corporate and government). The premier current awareness database of business information and intelligence including over 430 business newsletters, 11 worldwide news wires delivered in real-time, Dun & Bradstreet business reports, TRW business profiles, stock and commodity quotes, Investext company and industry reviews.

Nightly Computer Hotline

Wall Street On-Line Publishing
P.O. Box 6
Riverdale, NY 10471-0006

PH: (212) 884-5408

ONLINE
Cost: $125.00 annual fee
Compatibility: any PC or modem

Covers: stocks, market timing, options and futures and commodities. Market predictions and recommendations. Updated daily - Sunday through Thursday.

Nite-Line (CompuTrac)

Automated Data Collection
National Computer Network Corporation
1929 North Harlem avenue
Chicago, IL 60635

PH: (312) 622-6666

Cost: initiation fee (one time) $30.00
Standard Hrly. Rates -
Non-Prime-Time   Prime-Time 8AM - 6PM
                   All other times/days
Central Mon-Fri
Local Access

	Non-Prime-Time	Prime-Time
300 Baud-	$13.00 per hour	$26.00 per hour
1200 Baud-	$19.00 per hour	$34.00 per hour
2400 Baud-	$22.00 per hour	$37.00 per hour

More detailed pricing is available from the vendor.
Compatible with any basic desktop computer.

Covers: stocks, commodities/futures, mutual funds, and bonds. Nite-Line gives you access to the complete daily closing market information as well as up to 12 years of financial historical data from all U.S. and some Canadian exchanges on commodity future, futures options, stocks, indexes, and stock options. With data including high, low, close, open, interest, volume, bid, ask, settle, and more, you will have the information you need to accurately evaluate stock positions and portfolios, and make the most informed and timely trading decisions possible.

Option Pricing Model

Spreadware
P.O. Box 4552
Palm Desert, CA 92261-4552

PH: (619) 347-2365

SOFTWARE
Cost: $21.95 for software.
Compatibility: IBM/DOS compatible if requested
Macintosh

Covers: options. Spreadware Option Pricing Model us designed to estimate a call options theoretical price based on the price has been determined, up to five comparative analyses of the option can be simultaneously conducted to determine the effects of a change in any of the variables.

Options - 80 Advanced Stock Option Analyzer

Patrick N. Everett Ph.D.
P.O. Box 471
Concord, MA 01742

PH: (508) 369-1589

Cost: $170.00 for program (30 day money back guarantee)
Compatibility:IBM/DOS, Apple, Macintosh

Covers: stocks with charts. Program analyzes calls, puts, and spreads, does Black-Scholes modeling, and calculates market implied volatility. It plots annualized return on investment against expiration price of underlying stock, guiding the user to optimum investment. Unique algorithms account for future payments, as well as buying and selling costs and time value money.

Option Values and Arbitrage Software

Programmed Press
599 Arnold Road
W. Hempstead, NY 11552

PH: (516) 599-6527

SOFTWARE
Cost: $120.00
Compatibility: IBM/DOS, MacIntosh, TRS, Commodore

Options and futures valuation package. Evaluate price, risk, arbitrage and return on options and futures. Includes Black-Scholes, BOOKBINDER, Empirical P Models and Arbitrage.

Option Vue IV

Option Vue Systems International, Inc.
175 E. Hawthorne Parkway, Suite 180
Vernon Hills, Illinois 60061

PH: (800)733-6610
(708) 816-6610

Cost: Hook-up charges $895.00; futures option - $500.00/month; real-time - $500.00/month. Background data base updated daily, shipped monthly -$240.00 per year.
Compatibility : IBM/DOS

Covers: options. Online options analysis program. Fully equips you to trade every type of option and perform every type of options analysis ever conceived. Use it to test option strategies, find money making opportunities and avoid costly mistakes.

PC Software

TLM, Inc.
420 Westchester Avenue
Pt. Chester, NY 10573

PH: (800) 451-1392

SOFTWARE
Compatibility: IBM compatibles.
Cost: $89.00 +$5.00 postage and handling.
No online set up or additional fees.

Investments covered include options and index futures. TLM's proprietary trading model uses the high, low, and close of the index daily and generates 2-4 trading signals per month for options and 2 signals per month for futures trading. The simple manual explains how to make your trade and manage it when stops and limits.

Personal Hotline

Trendsetter Software
P.O. Box 6481
Santa Ana, CA 92706

PH: (800) 825-1852
(714) 547-5005
FAX: (714) 547-5063

SOFTWARE
Cost: $495.00 includes software, data files, documentation, and free technical support.
Macintosh product

Covers: stocks, futures, and options, and provides charts. Market timing and technical analysis software - stocks, futures, indexes, and spreads, one-program, one low price. Includes trading recommendations, superior graphics and speed, proven technical studies: oscillators, moving averages, Gann angles, stochastics, RSI, and more.

Personal Portfolio Manager

Prodata, Inc.
12101 Menaul Boulevard Northeast
Albuquerque, NM 87112

PH: (505) 294-1530

SOFTWARE
Cost: $49.95
Compatibility: IBM/DOS

Maintain multiple portfolios of stocks, bonds, options and money market funds. Performance reports include portfolio, individual stock, dividend and versus targets.

Personal Stock Technician

RazorLogic Systems
P.O. Box 335
Morgan Hill, CA 95038

Covers: stocks, mutual funds. Technical analysis and stock market tracking system. Generates buy and sell signals based on established criteria.

PH: (408) 778-0889

Cost: $99.50
Compatibility: IBM/DOS

Phase 3

Phase 3 Systems, Inc
504 Totten Pond Road
Waltham, MA 02154

PH: (617) 466-9800

Cost: Call salesperson for quote on pricing, service bureau vs. on-premises system. This is a very large system with many sub-systems.

Tandem Non-stop Systems. Securities processing, stocks, and bonds (municipal, corporate, and government), mortgage backs, treasuries, zeroes. Phase 3 is a real-time, integrated securities processing system for the brokerage and banking community. It provides all regulatory back office support systems for sales, order processing, and trading. For some, this is a complete on-premises system that customers license. For others, it is a service bureau relationship where costs vary according to volume.

PIMS Portfolio Information Management System

Atlantic Portfolio Analytics and Management, Inc.
201 E. Pine Street, Suite 600
Orlando, FL 32801

PH: (407) 843-7110 ext 333
FAX: (407) 843-7399

SOFTWARE
Cost: single user $25,000 multi-users $99,500
Compatibility: IBM/DOS

Covers: asset-backed securities, stocks, futures/commodities, municipal and government bonds. A multi-user software system that documents and controls transactions and positions in actively managed portfolios of assets, liabilities, and hedges. PIMS online queries will completely research all past activities and positions to the trade ticket-level in seconds. It facilitates everything from basic buy/sell transactions and fails, to pool substitutions and optimal good millions delivery allocations.

"Pink Sheets"

National Quotation Service
National Quotation Bureau, Inc.
The Harborside Financial Center
600 Plaza Three
Jersey City, NJ 07311

PH: (201) 435-9000
(201) 435-0713
FAX: (201) 435-9000

NOT AVAILABLE ONLINE. NO SOFTWARE
AVAILABLE
PRINTED DAILY HARDCOPY
Cost: $744 annually

The most complete quotation service of non-exchange traded stocks and bonds available. For daily information and pricing, bonds are printed on "yellow sheets" and stocks are printed on "pink sheets." Quotation service contains indicated Bid, Ask, Market Maker with phone numbers, Symbol, and Security Description. Contains over 10,000 stocks and 3,000 bonds.

Pocket Quote Pro

Telemet America, Inc.
Broadcasting House
325 First Street
Alexandria, VA 22314

PH: (800) 368-2078
(703) 548-2042

Covers: stocks, commodities, mutual funds ($10.00 extra), options and indices are real-time. At the touch of a button you get unlimited quotes on stocks, options, futures, & news headlines in a pocket size format

Cost: Hook-up charges	$395.00
For hand held unit	$354.00 per year
Basic monthly charge	$345.00 per year
Online charges per minute	n/a
NY & AM	$27.50 additional for real time quotes
NASDAQ	$16.00 additional for real time quotes

Includes: delayed stock quote service on stock & commodities.
Compatibility : IBM/DOS , Macintosh, others.

Portfolio Accounting Management System (PAMS)

Information Resource Management, Inc.
1800 East Denison Road
Suite 100
Naperville, IL 60565

PH: (312) 369-5757

SOFTWARE
Cost: $5,000.00
Compatibility: IBM/DOS, Unix, Xenix

Realtime information and reporting on security portfolios. Has many retrieval displays and parameter driven reporting. Provides reports and tax schedules.

Portfolio Analyzer

Hamilton Software, Inc.
6432 East Mineral Place
Englewood, CO 80112

PH: (303) 795-5572
(303) 770-9607

SOFTWARE
Cost: $79.00
Compatibility: IBM/DOS

Provides maintenance and analysis of investment portfolios containing stocks, bonds, options, savings accounts, annuities, collectibles and others. Tracks performance of investments individually and in groups. Provides year-to-date tax liability and schedules B and D.

Portfolio Management

Spreadware
P.O. Box 4552
Palm Desert, CA 92261-4552

PH: (619) 347-2365

SOFTWARE
Cost: $24.95 for software.
Compatibility: IBM/DOS compatible if requested, Macintosh

Covers stocks, options and bonds. Spreadware Portfolio Management is designed to manage and analyze a personal portfolio. The program will record routine investment transactions, as well as analyze the position of the portfolio. Individual investments can be analyzed to determine the break-even price and required role of return price, taking transaction fees, taxes, and other expenses into account.

Portfolio Management System

SunGard Financial Systems, Inc.
1 Corporate Drive, Andover Corporate Center
Andover, MA 01810

PH: (508) 691-6000

SOFTWARE
Cost: $10,000.00 - $200,000.00
Compatibility: IBM/DOS

Online investment securities accounting package. Automates accounting functions and provides reporting for investment instruments like stocks, U.S. Treasury, municipal securities, variable rate, callable, mortgage backed securities, zero coupon bonds, repurchase agreements and others.

Portfolio Tracking System

SCIX Corporation
2010 Lacomic Street
Williamsport, PA 17701

PH: (717) 323-3276

SOFTWARE
Cost: $765.00
Compatibility: IBM/DOS

Portfolio tracking system that can handle stocks, bonds, options, mutual funds and futures. Can select quotes from seven data vendors. Also supports money market funds, T-bills and commercial paper investments.

PORTIAsa Portfolio Reporting, Trading, and Investment Analysis (1-3 users)

Technical Data Software
11 Farnsworth Street
Boston, MA 02210

PH: (617) 345-2700
FAX: (617) 951-2520

Cost: Base system $7500 includes the following: securities transactions, reporting and other, also optional features range from $1000 to $5000.

Covers: futures, stocks and options, all types of bonds, and agencies. PORTIAsa runs a local area network of personal computers, which allows multiple users to simultaneously enter, access, and analyze up-to-the-second investment information. Portfolio managers and other investment professionals can perform ad hoc reporting, compute statistics, calculate straight line or scientific amortization/accretions, and analyze portfolios quickly, easily, and independently.

Prodigy

Prodigy Services Company
445 Hamilton Avenue
White Plains, NY 10601

PH: (914) 993-8000
 (800) 776-3460

ONLINE
Cost: Hook-up charges $49.95
Basic monthly charge $12.95
Stock quote service (delayed 15 minutes) at no additional cost.
Interactive stock data available.

Covers: stocks, mutual funds, chart service, listed bonds, gold, currencies, Dow Jones News Service. A general on-line information service which offers general news relating to national and world events, financial issues, sports, weather, etc. Stock quotes, investment recommendations pulled from newsletters, brokerage reports and other experts, mutual fund closing prices and bond closing prices are all included in basic service. Upgrades available for an additional fee.

The Professional Portfolio

Advent Software, Inc.
512 Second Street
San Francisco, CA 94107

PH: (415) 543-7696
 (212) 398-1188
FAX: (415) 543-5070

Cost: approximately $7,700.00.
Compatibility: IBM/DOS

A complete software package that provides portfolio tracking and in-depth analysis for money managers and large portfolios.

Professional Trader's Daily

CISCO
327 S. LaSalle Street, Suite 1133
Chicago, IL 60604

PH: (312) 922-3661
(800) 666-1223

ONLINE
Cost: $75.00 initial set up + monthly charge - $200.00
Fax available for additional $150.00. per minute $0.125

Covers: bonds, S&P, Yen, gold, crude oil, soybean futures. Designed for experienced traders, it blends the interactive thought processes seasoned traders with the quantitative powers of a computer. For the 1st time, a computer has been taught how to understand markets, interpret them and report information to you in terms that you as a trader can understand and use. The result is a powerful, yet objective analysis report, available each day on the major futures markets. Some of the information provided is: current condition of the market (trending or bracketing), recommended strategy to fit current market conditions, tomorrow's outlook, high-probability break-out alerts and more.

Profit Taker

Emerging Market Technologies, Inc.
1230 Johnson Ferry Road
Suite F-1
Marietta, GA 30068

PH: (404) 973-2300
FAX: (404) 973-3003

SOFTWARE
Cost: Contact Vendor
Compatibility: IBM/DOS

Technical and fundamental analysis of commodities.

Program Writer II

Technicom, Inc.
736 NE 20th Avenue
Ft. Lauderdale, FL 33304

PH: (305) 523-5394
FAX: (305) 523-3245

SOFTWARE
Cost: $995.00 for package.
Compatibility : IBM

Covers: commodities and futures. Provides you with a complete and powerful shell that contains all the features of historical testing, automatic optimization, graphics, data management, and automatic daily trading recommendations.

PROMT

Thomson Financial Network
11 Farnsworth Street
Boston, MA 02210

PH: (617) 345-2000
(800) 662-7878
FAX: (617) 330-1986

ONLINE
Cost: Online charges per hour ; $105.00Compatibility
with any PC with a modem or call (800) 662-7878.

Provides abstracts, excerpts, and in some cases, full text
articles from the world's major newspapers and business publications as well as a vast pool of local and
regional sources, industry newsletter, key trade journals, and other specialist publications. PROMPT primarily covers product and company issues. There are
currently 400,000 records in the database and approximately 4500 records are added each week.

Quant IX Portfolio Evaluator Version 3.16

Quant IX Software
5900 N. Port Washington Road
Suite 142A
Milwaukee, WI 53217

PH: (800) 247-6354
(414) 961-1991

SOFTWARE
Cost: $89.00
Compatibility: IBM/DOS 3.1 or higher

Consists of a portfolio manager and/or security analyzer. Automatic pricing through either Compuserve or
Warner. Security analysis includes ratio analysis, security valuation models, diversification analysis and
"what-if" testing. Has built-in communications program. Online bulletin board is available.

Quickplot/Quick Study

CSI Data Retrieval Service
200 W. Palmetto Park Road
Boca Raton, FL 33432

PH: (800) 327-0175
(407) 392-8663
FAX: (407) 392-1379

SOFTWARE
Cost: $195.00 hookup plus basic monthly charge from
$33.00 (depends on quantity collected daily. Stock
quote service @ close. $195 includes Quicktrieve and
QuickManager (must have these to work) .
Compatibility : IBM Apple

Covers: stocks, futures. Used for graphically analyzing
and manipulating data bank information. Lets you choose
among calculations for moving averages, RSI, CCI,
Detrend, On-Balance Volume, MACD, Stochastics,
and others. Includes Quicktreive/QuickManager.

Quicktrieve/Quick Manager

CSI Data Retrieval Service
200 W. Palmetto Park Road
Boca Raton, FL 33432

PH: (800) 327-0175
(407) 392-8663
FAX: (407) 392-1379

SOFTWARE
Cost: $39.00 hookup and basic monthly charge from $33.00 (depends on quantity collected daily)
Compatibility : IBM Apple

Covers: stocks and mutual funds. The software that interacts with the CSI data retrieval service and captures historical data as well as daily data that is tailored to each individual portfolio. This data includes the open, high, low, and closing prices as well as volume and open interest. Also maintains historical files and provides the user the flexibility to move, copy, print, create, delete, condense and edit one's own private data bank as well as convert these files to any popular format including ASCII, CompuTrac and MetaStock.

Quotdial

Quotron Systems, Inc.
5454 Beethoven Street
Los Angeles, CA 90066

PH: (213) 827-4600
(800) 366-6729
FAX: (800) 366-6702

Cost: Hook-up charges $50.00 registration fee, monthly charge $10.00 minimum, online charge $10.00 per hour, stock quote service at no additional cost for delayed or after market service, and at an additional charge of $30.00 per hour plus exchange fees for immediate. Provides chart services at an additional cost of $5 per month. Dow Jones News Retrieval available for $175.00 a month.
Compatibility with any PC or video terminal and modem.

Covers stocks, bonds, mutual funds, options, commodities, and charts. A real-time and after hours dial-up financial information service available to PC and video display users. Offers access to the industry's most complete and reliable source of price and market data on over 160,000 securities. Tracks leading market indicators and statistics, most actively traded issues, dividends and earnings information, as well as earnings forecasts. It monitors trading activity for up to 40 financial instruments on a last sale and net charge basis, and reviews price movement of selected stocks, commodities, and market indexes with intra-day graphs.

The Quote Exporter

Fossware
1000 Campbell Road
Suite 208—626
Houston, TX 77055

PH: (713) 467-3195

Cost: $99.00 (available in 30 day free trial basis)
Compatibility: IBM Compatible

Covers: options, stocks, and commodities. For use with CompuTrac. The Quote Exporter is a companion program to The Quote Monitor. It provides a bridge between quote retrieval and analysis. It transfers data saved by TQM (either intra-day or closing bar data) to any of a number of technical analysis programs.

Quote Line

Technical Tools
334 State Street, Suite 201
Los Altos, CA 94022

PH: (415) 948-6124

SOFTWARE
Cost: $50.00 hook-up charge. Online charges per minute
are at long-distance call rate, calls are usually under 1
minute. Monthly Charges are

180 contracts per day	$35.00/month
275 contracts per day	$45.00/month
00 contracts per day	$55.00/month

A dial-up electronic data service which provides daily
end-of-day price information for futures contracts traded
on US and Canadian exchanges. Data is available by
4:00 PM Pacific time and operational 23 hours a day.

Quote Master

Strategic Planning Systems, Inc.
21021 Soledad Canyon Road, Suite 504
Santa Clarita, CA 91351

PH: (800) 488-5898
(805) 254-5897

Cost: Quote Master $395.00; Quote Master Professional
$495.00 - Telemet receiver-$325.00; FNN receiver-
$350.00; History data $59.95.
Macintosh compatible

Covers: stocks, commodities, mutual funds, options,
futures, indexes, and provides chart service.FNN signal
and Telemet America broadcast market information
directly as it happens via satellite and FM, the receiver
picks up the information and with Quote Master passes
the information directly to your computer.

The Quote Monitor

Fossware
1000 Campbell Road, Suite 208-626
Houston, TX 77055

PH: (713) 467-3195

Cost: $295.00 (available on a 30 day free trial basis)
Compatibility: IBM Compatibles

Covers: options, stocks, and commodities/futures. For
use with CompuTrac. The Quote Monitor is designed to
monitor current day activity in the financial markets. It
provides quotation retrieval and graphics. It generates
both text and graphic displays from quotes received
over an FM radio or satellite broadcast. TQM allows
you to follow intra-day activity on issues of specific
interest as well as the broader market.

Quotrek

Financial News Network - Data Broadcasting Corp.
1900 S. Norfolk
San Mateo, CA 94403

PH: (800) 367-4670

Cost: $495.00 for unit or free if you trade in existing quote device from a competitor, $351.00 basic monthly charge for all markets, stock quote service (immediate) at no additional cost, interactive stock data.

Covers: stocks, commodities, mutual funds, market timing, municipal, corporate, government, and foreign bonds, with news via Dow Jones News Alert. Hand held portable unit giving real-time quotes from all major US futures, options, and equities exchanges plus 20 major market indices.

Radio Exchange

Telemet America
325 First Street
Alexandria, VA 22314

PH: (800) 368-2078
(703) 548-2042

Cost: Hook-up charges $349.00 for the box, basic monthly charge of $33.25, includes stock quote service delayed at no additional cost, immediate at: $330/yearly (NYSE & AMEX) ; $192/yearly NASDAQ; $144/yearly options; $ 960/CBT.
Compatibility :IBM/DOS.

Covers: stocks, commodities, mutual funds, market timing, chart service. Links your PC to all major securities exchanges and McGraw Hill Headlines news. Hailed by leading computer magazines and investor services as the "best value" in quotes today.

The Retriever Plus

NewTek Industries
P.O. Box 46116
Los Angeles, CA 90046

PH: (213) 874-6669

SOFTWARE
Cost: $79.95
Compatibility: IBM PC/XT/AT and compatibles

"A modem program automated to go online with Track Data, a vendor of historical market data. The automation removes the need to repeatedly enter ID, passwords, account information and the details of a download order while the user is online and is prone to make errors. It maintains a portfolio file with file names and symbols. Stocks, commodities on all the major exchanges are available, as well as over 1,300 mutual funds and the most commonly used indices."

Reuters

Dialog Information Services, Inc.
3460 Hillview Avenue
Palo Alto, CA 94304

PH: (800) 334-2564
(415) 858-3810
FAX: (415) 858-7069

ONLINE
Cost: Standard Service Plan: $45.00 for the first password
$25.00 for each additional password
$35.00 annual fee for each password
Online charges: $1.60 per minute or $96.00 per hour
Compatibility: IBM/DOS, MacIntosh

Complete text of news releases from the Reuter Business Report and the Reuter Library Service newswires. Updated continuously. Provided by Reuters U.S., Inc., New York, NY.

Right Time

T.B.S.P. Inc.,
(The Better Software People)
610 Newport Center Drive,
Suite 1120
Newport Beach, CA 92660

PH: (714) 721-8603
(800) 755-TBSP
FAX: (714) 721-8635

SOFTWARE
Cost: $599.00 each for Stock program, Stock Program/ Long Term, Futures Program, Index Program, Index Program/Long Term, Mutual Fund Program; $999.00 each for Day Trading Programs on Stock, Futures, and Indexes.
In combinations of 2/$999.00, 3/$1399.00, 4/$1699.00, 5/$1999.00, 6/$2399.00. Compatibility: IBM, Macintosh, & Apple compatibles.

Covers: include stocks, mutual funds, indexes, futures. A computerized trading system which was developed by an expert portfolio manager for his own personal use. The only software that analyzes volume/price, support/ demand, and global market trends and all at the same time. You can retrieve and update signals for your stocks, commodities, indices, or funds from several different vendors in less than 5 minutes a day. The software that generates profitable buy/sell signals by combining artificial intelligence with technical analysis.

SBBI/PC

Ibbotson Associates, Inc.
8 S. Michigan Avenue, 7th Floor
Chicago, IL 60603

PH: (312) 263-3435
FAX: (312) 263-1398

SOFTWARE
Cost: $435.00, $985.00 with quarterly updates, $1485.00
with monthly updates. Compatibility: IBM compatibles

Includes: stocks and bonds (corporate and government).
Specially designed software to quickly and easily compute summary statistics, prepare graphs and perform statistical analysis over any sub-period. Available in Lotus format.

SDC Risk, SDC Risk/OTC, SDC Sentry, SDC Gards

Systems Development Corporation
141 West Jackson Blvd., Suite 1240 A
Chicago, IL 60604

PH: (312) 408-1111
FAX: (312) 408-1818

Cost: Call for quotes on system
Compatibility: your hardware or need, they will install
their hardware.

Covers: options, stocks, commodities/futures. SDC's systems the full spectrum of hedging/options support as well as attendant risk management functions across equities, futures, listed options,cash, and OTC instruments, whether fixed income or foreign exchange. COMMENTS: in process of developing stand alone system of RISK for individual investor by Summer 1991.

SDS2 Money Service

Reuters Information Services
15303 Dallas Parkway, Suite 510, LB53
Dallas, TX 75248

PH: (800) 441-2645
(214) 661-2645
FAX: (214) 991-3267

Cost: Basic monthly charge $550.00 + exchange fees,
and up. Example: for $1000.00 you get domestic equities, fixed income news.Online charges per minute
vary.

Covers: stocks, commodities, bonds (municipal, corporate, government and foreign) , and options. A comprehensive investment service. Provides quotes, complete news coverage, technical charting, color graphics with advanced analytics, and market reports. COMMENTS: several other services available including hardware.

SEC Online

Thomson Financial Network
11 Farnsworth Street
Boston, MA 02210

PH: (617) 345-2000
(800) 662-7878
FAX: (617) 330-1988

ONLINE
Cost: Online charges per hour $120.00
Compatible with any PC with a modem or call (800) 662-7878.

Provides the full text documents filed with the SEC by companies traded on the New York and American Stock Exchanges, including annual reports, 10-K's, 10-Q's, and proxy statements.

Securities Accounting

Synon Corporation
5 The Mountain Road
Framingham, MA 01701

PH: (508) 620-8800

SOFTWARE
Cost: Contact Vendor
Compatibility: IBM/DOS, NCR Tower, Digital MicroVax

Provides functions to manage and control an institution's investment portfolio. Computes and posts all accounting transactions. Debt and equity instruments are supported. Interfaces to Lotus 1-2-3 and in-house systems.

Signal

FNN Data Broadcasting Corp.
1900 S. Norfolk Street
San Mateo, CA 94403

PH: (800) 367-4670
FAX: (415) 574-4621

Cost: hardware charges, $595.00 for receiver or $395.00 w/annual pre-paid subscription, hook-up charges $100.00 but waived with pre-paid annual fee, basic monthly charge $160.00 + exchange fees, online charges per minute n/a. Immediate stock quote service at no additional cost.

Covers: stocks, commodities, mutual funds, and news (Dow Jones $20.00 per month extra). Online Real-time data for over 40,000 stocks, commodities, options, indexes, mutual funds, and money-market funds. Gives instant compatibility with over 60 analytical software packages to run real-time analyses, and charts.

SmartBox III

Research Department, Inc.
200 W. Adams
Chicago, IL 60606

PH: (800) 231-9723
 (312) 407-5703

Cost: Hook-up charges $95.00
 Basic monthly charge $99.00 per month
Stock quote service available (delayed 10 minutes) for
commodities
Stock quote service available (delayed 15 minutes) for
stocks

Includes: research, quote and news. Covers: stocks, commodities, mutual funds, government bonds, research, domestic and international news. Expert analysis on financial and agricultural markets, both fundamental and technical. Up to 35 pages available everyday. In addition it provides 10 pages of news highlights daily as well as quotes.

Spectrum Gateway

CDA Investment Technologies, Inc.
1355 Piccard Drive
Rockville, MD 20850

PH: (301) 975-9600
FAX: (301) 590-1350

Cost: basic monthly charge $300.00 plus Quotron vendor fee or whatever database service you choose.

Covers: stocks and convertibles. Easy access to find the exact information you need on 7500 listed and unlisted common stocks and convertible issues held in the portfolios of over 2300 institutions. Coverage includes 13(F) filers, U.S. & European investment companies, 5% owners, private portfolio maintenance, and a system to retrieve your own historical trades and inquiries.

Spectrum Ownership Profile

1355 Piccard Drive
Rockville, MD 20850

PH: (301) 975-9600
FAX: (301-590-1350

Costs: online charges -$53.00 per hour, monthly charge $1800.00. Compatibility with any active terminal.

Covers: stocks. A comprehensive review of a company's ownership based on: 13F Institutional Common Stock Holdings, U.S. Institutional Convertible Holdings, U.S. Investment Company Holdings, Europlan Investment Company Holdings, 13D & 13G five percent Beneficial Ownership, 14D-1 Tender OFfers, Forms 3&4 Insider Ownership. All of this data is updated daily.

Splot!

Data Base Associates
P.O. Box 1838
Honolulu, HI 96805

PH: (808) 926-5854
FAX: (808) 926-5851

SOFTWARE
Cost: $125.00
Compatibility: IBM/DOS

Stock and portfolio plotting program for independent investors. Imports data from Dow Jones News Retrieval, CompuServe, Lotus Signal, X-press Executive, and X-press X-change. Printing compatibility for all Hewlett-Packard or Epson compatible printers. Can edit imported data or create stock data files without outside data sources.

Spreadware Option Pricing Model

Spreadware
P.O. Box 4574
Hayward, CA 94540

PH: (415) 794-4388

SOFTWARE
Cost: $18.95
Compatibility: MacIntosh

Estimates a call option's theoretical price based on Black-Scholes Option Pricing Model. Supports 5 comparative analyses of the option.

Spreadware Portfolio Management

Spreadware
P.O. Box 4574
Hayward, CA 94540

PH: (415) 794-4388

SOFTWARE
Cost: $24.95
Compatibility: MacIntosh

Package manages security transactions for a portfolio. Individual securities can be analyzed to determine the break-even price and required rate of return price, taking transaction fees, taxes and other expenses into account.

STARS Securities Trading Accounting and Reporting System

Equitable Capital Management Corporation
305 Madison Avenue
New York, NY 10165

PH: (212) 972-1860

Very large system - substantial application package - license fee is in the mid to upper six figures. Can work with client's existing hardware or software, or make a recommendation on hardware.STARS supports every major type of investment vehicle in today's marketplace.STARS is a comprehensive and integrated trading, portfolio management and investment accounting system which is suitable for any large money manager, insurance company or pension organization.

Stock and Futures Analyzer/Optimizer

N-Squared Computing
5318 Forest Ridge Road
Silverton, OR 97381

PH: (503) 873-4420
(214) 680-1445
FAX: (214) 680-1435

SOFTWARE
Cost: $595.00
Compatibility: IBM/DOS

A complete technical analysis graphics package designed for use by the advanced technician. Allows you to create, optimize, back-test, and visually verify any indicator that you can create using simple easy to follow prompts from N-Squared's powerful Create Indicator module.

Stock Charting

Diamond Head Software
35 E. Pierson Street
Phoenix, AZ 85012

PH: (808) 735-1891

SOFTWARE
Cost: $70.00
Compatibility: IBM/DOS

Covers: stocks. A technical analysis package that provides a price-bar and volume-bar chart. Can access the Warner Computer System data base and automatically retrieve the data. Manual data entry also supported.

Stock Data Corp

Stock Data Corp
905 Bywater Road
Annapolis, MD 21401

PH: (301) 280-5533

SOFTWARE
Cost: basic monthly charge of $45.00 + 10.00 for modem Includes stock quote service at close at no additional cost.
Compatibility : IBM

Covers: stocks. Download the entire 3 US markets (9000) issues in 5 minutes by modem or mailed weekly. Gives high, low, close and volume and will also create data for your favorite spreadsheets or charting programs, and design performance service to your specifications.

Stock/Expert

Hawkeye Grafix
Box 1400
Oldsmar, FL 34677

PH: (813) 855-8687

SOFTWARE
Cost: $988.00
 $ 50.00 - 30 day demo
Compatibility: IBM/DOS

Covers: stocks. Recommends what stocks to purchase and when based on 'expert' rules in the package. Provides portfolio support to group multiple accounts. Fetches stock closing data daily with online hookup using a modem.

The Stock Manager

Omni Software Systems, Inc.
146 North Broad Street
Griffith, IN 46319

PH: (219) 924-3522

SOFTWARE
Cost: $250.00
Compatibility: IBM/DOS

Covers: stocks. Portfolio management package that evaluates investment information. Offers accounting and controls for the securities portfolio. Prepares information for year end tax return.

Stock Market Software

Programmed Press
599 Arnold Road
W. Hempstead, NY 11552

PH: (516) 599-6527

SOFTWARE
Cost: $120.00
Compatibility: IBM/DOS, MacIntosh, TRS

Covers: stocks. Evaluates price, risk and return on investment in common stock.

Stock Master

Generic Computer Products, Inc.
P.O. Box 790, Dept. DD-17
Marquette, MI 49855

PH: (906) 249-9801

SOFTWARE
Cost: $49.95
Compatibility:

Covers: stocks, mutual funds. Stock market investment aid for the casual investor. Transactions are saved for later display of stock or mutual fund status.

StockMate

StockMate Financial Systems, Inc.
17981 Skypark Circle, Suite M
Irvine, CA 92714

PH: (714) 553-8814
Costs: Typical StockMate pricing per terminal, excluding exchange fees, would be:
screens

Hardware	data feed +	software	Per mo/ per terminal
4	$42.00	$75.00	$117
8	$25.00	$75.00	$100
16	$17.00	$75.00	$92

Compatibility: IBM/DOS

StockMate is a complete quotation and information solution for the brokerage industry. Combining S&P Ticker III, the world's most powerful real-time digital feed, with he latest hardware, a StockMate system can save you up to 50% compared with rental quotation systems.

Stock Option Analysis Program (SOAP)

H & H Scientific, Inc.
13507 Pendleton Street
Ft. Washington, MD 20744

PH: (301) 292-2958

SOFTWARE
Cost: $150.00
Compatibility: IBM/DOS, MacIntosh

Covers: stocks. Uses Black-Scholes model to calculate fair prices for stock options. Expected profit or loss calculated and graphed. Manual input of automatic retrieval from a Dow Jones or Warner Communications interface.

Stock Option Scanner (SOS)

H & H Scientific, Inc.
13507 Pendleton Street
Ft. Washington, MD 20744

PH: (301) 292-2958

SOFTWARE
Cost: $150.00
Compatibility: IBM/DOS, MacIntosh

Covers: stocks. Scans options and identifies those which are expected for further analysis. Use stand alone or as a front-end filter for the Stock Option Analysis Program from H & H Scientific, Inc. Manual entry of data or automatic download from Dow Jones or Warner Communication.

Stock Portfolio Reporter

Micro Investment Systems, Inc.
P.O. Box 8599
Atlanta, GA 30306

PH: (404) 378-7535

SOFTWARE
Cost: $279.00
Compatibility: IBM/DOS

Covers: stocks. Maintains up to 200 stocks in a portfolio. Updates market prices using Dow Jones News/ Retrieval. Adjusts for stock splits and dividends.

Stock Portfolio System

Smith Micro Software
21062 Brookhurst Street, #106
Huntington Beach, CA 92646

PH: (714) 964-0412

SOFTWARE
Cost: $185.00 - Apple
 $225.00 - MacIntosh and IBM/DOS
Compatibility: IBM/DOS, MacIntosh

Covers: stocks, mutual funds. Personal investment accounting, control and record keeping package. Covers stocks, bonds, options, multiple CD, mutual funds, bank credit union nd money market accounts. Has interface to Smith Micro's Market Link software.

StockCraft Version 2.0

Decision Economics, Inc.
14 Old Farm Road
Cedar Knolls, NJ 07927

PH: (201) 539-6889

SOFTWARE
Cost: Contact Vendor
Compatibility: Apple

Covers: stocks, mutual funds. Stock market system with portfolio management, technical analysis and optimized trading strategy. Includes a VisiCalc interface.

Stockfolio

Zephyr Services
1900 Murray Avenue
Pittsburgh, PA 15217

PH: (412) 422-6600

SOFTWARE
Cost: $29.95
Compatibility: IBM/DOS, Apple II

Covers: stocks. Maintains a portfolio for up to 40 stocks and will retrieve the latest price for all stocks. Provides portfolio summary and averages.

Stockpak II

Standard & Poor's Corporation
25 Broadway
New York, NY 10004

PH: (212) 208-8581

SOFTWARE
Cost: Contact Vendor
Compatibility: IBM/DOS, Apple II, Apple III

Covers: stocks. Fundamental analysis that provides monthly, bi-monthly and quarterly updated financial facts on over 4,700 companies that trade on the three major stock exchanges. Downloads data from S&P's Stock Guide Database. Transfers data into spreadsheets (such as Lotus 1-2-3) and/or custom programs.

Stock Watcher

Micro Trading Software
P.O. Box 175
Wilton, CT 06897-9890

PH: (203) 762-7820

SOFTWARE
Cost $119.00
Compatibility: Macintosh

For investments including futures, stocks, commodities, mutual funds, and provides chart service. Stock Watcher provides clear, concise charts to aide the decision making process and to track investment returns. It has the capability to organize large amounts of data quickly. Stock Watcher has the flexibility of tracking your investments on a daily, weekly, and monthly basis using data, which is downloaded by modem, from data services.

The Structured Financing Workstation

Wall Street Analytics, Inc.
33-41 85th Street
Jackson Heights, NY 11372

PH: (718) 446-5268
Costs: royalty-free permanent license $250,000;
non-issuer permanent license $49,500 + 4 basic points on the market price of all mortgage-backed securities issued.
special thrift license $39,500
Compatibility: IBM/DOS

Covers: mortgage-backed securities. The Structured Financing Workstation provides a system for structuring or analyzing mortgage-backed securities including highly complex derivative products such as CMO/REMICs and Residuals. CMO analysis system supports many major bond structures including floating coupon bonds, IO-strips, PO-strips, accrual ("Z") bonds, both jump and regular, multiple layers of PAC's TAC' and companions.

Swing Catcher

Trend Index Company
Box 5
Altoona, WI 54720-0005

PH: (715) 833-1234
Cost: $995.00
Compatibility: IBM/DOS compatible

Covers stocks, commodities, and has chart service. The major features: catches almost every price swing, be it minor, medium, or major trend; you can have very low drawdowns - "Drawdown Minimizer Logic"; AutoRun or Manual; you can trade all markets; unique methodology and new techniques; small or large traders; only three (5%) of the sixty + varied automatic indicators and pattern techniques are adjustable or optimizable; comprehensive automatic P&L back-testing report capabilities, and more.

The Do-It-Yourself Guide to Investment Information

The Technical Databridge

Savant Corporation
11211 Katy Freeway
Suite 250
Houston, TX 77079

PH: (800) 231-9900
(713) 973-2400

SOFTWARE
Cost: $145.00
Compatibility: IBM/DOS

For users of the Technical Investor. Provides data transfer between The Technical Investor and Lotus 1-2-3 and other spreadsheet programs.

The Technical Investor

Savant Corp.
11211 Katy Freeway, Suite 250
Houston, TX 77079

PH: (800) 231-9900
(713) 973-2400

SOFTWARE
Cost $395.00
Compatibility: IBM/DOS

Over 30 different types of standard technical analysis indicators plus user-defined equations. It's self-contained database allows you to store technical price and volume data for stocks, mutual funds, market indices, options, commodities, bonds, warrants, treasuries and more. Includes communications to retrieve prices from Warner, Dow Jones or Track Data. The most powerful feature is the automatic charting capability. At the touch of a key it can produce literally hundreds of graphs on your monitor or printer

The Technical Selector

Savant Corporation
11211 Katy Freeway
Suite 250
Houston, TX 77079

PH: (800) 231-9900
(713) 973-2400

SOFTWARE
Cost: Contact Vendor
Compatibility: IBM/DOS

Covers: stocks, market timing. Optional security filter for Savant's The Technical Investor. Uses certain technical analysis studies to select stocks, mutual funds, options, etc. Creates lists of securities that pass each filter.

Telechart 2000

Worden Brothers
111 Cloister Ct., Suite 104
Chapel Hill, NC 27514

PH: (919) 490-5250

ONLINE
Cost: hook-up charges $19.00 plus shipping cost $5.00, basic monthly charge based on stocks followed -
45 daily   - $12.42/month
100 "   - $18.00/month
500 "   - $30.00/month
45 weekly   - $5.85
1.25 cents 1st 50, .5 cents after 50
Price includes: stock quote service at close.
Compatibility : IBM/DOS, MacIntosh, Others

Covers: stocks and includes charts. Downloads prices and maps stock quotes into colorful bar charts. Maps moving averages, trend lines and prices, and offers technical indicators ranging from stochastics to the relative strength index. Comments: 60 day money back guarantee $15.00 free credit usage. Use modem and 1-800 number.

Telescan Analyzer/Edge

Emerging Market Technologies, Inc.
1230 Johnson Ferry Road
Suite F-1
Marietta, GA 30068

PH: (404) 973-2300
FAX: (404) 973-3003

SOFTWARE
Cost: Contact Vendor
Compatibility: IBM/DOS

Technical/Fundamental analysis covering stocks indexes, and mutual funds. The Edge product adds searches on more than 10,000 stocks and industry groups.

Telescan Edge

Telescan, Inc.
10550 Richmond Avenue, Suite 250
Houston, TX 77042

PH: (800) 324-8353
(713) 952-1060

SOFTWARE
Cost: $249.00, no monthly charge, online charge per minute 60 cents Prime time, 30 cents non-prime
Compatibility - IBM with modem

Includes stock quote service at no additional cost, (delayed with 20 minute updates) , chart services at additional 10 cents per, additional charge for searches, $2.00 prime time, $1.00 non prime. Types of investments covered: stocks, options, mutual funds, industry groups, indexes and charts. A critically acclaimed stock analysis and stock search program. Retrieves graphs in 4-8 seconds. It uses over 100 technical and fundamental indicators to analyze a database on over 11,000 stocks, 35,000 options, 1800 mutual funds, 197 industry groups and 560 indexes with information dating back 17 years. Also provides insider trading analysis, inflation adjustment, earnings estimates, news retrieval and online investment newsletters at an additional charge.

Telescan ProSearch

Telescan, Inc
10550 Richmond Avenue, Suite 250
Houston, TX 77042

PH: (800) 324-8353
(713) 952-1060

SOFTWARE
Cost: $395.00, no monthly charge, online charge per minute, 60 cents prime time, per graph $3.10, per search 2.00; 30 cents non-prime, per graph; $1.00, per search 10 cents. Compatibility: IBM with modem

Includes stock quote service at no additional cost, (delayed with 20 minute updates) , chart services at additional 10 cents per, additional charge for searches, $2.00 prime time, $1.00 non prime. A stock search program designed for serious investors as a tool for identifying stocks to meet virtually any investment goal as defined by a very wide range of fundamental and technical indicators (over 100 in all) . It uncovers stocks at the beginning of a trend reversal using a unique pattern recognition feature. It also returns up to 200 stocks for each search using up to 30 indicators and ranking them in order of how well they fit the search criteria. Portrays history and potential of a stock at a glance in a tabular report, offers free online support from a ProSearch expert and more.

The Timing Report

Timing Financial Services, LTD
10410 North 31st Avenue, Suite 404
Phoenix, AR 85051

PH: (602) 942-3111
(800) 779-5000 (DTN phone)

Cost: DTN approximate cost of installation $300.00 and $35.00 per month. Delayed stock quote service available for $49.00 quarterly. Compatibility: need DTN unit.

The Timing Report is transmitted daily via DTN(a delayed quote service) and is 5 (quote machine size) pages long. This service blends the fundamental and technical analysis of Timing editor, William Jaeger and Elliott Wave expert, Brent Harris with the fundamental (weather) analysis of Cliff Harris to aid you in trading decisions as well as planning one's business or marketing decisions.

Track Online

Track Data Corp.
61 Broadway
New York, NY 10006

PH: (718) 522-6886
Cost: minimum monthly charge $18.00, online charges per minute .36 cents
Compatibility: IBM compatibles.

Includes: options, stocks, commodities/futures, and indices. For use with CompuTrac. Track/Online offers a broad range of third party financial databases to keep you on top of your investments, research market trends, and spot investment opportunities.

Tradeline Securities Pricing

IDD Information Services
Two World Trade Center
New York, NY 10048

PH: (212) 432-0045
FAX: (212) 912-1457

Cost: $15,000.00 annually for unlimited usage.
Compatibility: IBM compatibles

Covers stocks, all bonds except foreign, options, and mutual funds. Provides as much as 15 years of daily price and dividend information on over 110,000 securities traded on all major North American exchanges and over the counter. The database also provides historical values on over 200 indexes. Securities information includes descriptive price (high-low-close) , volume, and dividend/interest data.

Trade Station

Omega Research, Inc.
3900 N.W. 79th Avenue
Suite 520
Miami, FL 33166

PH: (800) 556-2022
 (305) 594-7664
FAX: (305) 477-7808
Cost: $1895.00 plus data charges
Compatibility:

The first only real-time analysis program ever developed that lets you computer automate and track your own custom trading strategies without programming knowledge. It will: 1) Scan dozens of markets simultaneously, alerting you to buy or sell opportunities based on your own custom strategies. 2) Instantly chart, in real-time any custom technical indicator you wish to monitor. 3) Automate any intra-day systems you're currently trading; generating its buy/sell orders, protective stops and even tracking its open position profit or loss - all on a tick by tick basis.

TValue

Emerging Market Technologies, Inc.
1230 Johnson Ferry Road
Suite F-1
Marietta, GA 30068

PH: (404) 973-2300
FAX: (404) 973-3003

SOFTWARE
Cost: $129.00
Compatibility: IBM/DOS

Program for IRR, compound interest and loan amortization calculations.

Update

Automated Data Collection
Micron, Inc.
10045 Waterford Drive
Ellicott City, MD 21043

PH: (301) 461-2721

Cost: $298.00
Compatibility: IBM compatibles

Covers: stocks and commodities. For use with CompuTrac. Micron's product update uses the Signal receiver to gather daily data and update CompuTrac's data files. Final data is available from Signal approximately one hour after the market closes. Users will be able to collect a huge database on as many issues as the desire. Update can operate unattended. It automatically rolls symbols for one or two year commodity contracts to the closer in symbol at the date specified.

Value Line Software

711 Third Avenue
New York, NY 10017

PH: (800) 654-0508
(212) 687-3965

SOFTWARE
Cost: $281.00 a year with quarterly updates; $396.00 a year with monthly updates; $1500 a year with weekly updates
Compatibility: IBM/DOS, Macintosh

A powerful, easy to use database program that provides an integrated system for selecting stocks and analyzing investment performance over time. Contains information on approximately 1600 widely traded companies. Value/Screen II is a massive compilation of annual and quarterly financial records maintained by Value Line Publishing, Inc.

Value/Screen II

ValueLine Publishing, Inc.
711 Third Avenue
New York, NY 10017

PH: (800) 654-0508
(212) 687-3965

SOFTWARE
Cost: Contact Vendor
Compatibility: IBM/DOS

Covers: stocks. Database screening from a 1,600 stock database covered in the Value Line investment survey. Reports on individual stocks and groups of stocks.

Vickers Stock Research

Vickers Online
226 New York Avenue
Huntington, NY 11743

PH: (800) 832-5280 (in NY)
(800) 645-5043

ONLINE
Cost: annual $50.00, online charges per minute $1.00.
Compatibility: any PC with modem.

Covers: stocks. A menu-driven online dial-up service. Consists of institutional portfolio information. It lists the institutions alphabetically and shows all stocks owned, trading activity, four years of history, insider information (who's buying and selling and how much). Also gives 144 & 13D listings.

Vu/Text

Knight Ridder
325 Chestnut Street
Suite 1300
Philadelphia, PA 19106

PH: (800) 323-2940
(215) 574-4400

Cost: $50.00 hook-up charge. Online charges from $1.90 per minute. Vu/Quote a 20 minute delayed stock quote service is also available for $1.10 per minute.
Compatibility: almost any PC with a modem.

Covers: stocks and news. "The world's largest U.S. Newspaper Databank." Provides full text on over 70 newspapers, 9 magazines, 5 news and business wires and over 200 regional publications. Also offers over 300 Canadian databases and Maritime information.

Wall Street Techniques

Smith Micro Software
21062 Brookhurst Street, #106
Huntington Beach, CA 92646

PH: (714) 964-0412

SOFTWARE
Cost: $295.00
Compatibility: IBM/DOS

Covers: stocks, chart service. Technical analysis and charting system from manually entered data or automatic via the Dow Jones. Interfaces to Lotus 1-2-3, Smith Micro's Stock Portfolio System and Market Link.

WealthBuilder

Money Magazine and Reality
Technologies
3624 Market Street
Philadelphia, PA 19104

PH: (800) 346-2024
(215) 387-6055
FAX: (215) 387-2179

SOFTWARE
Cost: $208.50
Compatibility: IBM/DOS Macintosh

Covers: stocks, mutual funds and bonds(municipal, corporate, and government) . The complete personal planning and investment system. It gives you a comprehensive financial plan based on your own personal goals plus a strategy to achieve them based on your optional asset allocation. Gives performance information on up to 1200 mutual funds and 10,000 stocks and bonds.

WealthStarter

Money Magazines and Reality Technologies
3624 Market Street
Philadelphia, PA 19104

PH: (800) 346-2024
(215) 387-6055
FAX: (215) 387-2179

SOFTWARE
Cost: $59.95
Compatibility: IBM/DOS and Macintosh

A budgeting, savings and investment system for fast results that really work. Helps you to organize your finances, define your goals, and then create a savings strategy to achieve your goals. Also gives expert financial guidance on CD's, mutual funds, bonds, real estate, precious metals, stocks, money market funds and more.

World Equities Report

Dow Jones & Co., Inc.
One S. Wacker Drive
Chicago, Ill 60606

PH: (800) 223-2274
(212) 416-2420 ext 937 (NY)
(312) 750-4000

ONLINE
Cost: basic monthly charge-$677.00
Compatibility : Quotron

Covers: news. An international version of the Dow Jones "broadtape". Operates through Quotron - 24 hours a day Mon-Fri until 1600 Greenwich Mean Time on Saturday. Tightly focused on news that helps equities traders and investors.

"Yellow Sheets"

National Quotation Service
National Quotation Bureau, Inc.
The Harborside Financial Center
600 Plaza Three
Jersey City, NJ 07311

PH: (201) 435-9000
(201) 435-0713
FAX: (201) 435-9000

NOT AVAILABLE ONLINE. NO SOFTWARE
AVAILABLE
PRINTED DAILY HARDCOPY
Cost: $744 annually

The most complete quotation service of non-exchange traded stocks and bonds available. For daily information and pricing, bonds are printed on "yellow sheets" and stocks are printed on "pink sheets." Quotation service contains indicated Bid, Ask, Market Maker with phone numbers, Symbol, and Security Description. Contains over 10,000 stocks and 3,000 bonds.

YEN

Emerging Market Technologies, Inc.
1230 Johnson Ferry Road
Suite F-1
Marietta, GA 30068

PH: (404) 973-2300
FAX: (404) 973-3003

SOFTWARE
Cost: $195.00
Compatibility: IBM/DOS

Computes theoretical value of new NIKKEI options (warrants).

YLDEX

Pacific Bond Research
520 Clayton Street, #4
San Francisco, CA 94117

PH: (415) 621-7190

SOFTWARE
Cost: Contact Vendor
Compatibility:

Covers: bonds. Package for calculation and analysis of fixed income securities. Functions include: fixed income trading, fixed income accounting, fixed income investment analysis and performance evaluation.

Performance Rating Services

This small section lists services that provide information ranking the performance of mutual funds, stocks, and even the investment advice of newsletters.

TABLE OF CONTENTS

CDA Mutual Fund Report

CDA Investment Technologies, Inc.
1355 Piccard Drive
Rockville MD 10850

PH: (800) 232-2285
(301) 975-9600
FAX: (301) 590-1350
Cost: $275.00 annual

Covers: mutual funds, A comprehensive monthly service which analyzes the performance risk posture and percentile rankings of over 1500 funds. Cornerstone of report is the "CDA Rating", an overall rating of each funds that takes into account all aspects of performance and risk. Covers funds in 8 investment objective categories.

CTCR Commodity Traders Consumer Report

Bruce Babcock
1731 Howe Avenue, Suite 149
Sacramento, CA 95825

PH: (916) 677-7562 or
(800) 999-CTCR
FAX: (916) 672-0425
Cost: $168.00 annually
Frequency: every two weeks
Date of first issue: 4/83

Covers: commodities. Monitors major commodity trading advisory services - both their letters and hotline and summarizes the results of their recommendation. Designed to make you a smarter consumer and better trader in the exciting world of commodity trading.

Fund Performance Chartbook

Bert Dohmen
Wellington Financial Corporation
6600 Kalanianole Highway
Suite 114C
Honolulu, HI 96825-1299

PH: (808) 396-2220
(800) 992-9989
FAX: (808) 396-8640
Cost: $25.00
Frequency:
Date of first issue:

Covers: mutual funds. Over 100 charts showing relative performance versus S&P 500. The charts cover the last 5-1/2 years.

Hulbert Financial Digest

Mark Hulbert
316 Commerce Street
Alexandria, VA 22314

PH: (703) 683-5905
Cost: $135.00 year
Frequency: monthly
Date of first issue: 6/80

Tracks the performance of 125 financial newsletters. Gives a percentage rating on each based on following their recommendations. In January issue, he rates the performance of each newsletter going back to 1980.

Lipper Analytical Service Mutual Fund Profile

Standard & Poor's
25 Broadway
New York, NY 10004

PH: (800) 221-5277
(212) 208-8812
Costs: $125.00 yearly
Frequency of update: quarterly

Investments/services rated: mutual funds. Lists over 800 mutual funds and provides: performance rankings, portfolio managers, telephone numbers. Gives top performers for 1,5, & 10 years and other statistics.

Money Manager Previews

Wall Street Transcript / Richard Holman
99 Wall Street
New York, NY 10005

PH: (212) 747-9500
FAX: (212) 668-9842
Cost: $2600.00
Frequency: Weekly
Date of first issue: 1987

Weekly magazine. Covers: money manager interviews. Features interviews and discussions with leading money managers and portfolio strategists throughout the world.

Money Manager Verified Ratings

Norman Zadeh
P.O. Box 7634
Beverly Hills, CA 90212

PH: (213) 305-9300
FAX: (213) 273-7941
Cost: $200.00 per year
Frequency: monthly
Date of first issue: 1984

Covers: Money Manager Ratings. Requires money managers to specify a $1,000,000+ account at the beginning of each year and then send copies of brokerage statements to verify performance. Rates the best managers in several different categories: traditional buy and hold, mutual fund timers, small accounts, short selling and more.

Morningstar Mutual Fund Values

Morningstar, Inc.
53 W. Jackson Blvd
Chicago, Il 60604

PH: (800) 876-5005
FAX: (312) 427-9215
Cost: $395.00
Frequency of update: every 2 weeks - new issue on rotation basis, takes about 20 weeks to get back to a particular mutual fund.

Investments/services rated: mutual funds. Over 1000 funds evaluated by performance and risk data, portfolios, operations information, investment criteria, analyst commentary and Morningstar's investment recommendations.

The Mutual Fund Directory

Investment Company Institute
Probus Publishing Company
118 N. Clinton Street
Chicago, IL.

Published 1990
Cost: $18.95

Subjects addressed: mutual funds. Over 2500 identified, described, and categorized.

The Mutual Fund Encyclopedia

Gerald W. Perritt
Dearborn Financial Publishing, Inc.
520 N. Dearborn Street
Chicago, IL 60610

Published 1990
Cost: $27.95

Profiles 1100 mutual funds detailing objectives and strategies, financial statistics, current yields, portfolio turnover rate, year by year and 5 year average returns and more.

Mutual Fund Fact Book

Investment Company Institute
1600 M Street
Washington, D.C. 20036

PH: (202) 293-7700
(202) 955-3536
Published every May for the previous year.
Cost: $9.95

Covers mutual funds. The book includes: facts and figures on mutual fund investing, information on the assets of mutual funds, the sales redemption value, a historical background on mutual funds and recent trends affecting various funds.

Mutual Fund Forecaster

The Institute for Econometric Research
3471 N. Federal Highway
Ft. Lauderdale, FL 33306

PH: (800) 327-6720
(305) 503-9000
Cost: $100.00 per year
Frequency of update: monthly

Covers: mutual funds. Provides data on over 450 mutual funds including performance projections, risk rating, buy/sell records, loads/no load yield data and phone data, ranks funds in categories such as best buy, buy, hold, sell, etc.

1993 Mutual Funds Almanac

Babson - United Investment Advisors, Inc.
101 Prescott Street
Wellesley Hills, MA 02181

PH: (617) 235-0900
FAX: (617) 235-9450
Cost: $32.00
Date of first publication: 1991

Covers: mutual funds. An indispensable reference book of concise, accurate mutual funds information. Includes performance statistics for the past 10 years on 2100 funds, fund objectives, total assets, net asset value, sales charges, expense rations, minimum investments, addresses and straight talk about the mutual funds industry.

Nelson's Directory of Investment Managers

Nelson Publications
1 Gateway Plaza
Port Chester, NY 10573

PH: (800) 333-6357
FAX: (914) 937-8908
Published: 1991
Cost: $325.00

Subjects addressed: investment managers. In depth profiles of over 2000 money management firms... including 1, 3, 5 and 10 year performance results. Six fact filled sections: Section 1 - In-depth profiles of each money manager; Section 2 - Geographic listing of manager arranged by state; Section 3 - Rankings of all firms by asset size; Section 4 - Listing of firms by type of organization; Section 5 - Index of firms by specialized investment services offered; Section 6 - 1, 3, 5 and 10 year performance rankings of all firms by asset class.

Trading Advisor

Richard Luna
1737 Central Street
Denver, CO 80211

PH: (303)433-3202
(800)950-9339
FAX: (303)433-2731
Cost: $295.00 per year
Frequency: monthly
Date of first issue: 1986

Includes: fundamental analysis. Covers: Commodity Trading Advisors. The leading source of Commodity Trading Advisor information in the nation with both an extensive data base and a large number of accounts traded with Commodity Trading Advisors. Newsletter profiles specific Trading Advisors and includes their performance. Rates the top Commodity Trading Advisors for the past three years and gives pertinent data and key statistics on them. (Follows over 75 advisors.)

Value Line Convertibles

Value Line Publishing
711 Third Avenue
New York, NY 10017-4064

PH: (800) 633-2252
(800) 634-3583
(212) 687-3965
Cost: $445.00 annual
Frequency of update: weekly

Investments/services rated: convertible stock & warrants. Each week this service evaluates 585 convertibles, 95 warrants and their underlying common stocks, issues that trade on the Big Board, the AMEX and Over the Counter. You'll clearly see which convertibles and options Value Line feels are undervalued, which are overvalued, and by how much.

Value Line Options

Value Line Publishing
Allan S. Lyons - editor
711 Third Avenue
New York, NY 10017-4064

PH: (800) 633-2252
(800) 634-3583
(212) 687-3965
Cost: $445.00 annual
Frequency of update: weekly

Investments/services rated: options. Each issue brings a complete listing of all options recommended for buying or selling along with full evaluations on every issue they follow. Each recommendation includes the price at which to buy the stock and the price at which to sell the call. Also included are daily price charts for every stock on which listed options trade.

Weisenberger Management Results

Warren, Gorhamm, & Lamont, Inc.
One Penn Plaza
New York, NY 10119

PH: (800) 950-1209
(617) 423-2020
Cost: $150.00 annual
Frequency of update: monthly

Types of investments rated: mutual funds. Performance reviews of open and closed-end funds. Gives total return and rank by objective as well as asset breakdown and top 20 performers for current year, five-year, and ten-year periods.

The Zweig Performance Ratings Report

Dr. Martin E. Zweig
P.O. Box 360
Bellmore, NY 11710

PH: (800) 633-2252 ext 9000
FAX: (516) 785-0537
Cost: $205.00 yearly
Frequency of update: bi-monthly

Investments/services rated: stocks. Rates 3400 stocks from 1 (the top 5%) down to 9 (the worst 5%) for expected price performance over the next 6-12 months.

Stock and Bond Research Publications

This section lists the few comprehensive stock and bond services that provide information on a broad range of companies. For investors making their own investment decisions, a comprehensive informational source is invaluable.

We have attempted to limit this section to those services that provide information and not necessarily advice on numerous corporations.

TABLE OF CONTENTS

The Blue Book of CBS Stock Reports

Marpep Publishing Limited
133 Richmond Street West
Suite 700
Toronto, Ontario M5H3M8

PH: (416) 869-1177
Cost: $279.00
Frequency: every two weeks
Date of first issue: 1941

Includes: fundamental analysis and technical analysis. Covers: Canadian stocks, charts. Statistical financial analysis on Canadian stocks. Provides buy, sell, hold recommendations as well as five year performance data and company description.

The Fundamental Story

Investor's Daily
P.O. Box 240058
Los Angeles, CA 90024-0058

PH: (800) 235-2888
Cost: $15.00/story
Frequency :every 2 weeks
(Price decreases with volume - example
5 stories @ $10 each)
First published: October 1990

Includes: fundamental analysis, earnings analysis, charts, and covers all markets. Number of stocks covered:128 currently but 550 when complete. Clear, comprehensive 2 page reviews of companies with a high ranking in earnings per share growth. You'll get basic facts plus color pictures of company's products presented in an objective way with no recommendations.
Comments: Next day delivery available for $7.00 extra.

Investext

Thomson Financial Networks
11 Farnsworth Street
Boston, MA 02210

PH: (800) 662-7878
(617) 345-2000
(800) 627-8984
FAX: (617) 330-1986
Cost: $5.95 per page plus $5.00 handling charge

Includes: fundamental analysis, company and industry reports. Complete text of company and industry reports written by analysts at more than 125 of the world's leading investment banks, and consulting and research firms. Currently includes 200,000 reports covering 14,000 companies and 53 industries. Available as a database service (see Computer and Quote Chapter) as well as fax or mail services.

Market Guide

Market Guide, Inc.
49 Glen Head Road
Box 106
Glen Head, NY 11545

PH: (516) 759-1253
FAX: (516) 676-9240
Cost: $245.00
Frequency: Weekly
Date of first issue: 1983

Comprehensive research reports on 800 companies. Criteria for being put in the guide is one or more of the following: significant investor interest, financial strength, high growth rating, high yields, or low price/earnings ratio.

Moody's Bond Record

Moody's Investor Service
99 Church Street
New York, NY 10007

PH: (800) 342-5647 ext 0435
(212) 553-0435
FAX: (212) 553-4700
Frequency: monthly
Cost: $249.00 year
First published: 1969

Regular features: bond analysis. The most comprehensive and authoritative source of statistical data on 56,000 corporate, convertible, government, municipal, environmental control revenue, and international bonds, plus preferred stocks and commercial paper.

Moody's Bond Survey

Moody's Investor Service
99 Church Street
New York, NY 10007

PH: (800) 342-5647
(212) 553-0300
FAX: (212) 553-4700
Frequency: weekly
Cost: $1175.00 year
First published: 1981

Regular features: bond analysis and market update. Gives trends and prospects for the market and for individual bonds. Economic and market condition commentary and opinions, information on factors and issues which influence values of bonds, commercial paper and other debt instruments.

Moody's Dividend Record

Moody's Investor Service
99 Church Street
New York, NY 10007

PH: (800) 342-5647
(212) 553-0300
FAX: (212) 553-4700
Frequency: quarterly
Cost: $460.00 year

Outstanding Feature Issues: Tax Status Supplements (Jan-Feb-March); Annual Dividend Record - compilation of full years dividend information. Detailed reports of current dividend data covering over 18,300 stocks and Unit Investment Trusts.

Moody's Handbook of Common and OTC Stocks

Moody's Investor Service
99 Church Street
New York, NY 10007

PH: (800) 342-5647 ext. 0435
(212) 553-0300
FAX: (212) 553-4700
Cost: $299.00 annually
Frequency: quarterly

Includes: fundamental analysis, earnings analysis, P/E ratio, and covers the NY/OYC/AM markets. Number of stocks covered: 2200. Concise overview of 2200 corporations in an easy access format for instant facts, stock performance trends and financial summaries. Comments: May be ordered separately - common stocks - $210.00 covers all NYSE issues and some major ASE issues.
OTC - $149.00 covers all 600 OTC issues.

Moody's Industrial Manual and News Report

Moody's Investor Service
99 Church Street
New York, NY 10007

PH: (800) 342-5647 ext 0435
(212) 553-0300
FAX: (212) 553-4700
Cost: $1250.00
Frequency: annual with twice weekly updates
First published: 1900

Includes: fundamental analysis, P/E ratio, earnings analysis, and covers the NY and AM markets.
The most comprehensive resource for full financial and operating data of every industrial corporation in the New York and American stock exchanges. Over 500 on regional exchanges. Provides in-depth analyses, detailed financial and stock performance data, history and background on the country's top corporations on the leading national and regional exchanges. Includes dividend information, Moody's ratings and more.

Moody's Industry Review

Moody's Investor Services
99 Church Street
New York, NY 10007

PH: (800) 342-5647
(212) 553-0300
FAX: (212) 553-4700
Frequency: every two weeks
Cost: $450.00 annually

Regular features: company reviews. Comparitive statistics and rankings of 4000 leading corporations in 145 industry groups. Every two weeks receive approximately 10 industry reviews. Each is a profile on an industry including company's trading symbol and exchange, 52 week stock price range, earnings per share, book value, stockholder's equity, long term debt, and much more.
COMMENTS: Statistics, rankings and index are all updated twice a year.

Moody's International Manual and News Reports

Moody's Investor Service
99 Church Street
New York, NY 10007

PH: (800) 342-5647 ext 0435
(212) 553-0300
FAX: (212) 553-4700
Cost: $1795.00 annually
Frequency: annual/update 2xWK
First published: 1900
Number of stocks covered: 5000
Markets covered: International Chart services.

Includes: fundamental analysis
The only comprehensive reference source of financial and business data on over 5000 international corporations, incorporated outside of the U.S. and their global units. Includes full company history; up to 7 years of income accounts and balance sheets, descriptions of principle business activities, subsidiaries and properties, capital structure, including long term debt and capital stock, dividend record, officers, directors, and much more.

Moody's Municipal and Government Manual and News Reports

Moody's Investor Service
99 Church Street
New York, NY 10007

PH: (800) 342-5647 ext 0435
(212) 553-0300
FAX: (212) 553-4700
Cost: $1650.00 annually
Frequency: annual/update 2xWK
First published: 1900

Includes: fundamental analysis and bonds analysis. Complete coverage of over 15,000 bond issuing municipalities and government agencies. You get full descriptions and Moody's ratings on bond issues of state agencies such as housing authorities, colleges and universities, counties, cities, federal agencies and of the US government itself. In depth information includes three year growth of tax collections, assessed value and tax rates, schedule of bonded debt, including bond amounts, interest rates, redemption features, and due dates, operating revenues, debt service and more.

Moody's OTC Industrial Manual and News Reports

Moody's Investor Service
99 Church Street
New York, NY 10007

PH: (800) 342-5647 ext 0435
(212) 553-0300
FAX: (212) 553-4700
Cost: $1150.00
Frequency: Annual/update 2xWK
First published: 1900

Includes: fundamental analysis, earnings analysis, P/E/ratio, and covers the OTC market. The biggest single resource today for full financial and operating data of over 3200 OTC industrial companies. You get detailed company history; up to 7 years of income accounts and balance sheets; 7 year comparisons of statistical records, financial and operating ratios & analysis of operations for many companies, dividend history, officers, directors, and more.

Moody's OTC Unlisted Manual and News Reports

Moody's Investor Service
99 Church Street
New York, NY 10007

PH: (800) 342-5647 ext 0435
(212) 553-0300
FAX: (212) 553-4700
Cost: $1025.00 annually
Frequency: annual/update 2xWK
First published: 1900

Includes: fundamental analysis. A unique reference for dozens of hard to get financial facts and corporate data on 2000 unlisted OTC companies. Gives you verified facts such as 2 years worth of income accounts and balance sheets, place and date of incorporation, company history, mergers and acquisitions, long-term debts, capital stock, subsidiaries, transfer agent and more.

Moody's Public Utility Manual and News Reports

Moody's Investor Service
99 Church Street
New York, NY 10007

PH: (800) 342-5647 ext 0435
(212) 553-0300
FAX: (212) 553-4700
Cost: $1025.00 annually
Frequency: annual updates 2xWK

Includes: fundamental analysis; industry analysis (Public utilities). A comprehensive resource of full financial and operating data of all US public utilities. You get company history and detailed chronology of mergers and acquisitions up to 7 years of income accounts and balance sheets, 7 years of comparisons of statistical records, financial and operating ratios, complete details of all debt and capital stock, Moody's rating, dividend history and more.

Moody's Transportation Manual and News

Moody's Investor Service
99 Church Street
New York, NY 10007

PH: (800) 342-5647 ext 0435
(212) 553-0300
FAX: (212) 553-4700
Cost: $1025.00 annually
Frequency: annu Reportsal/ weekly updates

Reports include: fundamental analysis and industry analysis (Transportation). A comprehensive resource of full financial and operating data of all US companies in every phase of transportation. Includes up to 7 years of income accounts and balance sheets, description of business, subsidiaries, complete details of all debt and capital stock, Moody's ratings, dividend history, officers, directors, and more.

"National Quotation Service"

National Quotation Service
National Quotation Bureau, Inc.
The Harborside Financial Center
600 Plaza Three
Jersey City, NJ 07311

PH: (201) 435-9000
(201) 435-0713
FAX: (201) 435-9000

NOT AVAILABLE ONLINE. NO SOFTWARE
AVAILABLE
PRINTED DAILY HARDCOPY
Cost: $744 annually
Frequency: Daily

The most complete quotation service of non-exchange traded stocks and bonds available. For daily information and pricing, bonds are printed on "yellow sheets" and stocks are printed on "pink sheets." Quotation service contains indicated Bid, Ask, Market Maker with phone numbers, Symbol, and Security Description. Contains over 10,000 stocks and 3,000 bonds.

Nelson's Directory of Investment Research

Nelson Publications
1 Gateway Plaza
Port Chester, NY 10573

PH: (800) 333-6357
FAX: (914) 937-8908
Published: 1991
Cost: $450.00

Subjects addressed: stock analysis. Nelson's Directory is published in two volumes. Volume #1 contains expanded research and financial information on over 5,000 U.S. public companies. Volume #2 contains comprehensive information on over 4000 foreign-based public companies. And, of course analyst coverage of all 9000 companies, important stock data and research reports on each company.

"Pink Sheets"

National Quotation Service
National Quotation Bureau, Inc.
The Harborside Financial Center
600 Plaza Three
Jersey City, NJ 07311

PH: (201) 435-9000
(201) 435-0713
FAX: (201) 435-9000

NOT AVAILABLE ONLINE. NO SOFTWARE
AVAILABLE
PRINTED DAILY HARDCOPY
Cost: $744 annually
Frequency: Daily

The most complete quotation service of non-exchange traded stocks and bonds available. For daily information and pricing, bonds are printed on "yellow sheets" and stocks are printed on "pink sheets." Quotation service contains indicated Bid, Ask, Market Maker with phone numbers, Symbol, and Security Description. Contains over 10,000 stocks and 3,000 bonds.

Special Situations Report

Individual Investor / Financial Data Systems, Inc.
P.O. Box 92000
Collingswood, NJ 08108

PH: (212) 689-2777
FAX: (609) 858-2007
Cost: $150.00
Frequency: Monthly

Covers: stocks. In-depth confidential reports on the "single most promising stock Individual Investor sees in the market." Follow ups and updates are also provided on all previously recommended stocks along with buy/sell/hold advice.

Standard and Poor's Blue List of Current Municipal and Corporate Offerings

Standard and Poors
25 Broadway
New York, NY 10004

PH: (212) 208-8471
FAX: (212) 412-0498
Cost: $599.00 per year
Frequency: Daily publication
Date of first issue: 1935

Covers: municipal bonds and corporate bonds. Reports municipal and corporate bond offerings in the secondary market.

Standard and Poor's Bond Guide

Standard and Poors
25 Broadway
New York, NY 10004

PH: (212) 208-8000
(212) 208-8769
Cost: $185.00 per year
Frequency: Monthly
Date of first issue: 1942

Financial summaries on over 6000 bonds. Includes Standard and Poors ratings - both current and prior, balance sheet data, high-low price range YTD, current price, yield and YTM, and interest payment dates.

Standard and Poor's Corporation Records

Standard and Poors
25 Broadway
New York, NY 10004

PH: (212) 208-8363
FAX: (212) 412-1459
Cost: $1435.00 per year
Frequency: updated twice a month and published quarterly
Date of first issue: 1915

Financial data on almost 11,000 companies. Information includes: long-term debt, outstanding shares, corporate background, incorporation date and merger and acquisition data, stock data, earnings and finance information and annual report.

Standard & Poor's Credit Week

Standard & Poor's
25 Broadway
New York, NY 10004

PH: (800) 777-4858
(212) 208-8768
Cost: $1695.00 year
Frequency: weekly

Regular features: bond analysis. Focuses on trends and outlooks for fixed income securities including corporate and government bonds and money market instruments. Offers the latest info on S&P's new and changed ratings for corporate, municipal and structured issuers.

Standard and Poor's Dividend Record

Standard and Poors
25 Broadway
New York, NY 10004

Reports information on corporate dividends.

PH: (212) 208-8369
Cost: Daily publication - $735.00 per year
Weekly publication - $370.00 per year
Quarterly publication - $145.00 per year
Frequency: Daily, Weekly, or Quarterly
Date of first issue: 1931

Standard & Poor's Industry Reports

Standard & Poors
1221 Avenue of the Americas
New York, NY 10020

PH: (212) 512-4900
(212) 208-8768
(800) 525-8640
Cost: $225.00 annually
Frequency: annual with updates every two weeks
First published: 1935

Includes: fundamental analysis. Helps you gauge the investment merits of entire industry groups. They cover more than 30 business sectors from Aerospace to Utilities. Every report contains a comparison of industry performance vs. the S&P 500, a side-by-side look at representative companies, stock performance and more.

Standard & Poor's Stock Reports

Standard & Poors
1221 Avenue of the Americas
New York, NY 10020

PH: (212) 512-4900
(212) 208-8768
(800) 525-8640
Cost: $1035.00 year for NY exch.
$ 835.00 year for Am exch
$835.00 year for OTC exch
Frequency: Annual /weekly updates
Number of stocks - over 4000; exchanges - NY, AM, OTC

Includes: earnings analysis, P/E ratio, charts, and fundamental analysis. Each 2 page report is a succinct profile of the companies' activities and financial position supported by extensive statistics that facilitate - quick year to year comparisons. Stock reports are alphabetically assembled in 3 4-volume sets and are provided in permanent 3 ring binders. Additional information included: dividend information, S&P ranking, summary of business orientations and product line and much more.

Stock Guide

Standard & Poor's
25 Broadway
New York, NY 10004

PH: (212) 208-8786
Cost: $112.00 annually

Monthly periodical. Information on stock investment data and mutual fund review.

Unique 260 page guide to investment data on over 5300 common and preferred stocks, listed and OTC, providing rapid reviews of all issues with 48 items of data on each. Data includes: S&P earnings and dividend rankings, S&P earnings estimates, monthly high/low prices and volume, stock symbol, historical price ranges, summaries of financial positions and more. Also includes performance summary of over 500 mutual funds.

The Value Line Investment Survey Line Publishing

Value Line Publishing
711 Third Avenue
New York, NY 10017

PH: (800) 633-2252 ext 2683
(212) 687-3965
FAX: (212) 661-2807
Cost: $525.00 annually
$65.00 for a 10 week trial
Frequency: weekly
First published: 1931

Includes: fundamental and technical analysis, P/E ratio, and charts, and covers the NY and AM markets.

2000 page reference library included. Ranks 1700 stocks from best to worst for relative year ahead performance. 15 years past performance and 3-5 year future projection.

Comments: No risk money back guarantee

The Value Line OTC Special Situations Service

Value Line Publishing
711 Third Avenue
New York, NY 10017

PH: (800) 535-9645
Cost: $390.00 annually
Frequency: twice monthly
Date of first issue: 1951

Covers: stocks. A detailed 4 page report on a "Special Situation" chosen for its' chance to rise sharply in price. Also includes updates and reviews on previous recommendations.

Vector Vest Stock Advisory

Vector Vest
3604 North Fork
P.O. Box 577
Bath, OH 44210-9910

PH: (800) 533-3923
(216) 668-2814
(800) 237-8400
Cost: $395.00 annually
Frequency: weekly
Date of first issue: 1978

Includes: technical and fundamental analysis. Covers: stocks. A complete guide to safer, more profitable stock investing which gives specific buy, sell and hold recommendations. Also ranks stocks (best - worst) in several different categories from Relative Value and Relative Safety to stocks under $20.

"Yellow Sheets"

National Quotation Service
National Quotation Bureau, Inc.
The Harborside Financial Center
600 Plaza Three
Jersey City, NJ 07311

PH: (201) 435-9000
(201) 435-0713
FAX: (201) 435-9000

NOT AVAILABLE ONLINE. NO SOFTWARE
AVAILABLE
PRINTED DAILY HARDCOPY
Cost: $744 annually
Frequency: Daily

The most complete quotation service of non-exchange traded stocks and bonds available. For daily information and pricing, bonds are printed on "yellow sheets" and stocks are printed on "pink sheets." Quotation service contains indicated Bid, Ask, Market Maker with phone numbers, Symbol, and Security Description. Contains over 10,000 stocks and 3,000 bonds.

Brokerage Research Publications

Many portfolio managers and investors have realized that major brokerage firms provide outstanding and comprehensive stock and bond research. Major Wall Street forms devote millions of dollars to providing their clients with superior research in exchange for their transactional business.

The good news is that most of this research is available to clients without charge. Most major firms will even provide prospective clients with samples of their research in exchange for the opportunity to solicit their business.

The firms whose research is listed are under no obligation to provide investors with free information and advice. Of course, an investor requesting information is doing so with the understanding that his investment business will probably be solicited. Most investors do business where they receive the best advice. The contacts listed for each firm are not obligated to send stock and bond research pieces to potential investors. However, most firms do send complimentary information to prospective clients.

Portfolio managers have encountered problems finding out exactly what research their brokers have available. This guide has provided a listing of the more important research pieces published by each of the major Wall Street brokerage houses. Each publication is described and the information contained is briefly listed. The focus of each research piece is described: stocks (large, medium, small, preferred, or foreign), bonds (municipal, corporate, convertible, government, or foreign), or economic information. Most of the listings in this chapter focus on stocks and bond. Many useful and comprehensive publications are listed.

This section will be expanded in the future to include regional and smaller brokerage firms. Readers are urged to use the reply card to send in listings of research pieces that should be included.

Bond Market Comments

Dean Witter
530 Providence Towers East
5001 Spring Valley Road
Dallas, TX 75244

PH: (800) 827-2211
(214) 770-9724
Monthly publication approximately 2 pages.

Covers bonds and interest rates.
Includes commentary on the tax-free municipal bond market and interest rates. Also contains highlights of attractive municipal issues.

Market View

Dean Witter
530 Providence Towers East
5001 Spring Valley Road
Dallas, TX 75244

PH: (800) 827-2211
(214) 770-9724
Monthly publication approximately 7 pages.

Covers stocks (blue chip, small capital stocks and foreign),economic analysis. asset allocation.
Includes economic commentary, top technical and fundamental stock recommendations, asset allocation, economic numbers to be released, and closed and fund updates.

Market Watch

Dean Witter
530 Providence Towers East
5001 Spring Valley Road
Dallas, TX 75244

PH: (800) 827-2211
(214) 770-9724
Weekly publication approximately 75 pages.

Covers stocks (blue chip and small capital stocks).
Includes opinion changes on stocks; industry views and comments; market comments; analysis of performance of stocks and industries; technical comments, stock highlights, top stock recommendations; other available research reports; and upcoming economic numbers.

Monthly Investment Strategy

Dean Witter
530 Providence Towers East
5001 Spring Valley Road
Dallas, TX 75244

PH: (800) 827-2211
(214) 770-9724
Monthly publication approximately 50 pages.

Covers bonds and interest rates, economic analysis, stocks (blue chip and small capital stock), and asset allocation. Contains economic analysis; asset allocation; sector and industry analysis; model portfolio charts on stocks, bonds, the dollar, global equity markets, inflation, monetary numbers, economic numbers and corporate profits; and market valuation.

Monthly Statistical Review

Dean Witter
530 Providence Towers East
5001 Spring Valley Road
Dallas, TX 75244

PH: (800) 827-2211
(214) 770-9724
Monthly publication approximately 60 pages.

Covers stocks (blue chip and small capital stocks). Contains statistics on all stocks followed by Dean Witter's research department.

Weekly Technical Perspective

Dean Witter
530 Providence Towers East
5001 Spring Valley Road
Dallas, TX 75244

PH: (800) 827-2211
(214) 770-9724
Weekly publication approximately 10 pages.

Covers stocks, economic analysis, commodities Includes technical indicators for the market; put/call ration; investor sentiment; uptick/downtick ratio; index futures; institutional liquidity; CRB, stock bond and oil indexes; and top stock recommendations.

Merrill Lynch Market Letter

Merrill Lynch
2000 Premier Place
5910 N. Central Expressway
Dallas, TX 75206

PH: (800) 999-3056
(214) 750-2034
Cost: $35.00 a year
A bi-weekly publication approximately 6 pages .

Covers bonds and interest rates, stocks (blue chip and small capital stocks), and economic analysis. A brief update on economic developments and interest rates. Focuses on Merrill Lynch's top stock recommendations and special industry stock recommendations. Includes highlight of upcoming economic numbers.

Monthly Research Review

Merrill Lynch
2000 Premier Place
5910 N. Central Expressway
Dallas, TX 75206

PH: (800) 999-3056
(214) 750-2034
A monthly publication approximately 125 pages.

Covers bonds and interest rates, stocks (blue chip, small capital stocks, and foreign stocks), economic analysis, and asset allocation. Includes economic statistics and forecasts; interest rate analysis; foreign country economic statistics; market data; industry analysis and rankings; stock rankings; stock statistics; pricing, earnings P/E multiples, dividends, forecasts and return on equity, organized by industry; closed-end funds statistics; convertible securities statistics, and international company statistics.

Research Highlights

Merrill Lynch
2000 Premier Place
5910 N. Central Expressway
Dallas, TX 75206

PH: (800) 999-3056
(214) 750-2034
A weekly publication approximately 20 pages.

Covers bonds and interest rates, stocks (blue chip, small capital stocks, and foreign stocks), economic analysis, and asset allocation. A condensed piece with economic and interest rate analysis, industry comments, technical comments, top recommendations in stocks, and global comments.

Nelson's Directory of Investment Research

Nelson Publications
One Gateway Plaza
Port Chester, NY 10573

PH: (914)937-8400
(800)333-6357
FAX: (914)937-8908
Cost: $435.00
Frequency: annually
Date of first issue: 1975

Covers: U.S. and foreign stocks. A 2 volume directory of research on over 9000 stocks (5000 U.S. companies and 4000 foreign companies). Includes 5 year historical sales data, net income, EPS and 5 year growth rate, description, address, phone and fax numbers of each business. The directory also provides extensive analyst coverage information and geographical and industry groupings.

Futures - Agricultural Report

Prudential Securities, Inc.
10440 North Central Expressway
Suite 1600
Dallas, TX 75231

PH: (214)373-2700
(800)527-1320
FAX: (214)373-2788
Cost: Free
Frequency: monthly
Date of first issue: 1988

Covers: futures spreads. Gives current positions, closed out positions, market commentary and forecasting, details on current spread opportunities and an extensive review of technical data on the major futures.

Futures - Option Strategist

Prudential Securities, Inc.
10440 North Central Expressway
Suite 1600
Dallas, TX 75231

PH: (214)373-2700
 (800)527-1320
FAX: (214)373-2788
Cost: Free
Frequency: monthly
Date of first issue: 1989

Covers: options on futures. Includes charts and analysis of oil, bonds, Eurodollars, S&P 500, Yen, Mark, Swiss Franc, British Pound, Canadian Dollar, Gold, Silver, Gasoline, Soybean, Corn, Wheat, Sugar, Coffee, and Cotton.

Futures - The Technical Analyst

Prudential Securities, Inc.
10440 North Central Expressway
Suite 1600
Dallas, TX 75231

PH: (214)373-2700
 (800)527-1320
FAX: (214)373-2788
Cost: Free
Frequency: periodically
Date of first issue: 1989

Covers: futures and commodities. Includes charts, spreads, and analysis for T-Bills, Eurodollar, S&P 500, British Pound, Yen, Swiss Franc, Canadian Dollar, Deutsche Mark, Gold, Silver, Platinum, Oil, Heating Oil, Wheat, Corn, Oats, Soybean, Cotton, Cattle, Feeders, Hogs Bellies.

The International Interest Rate Weekly

Prudential Securities
10440 North Central Expressway
Suite 1600
Dallas, TX 75231

PH: (214)373-2700
 (800)527-1320
FAX: (214)373-2788
Cost: Free
Frequency: weekly

Covers: Bonds and Interest rates. Commentary and forecast on interest rates - domestic and international written by Prudential's staff analysts.

Asset Allocation/Equity Valuation

PaineWebber
5151 Beltline, Ste 101
Dallas, TX 75248

PH: (800) 288-1515
(214) 934-3434
FAX: (214) 450-4350
Monthly publication approximately 10 pages.

Covers bonds and interest rates, economic analysis, and asset allocation.

Includes expected rates of return on T-bills, 10 year bonds and stocks. Asset Allocation analysis: vs. bonds, stocks vs cash, bonds vs cash. Quantitative analysis: Equity Valuation model.

Focus List

PaineWebber
5151 Beltline, Ste 101
Dallas, TX 75248

PH: (800) 288-1515
(214) 934-3434
FAX: (214) 450-4350
Monthly publication approximately 6 pages.

Covers stocks (blue chip and small capital stocks). Lists the top recommendations by PaineWebber for value and timeliness. Decisions for recommendations are made by PaineWebber's research policy committee. Also includes technical recommendations.

Investment Strategy Pyramid

PaineWebber
5151 Beltline, Ste 101
Dallas, TX 75248

PH: (800) 288-1515
(214) 934-3434
FAX: (214) 450-4350
Monthly publication approximately 6 pages.

Covers stocks (blue chip and small capital stocks). Contains rankings of approximately 330 stocks based on value and price momentum. This publication also ranks 40 industries based on value and price momentum.

Portfolio Manager's Spotlight

PaineWebber
5151 Beltline, Ste 101
Dallas, TX 75248

PH: (800) 288-1515
(214) 934-3434
FAX: (214) 450-4350
Monthly publication approximately 30 pages.

Covers bonds and interest rates, stocks (blue chip and small capital stocks), economic analysis and asset allocation. This is a narrative piece that includes PaineWebber's asset allocation model and in-depth explanations of current industrial and economic trends. Includes explanations of ranking changes on stocks.

Statistical Summary

PaineWebber
5151 Beltline, Ste 101
Dallas, TX 75248

PH: (800) 288-1515
(214) 934-3434
FAX: (214) 450-4350
Monthly publication approximately 40 pages.

Covers stocks (blue chip and small capital stocks).
Contains statistics on 638 stocks followed by PaineWebber including earnings, dividends, 52 week range, performance, price to earnings, beta, book value, shares, market value, institutional ownership, trading volume, and debt to equity. Also includes PaineWebber's ranking of each stock. Organized by the industry.

Futures Monthly Report

Prudential Securities
10440 N. Central Expressway, Ste. 1600
Dallas, TX 75231

PH: (214) 373-2700
Monthly publication approximately 20 pages.

Covers bonds and interest rates, economic analysis, and commodities.
Fundamental and technical analysis including global yield comparisons, currency analysis, interest rate analysis, and yield spreads. Also covers oil and metals.

Quantitative Monthly

Prudential Securities
10440 N. Central Expressway, Ste. 1600
Dallas, TX 75231

PH: (214) 373-2700
Monthly publication approximately 65 pages.

Covers economic analysis and stocks (blue chip and small capital stocks).
Includes Prudential's view of the market and economy along with industry rankings and Model Portfolio Section. Blue chip and small capital stocks are ranked and listed by industry. New buy and sell recommendations are listed. Earnings, dividends, value, and correlations are graphed in the final section.

Research Weekly

Prudential Securities
10440 N. Central Expressway, Ste. 1600
Dallas, TX 75231

PH: (214) 373-2700
Weekly publication approximately 25 pages.

Covers stocks (blue chip and small capital stocks, and economic analysis.
Includes explanations of economic trends, industrial changes and a detailed explanation of changes in stock recommendations.

Strategy Weekly

Prudential Securities
10440 N. Central Expressway, Ste. 1600
Dallas, TX 75231

PH: (214) 373-2700
Weekly publication approximately 40 pages.

Covers bonds and interest rates, stocks (blue chip and small capital stocks), economic analysis, and asset allocation. Contains economic and industrial analysis with asset allocation structure. Also includes economic charts and Prudential's top recommendations put into model portfolios.

The Recommended List

Shearson Lehman Bothers
12222 Merit Drive, Suite 1250
Dallas, TX 75251

(800) 766-1088
(214) 387-8989
Monthly publication approximately 4 pages.

Covers stocks - blue chip and small capital stocks. Includes Shearson's top stock recommendations organized by industry with price performance, earnings, price 52 week range and dividend yield.

Research Universe

Shearson Lehman Bothers
12222 Merit Drive, Suite 1250
Dallas, TX 75251

(800) 766-1088
(214) 387-8989
Monthly publication approximately 90 pages.

Covers stocks - blue chip, small capital stocks, and foreign stocks; economic analysis; mutual funds (closed end).Includes Shearson's top stock recommendations, guided portfolios, listings of all stocks followed by Shearson, projected growth, P/E analysis, return models, beta coefficients, closed-end fund analysis, and economic analysis.

Ten Uncommon Values

Shearson Lehman Bothers
12222 Merit Drive, Suite 1250
Dallas, TX 75251

(800) 766-1088
(214) 387-8989
Annual publication approximately 8 pages.

Covers blue chip stocks.
Includes an annual listing of Shearson's top ten stock recommendations updated each mid-year.

Weekly Portfolio Summary

Shearson Lehman Bothers
12222 Merit Drive, Suite 1250
Dallas, TX 75251

(800) 766-1088
(214) 387-8989

Weekly publication: regular version is approximately 60 pages, condensed approximately 4 pages.

Covers bonds and interest rates; stocks - blue chip and small capital stocks, economic analysis, and asset allocation.
Divided into sections that include Strategy (asset allocation), Sector Analysis (industry groups), Technical Analysis, Global Strategy, Political Analysis, Economics, and comments on individual stocks.

Yield Curve

Shearson Lehman Bothers
12222 Merit Drive, Suite 1250
Dallas, TX 75251

(800) 766-1088
(214) 387-8989
Weekly publication approximately 13 pages.

Covers bonds and interest rates, corporate, municipals, government, annuities, preferred stock, money market. Economic analysis.
Includes a comprehensive bond market analysis, with an economic outlook, historical charts, yield curve charts, value matrix and analysis, and comments on specific bonds.

Closed-End Country Funds

Smith Barney
1660 One Galleria Tower
13355 Noel Road
Dallas, TX 75240

(800) 442-1357 TX
(800) 527-4175 US
(214) 450-6632
Approximately 45 pages.

Covers economic analysis, and foreign stocks.
Includes net asset values, premiums and discounts, holdings of funds and allocations.

Convertibles

Smith Barney
1660 One Galleria Tower
13355 Noel Road
Dallas, TX 75240

PH: (800) 442-1357 TX
(800) 527-4175 US
(214) 450-6632
Approximately 50 pages.

Covers convertible bonds and economic analysis. Includes a comprehensive listing of convertible bonds and preferred stocks; conversion prices, prices, symbols, issue size ratings, yield, pay dates, breakeven, call price, and industry. Also gives market comment and warrant listings.

Credit Market Comment

Smith Barney
1660 One Galleria Tower
13355 Noel Road
Dallas, TX 75240

PH: (800) 442-1357 TX
(800) 527-4175 US
(214) 450-6632
Approximately 10 pages.

Includes bonds and interest rates, and economic analysis.
Includes costs on yield changes for bond types, foreign spreads, corporate yields, economic data, industry and credit market comments, and upcoming economic numbers.

Futures Market Analysis/A Technical Overview

Smith Barney
1660 One Galleria Tower
13355 Noel Road
Dallas, TX 75240

PH: (800) 442-1357 TX
(800) 527-4175 US
(214) 450-6632
Weekly publication approximately 4 pages.

Includes charts, comments, and momentum of currencies, energy, metals, and bonds.

Portfolio Strategist

Smith Barney
1660 One Galleria Tower
13355 Noel Road
Dallas, TX 75240

PH: (800) 442-1357 TX
(800) 527-4175 US
(214) 450-6632
Weekly publication approximately 30 pages.

Includes bonds and interest rates, stocks (blue chip, small capital stocks, and foreign), economic analysis and asset allocation.Includes: top stock recommendations, asset allocation model, company comments; global markets report, technical reports on currencies, gold, and bonds; quantitative analysis, earnings estimate changes, closed-end country funds comments, and economic data.

Research Week

Smith Barney
1660 One Galleria Tower
13355 Noel Road
Dallas, TX 75240

PH: (800) 442-1357 TX
(800) 527-4175 US
(214) 450-6632
Weekly publication approximately 80 pages.

Includes stocks (blue chip) and economic analysis. Includes top stock recommendations, changes in recommendation, industry analysis, comments on specific industries and companies, and a listing of other available research reports.

Statistical Summary

Smith Barney
1660 One Galleria Tower
13355 Noel Road
Dallas, TX 75240

PH: (800) 442-1357 TX
(800) 527-4175 US
(214) 450-6632
Monthly publication approximately 50 pages.Includes stocks (blue chip, small capital stocks and foreign).

Includes top stock recommendations statistics on approximately 700 stocks followed by Smith Barney; 52 week range, earnings, growth, estimates, dividend, and current opinion. Also includes listings of closed-end country funds and international companies.

Investext

Thomson Financial Networks
11 Farnsworth Street
Boston, MA 02210

PH: (800)662-7878
(617)345-2000
(800)627-8984
FAX: (617)330-1986
Cost: $5.95 per page plus $5.00 handling charge

Includes: fundamental analysis, company and industry reports. Complete text of company and industry reports written by analysts at more than 125 of the world's leading investment banks, and consulting and research firms. Currently includes 200,000 reports covering 14,000 companies and 53 industries. Available as a database service (see Computer and Quote Chapter) as well as fax or mail services.

Brochures and Pamphlets on Investing

One of the most difficult processes for new investors is gathering the right information so mistakes are avoided. This guide is extremely useful as an information gathering tool. This section is designed for investors who want information on specific types of investing or financial planning subjects.

The brochures and pamphlets listed are available free to potential clients. The major brokerage houses and discount brokerages have compiled numerous publications to guide their customers when making investment decisions. Again, the firms listed are under no obligation to provide free information. However, most firms will provide information free to prospective clients.

Before making crucial investment and financial planning decisions, investors should design a plan for investing and make sure they understand what they are buying. This chapter provides listings of publications that can help investors in financial planning and selecting investments.

Investing for Safety & High Return

Charles Schwab
101 Montgomery Street
San Francisco, CA 94104

PH: (800)435-4000
Cost: Free
Date of first issue: 1990

Includes: Fundamental analysis. Covers: municipal bonds, corporate bonds, government bonds, zero-coupon bonds, Treasury bonds, CD's. Gives basic investment rules when dealing with fixed income investments as well as descriptions and helpful advice about each instrument.

Maximizing Your Retirement Plan Distribution

Charles Schwab
101 Montgomery Street
San Francisco, CA 94104

PH: (800) 435-4000
Date of publication: 1991

Includes explanations of a retirement plan distribution, options for rollover or forward averaging, and terms associated with retirement distributions.

Selecting Investments for Safety and Return

Charles Schwab
101 Montgomery Street
San Francisco, CA 94104

PH: (800) 435-4000
Date of publication: 1990

Areas covered by brochure: Bonds (municipal, corporate, government, zero-coupon), stocks, general investing, and financial planning.
Includes explanations of investment terms, portfolio allocation, goal setting, bond pricing, tax-exempt securities, and mutual fund alternatives.

IRA Rollover - Making Sense Out of Your Lump-Sum Distribution

Dean Witter
530 Providence Towers East
5001 Spring Valley Road
Dallas, TX 75244

PH: (800) 827-2211
(214) 770-9724
Date of publication 1988

Areas covered by brochure: financial planning.
Includes a discussion of options relating to retirement distributions and explains factors to be considered in rolling over a distribution.

Retirement Investment Strategies

Dean Witter
530 Providence Towers East
5001 Spring Valley Road
Dallas, TX 75244

PH: (800) 827-2211
(214) 770-9724
Date of publication 1989

Areas covered by brochure include mortgage backed securities, bonds(corporate, government, and zero-coupon), stocks, general investing and financial planning.

Includes a discussion of retirement plans and types of investments: money market funds, CD's, mutual funds, bonds, stocks, unit trusts, limited partnerships, covered options, and preferred stocks.

Collateralized Mortgage Obligations - Taxable Fixed Income

Dean Witter
530 Providence Towers East
5001 Spring Valley Road
Dallas, TX 75244

PH: (800) 827-2211
(214) 770-9724
Date of publication 1990

Areas covered by brochure: mortgage backed securities.

Includes an explanation of collateralized mortgage obligations, average life, maturity factors and prepayment assumptions.

How to Make the Most of Your Retirement Plan Distribution

Merrill Lynch
2000 Premier Place
5910 N. Central Expressway
Dallas, TX 75206

PH: (800) 999-3056
(214) 750-2034
Date of publication: 1988

Covers financial planning.

Includes an explanation of retirement distribution, alternatives, tax considerations and calculations, and rollover alternatives.

How Municipal Bonds Can Help You Reach Financial Goals

Merrill Lynch
2000 Premier Place
5910 N. Central Expressway
Dallas, TX 75206

PH: (800) 999-3056
(214) 750-2034

Covers municipal bonds.

Includes a brief introduction to the municipal market, explanations of terms, types of municipal bonds, tax-exempt status, and factors that determine a bond's price and yield.

How to Read a Financial Report

Merrill Lynch
2000 Premier Place
5910 N. Central Expressway
Dallas, TX 75206

PH: (800) 999-3056
(214) 750-2034
Date of publication: 1973/1990

Covers corporate bonds and stocks.
Includes an explanation of corporate financial statements: consolidated balance sheets, income statements, cash flow statements and changes in shareholder's equity.

How to Take Control of Your Financial Future - Choosing an Annuity That's Right for You

Merrill Lynch
2000 Premier Place
5910 N. Central Expressway
Dallas, TX 75206

PH: (800) 999-3056
(214) 750-2034
Date of publication: 1988

Covers annuities.
Includes types of annuities, tax-deferred explanations and advantages, and factors to consider when investigating an annuity.

IRA Sourcebook (1991 update)

Merrill Lynch
2000 Premier Place
5910 N. Central Expressway
Dallas, TX 75206

PH: (800) 999-3056
(214) 750-2034
Date of publication: 1988/1991

Covers IRA's.
Includes an explanation of Individual Retirement Accounts, deductibility, tax deferral, Form 8606 non-deductible contributions, and withdrawal requirements.

Merrill Lynch Guide to Collateralized Mortgage Obligations

Merrill Lynch
2000 Premier Place
5910 N. Central Expressway
Dallas, TX 75206

PH: (800) 999-3056
(214) 750-2034
Date of publication: 1988

Covers mortgage backed securities.
Includes explanations of the collateralized mortgage obligations, asset collateralization, and terms associated with CMO bonds.

Qualified Retirement Plans for Business

Retirement Builder - Guidebook to Planning Financial
Security
Merrill Lynch
2000 Premier Place
5910 N. Central Expressway
Dallas, TX 75206

PH: (800) 999-3056
(214) 750-2034
Date of publication: 1987/1988

Covers financial planning.
Includes explanation of types of qualified retirement
plans, their advantages and special factors relating to
plan establishment and maintenance.

Retirement Builder - Guidebook to Planning Financial Security

Merrill Lynch
2000 Premier Place
5910 N. Central Expressway
Dallas, TX 75206

PH: (800) 999-3056
(214) 750-2034
Date of publication: 1990

Covers financial planning.
Includes retirement planning explanations, financial
planning guidelines, income needs analysis, and financial planning calculation charts.

Short-Term Fixed-Income Investments for Businesses & Financial Institutions

Merrill Lynch
2000 Premier Place
5910 N. Central Expressway
Dallas, TX 75206

PH: (800) 999-3056
(214) 750-2034
Date of publication: 1990

Covers bonds (municipal, corporate, government, and
zero-coupon), and general investing.
Includes explanations of money market instruments,
tax-exempt money market instruments, and tax-advan-
tages money market instruments.

Tax Saving Ideas for Investors

Merrill Lynch
2000 Premier Place
5910 N. Central Expressway
Dallas, TX 75206

PH: (800) 999-3056
(214) 750-2034
Date of publication: 1987/1990

Covers municipal bonds, stocks, general investing and financial planning.
43 tax saving ideas are presented with a focus on personal investing.

Consumer Guide to Mutual Funds

PaineWebber
5151 Beltline, Suite 101
Dallas, TX 75248

PH: (800) 288-1515
(214) 934-3434
FAX: (214) 450-4350
Date of publication 1988

Covers mutual funds and financial planning.
Includes a discussion of mutual fund yield and total return, and explanations of selection criteria.

The Investor's Guide to Certificates of Deposit

PaineWebber
5151 Beltline, Suite 101
Dallas, TX 75248

PH: (800) 288-1515
(214) 934-3434
FAX: (214) 450-4350
Date of publication 1990

Covers financial planning and certificates of deposit.
Includes a discussion of CD's their features, FDIC insurance, insurance limits, and investing information.

The Investor's Guide to Ginnie Maes

PaineWebber
5151 Beltline, Suite101
Dallas, TX 75248

PH: (800) 288-1515
(214) 934-3434
FAX: (214) 450-4350
Date of publication 1990

Covers mortgage-backed securities.
Includes an explanation of the terms associate with Government National Mortgage Association (GNMA) bonds, explanation of common questions, and a list of features of GNMA bonds.

The Investor's Guide to Government Securities

PaineWebber
5151 Beltline, Suite 101
Dallas, TX 75248

PH: (800) 288-1515
(214) 934-3434
FAX: (214) 450-4350
Date of publication 1989

Covers government bonds.
Includes a brief explanation of most types of government bonds and a table showing the features of the different types of bonds.

An Investor's Guide to Tax-Exempt Securities

PaineWebber
5151 Beltline, Suite 101
Dallas, TX 75248

PH: (800) 288-1515
(214) 934-3434
FAX: (214) 450-4350
Date of publication 1990/91

Covers: municipal bonds.
Includes an introduction and definition of tax exempt municipal bonds, explanation of safety, special features, taxable equivalent yield calculations, and a comprehensive glossary of terms used in municipal investing.

The Investor's Guide to Tax-Free Zero Coupon Municipal Bonds

PaineWebber
5151 Beltline, Suite 101
Dallas, TX 75248

PH: (800) 288-1515
(214) 934-3434
FAX: (214) 450-4350
Date of publication 1988

Covers municipal bonds and zero coupon.
Includes a brief discussion of zero coupon municipal (tax-free) bonds and an explanation of their features.

The Investor's Guide to Treasury Zeros

PaineWebber
5151 Beltline, Suite 101
Dallas, TX 75248

PH: (800) 288-1515
(214) 934-3434
FAX: (214) 450-4350
Date of publication 1988

Covers government and zero-coupon bonds.
Includes a brief discussion of U.S. government zero-coupon bonds, their yields and pricing calculations.

Managing Your Retirement Plan Distribution: Tax Alternatives

PaineWebber
5151 Beltline, Suite 101
Dallas, TX 75248

PH: (800) 288-1515
(214) 934-3434
FAX: (214) 450-4350
Date of publication 1988

Covers financial planning.
Includes an explanation of distribution tax alternatives, rollover options, penalties, and stock rollovers.

Municipal Bonds Investing for Tax-Free Income

PaineWebber
5151 Beltline, Suite 101
Dallas, TX 75248

PH: (800) 288-1515
(214) 934-3434
FAX: (214) 450-4350
Date of publication 1988

Covers municipal bonds and financial planning.
Includes advantages of municipal securities, definitions of terms used in bond investing, ratings explanations, and types of municipal bonds.

The PaineWebber Guide to Retirement Plans

PaineWebber
5151 Beltline, Suite 101
Dallas, TX 75248

PH: (800) 288-1515
(214) 934-3434
FAX: (214) 450-4350
Date of publication 1990

Provides information on general investing and financial planning. Includes an explanation of retirement plan types, maximum contributions, special retirement, plan features, and a chart describing SEP, profit sharing, money purchase, 401K, CODA-SEP, and defined benefit pensions.

The PaineWebber Retirement Plan Distribution Investor's Guide

PaineWebber
5151 Beltline, Suite 101
Dallas, TX 75248

PH: (800) 288-1515
(214) 934-3434
FAX: (214) 450-4350
Date of publication 1990

Provides information financial planning. Includes a discussion of distribution tax alternatives, rollover advantages, tax averaging, and IRA explanations.

Retirement Planning - For the Self-Employed Professional and Small Business Owner

PaineWebber
5151 Beltline, Suite 101
Dallas, TX 75248

PH: (800) 288-1515
(214) 934-3434
FAX: (214) 450-4350
Date of publication 1987

Provides information on general investing and financial planning. Includes explanations of types of plans including SEP, money purchase, defined benefit, 401K and profit sharing.

Stock Market Investing - The Definitive Guide for Paine Webber Clients

PaineWebber
5151 Beltline, Suite 101
Dallas, TX 75248

PH: (800) 288-1515
(214) 934-3434
FAX: (214) 450-4350
Date of publication 1990

Covers stocks.
Includes stock market historical performance, dividend explanation, and a discussion of PaineWebber's research.

Mortgage Collateralized Bonds

Prudential Securities
10440 N. Central Expressway
Suite 1600
Dallas, TX 75231

PH: (214)373-2700
FAX: (214)373-2788
Cost: Free
Date of first issue: 1991

Covers: mortgage backed securities. An investor's guide to MCB's. Gives highlights and features as well as redemption information and explanation of how MCB's work.

Municipal Bonds: Investing For Tax-Free Income

Prudential Securities
10440 N. Central Expressway
Dallas, TX 75231

PH: (214)373-2700
FAX: (214)373-2788
Cost: Free
Date of first issue: 1991

Covers: municipal bonds and zero-coupon bonds. An informative booklet discussing the "why's" and "how-to's" of municipal bond investing. Gives features of muni bonds, and discusses the different forms and types of muni bonds.

Overview: Meeting Your Retirement Objectives

Prudential Securities
10440 N. Central Expressway
Suite 1600
Dallas, TX 75231

Covers: retirement planning. A booklet describing the different types of qualified plans and investment products suitable for these plans.

PH: (214)373-2700
FAX: (214)373-2788
Cost: Free
Date of first issue: 1986

Retirement Plan Distribution Analysis

Prudential Securities
10440 N. Central Expressway, Suite 1600
Dallas, TX 75231

A brief booklet that helps calculate distribution tax alternatives.

PH: (214) 373-2000

Tax-Deferred Annuities

Prudential Securities
10440 N. Central Expressway
Suite 1600
Dallas, TX 75231

Covers: annuities. A helpful guide explaining the benefits and features of annuities. Gives you the when, how-to and why's of buying annuities and discusses the annuitization options.

PH: (214)373-2700
FAX: (214)373-2788
Cost: Free
Date of first issue: 1986

Zero Coupon Bonds

Prudential Securities
10440 N. Central Expressway
Suite 1600
Dallas, TX 75231

Covers: zero-coupon bonds. An informative brochure for zero coupon bond investors. It explains how your money grows, gives a definition of zero's, shows how they should fit in your financial plan, summarizes the different types of zeros and briefly discusses tax implications.

PH: (214)373-2700
FAX: (214)373-2788
Cost: Free
Date of first issue: 1991

Federally Insured CD's

Shearson Lehman Brothers
12222 Merit Drive, Suite 1250
Dallas, TX 75251

1 (800) 766-1088
(214) 387-8989
Date of publication: 1990

Covers certificates of deposit.
A brief explanation of CD's, federal insurance, and investment considerations.

A Guide to Option Writing

Shearson Lehman Brothers
12222 Merit Drive, Suite 1250
Dallas, TX 75251

1 (800) 766-1088
(214) 387-8989
Date of publication: 1990

Covers stocks.
Includes a brief discussion of option writing to increase returns on current stock holdings, call premium calculations, and a short glossary of relevant terms.

A Guide to Successful Investment Management

Shearson Lehman Brothers
12222 Merit Drive, Suite 1250
Dallas, TX 75251

1 (800) 766-1088
(214) 387-8989
Date of publication: 1988

Covers stocks and bonds.
A brief discussion of money managers, selection criteria, and investment styles.

Investing Your Lump Sum Distribution

Shearson Lehman Brothers
12222 Merit Drive, Suite 1250
Dallas, TX 75251

1 (800) 766-1088
(214) 387-8989
Date of publication: 1988

Covers mortgage-backed securities, bonds (corporate, government, zero-coupon), general investing and financial planning.
Includes financial planning advice, rates of return comparisons, analysis of bond yields, discussions of common investing questions, portfolio suggestions, conservative, moderate, and aggressive investments with risk level discussions.

Lump Sum Distribution - How to Make the Most of Them

Shearson Lehman Brothers
12222 Merit Drive, Suite 1250
Dallas, TX 75251

1 (800) 766-1088
(214) 387-8989
Date of publication: 1989

Covers financial planning.
Includes explanations of retirement distribution alternatives, tax considerations and explanations, and financial planning considerations.

Managing Your IRA

Shearson Lehman Brothers
12222 Merit Drive, Suite 1250
Dallas, TX 75251

1 (800) 766-1088
(214) 387-8989
Date of publication: 1990

Covers mortgage backed securities, bonds (corporate, government, zero-coupon), stocks, general investing, and financial planning.
Includes a discussion of investments suited for individual retirement accounts, including stocks, bonds, mutual funds, CD's, covered options, and financial planning considerations.

Municipal Bonds - Now More Than Ever - An Investor's Guide to Municipal Bonds

Shearson Lehman Brothers
12222 Merit Drive, Suite 1250
Dallas, TX 75251

1 (800) 766-1088
(214) 387-8989
Date of publication: 1990

Covers municipal bonds and financial planning.
Includes an explanation of municipal bonds, tax-exempt status, factors determining the price and yield of a bond, taxable equivalent yields, and tax brackets.

Professional Portfolio Management - Making the Right Choice

Shearson Lehman Brothers
12222 Merit Drive, Suite 1250
Dallas, TX 75251

1 (800) 766-1088
(214) 387-8989
Date of publication: 1990

Covers stocks, bonds, and financial planning.
includes a discussion of money managers, selection criteria, risk vs return, and different money manager styles.

Triple Appeal of Convertible Securities

Shearson Lehman Brothers
12222 Merit Drive, Suite 1250
Dallas, TX 75251

1 (800) 766-1088
(214) 387-8989

Covers bonds and stocks.
A brief explanation of convertible securities and their features, along with a glossary of relevant terms for convertible securities investors.

Zero Coupon Treasuries

Shearson Lehman Brothers
12222 Merit Drive, Suite 1250
Dallas, TX 75251

1 (800) 766-1088
(214) 387-8989
Date of publication: 1988

Covers bonds (government and zero coupon), and financial planning.
Includes a brief discussion of U.S. Treasury zero-coupon bonds, an explanation of relevant terms, and a pricing chart.

A Lifetime Strategy for Investing in Common Stocks

American Association for Individual Investors
625 N. Michigan Avenue
Chicago, IL 60611

PH: (312)280-0170
Cost: Free
Date of first issue: 1981

Covers: stocks. Attempts to explain stock market risk and its relationship to returns.

Magazines, Newspapers and Periodicals

Before ordering a financial publication, it helps to know its major features, frequency, price, and how to order.

Included in this section are most of the major periodicals, magazines, and newspapers designed to help investors.

Investors who specialize in certain types of investments will benefit from unfamiliar listings that focus on one or more subjects.

TABLE OF CONTENTS

America's Finest Companies

Bill Staton Enterprises
Author - Bill Staton
300 East Blvd., Suite B-4
Charlotte, NC 28203

PH: (704) 335-0276
Cost: $11.95 post-paid
Date of first issue: 1991 with annually updates
thereafter
Annual periodical. Includes: earnings analysis.

Over 225 companies with superior records of annual earnings and dividend increases - including 53 with 30 or more years of higher earnings and dividends. Also includes stock symbols, yields, earnings, financial strengths ratings, dividend ratings, dividend reinvestment plan availability, addresses, and phone numbers.

Back-up Tables - Statistical Reports - Closed-end and Open-end Investment Companies

Investment Company Institute
1600 M Street, N.W, Suite 600
Washington, D.C. 20036

PH: (202) 293-7700
Cost: $50.00 annually
Date of first issue: 1989
Monthly periodical. Includes: technical analysis.

Covers mutual funds and bonds, uses tables and graphs. Monthly closed-end report includes total underwritings and new issues for bond and equity categories. There is also an annual survey of closed-end funds providing outstanding assets, annual volume of underwritings, and selected data on a per fund basis. Monthly open-end fund (back-up) tables include the same data as in "Trends in Mutual Fund Activity," except that it is classified by investment objective within method of sale and by asset size.

Barron's National Business & Financial Weekly

Dow Jones & Company, Inc
P.O. Box 7014 Chicopee, MA 01021-9901
200 Burnett Road, Chicopee, MA 01020

PH: (800) 328-6800 subscriptions
(800) 628-9320 info
FAX: (413) 592-4782
Cost: $109.00 annually
Date of first issue: May 1921
Weekly magazine. Regular features: company reviews, market update, stock choices, mutual fund review, bond analysis, money manager interviews.

Special feature issue: Barron's Lipper Gauge - a quarterly report on mutual fund performance, February, May, August, & November.

Continual flow of reliable info on virtually all investment areas. Includes facts, figures, exclusive statistics on the whole range of markets and spotlights individual companies and industries.

Blue Sky Guide

Investment Company Institute
1600 M Street, N.W, Suite 600
Washington, D.C. 20036

PH: (202) 293-7700
Cost: $600.00 initial subscription
$300.00 renewal for updates annually
Date of first issue: 1981
Semi-annual periodical. Includes: fundamental
analysis.

Covers mutual funds. A two-volume reference compendium of registration and regulatory requirements contained in the 50 states' securities laws offering mutual funds and their sales agents.

Bond Guide

Standard & Poor's
25 Broadway
New York, NY 10004

PH: (212) 208-8786
Cost: $185.00 annually

Monthly periodical.

Includes: bond analysis. 224 page guide with 41 columns of descriptive and statistical data on more than 5900 corporate bonds, 650 convertibles, and 280 Canadian and foreign issuers. All registered and coupon bonds identified. Features include S&P debt rating, capitalization data, debt to capital ratios and much more. A special feature, CreditWatch, focuses on fixed income issuers under surveillance for possible ratings changes by S&P' analytical staff.

Bond World

American Banker - Bond Buyer and International Financing Review
1 State Street Plaza
New York, NY 10004

PH: (800) 221-1809
(212) 943-7869
FAX: (212) 943-8216
(800)235-5552
Cost: $795.00
Frequency: Weekly
Date of first issue:

Weekly periodical.
Covers: municipal bonds, corporate bonds, government bonds, foreign bonds, and treasuries. Covers all fixed-income markets including treasuries and corporates. Deals with interest rate trends, investment allocation and deals.

Business International

Business International Corporation and Shirley Dreyfus
215 Park Avenue South
15th Floor
New York, NY 10003

PH: (212) 460-0600
Cost: $650.00
Frequency: Weekly
Date of first issue: 1954

Weekly magazine.
An international trade and investment magazine. Provides global business information, management and marketing techniques and globalization strategy.

Business International Money Reporter

Business International Corporation and Michael Williams
215 Park Avenue South
15th Floor
New York, NY 10003

PH: (212) 750-6300
Cost: $825.00
Frequency: Weekly
Date of first issue: 1975

Weekly magazine.
"A magazine covering performance evaluations, capital restructuring, cash management, exposure management, financing, government regulations, global markets and currency forecasting for corporate financial managers."

Business Week Magazine

McGraw-Hill
1221 Avenue of the Americas
New York, NY 10020

PH: (212) 512-2511
Cost: $39.95 annually
Date of first issue: 1931
ISSN# 0007-7135

Weekly magazine.
Regular specialized features include company reviews and stock choices. Departments include: Cover Story, Top of the News, International, Economic Analysis, Government Industries, The Corporation, People, Finance, Science & Technology, Information Processing, Design, Marketing, and Personal Business. Features include: Business Week Index, Reader's Report, Corrections & Clarifications, Books, Index to Companies, and Editorials.

CDA Mutual Fund Report

CDA Investment Technologies, Inc.
1355 Piccard Drive
Rockville, MD 20850

PH: (800) 232-2285
Cost: $275.00 annually
Date of first issue: 1976

Monthly periodical.
Includes: technical analysis.
Covers mutual funds. This service analyzes the performance, risk posture and percentile rankings of over 1,500 funds. Cornerstone of this report is the "CDA Rating", an overall rating of each fund that takes into account all aspects of performance and risk. Rates of return are calculated for 22 time periods (including bull and bear markets) and each report is mailed 3 days after month-end.

Consensus - National Futures and Financial Weekly

Consensus, Inc.
P.O. Box 411128
Kansas City, MO 64141

PH: (816) 471-3862
FAX: (816) 221-2045
Cost: $365.00 annually
Date of first issue: 1971

Weekly newspaper.
A unique investment newspaper covering commodities, stock indices, currencies, gold, silver, oil, T-bills. Gives you current market letters of brokerage firms, special reports from brokerage firms, graphic consensus index, weekly price quotes of all major futures markets and comprehensive charting of all actively traded futures. Includes free index hotline.

The Economist

Rupert Pennant-Rea
10 Rockefeller Plaza
New York, NY 10020

PH: (212) 541-5730
FAX: (212) 541-9378
Cost: $98.00
Frequency: Weekly
Date of first issue: 1843

Weekly magazine.
An international magazine reporting news, world affairs, business and finance.

Financial Analysts Journal

Association for Investment Management and Research
P.O. Box 3668
Charlottesville, VA 22903

PH: (800) 247-8132
(212) 953-5700
(203)227-4272
FAX: (203) 629-3755
Cost: $150.00 annually
 $48.00 if a member of AIMR
Frequency: Bi-monthly
Date of first issue: 1945

Includes: fundamental analysis. Covers: general investment information. "A practitioner-oriented journal dedicated to the needs of investment professionals...it includes articles describing research in the fields of portfolio management, asset allocation, global investing and security analysis, among others."

Financial Executive

Financial Executives Institute
10 Madison Avenue Box 1938
Morristown, NJ 07962-1938

PH: (201) 898-4642
(212) 689-5777
FAX: (201) 898-4649
Cost: $40.00 annually
Date of first publication: 1934 (formerly Controller)

Bi-monthly magazine.
Regular specialized features: corporate financing and reporting.
An award winning publication in which business executives write articles for senior financial executives in major corporations about both corporate finance and corporate reporting developments. Covers cash management, pension fund management, international finance, information technology, new financial instruments, developments at the SEC & FASB, risk management, investment strategy, and much more.

Financial Freedom Report

Mark O. Haroldsen, Inc.
2450 E. Fort Union Blvd.
Salt Lake City, UT 84121

PH: (801) 943-1280
Cost: $48.00 annually
Date of first publication: 1976

Monthly magazine.
The magazine for high profit investors. Designed for the highly motivates individual who is seeking to establish his own financial freedom, The main emphasis is real estate and income property, but other areas are also examined.

Financial Planning

Securities Data Company, Inc.
40 West 57th Street
8th Floor
New York, NY 10019

PH: (212) 765-5311
(404) 395-1605
FAX: (212) 765-6123
Cost: $48.00
Frequency: Monthly
Date of first issue: 1972

Monthly magazine. Covers: stocks, mutual funds, and assorted investments. "A business magazine for professionals in the financial services industry - financial planners, bankers, insurance agents, stock brokers, lawyers, accountants, securities broker/dealers."

Financial World

Financial World Partners
1328 Broadway
New York, NY 10001

PH: (212) 594-5030
(800) 666-6639
Cost: $39.00 annually

Bi-weekly magazine.
Regular features include company reviews, market update, stock choices, and mutual fund review
Departments: Editor Page, Market Watch, Company Watch, Technology Watch, Systems User, Institution Watch, Financial Planner, Mutual Fund Watch. Columns: Economic Currents, Special Situations, and Speaking Out.

Forbes, Inc.

Malcolm G. Forbes, Jr.
60 Fifth Avenue
New York, NY 10011

PH: (800) 356-3704 subscriptions
(212) 620-2200
Cost: $52.00 annually
Date of first issue: 1917

Bi-monthly magazine.
Regular features: company reviews, international news, and government news.
Outstanding feature issues: Highest Paid CEO's, Annual Forbes 400 (richest Americans), Special Report on International Business, Earnings Forecast for Forbes 500, Annual Mutual Fund Survey, Annual Report on American Industry, Annual Directory Issue.

Short articles of interest to business and financial executives. Gives prospects for industries and individual companies, various financial statistics including the Dow and 5 other major indexes.

Fortune

The Time, Inc. Magazine Co. - James McManus - Editor
Time & Life Building
Rockefeller Center
New York, NY 10020-1393

PH: (212) 522-1212
(800) 633-9970 subscriptions
(800) 621-8000
Cost: $49.95 annually
Date of first issue: Feb 1930

Bi-monthly magazine.
Regular features: company reviews, industry spotlights, market updates, and current news.
Outstanding feature issues: Fortune 500 - (April), The Global 500 - (July), Investor's Guide - (Fall), Service 500 - (June).
Business magazine covering world news, investments, business and company reviews.

Futures

Merrill J. Oster/Oster Publications
219 Parkade
Cedar Falls, Iowa 50603

PH: (319) 277-6341
(800) 635-3931 circulation
(800) 221-4352 ext 645
FAX: (319) 277-7982
Cost: $39.00 annually
Date of first issue:1981 changed from Commodities Magazine

Monthly magazine.
Regular features: market update.
Explores "what, when, & where" of market developments and explains exactly how they will influence future market opportunities. In depth, on-target market news needed to make more informed and more profitable trading decisions.

Global Finance

Global Information, Inc.
55 John Street
7th Floor
New York, NY 10038

PH: (212) 766-5868
FAX: (212) 766-8014
Cost: $60.00
Frequency: Monthly
Date of first issue: 1987

Monthly magazine. An international finance magazine for institutional investors. Covers investing on a large scale. Chapters include: equities, derivatives, mergers and acquisitions, real estate, currencies and more.

Institutional Investor

Institutional Investor
488 Madison Avenue
New York, NY 10022

PH: (212) 303-3300
(800) 437-9997
Cost: $295.00
Frequency: Monthly
Date of first issue: early 70's

Monthly magazine. A magazine which focuses on finance and investing.

Investment Advisor's Guide

Investment Company Institute
1600 M Street, N.W, Suite 600
Washington, D.C. 20036

PH: (202) 293-7700
Cost: $500.00 initial subscription
$200.00 renewals annually

Semi-annual periodical.
Includes: fundamental analysis. Covers regulations. A two-volume reference publication containing information relating to regulation of investment advisors by the SEC, under ERISA, and in all 50 states.

Investment Dealers' Digest

Investment Dealers' Digest, Inc.
150 Broadway
New York, NY 10038

PH: (212) 227-1200
Cost: $375.00 annually
Date of first issue: 1935

Weekly magazine.
Regular features: company reviews, stock choices, bond analysis, stories about firms and exchanges, and market updates. Regular columns: The Week on Wall Street; Firms and Exchanges; Street Names; The Week in Finance; Corporate Finance; For Reference; Issues in Registration, Securities Registered Last Week; Weekly Review of Offerings; Corporate Monthly Roundup; Municipal Market Data; Corporate Market Data; Calendar of Offerings.

Investor's Business Daily

Investor's Daily Inc.
1941 Armacost Avenue
Los Angeles, CA 90025

PH: (213) 207-1832
(800) 443-3113 subscriptions
East Coast: (800) 831-2525
West Coast: (800) 831-2525
Midwest: (800) 992-2126
CA: (800) 621-7863

Illinois: (312) 229-0402
FAX: (213) 473-7551
Cost: $139.00 annually
Date of first issue: April 1984

Daily newspaper.
Regular features: company reviews, market update, stock choices, mutual fund review, bond analysis, and money manager interviews.

Journal of Futures Markets

John Wiley & Sons
605 Third Avenue
New York, NY 10158

PH: (212) 850-6000
Cost: $225.00 annually

Bi-monthly magazine.
Contemporary articles on the futures markets including practical information, theory, corporate hedging, strategy, tax implications, trading analysis, and commodity portfolio optimization.

The Journal of Portfolio Management

Institutional Investor
488 Madison Avenue
New York, NY 10022

PH: (212) 303-3300
(800) 437-9997
Cost: $195.00
Frequency: quarterly
Date of first issue: 1974

Quarterly magazine.
An analytical publication focusing on portfolio management and investment systems.

The Market Chronicle

William B. Dana Co.
213 Silver Beach Avenue
Daytona Beach, FL 32118

PH: (800) 962-3262
Cost: $120.00 annually
Date of first issue: 1960

Weekly newspaper.
Features: company reviews.
A 24 page newspaper which covers company reviews, i.e. general press releases. Also discusses new products on the market.

Money

William S. Myers - Publisher
Jason McManus - Editor
Time & Life Building
Rockefeller Center
New York, NY 10020

PH: (800) 633-9970 subscriptions
(212) 522-1212
Cost: $35.95 annually
Date of first issue: October 1972

Monthly magazine, 2 issues in the fall
Outstanding feature issues: Special year end issue (deals with something different each year) November
Offers solid investment advice on a wide variety of investments. Gives performance data and helpful how-to's for personal investing.

Money Manager Portfolios

H.F. Pearson & Company, Inc.
33 Queen Street
Syosset, NY 11791

PH: (516) 921-7070
Cost: $800.00 annually
Date of first issue: 1980

Quarterly periodical.
Includes: common stock holdings.
The most comprehensive single publication listing all common stock holdings of over 2,500 lending institutions. Includes all institutions filing 13-Fs. Also covers 900 insurance companies, 200 Canadian funds and 300 foreign funds. Each quarterly publication is available in two versions: 1) catalogued by security, 2) catalogued by portfolio.

Money Manager Previews

Wall Street Transcript / Richard Holman
99 Wall Street
New York, NY 10005

PH: (212) 747-9500
FAX: (212) 668-9842
Cost: $2600.00
Frequency: Weekly
Date of first issue: 1987

Weekly magazine.
Covers: money manager interviews. Features interviews and discussions with leading money managers and portfolio strategists throughout the world.

Moody's Bond Record

Moody's Investor Service
99 Church Street
New York, NY 10007

PH: (800) 342-5647 ext 0435
(212) 553-0435
FAX: (212) 553-4700
Cost: $249.00 annually
Dat of first issue: 1969

Monthly periodical.
Regular features: bond analysis
The most comprehensive and authoritative source of statistical data on 56,000 corporate, convertible, government, municipal, environmental control revenue, and international bonds, plus preferred stocks and commercial paper.

Moody's Bond Survey

Moody's Investor Service
99 Church Street
New York, NY 10007

PH: (800) 342-5647
(212) 553-0300
FAX: (212) 553-4700
Cost: $1175.00 annually
First issue: 1981

Weekly periodical.
Regular features: bond analysis and market update.
Gives trends and prospects for the market and for individual bonds. Economic and market condition commentary and opinions, information on factors and issues which influence values of bonds, commercial paper and other debt instruments.

Moody's Dividend Record

99 Church Street
New York, NY 10007

PH: (800) 342-5647
(212) 553-0300
FAX: (212) 553-4700
Cost: $460.00 annually

Quarterly periodical.
Outstanding Feature Issues: Tax Status Supplements (Jan-Feb-March). Annual Dividend Record - compilation of full years dividend information.
Detailed reports of current dividend data covering over 18,300 stocks and Unit Investment Trusts.

Moody's Industry Review

99 Church Street
New York, NY 10007

PH: (800) 342-5647
(212) 553-0300
FAX: (212) 553-4700
Cost: $450.00 annually

Bi-weekly periodical.
Regular features: company reviews.
Comparative statistics and rankings of 4000 leading corporations in 145 industry groups. Every two weeks receive approximately 10 industry reviews. Each is a profile on an industry including company's trading symbol and exchange, 52 week stock price range, earnings per share, book value, stockholder's equity, long term debt, and much more.
COMMENTS: Statistics, rankings and index are all updated twice a year.

Mutual Fund Fact Book

Investment Company Institute
1600 M Street, N.W, Suite 600
Washington, D.C. 20036

PH: (202) 293-7700
Cost: $15.00 annually
Date of first issue: 1988/1989 revised

Annual periodical.
Includes: fundamental analysis.
Covers mutual funds. An annual reference guide which includes annually-updated facts and figure on the U.S. mutual funds industry, including trends in sales, assets, exchanges, and performance. It also outlines the history and growth of the fund industry and its policies, operations, regulation, services, and shareholders.

National Farm Finance News

Dorset Group, Inc.
New York, NY 10001

PH: (212) 563-4273
(800) 327-6346 subscriptions
Cost: $100.00 annually
Date of first issue 1987

Twice a month newspaper.
National Farm Finance News reports on the nation's farm economy. It typically addresses the community of agricultural bankers, foreign bankers and farm home administrators. The newspaper reports on commodity/futures marketing. Several departments include: Biotechnology, Energy/Environment, Mortgages, Earnings, Farm Management, and Book Review.
Features: Commodity/futures markets and company reviews.

The New York Times

229 W. 43rd Street
New York, NY 10036

PH: (800) 631-2500
Cost: $343.20 annually
Date of first publication: 1851

Daily newspaper.
Regular features: economic comments, CD and mortgage rate listings, stock market comments and company reviews.

Oil and Gas Investor

Hart Publications, Inc.
1900 Grant Street, Suite 400
P.O. Box 1917
Denver, CO 80201

PH: (800) 832-1917
(303) 832-1917
Cost: $132.00 annually
$216.00 two years
Date of first publication: 1981
ISSN# 0744-5881

Monthly magazine.
Regular specialized features: company reviews, stock choices, oil and gas investments, and interviews.
The magazine identifies the trends and where the money flows in the oil and gas industry. Investor covers all the major exploration areas, from the Arkansas Basin in Oklahoma, to the Gulf of Mexico, to emerging international plays. Oil and Gas features prominent, interviews with executives of oil and gas companies to find out what makes them successful. Investment Opportunities are identified in drilling ventures, acquisitions, stocks, public funds, and foreign exploration deals.

The Oil Daily

The Oil Daily Co.
1401 New York Avenue N.W.
Washington, DC 20005

PH: (202) 662-0700
(800) 621-0050
FAX: (202) 783-5918
Cost: $597.00 for the daily publication
$397.00 for the weekly publication
Frequency: Monday - Friday
Date of first publication: 1951

Covers: energy industry. A daily newspaper serving the energy industries. Includes tables with the Nationwide Rack Price Survey by company, Global Spot Market Price Review and Spot Cash Markets. Also includes world news items relevant to the energy industry.

On The Wires

Dow Jones News Services
Dow Jones and Company, Inc.
P.O. Box 300
Princeton, NJ 08543-0300

PH: (800) 223-2274
Cost: Free
Frequency: Monthly
Date of first issue:

Monthly periodical. Highlights from the prior broad tape news.

OTC Review

OTC Review, Inc.
37 East 28th
Room 706
New York, NY 10016

PH: (212) 685-6244
FAX: (212) 685-8882
Cost: $84.00
Frequency: Monthly
Date of first issue: 1951

Monthly magazine. "A business and finance magazine featuring investigative reports, company profiles, financial highlights, mergers and acquisitions, foreign investments, statistics and ratings."

The Outlook

Standard & Poor's
25 Broadway
New York, NY 10004

PH: (800) 777-4858
(212) 208-8768
Cost: $280.00 annually

Weekly periodical.
Regular features: stock choice and market update
Analyzes and projects business and stock market trends.
Brief data on individual securities with buy recommendations. Also includes current S&P market indexes.

Pensions & Investments

Crain Communications, Inc.
740 Rush Street
Chicago, IL 60611-2590

PH: (312) 649-5200
(800) 678-9595
FAX: (313) 446-0961
Cost: $135.00 annually
Date of first issue: 1961

Bi-Weekly newspaper.
Regular specialized issues include company reviews, stock articles, bond articles, pension funds, real estate, money manager interviews, and stock and bond indexes.
The newspaper of corporate and institutional investors. Departments include: Frontlines, P&I Indexes, Valuation Index, Commentary, From the Editor, Letter to the Editor, People, Portfolio Management, Money Movers, Classifieds. Also included are articles on financing, international issues, real estate. and special reports.

Pensions and Investments

Crane Communications
740 Rush Street
Chicago, IL 60611

PH: (312) 649-5200
(312) 649-5378
Cost: $135.00 annually
Date of first issue: 1973
Twice a month newspaper.

This newspaper covers corporate and institutional investing, benefits, corporate finance and more.

Pension World

6255 Barfield Road
Atlanta, GA 30328

PH: (404) 256-9800
Cost: $60.00 annually
Date of first issue: 1964

Monthly magazine.
This international magazine is directed towards pension fund investors. Regular features include: coverage of the stock market, employee benefits and more.
Comments: 30,000 in circulation.

Personal Investor

Plaza Communications, Inc.
18818 Teller Avenue, Suite 280
Irvine, CA 92715

PH: (714) 851-2220
(619) 745-2809 subscription
Cost: $9.97 annually
$14.97 for two years
Date of first issue: April 1985
ISSN# 0747-3044

Bi-monthly magazine.
Regular specialized features: company reviews, stock choices, bond analysis, mutual fund review.
The How-To magazine of investment success. Contents include: OUTLOOKS - stocks, mutual funds, retirement, personal finance; SPECIAL FEATURES; DEPARTMENTS - Letters - comments from our readers, Oddlots, Fundscope - The hottest mutual funds, Closed-End Corner - Shopping for bargains, Computerline - sleuthing for stocks on a computer, Index - a listing of companies mentioned in this issue, Trends - The big picture, Personal Advisor - the pro's top picks, and It's Only Funny.

Perspective on Mutual Fund Activity

Investment Company Institute
1600 M Street, N.W, Suite 600
Washington, D.C. 20036

PH: (202) 293-7700
Cost: $30.00 annually
Date of first issue: 1983

Annual periodical.
Includes: technical analysis.
Covers mutual funds and uses graphs.
An annual analysis by the Institute's research department of recent economic trends and their impact on the mutual fund industry. Includes numerous statistical groups.

Security Traders' Monthly

Investment Dealers' Digest, Inc.
#2 World Trade Center, 18th Floor
New York, NY 10048

PH: (212)227-1200
Cost: $76.00 per year
Frequency: Monthly
Date of first issue:

Monthly magazine.
News of general interest to securities traders including: monthly news review, 'Market Movers In the News,' 'For Your Information,' 'Changing Times,' 'The Buy Side,' and information about the various exchanges.

Spectrum Publications

CDA Technologies
1355 Piccard
Rockville, MD 20850

PH: (301) 975-9600
FAX: (301) 590-1350
Cost: from $250.00

Periodicals: quarterly and monthly depending on publication.
Covers: stocks and convertibles
Reports the holdings and changes in holdings of common stocks and convertibles as reported to the SEC. Publications include: Investment Company Stock Holdings Survey, 13(F) Institutional Portfolios, 5% Ownership Based on 13D, 13G, & 14D-1 FIlings, Insider Ownership Based on Forms 3&4, 13(F) Holdings Survey of COnvertible Bonds and Convertible Preferred Stocks, Institutional Holdings & Ownership Data of Worldwide Securities.

Standard & Poor's Credit Week

Standard & Poor's
25 Broadway
New York, NY 10004

PH: (800) 777-4858
(212) 208-8768
Cost: $1695.00 annually

Weekly periodical.
Regular features: bond analysis.
Focuses on trends and outlooks for fixed income securities including corporate and government bonds and money market instruments. Offers the latest info on S&P's new and changed ratings for corporate, municipal and structured issuers.

Standard & Poor's Emerging and Special Situations

Standard & Poor's
25 Broadway
New York, NY 10004

PH: (800) 777-4858
(212) 208-8768
Cost: $210.00 annually
First issue: 1982

Monthly periodical.
Regular features: stock choices and new issues.
Points out lesser known stocks which S&P's analysts deem to be overlooked and undervalued. Alerts investors to the growth situations that have appreciation potential. Also provides a regarded analysis of new issues before they go public.

Statistical Reports - Unit Investment Trusts

Investment Company Institute
1600 M Street, N.W, Suite 600
Washington, D.C. 20036

PH: (202) 293-7700
Cost: $50.00 annually
Date of first issue: 1985

Monthly periodical.
Includes: technical analysis. Covers investment trusts.
Monthly report that includes value and number of deposits of new trusts by type, maturity, and insurance feature.

The Stocks, Bonds, Bills & Inflation Yearbook

Ibbotson Associates, Inc.
8 S. Michigan Avenue, 7th Floor
Chicago, IL 60603

PH: (313) 263-3435
FAX: (312) 263-1398
Cost: $85.00 annually

Annual periodical
Covers: stocks, intermediate and long-term government bonds, long-term corporate bonds, U.S. T-Bills, and inflation. A hard bound reference book which provides high quality authoritative data on the most important U.S. asset classes. These monthly and annual data begin in 1926, giving a comprehensive historical view of the behavior of capital markets. Extensive graphs are included.
COMMENTS: Quarterly reports available for $585.00 includes Yearbook and Forecast Edition.
Monthly reports are available for $1085.00 - includes quarterly reports, Yearbook and Forecast Edition.

Stock Guide

Standard & Poor's
25 Broadway
New York, NY 10004

PH: (212) 208-8786
Cost: $112.00 annually

Monthly periodical.
Information on stock investment data and mutual fund review.
Unique 260 page guide to investment data on over 5300 common and preferred stocks, listed and OTC, providing rapid reviews of all issues with 48 items of data on each. Data includes: S&P earnings and dividend rankings, S&P earnings estimates, monthly high/low prices and volume, stock symbol, historical price ranges, summaries of financial positions and more. Also includes performance summary of over 500 mutual funds.

Taking Stock

Dallas Business Journal
Jack Bick - Editor
4131 N. Central Expressway, Suite. 310
Dallas, TX 75204-9699

PH: (214) 520-1010
Cost: $9.95 annually
Date of first issue: 1989

Annual periodical.
Regular features: company reviews.
Information about every public company in the DFW Metroplex area that has revenue of at least $10 million. Ranked by revenue (includes earnings, dividend information, number of employees, exchange and symbol, business description and chief executive) also listed alphabetically.

Technical Analysis of Stocks and Commodities

Technical Analysis, Inc.
3517 S. W. Alaska Street
Seattle, WA 98126

PH: (800) 832-4642
        (206) 938-0570
Cost: $64.95 annually
Date of first issue: 1982

Monthly magazine.
All about charts and computer applications that can help you profit in today's market. Includes cycles, charts, patterns, systems, real trades, statistics, psychology reviews, indicators and oscillators.

Trader's Magazine

Trader's Magazine, Inc.
40 West 57th Street
Suite 802
New York, NY 10019

PH: (212)265-4610
Cost: $60.00
Frequency: Monthly
Date of first issue: 1987

Monthly magazine. A magazine about people in the investment industry and their personalities.

Trends in Mutual Fund Activity - Statistical Reports - Open End Investment Companies

Investment Company Institute
1600 M Street, N.W, Suite 600
Washington, D.C. 20036

PH: (202) 293-7700
Cost: $120.00 annually
Date of first issue: 1981

Monthly periodical.
Includes: technical analysis.
Covers mutual funds and uses graphs.
Monthly news releases with accompanying tables describing mutual fund sales, redemptions, assets, cash positions, exchange activity, and portfolio transactions classified by investment objective, fund size, and method of distribution. Quarterly sales data for long-term funds is provided on a state-by-state basis. An annual report provides statistics on shareholder accounts, withdrawal accounts, and IRA and KEOGH assets and accounts.

USA Today

Gannett Company, Inc.
1000 Wilson Blvd.
Arlington, VA 22229

PH: (800) USA-0001
 (703) 276-3400
FAX: (301) 622-6039
Cost: $130.00
Frequency: Daily (M-F)
Date of first issue: 1982

Daily periodical.
A national newspaper. The second section is called "Money" and is devoted to financial news. Also gives NY, American, NASDAQ and Mutual fund quotes.

US News and World Report

Mortimer B. Zuckerman
2400 N. Street N.W.
Washington, DC 20037-1196

PH: (212) 326-5300
(202) 955-2000
(800) 234-2450
Cost: $39.00 annually and other special rates
Date of first issue: 1948

Weekly magazine.
Outstanding Feature Issues: Investment Outlook (December).
An independent news magazine serving 12 million readers by focusing on the events and forces that shape their lives." Organized into 6 distinct sections: Outlook, U.S. News, World Report, Business, News You Can Use, and Science and Society.

Wall Street Computer Review

Gralla Publications
1515 Broadway
New York, NY 10036

PH: (212) 869-1300
(212) 488-9001
FAX: (212) 553-4700
Cost: $65.00 annually
Date of first issue: 1983

Monthly magazine.
Regular features: company reviews.
Outstanding Feature Issues: Buying Guide - November or December
Gives readers the latest information on hardware and software developments that are crucial to a strong bottom line.

Wall Street Journal

Dow Jones & Company, Inc
World Financial Center
200 Liberty Street
New York, New York 10281

PH: (800) 628-9320
Customer Service: (212) 416-2000
Cost: $139.00 annually
Date of first issue: 10/21/29

Daily newspaper.
Regular features: company reviews, market update, stock choices, mutual fund review, bond analysis, and money manager interviews.
A daily newspaper of national and international news. Composed of three sections: 1) front-page news, 2) business - economic news - "Marketplace", 3) money rates, stock quotes, mutual funds, bonds - "Money & Investing."

Wall Street Transcript

Richard A. Holman
99 Wall Street
New York, NY 10005

PH: (212) 747-9500
Cost: $1890.00 annually
Date of first issue: 1964

Weekly newspaper.
Regular features: company reviews and money manager reviews.
Reproduces selected brokerage house reports on companies and individuals, discussions on a leading industry or topic by leading analysts, interviews with money managers and top CEO's. Options news, technical analysis.

Wiesenberger's Mutual Funds Panorama

Warren, Gorham, & Lamont, Inc.
210 South Street
Boston, MA 02111

PH: (800) 950-1209
(617) 423-2020
Cost: $50.00

Annual periodical.
Includes: fundamental analysis of mutual funds.
A statistical review of pertinent data concerning virtually all mutual funds registered for sales in the United States. Information provided includes: year of organization, primary objective, investment policy, statistical data, dividend data, fees & expenses, shareholder's services, information and complete list of addresses and phone numbers for funds.

Financial Television Programs

All news is investment relevant. This chapter does not attempt to list all news sources. While the Computer and Quote Services section provides online news services, television programs focusing on the financial markets can be an extremely valuable tool. Programs focused on investing usually give analysis and commentary that helps interpret the impact of news on the financial markets.

This section lists the major national programs and networks that concentrate on investment news and trends. Knowledge of the most popular programs allows an investor to choose the most appropriate. It could take weeks to find and review the most popular national investment programs. The Financial Television Programs chapter helps eliminate a time consuming search.

Each program and network is listed with a phone number or address for more specific program information and local times.

TABLE OF CONTENTS

Adam Smith's Money World

1329 Braddock Place
Alexandria, VA 22314

PH: (703) 739-5000
Broadcast Times: 8:30 pm
Broadcast Dates: Friday
Cable/Network: PBS

World economy and financial matters.

Business Day

One CNN Center
Atlanta, GA 30348

PH: (404) 827-1503
Broadcast Times: 7:30 am
Broadcast Dates: Monday - Friday
Cable/Network: CNN
Anchor/Editor: Stuart Varney

Economy, market activity, international and domestic events relevant to the investment community. Spotlights companies in the news and has special guests addressing specific topics.

Business Morning

One CNN Center
Atlanta, GA 30348

PH: (404) 827-1503
Broadcast Times: 6:30 am
Broadcast Dates: Monday - Friday
Cable/Network: CNN
Anchor/Editor: Stuart Varney and Deborah Marchine

International and domestic general business news.

CNBC/FNN

Consumer News and Business Channel/Financial News
Network
2200 Fletcher Avenue
Ft. Lee, NJ 07024

PH: (201) 585-2622
 (800) SMART-TV
Cable/Network: CNBC/FNN

Ongoing investment programming covering all investment subjects and news. Has constant market updates and non-stop ticker tape. Call 800-SMART-TV to order programming directory.

Headline News

One CNN Center
Atlanta, GA 30348

International news summary reports the latest business and financial news. Constant non-stop ticker.

PH: (404) 827-1500
Broadcast Times: every 1/2 hour - 15 minutes and 45 minutes after each hour
Broadcast Dates: Daily
Cable/Network: CNN

Market to Market

1329 Braddock Place
Alexandria, VA 22314

Weekly journal of the farming industry. Gives general economic news and figures also. Discusses current and pending legislation and programs affecting the farming industry. Also addresses current R&D, and gives a market overview and forecast of the commodities and futures markets.

PH: (703) 739-5000
Broadcast Times: Check Local Listing
Broadcast Dates: Check Local Listing
Cable/Network: PBS
Anchor/Editor: Mark Pearson

McNeil / Lehrer Newshour

1329 Braddock Place
Alexandria, VA 22314

General domestic and international news.

PH: (703) 739-5000
Broadcast Times: Check local listings
Broadcast Dates: Check local listings
Cable/Network: PBS
Anchor/Editor: Robert McNeil and Jim Lehrer

MoneyLine

One CNN Center
Box 105366
Atlanta, GA 30348

Economy, banking and Savings and Loan industries, insurance industry, personal finance. Data on major U.S. markets and stock closing prices. International and economic news. Comments: General financial news - both domestic and international.

PH: (404) 827-1503
Broadcast Times: 5:00 pm & 9:30 pm
Broadcast Dates: Monday - Friday
Cable/Network: CNN
Anchor/Editor: Lou Dobbs with Myron Kandell as an analyst

Money Week

One CNN Center
Atlanta, GA 30348

PH: (404) 827-1503
Broadcast Times: 3:30 am - Sunday
11:30 am - Sunday
7:30 am - Saturday
Cable/Network: CNN
Anchor/Editor: Lou Dobbs

Economy. Recap of the week's economic activity, indicators, news and market activity and wrap-up.

Nightly Business Report

1329 Braddock Place
Alexandria, VA 22314

PH: (703)739-5000
Broadcast Times: Check Local Listing
Broadcast Dates: Check Local Listing
Cable/Network: PBS
Anchor/Editor: Paul Kangas and Cassie Siefert

Information on the economy, Wall Street, stock market commentary and data. All other major markets including currencies and precious metals and company spotlights in the news.

The Wall Street Journal Report

30 Rockefeller Center
New York, NY 10012

PH: (212) 664-4444
Broadcast Times: 6:00 am
Broadcast Dates: Sunday
Cable/Network: NBC
Anchor/Editor: Consuela Mack

Economic news and data, pending legislation and important news of the week. Features guest speakers/ experts for commentary on current issues and conditions.

Wall Street Week

1329 Braddock Place
Alexandria, VA 22314

PH: (703) 739-5000
Broadcast Times: 6:30 pm - Friday
9:30 am - Sunday
Cable/Network: PBS
Anchor/Editor: Louis Rukeyser

Begins with recap of week's economic news and events and market activity. Then panelists and special guests discuss the economy and the markets.

Your Money

One CNN Center
Atlanta, GA 30348

PH: (404) 827-1503
Broadcast Times: 7:30 am - Sunday
 1:30 pm - Saturday
Cable/Network: CNN
Anchor/Editor: Stuart Varney

Money. Interest rates, mortgages, loans, education, market data and economic news. Helpful tips and information on all aspects of personal finances. Comments: Features question and answer segment for write-in viewers.

Books and Tapes on Investing

This is the largest section. There are thousands of good books published on the subject of investing and money. To avoid creating an infinite bibliography, this section has been limited to books that provide current or timeless information on investing and investment strategies. Biographies and books on predictions and economics are included only if they provide a focus on discussion of investing or strategy.

Investors are urged to use the cross reference to focus their search on specific investment areas. Stocks, bonds, options, futures and commodities, mutual funds, and financial planning books are all listed by subject in the cross reference section. Each book is described and a source to order the book is provided. In many cases, the source to order may not be the publisher. This was done to save time and provide easier ordering procedures. The price, original publishing date, date of most recent update, and how to order are listed with each book.

As more books are published on investing, it becomes crucial for investors not to waste their reading time. Before spending money on a book, check its description to make sure it is providing the desired information. Investors may also find better books on which to spend their time and money by having a large list of recognized books on investing. Again, none of the publications in this section are guaranteed or specifically recommended.

TABLE OF CONTENTS

1993 Stock Trader's Almanac

Hirsch Organization, Inc.
6 Deer Trail
Old Tappan, NJ 07675

PH: (201) 644-3400
Published 1992
Cost: $24.95

The Almanac is an annual appointment calendar that is also considered the "definitive reference work on seasonal trading patterns." It is famous for its market lore in the form of daily quotations. In addition, the 1992 edition of the "Almanac" contains: a directory of Seasonal Trading Patterns, a strategy planning and record section, updates of new techniques and tools, reminders of seasonal opportunities and dangers, monthly almanacs, every form needed for portfolio planning, recordkeeping and tax preparation.

ABC's of Agricultural Options

Commodities Education Institute
219 Parkade
Cedar Falls, IA 50613

PH: (800) 635-3936
(319) 277-6341
FAX: (319) 277-7982
Published 1991 updated
Cost: $55.00

VIDEO
Subjects addressed: trading analysis, options trading. Learn how, when properly managed, options can serve as "price insurance" in your marketing plan. You'll cover terminology, puts and calls, evaluating an options move versus a minimum price contract, and specific ways to determine whether to use options, futures, or the cash market.

ABC's of Price Risk Management

Commodities Education Institute
219 Parkade
Cedar Falls, IA 50613

PH: (800) 635-3936
(319) 277-6341
FAX: (319) 277-7982
Published 1990
Cost: $55.00

VIDEO
Subjects addressed: commodities trading. Learn how to use the marketing system to forward price the commodities you provide. Understand the terminology and basic principles behind hedging, futures trading, basis, mechanics of a brokerage account and controlling your pricing decisions.

ABC's of Technical Analysis

Commodities Education Institute
219 Parkade
Cedar Falls, IA 50613

PH: (800) 635-3936
(319) 277-6341
FAX: (319) 277-7982
Published 1991 updated
Cost: $55.00

VIDEO
Subjects addressed: commodities trading, trading analysis, technical analysis. Technical expert Wayne Purcell shows you how to use price charts and indicators in your trading. He'll help you understand trend lines, support/resistance, gaps, corrections, head & shoulders formations, reversals, RSI and other key tools.

Active Asset Allocation: State-of-the-Art Portfolio Policies, Strategies & Tactics

Robert D. Arnott & Frank J. Fabozzi, Editors
Probus Publishing Co.
1925 North Clybourn Avenue
Chicago, IL 60614

PH: (800) PROBUS-1
FAX: (312) 868-6250
ISBN: 1-55738-237-9
Published 1991
Cost: $65.00

Subjects addressed: investing theories. This revised edition is a comprehensive overview of the critical issues, theories and portfolio management practices that are successfully employed in today's domestic and global markets. The proven strategies and tactics presented here are the culmination of the expertise of eminent theoreticians and practitioners in the field. The nineteen authors focus on three major areas of asset allocation: policy asset mix and portfolio insurance, optimization and surplus management, tactical asset allocation. Comments: an institutional investor publication.

Active Total-Return Management of Fixed Income Portfolios

Ravi E. Dattatreya and Frank J. Fabozzi
Probus Publishing Co.
1925 North Clybourn Avenue
Chicago, IL 60614

PH: (800) PROBUS-1
FAX: (312) 868-6250
ISBN: 1-55738-049-X
Published 1989
Cost: $65.00

Presents guidelines that market participants can employ to enhance returns. The framework presented here is applicable to both active strategies and structured portfolio strategies. Contents include: the first generation: duration analysis; the second generation: parametric analysis; the other side of the equation: horizon return; making the right assumptions: internal and external consistency; options and their parametric characteristic; analysis of callable bonds; analysis of mortgage-backed securities; using futures and options to modify total returns.

The Adam Theory of Markets

Trend Research Ltd./J. Welles Wilder, Jr.
P.O. Box 128
McLeansville, NC 27301

PH: (919) 698-0500
Published 1986
Cost: $65.00

Subjects addressed: commodities trading, stock analysis, market analysis, technical analysis; uses charts. Presents a revolutionary concept about markets... about how markets really work and how they move relative to price and time.

Adjustable Rate Mortgages and Mortgage Backed Securities: The Complete Reference Guide for Originators, Issuers, and Investors

Jess Lederman and Margaret A. Celic, Editors
Business One Irwin
1818 Ridge Road
Homewood, IL 60430

PH: (708) 206-2700
(800) 634-3966
FAX: (708) 798-1490
ISBN: 1-55623-232-2
Published 1991
Cost: $90.00

The most comprehensive overview of the market for ARMs and ARM securities ever compiled. Includes important tables of historical ARM index values and more.

Advanced Commodity Trading Techniques

J.D. Hamon
Windsor Books
P.O. Box 280
Brightwaters, NY 11718

ISBN: 0-930233-06-9
Published 1986 (3rd edition)
Cost: $65.00

Information designed to create winning commodity traders with long-lasting profitable ventures into the futures market. Reports the findings of extensive research into the laws governing market phenomenon, conducted by the HAP Research Investment Study Group. Introduces several valuable new techniques developed as a result.

Advances and Innovations in the Bond and Mortgage Markets

Frank J. Fabozzi, Editor
Probus Publishing Co.
1925 North Clybourn Avenue
Chicago, IL 60614

PH: (800) PROBUS-1
FAX: (312) 868-6250
ISBN: 1-55738-016-3
Published 1989
Cost: $65.00

Frank J. Fabozzi has assembled the finest minds of institutional players in the debt markets to present state-of-the-art strategies and advanced analytical techniques for debt instruments. Topics include: the changing corporate bond market, agency Eurobond and foreign bond markets, mortgage-backed and asset backed securities, futures and interest rate agreements.

The Affluent Investor

NY Institute of Finance
Stephen P. Rappaport
2 Broadway
New York, NY 10004-2207
Published 1990
Cost: $24.95

Subjects addressed: investing theories, stock analysis, market analysis, bond analysis, trading analysis Investment strategies for all markets

After the Crash: New Investment Strategies for Survivors

Donna Sammons Carpenter
Contemporary Books
180 N. Michigan Avenue
Chicago, IL 60601

PH: (312) 782-9181
ISBN: 0-8092-4525-6
Published 1988
Cost: $7.95

Over 100 financial experts, basing their assessments on market conditions after the crash of 1987, offer the information you need to survive in today's turbulent economy. Assesses the damage, then analyzes the outlook for cash and cash equivalents, fixed-income instruments, equities, 100 hot stocks, real estate, and hard assets.

The Analysis and Forecasting of Long-Term Trends in the Cash and Futures Markets

Jake Bernstein
Probus Publishing Co.
1925 Clybourn Avenue
Chicago, IL 60614

PH: (800) PROBUS-1
FAX: (312) 868-6250
Published 1989
Cost: $137.50

Subjects addressed: market analysis, technical analysis. A purely technical approach to weathering today's market volatility. "This power packed information examines the various technical tools and methodologies by which long-range forecasts and trends can be determined."

Analysis of Financial Statements

Leopold A. Bernstein
Available through Business One Irwin
1818 Ridge Road
Homewood, IL 60430

PH: (708) 206-2700
(800) 634-3966
FAX: (708) 798-1490
ISBN: 0-87094-494-0
Published 1984 (2nd edition)
Cost: $39.50

Revised edition continues to provide the best information on the tools and techniques required to intelligently analyze financial statement: including the analysis of short-term liquidity, funds flow, capital structure, return on investments, and results of operations. For those who must make decisions based on financial data.

Analytical Methods for Successful Speculation

James E. Schildgen
Capital Futures Associates, LTD
P.O. Box 2618
Chicago, IL 60690

PH: (312) 274-9254
ISBN: 0-939397-00-5
Published 1986
Cost: $49.95

The complete book of trading systems, comprising all major technical and fundamental analytical methods applied to gold from 1975 to 1985. All methods are briefly yet clearly explained and objectively presented. Choose those that interest you most from over 40 systems. Illustrated with computer studies graphically portrayed.

Anatomy of a Crash - 1929

J.R. Levien
Fraser Publishing Company
P.O. Box 494
Burlington, VT 05402

PH: (802) 658-0322
037-9
Cost: $8.00

Compiled by Levien in 1966, offering a clear picture of the events that happened together with the idea of what people thought was happening. Actual material is taken from the pages of the New York Times during 1929. There is a chronology of financial events for the year and a listing of new articles during the Crash. None of the original data has been altered, no comments are given, and you may fit the facts into your own thinking mechanism.

The Arms Index (TRIN)

Richard W. Arms, Jr.
Business One Irwin
1818 Ridge Road
Homewood, IL 60430

PH: (800)634-3966
FAX: (708)748-1490
ISBN: 1-55623-101-6
Published: 1989
Cost: $62.50

Covers investing theories and market analysis. An in-depth look at how volume - not time - governs stock price changes. Shows you how the Arms Index helps you make more profitable market decisions. Uses Arms' own system to forecast the price changes of individual issues as well as market indexes.

Art of Contrary Thinking

Humphrey B. Neill
Caxton Printers, LTD
312 Main Street
Caldwell, ID 83605

PH: (800) 456-8791
ISBN: 0-87004-110-C
Cost: $4.95

Fifth enlarged edition. The originator of the Theory of Contrary opinion answers the questions: Contrary Opinion - What is it? What will it do for me? This is the workbook of Contrary Opinion, for anyone seeking to benefit from the contrary approach in analyzing trends.

The Art of Speculation

Philip L. Carret
Fraser Publishing Company
P.O. Box 494
Burlington, VT 05402

PH: (802) 658-0322
ISBN: 0-87034-050-6
Published 1924
Cost: $16.00

First written in 1924, this is a reprint of the revised 1930 edition. The author, the founder of the Pioneer Fund, is still alive and working in the investment arena today. Looking back in his book, Carret is more than ever convinced that speculation is an art rather than a science.

Assessing Risk on Wall Street

Thomas A. Rorro
Liberty Publishing Company, Inc.
440 S. Federal Highway
Suite B-3
Deerfield Beach, FL 33441

PH: (305) 360-9000
ISBN: 0-89709-134-5
Published 1984
Cost: $19.95

A novel look at investing from the perspective of both risk and profit potential. Starts with basic investment building blocks and progresses to the application of powerful statistical tools. Explains the techniques required to evaluate risk before the investment is made. Uses capital market line to illustrate performance.

Asset Allocation: Balancing Financial Risk

Roger C. Gibson
Business One Irwin
1818 Ridge Road
Homewood, IL 60430

PH: (708) 206-2700
(800) 634-3966
FAX: (708) 798-1490
ISBN: 1-55623-164-4
Published 1990
Cost: $34.50

The first comprehensive, practical book dedicated to asset allocation from a nationally recognized authority. Explains how to involve clients in the decision making process. Essential reading for anyone who advises individuals or small institutional clients regarding their investment of money.

Asset/Liability Management

Atsuo Konishi and Frank J. Fabozzi, Editors
Probus Publishing Co.
1925 North Clybourn Avenue
Chicago, IL 60614

PH: (800) PROBUS-1
FAX: (312) 868-6250
Published 1991
Cost: $69.95

Addresses "gap" management - that is, a bank's or thrift's ability to match maturities of its deposits with the length of its loan commitments and other liabilities. This book shows bank and thrift managers how to: measure interest rate risk exposure; use interest rate controls tools (futures, options, swaps, caps and floors); develop optimal strategies within the framework of the new capital guidelines for banks; develop and implement liability and funding strategies. The authors have combined the work of experts from every pertinent area of ALM to provide an all-inclusive, up-to-date picture of this rapidly growing field.

Asset/Liability Management Techniques

Bill Williams
Probus Publishing Co.
1925 North Clybourn Avenue
Chicago, IL 60614

PH: (800)PROBUS-1
FAX: (312)868-6250
Published:
Cost: $25.00

Learn how to: initiate effective short- and long-range matching techniques to attain or maintain asset/liability balance in the portfolio, recognize various types of swaps and how to use interest rate swaps to hedge against potential earnings losses, use options as an effective hedging tool, take a realistic approach to measuring the interest rate risk exposure presented by swaps.

Astro-Cycles & Speculative Markets

L.J. Jenson
Lambert Gann Publishing Company
P.O. Box O
Pomeroy, WA 99347

PH: (800)228-0324
Published 1978
Cost: $25.00

From the pioneer in American astro-research. Learn to pinpoint weeks in advance the Longitude and Latitude of where a trend will be centered, and how it will affect business, weather, or a natural disaster. A major contribution to scholarship in the field of economic forecasting.

The A-Z of Wall Street: 2,500 Terms for the Street Smart Investor

Sandra S. Hildreth
Longman Financial Services, Publisher
520 N. Dearborn Street
Chicago, IL 60610

Published: 1988
Cost: $12.50

Definitions. Written for both the individual investor and the investment professional, this book contains over 2,500 clearly written definitions of common investment words and phrases. Readers will find concise explanation of correction, initial public offering and zero coupon bond, as well as many new words tied to current events on Wall Street. Figures and stock pages from the Wall Street Journal and Standard and Poor's give further explanation.

Barron's Finance and Investment Handbook

John Downes and Jordan Elliot Goodman
Barron's (Publishing)
250 Wireless Blvd.
Hauppauge, NY 11788

PH: (516) 434-3311
Published 1986, 1990 (updated)
Cost: $26.95

The one indispensable desk reference for all your financial planning and personal investing needs. Dictionary of 2500 financial and investing terms, name, address, & phone numbers for NYSE, AMEX, OTC stocks, & mutual funds, historical market and economic data, how to read financial news, annual reports, ticker tape and much, much, more. Over 1200 pages.

Basic Gann Techniques

Commodities Education Institute
219 Parkade
Cedar Falls, IA 50613

PH: (800) 635-3936
(319) 277-6341
FAX: (319) 277-7982
Published 1990
Cost $55.00

VIDEO
Subjects addressed: investing theories, technical analysis Glen Ring reviews the technical approach to markets and basic Gann tools. Part of a series of 5 tapes available for $233.00.

The Basics of Investing

Benton E. Gup
John Wiley and Sons, Inc.
605 Third Avenue
New York, NY 10158-0012

PH: (212) 850-6418 orders
(212) 850-6233 info.
ISBN: 0-471-82146-2
Published 1986 (3rd edition)
Cost $44.95

Reviews securities, options, commodities, tax shelters, works of art, and more. Explains proven methods for analyzing investment opportunities, whether in stocks, oil wells, or diamonds. Examines timing techniques, and considers what to expect from stockbrokers, investment advisors, financial planners, and computer programs.

Beating the Dow

Michael O'Higgins/Harper Collins Publisher
10 E. 53rd Street
New York, NY 10022
Published 1991
Cost: $19.95

Subjects addressed: investing theories, stock analysis; uses charts. High return - low risk method for investing in the Dow Jones Ind. stocks with as little as $5000.00.

Behavior of Prices in Wall Street

Authur A. Merrill
Analysis PR.
3300 Darby Road #3325
Haverford, PA 19041

PH: (215) 642-2011
ISBN: 0-911894-49-7
Published 1966,1984 (revised 2nd edition)
Cost $38.00

Subject: market timing. This book concentrates on the profitable study of timing. The text of this book is addressed to non-mathematical investors. It is a concisely-written volume and is considered the classic guide to typical market behavior. Topics covered include: the Presidential Cycle, monthly, weekly, and daily patterns, holiday behavior, Dow Theory, the influence of Fed policy and much more.

Best Ways to Make Money Now

Editors of Money Magazine
Money Books
P.O. Box 2463
Birmingham, AL 35201

PH: (800)765-6400
Published 1991
Cost: $19.95

Discover the hottest investments of the decade, getting in on the European Boom, how to profit from the S & L crisis and how to make sure your money market funds are safe. Also covers college budgeting plans, home selling tips and more.

A Better Way to Make Money: A Simple and Practical Plan of Investing and Trading in Stock and Grain Markets

Burton H. Pugh
Lambert Gann Publishing Company
P.O. Box O
Pomeroy, WA 99347

PH: (800)228-0324
ISBN: 0-939093-09-X
Published 1948 (1956 reprint)
Cost: $20.00

Reprint of 1948 text tells specifically what kind of stocks to buy, and when to buy and sell them. Describes a simple system by which anyone can profit - without studying the latest financial news, earnings, or dividend rates, and without keeping abreast of the statistics, money market, crop situation, foreign trade, or politics.

Beyond the Investor's Quotient: The Inner World of Investing

Jacob Bernstein
John Wiley and Sons
605 Third Avenue
New York, NY 10158-0012

PH: (212) 850-6418 orders
(212) 850-6233 info.
ISBN: 0-471-82062-8
Published 1986
Cost: $19.95

The Investor's Quotient unraveled the mystery behind investor behavior; this work takes you one critical step closer to success as a trader or investor. Presents specific methods of self-analysis - proven techniques to help you find your direction, define your objectives, choose your methods, and keep your eye on long-term goals.

The Big Hitters: Interviews with the World's Foremost Market Movers

Kevin Koy
Intermarket Publishing Corp.
401 S. LaSalle Street
Suite 1100
Chicago, IL 60605

PH: (312) 922-4300
ISBN: 0-937453-00-5
Published 1986
Cost: $24.95

Meet the select few, and learn what distinguishes them from the crowd. Eleven trading and investment experts share their experiences, insights, and trading skills. Their market know-how and success strategies, spelled out in question-and-answer format, can become the cornerstone of your own trading approach and philosophy.

Blood in the Streets: Investment Profits in a World Gone Mad

James Dale Davidson & Sir William Rees-Mogg
Warner Books
66 5th Avenue
New York, NY 10103

PH: (800)638-6460
ISBN: 0-671-62735-X
Published 1985
Cost: $21.95

Also available in paperback
ISBN: 0-446-35316-7
Published 1988
Cost: $5.95

Using straightforward language, the authors provide a roadmap to understanding the relationships between politics, the mechanics of markets, and the way people respond to crisis. They uncover the hidden meanings behind current events and make specific recommendations for capitalizing on those events. Replete with revelations.

Bond Index Funds

Sharmin Mossavar-Rahmani
Probus Publishing Co.
1925 North Clybourn Avenue
Chicago, IL 60614

PH: (800) PROBUS-1
FAX: (312) 868-6250
ISBN: 1-55738-014-7
Published 1991
Cost: $65.00

Explains the bond indexing concept in detail and shows how it applies to a comprehensive overall investment strategy. Topics include: selecting an appropriate index, setting up and managing optimal index funds, actively managing enhanced index funds, implications of indexing for the fixed income market. Appendices include a detailed profile of the major U.S. institutional investments in bond index funds, as well as a special section on selecting an index fund advisor.

The Bond Book: Everything Investors Need to Know About Munis, Treasuries, GNMAs, Funds, Zeroes, Corporates, Money Markets and More

Annette Thau
Probus Publishing Co.
1925 North Clybourn Avenue
Chicago, IL 60614

PH: (800) PROBUS-1
FAX: (312) 868-6250
ISBN: 1-55738-248-4
Published 1991
Cost: $29.95

Subjects addressed: bond analysis. "The Bond Book" was written and developed for the individual who has some general knowledge in the financial markets but lacks the sophistication and confidence to develop active strategies in fixed income securities. The first section of this book serves as a refresher course, providing a general background of how the debt market works and the various types of risks involved. Part Two is devoted to the major types of fixed income instruments. Part Three shows the reader how to "put it all together" with state-of-the-art portfolio management geared specifically to the individual investor.

Bulls, Bears, and Dogs: A Stock Market Strategy

Jason E. Farber & Geoffrey R. Barger
Albright Press
12240 Blythen Way
Oakland, CA 94619

ISBN: 0-918301-00-9
Published 1984
Cost: $13.95
Also available in paperback
ISBN: 0-918301-25-4
Cost: $7.95

The keys to successful investing. Subjects covered include: buying and selling stocks; timing and cycles; market analysts, market services, and brokers; the effect of news on the market; money supply, interest rates, and the Federal Reserve; P/E ratios; contrary opinion; fundamental and technical analysis; the wave theories.

The Burning Match

J. F. Straw
301 Plymouth Drive N. E.
Dalton, GA 30721-9983

Subjects addressed: stock analysis. A booklet detailing how you can win (consistently) trading the stock markets.

PH: (404) 259-6035
Published 1990
Cost: $10.00

The Burning Match

J.F. (Jim) Straw
301 Plymouth Drive N.E.
Dalton, GA 30721-9983

PH: (404) 259-6035
Cost: $395.00 (includes four 1 hour tapes plus a 53 page workbook)

VIDEO
Learn how to select the stocks to trade, when to buy, when to sell short and how to earn a consistent 100% annualized yield on your trading activity--all by using the Burning Match principles.
Money back guarantee if after one year of trading this system you have not shown an effective annualized yield of 100%.
Comments: Taped from a 1988 seminar.

The Business One Irwin Business and Investment Almanac

Sumner N. Levine, Editor
Business One Irwin
1818 Ridge Road
Homewood, IL 60430

PH: (708) 206-2700
(800) 634-3966
FAX: (708) 798-1490
ISBN: 1-55623-532-1
Published Annually
Cost: $49.95

Subjects addressed: market analysis. Uses charts. Contains all new facts and figures on 1992's best investments. The book reviews the significant financial happenings in 1991 and tells what they mean for the serious investor. The 16th edition will save investors valuable time by providing: major and group stock market averages, charts for futures-traded commodities, price per earnings ratios.

The Business One Irwin Guide to Buying and Selling Treasury Securities

Howard M. Berlin
Business One Irwin
1818 Ridge Road
Homewood, IL 60430

Covers bond analysis. How to analyze, buy and sell T-bills, notes, and bonds. Details both conservative purchases with minimal risk, and indirect methods, such as futures and options.

PH: (800) 634-3966
(708) 206-2700
FAX: (708) 798-1490
ISBN: 1-55623-048-6
Published: 1988
Cost: $34.95

The Business One Irwin Guide to Using the Wall Street Journal

Michael B. Lehmann
Business One Irwin
1818 Ridge Road
Homewood, IL 60430

Covers the Wall Street Journal. Discover how to use the comprehensive information in The Journal to make more profitable business and investment decisions.

PH: (800) 634-3966
(708) 206-2700
FAX: (708) 798-1490
ISBN: 0-87094-923-3
Published 1990 (3rd edition)
Cost: $24.95

The Business One Irwin Investors Handbook 1993

Phyllis Pierce
Business One Irwin
1818 Ridge Road
Homewood, IL 60430

Covers stock analysis. Save time and make more informed investment decisions with all of the statistical information on the 1989 year-end closing prices from the NYSE, AMEX, and OTC at your fingertips.

PH: (800) 634-3966
FAX: (708) 798-1490
ISBN: 1-55623-309-4
Published 1990
Cost: $14.95

Business Week's Guide to Mutual Funds

J. Laderman
McGraw Hill, Inc.
11 West 19th Street
New York, NY 10011

PH: (800) 722-4726
(212) 512-4100
Published 1991
Cost: $24.95

Subjects addressed: mutual funds. Business Week's annual Mutual Fund Scoreboard combined with complete practical information covering the entire scope of mutual funds. "The result is the most comprehensive and current how-to-guide to mutual funds available today."

Charting Commodity Market Price Behavior

L. Dee Belveal
Available through Business One Irwin
1818 Ridge Road
Homewood, IL 60430

PH: (708)206-2700   (800)634-3966
FAX: (708)798-1490
ISBN: 0-87094-651-X
Published 1985
Cost: $40.00

Takes an in-depth look at the technical dynamics that energize commodity markets. Explains, illustrates, and demonstrates the principles of chart trading. Covers many specific applications and a wide range of trade quandaries. A definitive source on technical trading tactics in futures markets.

Choice Investing Strategies

Business One Irwin
1818 Ridge Road
Homewood, IL 60430

PH: (800) 634-3966
(708) 206-2700
FAX: (708) 798-1490
Published October 1990
Cost: $26.50

Subjects addressed: investing theories and strategies. Introduces the principle of lifelong investment, clearly illustrating the advantage of a long-term approach; provides 10 different strategies so readers can choose which option will best suit their needs. Offers step-by-step methodology on how to implement the appropriate financial strategies.

Classics: An Investor's Anthology

Charles D. Ellis with James R. Vertin
Business One Irwin
1818 Ridge Road
Homewood, IL 60430

PH: (708) 206-2700
(800) 634-3966
FAX: (708) 798-1490
ISBN: 1-55623-098-2
Published 1989
Cost: $37.70

Offers readers invaluable insights into the ideas and philosophies that have influenced investors for 60 years. "This is an outstanding effort to show how modern theory and practice have evolved," says Darwin Bayston of the Institute of Chartered Financial Analysts.

Climate: The Key to Understanding Business Cycles

Raymond H. Wheeler
Tide Press
P.O. Box 4224
Linden, NJ 07036

PH: (201) 862-0762
ISBN: 0-912931-00-0
Published 1983
Cost: $30.00

Edited by Michael Zahorchak, this volume summarizes Wheeler's extensive research with long climatic cycles and their relationship to the business cycle. Reveals the many remarkable discoveries he made over the course of his lifetime study of world climate and cultural activities back to the dawn of recorded civilization.

Closed End Funds

Frank Cappiello, W. Douglas Dint, Peter W. Maellem
International Publishing Company
625 N. Michigan, Suite 1920
Chicago, IL 60611

Published 1990
Cost: $24.95

Subjects addressed: closed end funds. Covers nearly 200 funds. Includes address and phone number, transfer agent, background investment objectives, portfolio composition, dividend distribution, management, shareholder reporting, capitalization, year-end and 5 year statistical history and performance ranking.

Commodities: A Chart Anthology

Edward D. Dobson
Traders Press, Inc.
P.O. Box 6206
Greenville, SC 29606

PH: (803) 288-3900
ISBN: 0-934380-02-3
Published 1981 (2nd edition)
Cost: $29.95

The largest compilation of commodity bar charts available. This collection of 1,107 charts and assorted material dealing with their interpretation is intended to serve as both a convenient reference on what markets have done in past years on a daily basis, and as a concise primer on the use of commodity bar charts.

Commodity Futures Trading with Moving Averages

Joseph R. Maxwell, Sr.
Speer Books
333 Ash Street
Red Bluff, CA 96080

ISBN: 0-917832-09-4
Published 1976
Cost: $14.00
Also available in paperback
Published 1975
Cost: $12.75

Presents the results of a study of moving averages as trading signals. This exhaustive research project answered - to the author's satisfaction - the question of whether the use of moving averages can be adopted as standard operating procedures for getting profitable trading signals. Tells how - and whether - to rely on averages.

Commodity Futures Trading Orders

Joseph R. Maxwell, Sr.
Speer Books
333 Ash Street
Red Bluff, CA 96080

ISBN: 0-917832-10-8
Published 1974
Cost: $13.00
Also available in paperback for $10.75

The trading order is a critically important element, and many speculators are not nearly enough acquainted with it. The difference between profit and loss often lies with a trading order. Learn every conceivable practical trading order from an expert and increase your profits.

Commodity Futures Trading with Point and Figure Charts

Joseph R. Maxwell, Sr.
Available through Fraser Publishing
P.O. Box 494
Burlington, VT 05402

PH: (802) 658-0322
ISBN: 0-917832-16-7
Published 1978
Cost: $14.00

To help futures traders break out of their over-reliance on bar charts, the author advocates point and figure charts for fast, accurate, and versatile market selections and predictions. Presents a clear explanation of the most commonly used point and figure charting methods - and takes the mystery out of this neglected art.

Commodity Speculation For Beginners: A Guide to the Futures Market

Huff and Marinacci
McGraw Hill, Inc.
11 West 19th Street
New York, NY 10011

PH: (800) 722-4726   (212) 512-4100
Published 1982
Cost: $5.95

Subjects addressed: commodities trading. A basic book covering commodity trading, the commodity exchange and trading floor. Also discusses hedging, speculating, fundamental and technical tools, charting, contracts and prices.

Commodity Spreads: A Historical Chart Perspective

Edward D. Dobson
Traders Press
P.O. Box 6206
Greenville, SC 29606

PH: (803) 288-3900
ISBN: 0-934380-00-7
Published 1983 (3rd edition)
Cost: $29.95

A convenient reference on commodity spread for interested traders, brokers, and analysts. Includes a series of articles on analyzing spread for lucrative speculation. Presents detailed, historical charts on seventeen popular commodities to permit informed decision making based on actual behavior patterns from past years.

Commodity Trading Manual

Chicago Board of Trade
Probus Publishing Co.
1925 North Clybourn Avenue
Chicago, IL 60614

PH: (800) PROBUS-1
FAX: (312) 868-6250
ISBN: 0-917456-00-9
Published 1991
Cost: $40.00, $7.95 for the workbook

Subjects addressed: commodities trading. "The definitive guide to the futures industry. A comprehensive textbook/reference guide on the futures industry covering many topics including: development of the marketplace, U.S. Futures exchanges, exchange floor operations, clearing operations, price analysis and regulation of futures trading among others."

Common Stock Price Histories, 1910-1987

Dennis E. Predeville
WIT Financial Publishers
1307 E 74th
Suite 1B
Anchorage, AK 99518

PH: (800) 422-1910
ISBN: 0-9618454-1-4
Published 1988 (2nd edition)
Cost: $39.95

The first book of its kind to provide long-term price histories of common stocks, some of which date back to 1910. Virtually all stocks on the New York and American Stock Exchanges plus over-the-counter issues are included. Over 4,000 charts - including 2,800 complete histories - are contained in this unique publication.

Common Stocks and Uncommon Profits

Philip A. Fisher
Business Classics
301 Henrik Road
Woodside, CA 95062

PH: (415) 851-3337
ISBN: 0-931133-00-9
Published 1984 (reprint of 1958 edition)
Cost: $21.95

Subject: stock analysis. Mr. Fisher tells in detail what to do and what not to do for maximum profits. His 10 "Don'ts" picture the popular regard for mathematical factors such as ratios, percentages, and dividend record. His 15 points to look for in a common stock stress fundamentals such as company quality, management competence, and competitive position - and ways to size up these factors most accurately.

The Complete Bond Book: A Guide to All Types of Fixed Income Securities

David M. Darst
McGraw-Hill Publishing Co.
1221 Avenue of the Americas
New York, NY 10020

PH: (800) 262-4729
ISBN: 0-07-017390-7
Published 1975
Cost: $44.95

Rapidly changing economic pressures and financial concerns require solid advice for investing in all types of fixed-income securities. Valuable step-by-step guidelines, worksheets, charts, simplified formulas, and other aids enable you to devise safe and sound strategies for profitable investments now and in the future.

The Complete Book of Bonds - How to Buy and Sell Profitably

Robert Lawrence Holt
Harper & Row
10 E. 53rd Street
New York, NY 10022

ISBN: 0-06-463713-1
Published 1980, 1985 (revised)
Cost: $8.95

Subjects addressed: bond analysis. Bond bible covering what they are, different types, how and where to buy, etc.

The Complete Guide to Closed-End Funds: Finding Value in Today's Stock Market

Frank Cappiello, W. Douglas Dent, and Peter W. Madlem
 International Publishing Corp.
625 N. Michigan Avenue
Chicago, IL 60611

PH: (312) 943-7354
ISBN: 0-942641-18-3
Published 1989
Cost: $21.50

Learn what a closed-end fund is, how to track the discount and utilize trading strategies from three experts. Provides information on more than 160 bond and equity funds, including year-end performance and fund background and investment objective. Participate in the bond and stock market with minimum risk.

A Complete Guide to the Futures Markets Fundamental Analysis, Technical Analysis, Trading, Spreads and Options

Jack O. Schwager
John Wiley & Sons
605 Third Avenue
New York, NY 10158-0012

PH: (212) 850-6418 (orders)
(212) 850-6233 (info)
Published 1984
Cost: $47.50

Subjects addressed: commodities trading, technical analysis; uses charts. A non-technical book for the intelligent layperson already familiar with the basic concepts of futures trading but interested in more detailed discussion of analytical techniques.

A Complete Guide to Trading Profits

Alexander P. Paris
Traders Press
P.O. Box 6206
Greenville, SC 29606

PH: (803) 288-3900
ISBN: 0-934380-05-8
Published 1970
Cost: $19.95

Reap the benefits of short-term trading by learning the most important basic principles of technical analysis and the basic systems of charting. Incorporate these new skills into whatever approach you're accustomed to. Written for the layman.

The Complete Investment Book: Trading Stocks, Bonds, and Options with Computer Applications

Richard Bookstaber
Scott, Foresman and Company
1900 E. Lake
Glenview, IL 60025

PH: (708) 729-3000
ISBN: 0-673-15952-3
Published 1985
Cost: $21.95

Application-oriented book develops all concepts directly into trading strategies. Computer programs in each chapter will convert past prices and other data into useful information. But this is not a manual for the use of computer programs; they are included as a tool both to illustrate and facilitate the strategies described.

The Complete Option Player

Kenneth R. Trester
Investrek
419 Main Street No 160
Huntington Beach, CA 92648

PH: (800) 334-0854
Published 1981 (2nd edition)
Cost: $16.95

Subject: options; uses charts. The book contains over 300 pages full on indispensable tables, charts, investment tools, illustrations and a gold mine of secrets and information on how to win big in the options game.

The Concise Handbook of Futures Markets: Money Management, Forecasting, and the Markets

Perry J. Kaufman, editor
John Wiley and Sons, Inc.
605 Third Avenue
New York, NY 10158-0012

PH: (212) 850-0012
ISBN: 0-471-85088-8
Published 1986
Cost: $29.95

Concise, paperback version of the definitive Handbook. Retains all of the analytic sections of the larger volume and other important background material. Includes chapters on hedging, options, financial markets, spreads, and technical analysis, as well as regulation, taxation, and computer application. Promotes logic above all.

Contrary Investing: The Insiders Guide to Buying Low and Selling High

Richard E. Band
McGraw-Hill Publishing Company
1221 Avenue of the Americas
New York, NY 10020

PH: (800) 262-4729
ISBN: 0-07-003604-7
Published 1985
Cost: $16.95

Applies contrary strategy to all investments: stocks, bonds, precious metals, commodities, futures, foreign currencies, real estate, and collectibles. Filled with helpful charts, lists, and tables, combines insightful analysis of historical trends in the economy with practical advice on making the most of current conditions.

Contrary Investing for the 90's (How to Profit by Going Against the Crowd)

Richard E. Band
St. Martin's Press, Inc.
174 5th Avenue
New York, NY 10010

PH: (212) 674-5151
FAX: (212) 420-9314
ISBN: 0-312-03804-6
Published 1990
Cost: $19.95

Covers: investing theories. Richard Band shows how the art of thinking for yourself against the pressure of the crowd has led contrarians to make huge profits in the stock market. The only book that applies a contrary strategy to all investments: stocks, bonds, precious metals, commodities, futures, foreign securities, currencies, real estate, and collectibles.

Contrary Opinion

R. Earl Hadady
Key Books Press
1111 S. Arroyo Parkway, Suite 410
Pasadena, CA 91105

PH: (818) 441-3863
ISBN: 0-9611390-0-5
Published 1983
Cost: $39.50

Subjects: commodities trading. R. Earl Hadady is generally identified as the leading authority on contrary opinion as applied to the commodity futures market. Contrary opinion is the essence of the commodity futures game. This once vague and often improperly used tool is brought into clear focus and presented in easy-to-understand quantitative terms so you can use what many consider the most powerful of all market tools.

Convertible Bonds

Thomas Noddings
Probus Publishing Co.
1925 North Clybourn Avenue
Chicago, IL 60614

PH: (800) PROBUS-1
FAX: (312) 868-6250
ISBN: 1-55738-148-8
Published
Cost: $32.50

"Convertible Bonds," shows how carefully selected convertibles can give an investor fixed income safety while providing stock market opportunity. The variety of convertible bond investment strategies presented here is designed to take full advantage of the low-risk, high-profit potential of these near-perfect securities. Topics include: undervalued convertible bonds, large-cap convertible bonds, medium- and small-cap convertible bonds, hedging convertible bonds.

The Crash and Its Aftermath: A History of Securities Markets in the United States, 1929-1933

Barrie A. Wigmore
Greenwood Publishing Group, Inc.
88 Post Road, W., Box 5007
Westport, CT 06881

PH: (203) 226-3571
ISBN: 0-313-24574-6
Published 1985
Cost: $50.95

Examines the various securities markets - not just stocks - over the full period of decline. Focuses on the broader structural changes that took place in the financial industry, rather than on the extreme instances of market changes and the hyperbole of unusual personalities and corruption. For students and practitioners alike.

Creating and Preserving Wealth

F. Bentley Mooney, Jr.
Probus Publishing Co.
1925 North Clybourne Avenue
Chicago, IL 60614

PH: (800)PROBUS-1
FAX: (312) 868-6250
ISBN: 1-55738-208-5
Published 1991
Cost: $34.95

Subjects addressed: investments.
This shows smart individuals how to reduce their risk level to the absolute minimum using state-of-the-art diversification and protection techniques. It includes an informative and easy-to-read question and answer section about how asset protection works, levels of risk and then covers other asset protection techniques, including estate planning, estate management, guardianship, transfer costs, life insurance trusts, special tax reductions, deferred payment possibilities and offshore tax havens.

Cross Currency Swaps

Carl R. Beidleman, Editor
Business One Irwin
1818 Ridge Road
Homewood, IL 60430

PH: (708) 206-2700
(800) 634-3966
FAX: (708) 798-1490
ISBN: 1-55623-316-7
Published 1991
Cost: $67.50

Written by two-dozen leaders in the industry, "Cross Currency Swaps" gives readers everything they need to effectively manage these complicated, but highly lucrative, instruments. Logically organized, this one-of-a-kind resource includes: the strategies and tactics of prominent international authorities based on their areas of expertise, step-by-step details of each of the various swaps tactics, an historical look at the development of the swaps market, the accounting and taxation treatments of swap transactions, the innovation of swap strategies so readers are prepared for the future.

Cybernetic Approach to Stock Market Analysis: Versus Efficient Market Theory

Jerry Felsen
CDS Publishing Company
1620 Gregg Avenue #14
Florence, SC 29501

ISBN: 0-916376-01-X
Published 1975
Cost: $20.00

Cybernetic concepts and artificial intelligence techniques applied to investment analysis. Explains the principles and philosophy underlying the cybernetic approach - in clear and simple language, without technical or mathematical details. Promotes powerful new security analysis and market timing techniques. For novice and pro.

Cyclic Analysis in Futures Trading: Contemporary Methods and Procedures

Jacob Bernstein
John Wiley & Sons
605 Third Avenue
New York, NY 10158-0012

PH: (212) 850-6418 orders
(212) 850-6233 info.
ISBN: 0-471-01185-1
Published 1988
Cost: $68.00

Subjects: commodities/futures trading. This book gives you many of the tips, techniques and tactics you need to develop effective strategies for profiting from cycles in futures markets of all types.

The Definitive Guide to Futures Trading

Larry Williams
Windsor Books
P.O. Box 280
Brightwaters, NY 11718

Subjects addressed: investing theories, commodities trading; uses charts. Larry Williams reveals his private trading secrets, thoughts and strategies which led to his $1.1 million profit.

Published 1988
Cost: $50.00

The Definitive Guide to Futures Trading, VolumeI

Larry Williams - Windsor Books
Probus Publishing Co.
1925 North Clybourn Avenue
Chicago, IL 60614

Subjects addressed: futures.

PH: (800) PROBUS-1
FAX: (312) 868-6250
ISBN: 0-930233-19-0
Published
Cost: $55.00

The Definitive Guide to Futures Trading, Volume II

Larry Williams - Windsor Books
Probus Publishing Co.
1925 North Clybourn Avenue
Chicago, IL 60614

Subjects addressed: futures.

PH: (800) PROBUS-1
FAX: (312) 868-6250
ISBN: 0-930233-36-0
Published
Cost: $55.00

Dictionary of Finance and Investment Terms

John Downes & Jordan Elliot Goodman
Barron's Educational Series, Inc.
P.O. Box 8040
250 Wireless Blvd.
Hauppauge, NY 11788

Defines new terminology and updates the traditional language of finance and investment. Basic enough for the student, yet comprehensive enough for the professional. Designed for investors of all types, and includes entries from accounting, consumer and business law, economics, taxation, and other related fields. Over 2500 terms.

PH: (800)645-3476
ISBN: 0-8120-2522-9
Published 1987
Cost: $8.95

Directional Movement Indicator (DMI)

Commodities Education Institute
219 Parkade
Cedar Falls, IA 50613

PH: (800) 635-3936
(319) 277-6341
FAX: (319) 277-7982
Published 1990
Cost: $55.00

VIDEO
Subjects addressed: investing theories, trading analysis, technical analysis. Combines Gann tools with DMI as an overbought/oversold trend indicator and to determine the likelihood of a trending versus a non-trending market. Glen Ring will package these indicators to develop a systematic, technical approach to the markets that will work. Set of 5 tapes in this series.

The Directory of Mutual Funds

Investment Company Institute
1600 M. Street
Washington, D.C. 20036

PH: (202) 293-7700
(202) 955-3536
Cost: $5.00

Covers mutual funds. Complete listing of the member 3,000 mutual funds.

Distressed Securities: Analyzing and Evaluating Market Potential and Investment Risk

Edward I. Altman
Probus Publishing Co.
1925 North Clybourn Avenue
Chicago, IL 60614

PH: (800) PROBUS-1
FAX: (312) 868-6250
ISBN: 1-55738-189-5
Published
Cost: $50.00

The definitive guide to the distressed securities market including: defaulted private trade debt, bank debt, defaulted straight debt securities, "Fallen Angels." An extensive appendix that includes a listing of bankruptcy analysts and firms that are restructuring or in default rounds out this text, making it a complete guide to the boom industry of the 1990s.

The Dividend Investor: A Safe and Sure Way to Beat the Market

Harvey C. Knowles, III and Damon H. Petty
Probus Publishing Co.
1925 North Clybourn Avenue
Chicago, IL 60614

PH: (800) PROBUS-1
FAX: (312) 868-6250
ISBN: 1-55738-243-3
Published 1992
Cost: $24.95

Subjects addressed: investing theories. "The Dividend Investor" employs a high-yield strategy based on the investment strategy of Ben Graham, the father of security analysis, as well as volumes of the authors' research and experience applying the theory to their clients' portfolios. This book comes complete with a step-by-step method to implement this proven strategy profitably, as well as detailed research explaining why dividends are sound investment indicators. The historical performance of investing in high-yield stocks is also illustrated to support variations of this high-yield strategy.

Dividends Don't Lie: Finding Value in Blue-Chip Stock

Geraldine Weiss & Janet Lowe
Longman Financial Services Pub.
520 N. Dearborn Street
Chicago, IL 60610

PH: (312) 836-0490
ISBN: 0-88462-115-4
Published 1988
Cost: $23.95, $12.95 paperback

Subjects addressed: stock analysis, market analysis, fundamental analysis; uses charts. Outlines the strategies that give investors excellent returns. Shows how to: spot high quality blue chip stocks, maximize profits and minimize risk, find bargains in the market, identify the 6 criteria for buying stocks and know the right time to buy and sell.

Dividend Potentials: A Seven-Year Survey Portraying Price Dividend Rations of High Grade Common Stocks as a Determinant for Investment Decisions

Duncan L. Marshall
Marshall Publishers
2990 Watson Street
Memphis, TN 38118

PH: (901)363-9738
ISBN: 0-9626505-1-X
Published 1989
Cost: $25.00

A seven-year study of investment grade stocks using dividend returns as a determinant for Buy & Sell signals. Fifty-four charts included to illustrate method, as well as Portfolio Allocation Model based on Dow Jones Industrials and an explanation of how to set up charts of your own to use the method.

Donoghue's Investment Tips for Retirement Savings

William E. Donoghue
Harper Collins Publishers, Inc.
10 E. 53rd Street
New York, NY 10022

PH: (802) 658-0322
ISBN: 0-06-096148-1
Published 1987 (2nd edition)
Cost $6.95

Presents tactics to help you avoid thousands of dollars in taxes and fees in preparing for your retirement. Includes do-it-yourself strategies for investors of all ages, essential details on retirement plans, and many more money-making ideas. Learn how to select and use the right investment tools for your retirement plan.

Don't Sell Stocks on Monday: An Almanac for Traders, Brokers and Stock Market Watchers

Yale Hirsch
Penguin Books
375 Hudson Street
New York, NY 10014

PH: (800) 631-3577
ISBN: 0-14-010375-9
Published 1987
Cost: $8.95

An insightful, up-to-date collection of prognostic tips based on more than 25 years of research. Theories and advice on investing - day-by-day, week-by-week, month-by-month, and year-by-year - are highlighted by vignettes from stock market history. Includes Hirsch's famous January Barometer Theory and 14 Forecasting Secrets.

The Dow Jones Averages: 1885-1992

Phyllis Pierce, Editor
Business One Irwin
1818 Ridge Road
Homewood, IL 60430

PH: (708) 206-2700
(800) 634-3966
FAX: (708) 798-1490
ISBN: 1-55623-512-7
Published 1991
Cost: $75.00

Subjects addressed: market analysis. "An essential tool for analyzing financial market history so you can better understand the trends of today's volatile markets. It's a one-of-a-kind compilation of every industrial, transportation, and utility average from the beginning of the 12-stock index through 12-31-92."

The Dow Jones Investor's Handbook 1992

Phyllis Pierce, editor
Business One Irwin
1818 Ridge Road
Homewood, IL 60430

PH: (708) 206-2700
(800) 634-3966
FAX: (708) 798-1490
ISBN: 1-55623-196-2
Published 1989
Cost: $13.95

Complete Dow Jones Averages through 1991, with earnings, dividend yield, and price-earnings ratio; 1991 records of common and preferred stocks and bonds on the New York and American Stock Exchanges, with highs and lows, net change, volume and dividend, and most active stocks; over 2,000 over-the-counter securities quotations.

The Dow Jones-Irwin Business and Investment Almanac

Edited by Sumner N. Levine
Business One Irwin
1818 Ridge Road
Homewood, IL 60430

PH: (708) 206-2700
(800) 634-3966
FAX: (708) 798-1490
ISBN: 1-55623-254-3
Published 1990 (4th edition)
Cost: $29.95

The most comprehensive single source of business and investment information available. "The business world's equivalent to a World Almanac," says Computer Book Review. It's all here, including future employment opportunities, U.S. demographics and employer benefits.

The Dow Jones-Irwin Guide to Bond and Money Market Investments

Marcia Stigum & Frank Fabozzi
Business One Irwin
1818 Ridge Road
Homewood, IL 60430

PH: (708) 206-2700
(800) 634-3966
FAX: (708) 798-1490
ISBN: 0-87094-892-X
Published 1986
Cost: $34.50

Explores interest-bearing IOUs - under-utilized instruments that offer attractive returns, low risk, high liquidity, and tax advantages. From certificates of deposit to Treasury bills, bond funds, and zeros, this clear treatment of long and short term debt securities provides investors with all of the necessary information.

The Dow Jones-Irwin Guide to Buying and Selling Treasury Securities

Howard M. Berlin
Business One Irwin
1818 Ridge Road
Homewood, IL 60430

PH: (708) 206-2700
(800) 634-3966
FAX: (708) 798-1490
ISBN: 1-55623-048-6
Published 1988 (2nd edition)
Cost: $27.50

Covers virtually every aspect of analyzing, buying, and selling T-bills, notes, and bonds - either as conservative purchases or by indirect methods such as futures and options trading. Find out why many consider Treasury securities a near-ideal investment instrument. Includes updated information on the Tax Reform Act of 1986.

The Dow Jones-Irwin Guide to Investing with Investment Software

Thomas A. Meyers
Business One Irwin
1818 Ridge Road
Homewood, IL 60430

PH: (708) 206-2700
(800) 634-3966
FAX: (708) 798-1490
ISBN: 0-87094-938-1
Published 1987
Cost: $32.50

A primer on how to select and use software for portfolio management, fundamental analysis, and technical analysis. Shows individual investors how to take advantage of investment software; what options, capabilities, and special features are available from different programs; and how to determine what kind of software you need.

The Dow-Jones - Irwin Guide to Municipal Bonds

Sylvan G. Feldstein & Frank Fabozzi
Business One Irwin
1818 Ridge Road
Homewood, IL 60430

PH: (708) 206-2700
(800) 634-3966
FAX: (708) 798-1490
ISBN: 0-87094-542-4
Published 1987 (2nd edition)
Cost: $39.95

Comprehensive overview of the types of bonds available, their unique features, and the markets in which they trade. Provides a clear framework for municipal bond analysis and establishes guidelines for evaluating the risks associated with these instruments, wit special attention to the potential credit impact of the new tax law.

The Dow Jones Guide to Mutual Funds: How to Diversify Your Investments for Maximum Return and Safety in Any Kind of Market

Donald D. Rugg
Business One Irwin
1818 Ridge Road
Homewood, IL 60430

PH: (708) 206-2700
(800) 634-3966
FAX: (708) 798-1490
ISBN: 0-87094-756-7
Published 1986 (3rd edition)
Cost: $27.50

Plan worry-free investments that will pay off in years to come. Here's a complete do-it-yourself program based on the intermediate to long-term trading of no-load mutual funds, which are among the best investment vehicles for independent investors. Straightforward with no gimmicks.

The Dow Jones-Irwin Guide to Put and Call Options

Henry A. Clasing, Jr.
Business One Irwin
1818 Ridge Road
Homewood, IL 60430

PH: (800) 634-3966
(708) 206-2700
FAX: (708) 798-1490
ISBN: 0-87094-148-8
Published 1978 (new edition will be out soon)
Cost: $37.50

Subjects addressed: options. Details how stock options are traded. Includes option strategies for the serious investor.

The Dow Jones-Irwin Guide to Retirement Planning

Ray Vicker
New American Library
1633 Broadway
New York, NY 10019

PH: (800) 526-0275
ISBN: 0-451-15767-2, sig
Published 1989
Cost: $4.95 (paperback)

Start a lifetime money management program that will turn a handful of dollars into a six-figure nest egg. Explains how to develop savings habits, organize records, estimates one's net worth, and make personal financial statements. Outlines investment strategies and describes potential health, insurance, and legal problems.

The Dow Jones-Irwin Guide to Stock Index Futures and Options

William Nix and Susan Nix
Business One Irwin
1818 Ridge Road
Homewood, IL 60430

PH: (708) 206-2700
(800) 634-3966
FAX: (708)798-1490
ISBN: 0-87094-482-7
Published 1984
Cost: $42.50

Outlines critical differences in stock index futures, futures options, and index options on major U.S. exchanges. Contains practical advice for beginning and veteran commodity traders, securities and options investors, financial executives, and institutional money managers looking for alternative risk management strategigies.

The Dow Jones-Irwin Guide to Trading Systems

Bruce Babcock, Jr. - Author
CTCR Pub
Business One Irwin
1818 Ridge Road
Homewood, IL 60430

Phone: (800) 634-3966
(708) 206-2700
FAX: (708) 798-1490
Published 1989
Cost: $55.00

Subjects addressed: commodities trading, analysis, technical analysis. Uses charts. Explains why a mechanical approach is best and teaches you how to choose the right system. You'll become a better system developer and a far more knowledgeable system buyer. Babcock presents historical tests of various trading system approaches in ten markets over a five year period.

The Dow Jones Municipal Bond Valuation Handbook

John A. Prestbo, editor
Business One Irwin
1818 Ridge Road
Homewood, IL 60430

PH: (708) 206-2700
(800) 634-3966
FAX: (708) 798-1490
ISBN: 0-87128-546-0
Published 1977
Cost: $9.95

A guide to market values of tax exempt securities for incomes, estate, and gift tax purposes. Based on the financial computing service Telstat and reworked into an easy-to-use format by Dow Jones, this important reference work makes sense of the major changes in U.S. tax code caused by the Tax Reform Act of 1976.

Dun & Bradstreet: Guide to $Your Investments$ 1992

Nancy Dunnan
Harper Collins Publishers, Inc.
10 E. 53rd Street
New York, NY 10022

PH: (800)242-7737
ISBN: 0-06-055184-4
Published 1992
Cost: $24.95

Explore the new trend toward diversification in investment portfolio and against individual ownership of stock. A new focus on hard assets and the increased attraction of CDs are covered and much more. In its 36th year, it remains a standard sourcebook for both advisors and investors.

Dying of Money: Lessons of the Great German and American Inflations

Jens O. Parsson
Wellspring Press
Page Road
Lincoln, MA 01773

ISBN: 0-914688-01-4
Published 1974
Cost: $18.00

Transforms the dry economic subject of inflation into a white-knuckles kind of blood chiller. Clear and fascinating, yet entirely technically valid, this book applies the lessons gleaned from the German inflation of 1923 to the American inflation that followed 1962. Charts out all possible prognoses for our country's economy.

Dynamics of Commodity Production Cycles

Dennis L. Meadows
MIT Press
55 Hayward Street
Cambridge, MA 02142

ISBN: 0-262-13141-2
Published 1970
Cost: $32.50

Employs industrial dynamics methodology to develop a general dynamic model of economic, biological, technological, and psychological factors that cause instability of commodity systems. Computer simulation experiments of alternative policies and structural changes reveal surprising implications for stabilization policies.

Dynamic Stock Option Trading

Joseph T. Stewart, Jr.
John Wiley and Sons, Inc.
605 Third Avenue
New York, NY 10158-0012

PH: (212) 850-6000
ISBN: 0-471-08670-3
Published 1981
Cost: $60.00

A reliable, easily understood way to time the buying and selling of options. Presents a proven system to measure, follow, and predict stock option movement. Includes checklists for buying and selling, forms to use, rules to obey, lessons in charting and analyzing trades, a method of self-appraisal, and a plan of action.

Economics of Futures Trading for Commercial and Personal Profit

Thomas A. Hieronymous
Commodity Research Bureau
75 Wall Street
22nd Floor
New York, NY 10005

PH: (800)446-4519
ISBN: 0-910418-03-9
Published 1977
Cost: $17.95

A 'How-to' book designed for those in the commodity trades, investors in futures contracts, and students of both. Combines a review of the economics behind the markets with an explanation of the techniques involved in using them. Appraises the performance of the system—and presents some startling recommendations for reform.

The Elliott Wave Educational Video Series

Robert Prechter, Jr.
P.O. Box 1618
Gainesville, GA 30503

PH: (800) 336-1618
(404) 536-0309
Published 1987
Cost: $1499

VIDEO
Uses charts; subjects addressed: investing theories. Set of 10 tapes providing professional instruction on Elliott Wave analysis complete with a set of workbooks containing all of the charts and graphics used during the actual presentation. Comments: taped from a 1987 seminar

Elliott Wave Principle

Frost & Prechter
New Classics Library, Inc.
P.O. Box 1618
Gainesville, GA 30503

PH: (800) 33-1618
Other: (404) 536-0309
ISBN: 0-932750-07-9
Published 1978, 1990 (6th edition)
Cost: $24.95

Covers: investing theories, stock analysis, market analysis, bond analysis, trading analysis, commodities trading, technical analysis; uses charts. The bible of wave analysis. A highly acclaimed must for every serious investor in stocks, bonds, and commodities.

Elliott Wave Principle, Expanded Edition

Frost and Prechter - New Classics Library
Probus Publishing Co.
1925 North Clybourn Avenue
Chicago, IL 60614

PH: (800) PROBUS-1
FAX: (312) 868-6250
ISBN: 0-932750-17-6
Published 1991
Cost: $27.50

Subjects addressed: investment..Learn to apply the principles of Elliott Wave analysis to stocks, bonds and commodities and improve investment returns. The authors cover terminology, rules and guidelines, alternation, correct counting, bear market limitations, charting the waves, wave personality, historical and mathematical background, the Fibonacci Sequence, the Coldel Rectangle, the Golden Spiral, ratio and technical analysis, time sequence, long-term waves, the Grand Supercycle, the Supercycle, Dow Theory, and more.

Encyclopedia of Stock Market Strategies

Edited by Investors Intelligence Staff
Chartcraft, Inc.
1 West Avenue
Larchmont, MY 10538

PH: (914) 834-5181
Published 1963
Cost: $60.00 supplements $12.50

Subjects: investing theories. Newly revised edition of the famous original Encyclopedia, now issued in a 3-ring binder which will be supplemented regularly. The investor, trader or technician now has access to the methods, theories, and thoughts of the world's most noted financial writers; all conceivable investment techniques are covered, in many cases by the originators, with purpose explained and method described.

The Encyclopedia of Technical Market Indicators

Robert W. Colby and Thomas A. Meyers
Business One Irwin
1818 Ridge Road
Homewood, IL 60430

PH: (800) 634-3966
FAX: (708) 798-1490
ISBN: 1-55623-049-4
Published 1988
Cost: $52.50

Covers market and technical analysis. Separates the myth from reality and shows you the true forecasting value of over 110 indicators. Calculate and interpret scores of widely followed technical market indicators and maximize profit.

Ethical Investing

Amy L. Domini & Peter D. Kinder
Addison-Wesley Publishing Co.
1 Jacob Way
Reading, MA 01867

PH: (800) 447-2226
ISBN: 0-201-10803-8
Published 1984
Cost: $17.95

How to invest for profit without sacrificing your principles. Traditional sources offer little help in screening companies' activities beyond the balance sheet. This is the first book to show you how you can improve the quality of your life as you improve the value of your portfolio. A practical, profitable, and ethical approach.

Eurodollar Futures and Options: Controlling Money Market Risk

Burghardt, Belton, Lane, Luce and McVey
Probus Publishing Co.
1925 North Clybourn Avenue
Chicago, IL 60614

PH: (800) PROBUS-1
FAX: (312) 868-6250
ISBN: 1-55738-159-3
Published 1991
Cost: $65.00

Subjects addressed: Eurodollar Futures and Options. "Learn how to fold futures and options into a portfolio of conventional and derivative interest rate products. Ideal for portfolio managers, traders and bankers."

The European Options and Futures Markets

A Probus Guide to World Markets
Probus Publishing Co.
1925 North Clybourn Avenue
Chicago, IL 60614

PH: (800) PROBUS-1
FAX: (312) 868-6250
ISBN: 1-55738-119-4
Published 1991
Cost: $75.00

Subjects addressed: European market analysis. This book provides on update of the futures and options trading markets in Europe and their contracts. This book describes both the unique opportunities and characteristics of futures and options markets in fourteen European countries: Austria, Belgium, Denmark, Finland, France, Germany, Ireland, Italy, Netherlands, Norway, Spain, Sweden, Switzerland, United Kingdom. Charts, graphs and tables, each market is presented: history of the market, organization of the market, overview of the products, detailed contract specifications, taxation, regulation, quote vendors, sources of information.

Extraordinary Investments for Ordinary Investors: Choosing the Best from the New Money Packages

Wayne F. Nelson
Putnam Publishing Group
200 Madison Avenue
New York, NY 10016'

PH: (800)631-8571
ISBN: 0-399-12991-X
Published 1984
Cost: $16.95

Takes the mystery out of the money world, including the four major new products: mutual funds, limited partnerships, unit trusts, and insurance. Filled with helpful charts, tables, and questionnaires - as well as a comprehensive appendix listing nearly 1,000 mutual fund choices along with their addresses and telephone numbers.

Extraordinary Popular Delusions and the Madness of Crowds

Charles MacKay
Buccaneer Books
P.O. Box 168
Cutchogue, NY 11935

ISBN: 0-89966-516-0
Published 1986
Cost: $36.95

A landmark study of crowd psychology and mass mania throughout history which includes accounts of classic scams such as the Mississippi Scheme, the South Sea Bubble, and Tulipmania. Also deals with fads and delusions such as Alchemy and the Philosopher's Stone, the Prophecies of Nostradamus, the Rosecrucians and astrology. Foreward by Bernard Baruch.

The 50 Plus Guide to Retirement Investing

Walter W. David
Business One Irwin
1818 Ridge Road
Homewood, IL 60430

PH: (800) 634-3966
FAX: (708) 798-1490
ISBN: 1-87094-951-9
Published 1987
Cost: $22.95

Covers investing theories. Plan a financial future that is comfortable and worry-free. Establishes firm guidelines for planning a retirement budget based on security, pension benefits and investment income.

Filtered Waves Basic Theory: A Tool for Stock Market Analysis

Arthur A. Merrill
Analysis Press
3300 Darby Road #3325
Haverford, PA 19041

PH: (215) 642-2011
ISBN: 0-911894-36-5
Published 1977
Cost: $15.00

A simple method of identifying and measuring market swings based on "filtered" analysis - ignoring all shifts below a specified percentage level. Examines every bull and bear market since 1898. Presents charts for the life expectancy of rallies and secondary reactions. Describes applications to individual stocks, and other uses.

Finance and Investment Handbook

John Downes & Jordan Elliot Goodman
Barron's
250 Wireless Blvd.
Hauppauge, NY 11788

PH: (916) 677-7562
Published1966,1990 (3rd edition)
Cost: $26.95

Subjects addressed: stock analysis, bond analysis, commodities trading. Dictionary of over 3000 key terms, complete lists of brokerage firms, MF, investment newsletters, magazines, and more. Directory of 4000 major corporations, also 30 key personal investment opportunities.

Financial Analyst's Handbook: Portfolio Management

Sumner N. Levine, editor
Business One Irwin
1818 Ridge Road
Homewood, IL 60430

PH: (708) 206-2700
(800) 634-3966
FAX: (708) 798-1490
ISBN: 0-87094-919-5
Published 1987 (2nd edition)
Cost: $ 80.00

Portfolio management and evaluation examined by 48 authorities. Includes sections on Liability and the Analyst, the SEC and Regulations, Investment Vehicles, Special Investment Vehicles, Analysis of Financial Reports, Economic Analysis and Timing, Mathematical Aids, Portfolio Management and Theories, and Information Sources.

Financial Futures and Investment Strategy

Arthur L. Rebell, Gail Gordon, & Kenneth B. Platnick
Available through Fraser Publishing
P.O. Box 494
Burlington, VT 05402

PH: (802) 658-0322
ISBN: 0-87094-491-6
Published 1984
Cost $40.00

Designed to help non-speculative professional money managers deal with the risks of today's volatile and unpredictable capital markets through the use of financial futures and options. Covers fundamentals and uses of these contracts. Recommends hedging — as distinguished from speculation - as a way to control market exposure.

Financial Futures Markets

Brendan Brown & Charles R. Geisst
St. Martin's Press, Inc.
175 Fifth Avenue
New York, NY 10010

PH: (800) 221-7945
ISBN: 0-312-28955-3
Published 1983
Cost $25.00

Details the financial futures trading, highlighting the key channels that link this new market and the conventional cash markets. Considers speculation, arbitrage, hedging, scalping, and brokering, Traders in currency, interest rate, and stock futures markets are described within an economics of financial futures trading.

The Financial Marketplace

S. Kerry Cooper & Donald R. Fraser
Available through Addison-Wesley Publishing Co., Inc.
1 Jacob Way
Reading, MA 01867

PH: (800) 447-2226
ISBN: 0-201-10548-9
Published 1986 (2nd edition)
Cost $23.95

Covers the full range of financial markets and instruments, as well as the most important participants. Emphasizes major innovations, including the financial futures markets. Examines the structure and role of the Federal Reserve System and the goals and methods of monetary control. A balanced blend of description and analysis.

Financial Options - From Theory to Practice

Stephen Figlewski, William Silber and Marti
Subrahmanyam
A Salomon Brothers Center Book
Business One Irwin
1818 Ridge Road
Homewood, IL 60430

PH: (800) 634-3966
FAX: (708) 798-1490
ISBN: 1-55623-234-9
Published 1990
Cost: $49.95

Covers investing theories and options. Focuses on the crucial relation between options theory and actual investing so that you can combine your knowledge of the two and make profitable trades. Explains option valuation theories clearly; concisely and with very little mathematics.

Financial Statement Analysis: Investor's Quick Reference

Rose Marie L. Bukics
Probus Publishing Co.
1925 North Clybourn Avenue
Chicago, IL 60614

PH: (800) PROBUS-1
FAX: (312) 868-6250
ISBN: 1-55738-183-6
Published 1991
Cost: $14.95

Subject addressed: investment. Shows the reader how to diagnose a company's financial health before it—and the investment in it—falters. Covers: preparation of financial statements, balance sheet use, income statements, changes in shareholder equity basics, and criticisms of note disclosures.

Financial Statement Analysis: Investor's Self-Teaching Seminars Series

Charles J. Woelfel
Probus Publishing Co.
1925 North Clybourn Avenue
Chicago, IL 60614

PH: (800) PROBUS-1
FAX: (312) 868-6250
ISBN: 0-917253-92-2
Published 1988
Cost: $24.95

Subjects addressed: investment.
This seminar aids investors in the essential basics of how to read, interpret and analyze company financial statements by using real-world examples and self-study exercises and problems. Also explained is horizontal and vertical analysis, common-size statements, financial ratios, liquidity, active ratios, profitability ratios, capital structure and solvency ratios.

The Flexible Choice: Hedging with CBOT Agricultural Options

Chicago Board of Trade
141 W. Jackson Blvd., Suite 2210
Chicago, IL 60604-2994

Published 1990
Cost: $3.00

Subjects addressed: commodities trading. Written for anyone wanting to establish prior to delivery, a selling or buying price for a cash commodity. Ten hedging strategies are described in the 58 page text and each one highlights its market objective, potential outcome, margin requirements, risks and advantages, disadvantages of using a particular strategy. Also included is a glossary of common futures and options terms.

The Flexible Choice: Trading with CBOT Agricultural Options

Chicago Board of Trade
141 W. Jackson Blvd., Suite 2210
Chicago, IL 60604-2994

Published 1990
Cost: $3.00

Subjects addressed: commodities trading. A 60-page text featuring 12 speculative strategies using CBOT agricultural contracts. Each one highlights its market objective, profit-potential, margin requirements and risk. Also includes a glossary of common futures and options terms.

The First Time Investor: Starting Out Safe & Smart

Larry Chambers and Kenn Miller
Probus Publishing Co.
1925 North Clybourn Avenue
Chicago, IL 60614

PH: (800) PRÓBUS-1
FAX: (312) 868-6250
ISBN: 1-55738-212-3
Published 1991
Cost: $22.95

Subjects addressed: investment.
The authors show how to choose investments that are both safe and profitable with an optimistic view of the markets. Information covers how the global economy affects investing, how to develop an investing plan, how to analyze investments using trend analysis, and includes in-depth coverage of stocks, mutual funds, municipal bonds, retirement planning and more.

Fixed Income Analytics

Ravi E. Dattatreya, Editor
Probus Publishing Co.
1925 North Clybourn Avenue
Chicago, IL 60614

PH: (800) PROBUS-1
FAX: (312) 868-6250
ISBN: 1-55738-163-1
Published 1991
Cost: $69.95

"Fixed Income Analytics" brings a much-needed order to the process of fixed income investment management, beginning with a detailed description of parametric analysis of securities and a discussion of various other advanced valuation technologies, such as yield surface and option adjusted spread analysis. In addition, it shows practitioners the various hedging, arbitrage and portfolio management implications of all new methods of fixed income valuation.

Fixed Income Calculations, Volume 1: Money Market Paper and Bonds

Marcia Stigum and Franklin L. Robinson
Business One Irwin
1818 Ridge Road
Homewood, IL 60430

PH: (708) 206-2700   (800) 634-3966
FAX: (708) 798-1490
ISBN: 1-55623-476-7
Published 1992
Cost: $62.50

The most significant feature of this problem-solving guide is its simple and easy-to-understand notation. It's organized for quick reference and includes key money market tables. Stigum and Robinson show readers how to quickly and accurately: compare discount instruments with interest-bearing instruments on a 360 or 365-day basis; calculate price-given yields and yield-given prices; calculate true yields to maturity; compute holding-period yields; calculate true break-even rates on shorts, reverses, long bonds, and foreign paper.

Fixed Income Mathematics, 2nd Edition

Frank J. Fabozzi
Probus Publishing Co.
1925 North Clybourn Avenue
Chicago, IL 60614

PH: (800) PROBUS-1
FAX: (312) 868-6250
Published 1993
Cost: $40.00

Subjects addressed: bond analysis. A complete guide to understanding the mathematical concepts and tools used to evaluate fixed income securities and portfolio strategies. Topics include: the time value of money, bond pricing and return analysis, bond price volatility, applications to bonds with embedded call options. Second edition, revised.

Fixed Income Portfolio Strategies

Frank J. Fabozzi, Editor
Probus Publishing Co.
1925 North Clybourn Avenue
Chicago, IL 60614

PH: (800) PROBUS-1
FAX: (312) 868-6250
ISBN: 1-55738-067-8
Published 1989
Cost: $69.95

Frank J. Fabozzi has combined the work of 46 of the nation's leading experts in fixed-income portfolio management to create a definitive guide to state-of-the-art technologies and innovations. This highly rigorous review builds on a critical five-stage process of asset management to address a plethora of important issues, including: indexing, immunization and dedicated strategies for insurance, portfolio insurance, bond analysis tools, international portfolios, strategies with interest rate control instruments.

Foreign Bonds - An Autopsy: A Study of Defaults and Repudiations of Government Obligations

Max Winkler
Ayer Company Publishers
P.O. Box 958
Salem, NH 03079

PH: (603) 898-1200
ISBN: 0-405-09308-X
Published 1933 (1976 reprint)
Cost: $25.50

Classic historical analysis, all the more meaningful in light of today's international financial uncertainty. Retraces the origins of the United States as bankers to the world up to the Depression era. Places modern events in perspective by reviewing default throughout recorded history, from ancient times to the 20th century.

Foreign Exchange Dealer's Handbook

Raymond G. F. Coninx
Business One Irwin
1818 Ridge Road
Homewood, IL 60430

PH: (708) 206-2700   (800) 634-3966
FAX: (708) 798-1490
ISBN: 1-55623-626-3
Published 1991
Cost: $75.00

This third edition takes into account a volatile economic climate and new financial products used in analyzing the many transactions that can now be handled by computer. Coninx gives readers a wide variety of formulas and equations to help avoid the pitfalls of modern trading. Topics include: exchange, spot, and forward rates, as well as interest arbitrage, swap transactions, and the calculation of compound interest; step-by-step instructions and detailed examples that show readers how to use valuable formulas and equations.

The Foreign Exchange Handbook

Julian Walmsley
Wiley-Interscience
1 Wiley Drive
Somerset, NJ 08873

PH: (201) 469-4400
ISBN: 0-471-86388-2
Published 1983
Cost: $75.00

Designed to help professional traders who are in the international markets. The first edition is on the background of the markets, the second sets out the calculations involved, and the third ties in financial futures and gold markets, payment systems, and exposure measurement and control.

Foreign Exchange & Money Markets: Managing Foreign and Domestic Currency Operations

Heinz Riehl & Rita M. Rodriguez
McGraw-Hill Publishing Company
1221 Avenue of the Americas
New York, NY 10020

PH: (800) 262-4729
ISBN: 0-07-052671-0
Published 1983
Cost: $44.95

Everything you need to know about how the foreign exchange and money markets function in order to successfully manage operations. Includes step-by-step explanations of the basic mechanics and inter-relationships, practical business applications, controlling the risks involved, and accounting systems to measure profitability.

45 Years in Wall Street

William D. Gann
Lambert Gann Publishing Company
P.O. Box O
Pomeroy, WA 99347

Published 1936, 1949, 1976 (reprint)
Cost: $30.00

Two complete works by Gann are reprinted here - 45 Years in Wall Street and New Stock Trend Detector - which, between them, review a series of panics and bull markets from 1929 to 1946, and interpret all events with the benefit of his long and profitable career on Wall Street. Written from practical application, not theory.

Frank Capiello's New Guide to Finding the Next Superstock

Frank Capiello
McGraw Hill, Inc.
11 West 19th Street
New York, NY 10011

PH: (800) 722-4726
(212) 512-4100
Published 1990
Cost: $12.60

Subjects addressed: stock analysis. "Reveals Capiello's method for selecting stocks poised for dramatic price increases - the Xeroxs and IBMs of tomorrow." It also shows you how to rate stocks to discover super stocks before other investors and covers lessons learned in the crash of 1987.

The Fundamentals of Investments

Gordon J. Alexander and William F. Sharpe /
Prentice Hall
15 Columbus Circle
New York, NY 10023

Published 1989
Cost: $52.00

Subjects addressed: investing theories, stock analysis, market analysis, bond analysis, earnings analysis, commodities trading, fundamental analysis, technical analysis, options. Minimal use of charts. Textbook covering the workings of the market, portfolio selection theories, common stocks and fixed-income section, taxation and inflation effects on investments.

Fundamentals of Municipal Bonds

Public Securities Association
40 Broad Street
12th Floor
New York, NY 10004-2373

PH: (212) 809-7000
ISBN: 0-9605198-1-5
Published 1987 (3rd edition)
Cost: $23.95

Covers every aspect of the municipal bond securities market - investor objectives and strategies; the roles of issuers, dealers, and bond brokers; much more. Valuable tables, charts, graphs, and analytical mathematical computations make this reference work for every investor. Revised edition deals comprehensively with recent developments.

Fundamentals of the Securities Industry

Allan H. Pessin
New York Institute of Finance
2 Broadway
New York, NY 10004

A comprehensive introduction to the ways of Wall Street by a 30-year veteran. Explains the nature of equities and their purposes - common standard resources to those new to the industry and the serious investor.

PH: (212) 344-2900
ISBN: 0-13-343906-2
Published 1985
Cost: $39.95

The Futures Game: Who Wins? Who Loses? Why?

Richard J. Teweles & Frank J. Jones
McGraw-Hill Publishing Company
1221 Avenue of the Americas
New York, NY 10020

Second edition of the best-selling "The Commodity Futures Game" is an updated reference to the entire field of futures and options trading. New sections on the latest proven techniques for trading in financial futures, as well as the history, mechanics, and use of futures options. Practical features of the original remain intact.

PH: (800) 262-4729
ISBN: 0-07-063728-8
Published 1987
Cost $47.95

Also available in paperback
ISBN: 0-07-063734-2
Published 1989
Cost: $19.45

The Futures Markets: Arbitrage, Risk Management and Portfolio Strategies

Daniel R. Siegel and Diane F. Siegel
Probus Publishing Co.
1925 North Clybourn Avenue
Chicago, IL 60614

Subjects addressed: futures trading. A comprehensive study of the futures markets covering: trading strategies used for arbitrage, hedging and speculation, theory of futures pricing, the mechanics of futures trading and more.

PH: (800) PROBUS-1
FAX: (312) 868-6250
ISBN: 1-55738-083-X
Published 1990
Cost: $47.50

Futures Techniques & Technical Analysis

Commodity Trend Service
P.O. Box 32309
Palm Beach Gardens, FL 33420

PH: (800) 331-1069
(407) 694-0960
FAX: (407) 622-7623

VIDEO
Subjects addressed: commodities trading, technical analysis. A 2 hour video of Joe Van Nice and Paul Wilcox revealing the latest tricks to profiting in commodities... how to spot "get rich quick" trades using stochastics, RSI, and ADX to spot price trends early and much more.

Gaining on the Market

Charles J. Rolo and Robert J. Klein
Little Brown & Co.
34 Beacon Street
Boston, MA 02106

Published 1988
Cost: $18.95

Subjects addressed: investing theories, market analysis, earnings analysis, trading analysis, fundamental analysis. Good book for the do-it-yourself investor. Shows how to: read a company's financial statement, analyze the value of a stock, read and understand market indexes, read and profit from financial news, buy gold, use options, choose and evaluate market newsletters, and choose a broker.

Getting Started in Bonds

Michael C. Thomsett
John Wiley & Sons
605 Third Avenue
New York, NY 10158-0012

PH: (212) 850-6418 orders
(212) 850-6233 info
Published 1991
Cost: $12.95

Subjects addressed: bond analysis. Complete non-technical guide to investing at all levels in corporate, federal, and municipal bonds.

Getting Started in Commodity Futures Trading

Mark J. Powers
Investor Publications, Inc.
219 Parkade
Cedar Falls, IA 50613

PH: (800) 553-1789
ISBN: 0-914230-01-8
Published 1983 (4th edition)
Cost: $12.95

An internationally respected expert applies theory and practical experience to commodity futures trading. Evaluates the relative risks/benefits of stocks and commodities. Examines commodity options and futures, as well as stock index futures. Presents valuable trading strategies and price forecasting techniques.

Getting Started in Futures

Todd Lofton
John Wiley & Sons
605 Third Avenue
New York, NY 10158-0012

PH: (212) 850-6418 orders
(212) 850-6233 info
ISBN: 0-471-61492-0
Published 1989
Cost: $32.95 (hard cover) $16.25 (soft cover)

Subjects: commodities/futures, options. How to make money in futures and options. This non-technical guide shows you how to play the futures markets in commodities, foreign currency, and interest rates, and how to handle options. He explains how to understand the prices in the newspaper and he covers buying and selling "long" and "short", what to expect from your broker, commissions, hedging, trading systems, "technical" tools, and basic trading strategies.

Global Bond Markets

Jess Lederman and Keith K. H. Park, Editors
Probus Publishing Co.
1925 North Clybourn Avenue
Chicago, IL 60614

PH: (800) PROBUS-1
FAX: (312) 868-6250
ISBN: 1-55738-153-4
Published 1991
Cost: $75.00

Provides comprehensive coverage of the world bond markets and related debt instruments. Among the many topics covered are: measuring the risk of foreign corporate and sovereign bonds; measuring global bond portfolio performance; high yield bond investment strategies; hedging global bond portfolios and currency risk; and operational considerations, including clearance and settlement difficulties, the role of the custodian and transactions costs.

Global Equity Markets

Jess Lederman and Keith K. H. Park, Editors
Probus Publishing Co.
1925 North Clybourn Avenue
Chicago, IL 60614

PH: (800) PROBUS-1
FAX: (312) 868-6250
ISBN: 1-55738-152-6
Published 1991
Cost: $75.00

This book is a thorough examination of the world's equity markets - from New York and London to Paris and Tokyo. Among the many topics covered are: new product innovations and developments in stock markets around the globe, risk reduction through global diversification, the international crash of 1987, corporate accounting practices for different countries, tactical asset allocation, comparison of international indices, hedging global equity portfolios and currency risks.

Global Investing: The Professional's Guide to the World Capital Markets

Ibbotson and Brenson
McGraw Hill, Inc.
11 West 19th Street
New York, NY 10011

PH: (800) 722-4726
 (212) 512-4100
Published 1991
Cost: $39.95

Subjects addressed: global investing. Uses charts. "Sound financial advice on building and maintaining diversified portfolios, based on field-tested economic analysis and historical evidence of capital markets throughout the world - including the boom of 1986-87 and the subsequent crash, as well as recent developments in Europe and on the Pacific Rim." "Incisive, intelligent, and packed with charts, tables and graphs." It shows the reader where money has been made in stocks, bonds, cash, gold and silver, options, futures and more.

The Global Investor: How to Buy Stocks Around the World

Thomas R. Keyes and David Miller
Longman Financial Services Publishers
520 N. Dearborn
Chicago, IL 60610

PH: (800)621-9621
ISBN: 0-88462-914-7
Published 1990
Cost: $29.95

Take advantage of a wealth of foreign investment opportunities by learning how to evaluate a foreign investment vehicle in terms of risks and potential rewards, how to calculate exchange rates and convert currencies quickly, and much more. Become an astute player.

Global Portfolios - Quantitative Strategies for Maximum Performance

Robert Z. Aliber and Brian R. Bruce
Business One Irwin
1818 Ridge Road
Homewood, IL 60430

PH: (800) 634-3966
FAX: (708) 798-1490
ISBN: 1-55623-337-4
Published 1991
Cost: $75.00

Covers stock and bond analysis, and global investing. Industry leaders show you how to develop and organize a global portfolio based on a specific objective. Covers everything from a basic introduction of quantitative global investing to asset allocation, optimal bond portfolios, optimal equity portfolios and the foreign exchange exposure decision.

Gold Futures: Facts and Figures; Trading Strategies and Tactics

Kevin Commins
Probus Publishing Co.
1925 North Clybourn Avenue
Chicago, IL 60614

PH: (800) PROBUS-1
FAX: (312) 868-6250
Published 1991
Cost: $39.95

Subjects addressed: gold futures. " The gold traders bible!" "A valuable reference for both the novice trader and the seasoned pro... required for anyone interested in precious metals."

Good Money: A Guide to Profitable Social Investing in the 90's

Ritchie P. Lowry
W. W. Norton Publishers
500 5th Avenue
New York, NY 10110

PH: (800) 223-2584
Published 1991
Cost: $23.00

Subjects addressed: investing theories. Is a how-to guide for both individual and institutional investors who want to do good socially while also doing well financially. Shows how socially screened investments can outperform those made only for profit. Illustrates how to match and balance financial goals with social preferences when making investment decisions.

Good Money's Social Funds Guide

Ritchie P. Lowry
Good Money Publications
P.O. Box 363
Worcester, VT 05682

PH: (800) 535-3551
(802) 223-3911
FAX: (802) 223-8949
Published 1982
Cost: $19.95

Subjects addressed: mutual funds analysis. A guide to social and environmental mutual funds. The guide includes descriptions and analyses of the social screens, investor costs and financial performance of socially-screened equity, bond, and money market mutual funds.

Graham & Dodd's Security Analysis

Sidney Cottle, Roger Murray, & Frank Block
McGraw-Hill
1221 Avenue of the Americas
New York, NY 10020
ISBN: 0-471-61844-6

PH: (800) 2-MCGRAW
(212) 512-2000
Published 1962, 1988 (5th edition)
Cost: $56.50

Subjects addressed: bond analysis, stock analysis, earnings analysis. Provides the principles and techniques to measure asset values and cash flows so that you can sharpen judgements of company earnings, refresh your insight into what individual companies are worth, and evaluate how much debt a leveraged company can service.

The Great Bull Market: Wall Street in the 1920s

Robert Sobel
W. W. Norton & Co., Inc.
500 5th Avenue
New York, NY 10110

PH: (800) 223-2584
ISBN: 0-393-09817-6
Published 1968
Cost: $5.95

The era of the 1920s was one of economic growth, and not merely tinsel and ballyhoo. For most of the period, stock market prices were not unreasonably high. Investment capitalism matured and took on its present-day power. It was Wall Street's silver age. But it was also an age of flagrant abuses and governmental incompetence.

The Greatest Money Book Ever Written

Bruce G. Gould
Gould Publications, Inc.
199/300 State Street
Binghamton, NY 13901

PH: (607) 724-3000
ISBN: 0-918706-42-4
Published 1985
Cost: $10.95

An unusually entertaining story about how to make large sums of money in extremely short periods of time. With a compelling blend of fact and fiction, the author creates people to illustrate principles and quotes actual price history to back up his beliefs.

Guide to Computer-Assisted Investment Analysis

William B. Riley, Jr. & Austin H. Montgomery, Jr.
 McGraw-Hill Publishing Company
1221 Avenue of the Americas
New York, NY 10020

PH: (800) 262-4729
ISBN: 0-07-052917-5
Published 1982
Cost $19.95

Interactive computer programs that make financial problem-solving less laborious and more realistic. Each chapter contains a description of the topic area; a brief examination of the theoretical constructs; a description and explanation of the relevant computer program; and examples, hand solutions, and computer runs.

A Guide to Money Market and Bond Investment Strategies

Dr. Carroll D. Aby, Jr.
Chartcraft, Inc.
1 West Avenue
Larchmont, NY 10538

PH: (914) 834-5181
Published 1989
Cost: $32.95

Subjects: bond investment, portfolio management, fixed income investments; uses charts. This book aims to acquaint the reader with up-to-date ideas and techniques that will promote financial survival in the current difficult climate. Chapter titles include: Money Market Strategy; Fundamentals of Bond Investment; Taxable Fixed Income Securities; Tax Exempt Bonds; Portfolio Management. Many charts and tables are included to ease comparisons between differing types of fixed income investments and to calculate real returns.

Guide to World Commodity Markets: Physical, Futures, and Options Trading

John Buckley, Editor
Beekman Publishers, Inc.
P.O. Box 888
Woodstock, NY 12498

PH: (914) 679-2300
ISBN: 1-85091-116-9
Published 1986 (5th edition)
Cost $70.00

Also available in text edition
ISBN: 0-8464-1361-2
Published 1989
Cost: $144.00

Fifth edition of this highly acclaimed guide has been thoroughly revised and updated. Provides a detailed survey of the physical and futures markets, and includes more comprehensive exchange details and additional trading members lists. Full information on 18 different commodity markets, in 21 countries and over 60 exchanges.

The Handbook for No-Load Fund Investors

Sheldon Jacobs, Editor
Business One Irwin
1818 Ridge Road
Homewood, IL 60430

PH: (708) 206-2700
 (800) 634-3966
FAX: (708) 798-1490
ISBN: 1-55623-528-3
Published 1991
Cost: $34.95

A complete text on mutual fund investing, performance data going back 10 years, and a complete directory of toll-free numbers.

The Handbook for No-Load Fund Investors - Tenth Edition

Sheldon Jacobs, Editor
Business One Irwin
1818 Ridge Road
Homewood, IL 60430

PH: (800) 634-3966
FAX: (708) 798-1490
ISBN: 1-55623-362-0
Published 1990
Cost: $34.95

Covers mutual fund analysis. The complete book on mutual fund investing to help you make the most profitable decisions. Includes how to pick the right fund for your situation, how to track performances, switching, profit-taking, mistakes to avoid, hidden charges, and more. Performance data going back 10 years, complete directory of no-load and low-load funds including toll-free numbers.

A Handbook for Professional Futures and Options Traders

Joseph D. Koziol
John Wiley and Sons, Inc.
605 Third Avenue
New York, NY 10158-0012

PH: (212) 634-3966
ISBN: 0-471-87423-X
Published 1987
Cost: $49.95

Compares trading and hedging techniques for the quantitative edge you need to succeed. Shows how to measure the risks as rewards in virtually every situation. Reviews the myriad forms of analysis - including technical, chart, fundamental, seasonal, cyclical, and spread. Also covers arbitrage, hedging, and foreign exchange.

The Handbook of the Bond and Money Markets

David M. Darst
McGraw-Hill Publishing Company
1221 Avenue of the Americas
New York, NY 10020

PH: (800) 262-4729
ISBN: 0-07-015401-5
Published 1981
Cost $53.50

Easy to use handbook helps the investor understand and take advantage of the many new developments in fixed-income securities. Presents clear information on all participants in the market, explains the forces affecting them, and provides specific techniques for formulating strategy and investing on a day-to-day basis.

The Handbook of Commodity Cycles: A Window on Time

Jacob Bernstein
John Wiley and Sons, Inc.
605 Third Avenue
New York, NY 10158-0012

PH: (212) 634-3966
ISBN: 0-471-08197-3
Published 1982
Cost: $68.50

Top commodity advisor shows how to use the fundamental but often overlooked principles of cyclic analysis for profitable short and long term trading. Examines the proven repetitive price patterns that can help lower investment risks. Discusses the history, current status, and probable future direction of market cycles.

The Handbook of Derivative Instruments

Atsuo Konishi and Ravi E. Dattatreya, Editors
Probus Publishing Co.
1925 North Clybourn Avenue
Chicago, IL 60614

PH: (800) PROBUS-1
FAX: (312) 868-6250
ISBN: 1-55738-154-2
Published 1991
Cost: $69.95

Subjects addressed: finance.
Professionals show how to model and effectively use futures and options to hedge both interest rates and equities. They also cover the neglected areas of hybrid derivatives, such as convertible bonds, warrants and American Trust Primes and Scores. Also shown is how derivative instruments can be applied to a wide range of real-life hedgin and arbitrage situations.

The Handbook of Economic Cycles: Jake Bernstein's Comprehensive Guide to Repetitive Price Patterns in Stocks, Futures and Financials

Jacob Bernstein
Business One Irwin
1818 Ridge Road
Homewood, IL 60430

PH: (708) 206-2700
(800) 634-3966
FAX: (708) 798-1490
ISBN: 1-55623-294-2
Published 1991
Cost: $65.00

Subjects addressed: commodities trading, stock analysis, trading analysis, currencies interest rates. Uses charts extensively. "Everything you need to use cyclical and seasonal analysis to improve your investment decision-making and results." "Jake Bernstein's comprehensive Guide to Repetitive Price Patterns in Stocks, Futures and Financials."

The Handbook of Financial Futures: A Guide for Investors and Professional Money Managers

Nancy Rothstein and James Little
McGraw Hill
1221 Avenue of the Americas
New York, MY 10020

PH: (800) 2-MCGRAW
(212) 512-2000
Published 1984
Cost: $74.95

Subjects addressed: commodities trading; uses charts. Designed to explain and illustrate important concepts and methods for the use and analysis of financial futures for hedging and trading purposes.

Handbook of Financial Market Indexes, Averages and Indicators

Howard M. Berlin
Business One Irwin
1818 Ridge Road
Homewood, IL 60430

PH: (800) 634-3966
FAX: (708) 798-1490
ISBN: 1-55623-125-3
Published 1990
Cost: $69.95

Covers market analysis. Understand the complex components that make up leading economic barometer and forecast market moves more accurately. Berlin shows you how over 200 major financial market averages and indexes in over 24 countries are constructed.

Handbook of Financial Markets and Institutions

Edward I. Altman, Editor
John Wiley and Sons, Inc.
605 Third Avenue
New York, NY 10158-0012

PH: (212) 850-6000
ISBN: 0-471-81954-9
Published 1987 (6th edition)
Cost: $90.00

Since it first appeared in 1925, the Financial Handbook has been an authoritative source of financial guidance for business and finance professionals. The updated, reorganized sixth edition focuses on domestic and international financial markets as well as investment analysis and strategies. Many new sections.

Handbook of Financial Markets: Securities, Options & Futures

Frank Fabozzi, and Frank G. Zarb
Business One Irwin
1818 Ridge Road
Homewood, IL 60530

PH: (708) 206-2700
(800) 634-3966
FAX: (708) 798-1490
ISBN: 0-87094-600-5
Published 1981, 1986 (updated)
Cost: $69.95

Subjects addressed: market analysis. Provides broad knowledge of these 3 financial markets for the experienced and novice investor. Discusses the available instruments in each investment field, the particular risks associated with each trend and the economic and market environments in which trades take place.

Handbook of Fixed Income Options: Pricing, Strategies & Applications

Frank J. Fabozzi, Editor
Probus Publishing Co.
1925 North Clybourn Avenue
Chicago, IL 60614

PH: (800) PROBUS-1
FAX: (312) 868-6250
Published 1989
Cost: $69.95

Strategies such as Caps and Floors, Swaps, Straddles, Covered Calls, and Compound Options are just a few of the strategies financial and investment professionals are now using to lower their borrowing costs, enhance their investment returns and protect the value of their fixed-income positions against adverse rate movements. This book is designed to acquaint financial professionals with the broad range of option-based strategies available, as well as the analytical tools needed to implement them successfully.

The Handbook of Fixed Income Securities

Frank J. Fabozzi
Business One Irwin
1818 Ridge Road
Homewood, IL 60430
ISBN: 1-55623-308-6

PH: (708) 206-2700
(800) 634-3966
FAX: (708) 798-1490
Published 1983, 1991 (3rd edition)
Cost: $75.00

Subjects addressed: bond analysis. Covers all instruments in the fixed income markets, techniques for evaluating them and portfolio strategies employing them. Fifty leading experts show how to take advantage of new opportunities in the market. Clear cut explanations of complicated bond mathematics.

Handbook of Interest and Annuity Tables

Jack C. Estes
McGraw-Hill Publishing Company
1221 Avenue of the Americas
New York, NY 10020

PH: (800)262-4729
ISBN: 0-07-019681-8
Published 1976
Cost $57.95

Quick-reference volume provides ready solutions to almost any type of investment or financial calculation - without technical complication. Reviews the various aspects of compound interest, then presents easy-to-use tables and explains the purpose of each. Lets you give accurate, authoritative answers simply by looking them up.

The Handbook of Mortgage-Backed Securities

Frank J. Fabozzi, Editor
Probus Publishing Co.
1925 North Clybourn Avenue
Chicago, IL 60614

PH: (800) PROBUS-1
FAX: (312) 868-6250
ISBN: 1-55738-257-3
Published 1992
Cost: $75.00

Subjects addressed: mortgage-backed securities. This newly updated and expanded third edition goes beyond the basics of these rapidly evolving securities. Topics in this comprehensive text include: collateralized mortgage obligations, stripped mortgage-backed securities, prepayment forecasting and valuation techniques, arbitrage, swap and portfolio management strategies, computer technology, taxation and accounting.

Handbook of U.S. Government and Federal Agency Securities And Related Money Market Instruments

First Boston Corporation
Probus Publishing Co.
1925 North Clybourn Avenue
Chicago, IL 60614

PH: (800) PROBUS-1
FAX: (312) 868-6250
ISBN: 1-55738-168-2
Published 1990
Cost: $32.50

Uses charts. Published biennially since 1922. Contains comprehensive and detailed factual information on the activities, instruments and institutions of the U.S. Government Securities markets. Covers marketable and nonmarketable securities of the government-sponsored enterprises, such as Freddie Mac; federal agencies, including HUD, SBA and FHA; international quasi-government institutions, the World Bank and Asian Development Bank; and money market instruments, Bankers' Acceptances, and Certificates of Deposits. The text covers the futures and options markets for government securities, Federal Reserve open market operations and the federal taxation of government securities.

Happiness Is A Stock That Let's You Sleep At Night

Ira Cobleigh
Donald I. Fine, Inc.
19 W. 21st, Suite 402
New York, NY 10010

PH: (212) 727-3270
Published 1989
Cost: $15.95

Subjects addressed: stock analysis, market analysis, bond, analysis, trading analysis, fundamental analysis. Tells investors how to build a "fortress portfolio" of stocks that will, over the long term, provide dependable growth, income, and let the investor sleep at night.

Hedging and Options Workshop

Wayne Purcell
Commodities Educational Institute
219 Parkade
Cedar Falls, IA 50613

PH: (800) 635-3936
FAX: (319) 277-7982
Published 1991
Cost: $198.00 (complete set); $55.00 (individual tapes
—4 total)

VIDEO
Subjects addressed: commodities trading, technical analysis. Uses charts. All the key pieces to build your own farm marketing plan. Coverage includes: ABC's of Price Risk Management - principles of hedging and futures trading; Managing Your Pricing Program; ABC's of Ag options; ABC's of Technical Analysis.

Hedging Financial Instruments: A Guide to Basis Trading for Bankers, Treasurers and Portfolio Managers

Jeff L. McKinzie and Keith Schap
Probus Publishing Company
1925 North Clybourn Avenue
Chicago, IL 60614

PH: (800) PROBUS-1
FAX: (312) 868-6250
ISBN: 0-917253-87-6
Published 1988
Cost: $47.50

The adept use of "basis trading" enables grain traders to remain relatively risk-free. This book shows how the same principles can be successfully applied to the management of financial assets, such as bonds, currencies, mortgage instruments, and CDs. Learn how to practice basis trading to enhance your investment returns.

Hedging - Principles, Practices, and Strategies for the Financial Markets

Joseph D. Koziol
John Wiley & Sons
605 Third Avenue
New York, NY 10158-0012

PH: (212) 850-6418 (orders)
(212) 850-6233 (info
INFO: (212) 850-6418
Published February 1990
Cost: $49.95

Subjects addressed: investing theories, commodities trading, trading analysis. Guide to successful hedging in financial and commodity markets. It presents an overview of hedging principles and specific applications for investors and portfolio managers.

High Performance Futures Trading

Joel Robbins
Probus Publishing Co.
1925 North Clybourn Avenue
Chicago, IL 60614

PH: (800) PROBUS-1
FAX: (312) 868-6250
ISBN: 1-55738-149-6
Published 1992
Cost: $42.50

Subjects addressed: investing theories, commodities trading. Minimal use of charts. Shows individual investors, futures/options traders, portfolio/fund managers and investment advisors how to understand and use the high performance trading systems developed by the experts and how to apply them successfully to their own individual programs.

High Performance Mutual Fund Selection and Timing Guide

Louis R. Liuzzi
Available through Fraser Publishing
P.O. Box 494
Burlington, VT 05402

PH: (802) 658-0322
Published 1986
Cost: $12.95

Presents the results of an extensive literature search effort that included many major classic and "how to" investment books, magazines and newspaper articles, current stock market newsletters, and other professional resources. Yields a simple, high performance mutual fund selection and timing system with relatively low risk.

High-Profit/Low Risk Options Strategies

Humphrey E.D. Lloyd
Windsor Books
P.O. Box 280
Brightwaters, NY 11718

Published 1984
Cost: $34.95

Begins with an analysis of spread trading in listed options; then describes fully and partially hedged opportunities available using common stock warrants and convertibles. Finally, introduces stock futures and commodities and considers the opportunities presented by options on stock futures, stock indexes, and commodity futures.

The High Yield Debt Market

Edward I. Altman, Editor
Business One Irwin
1818 Ridge Road
Homewood, IL 60430

PH: (800) 634-3966
FAX: (708) 798-1490
(708) 206-2700
Published 1990
Cost: $47.50

Subjects covered: bond analysis. A Saloman Brothers Center Book. The definitive book on high yield debt securities... or junk bonds. Eminent authorities show you how to determine to volatility of a junk bond, measure the risk of default, value a high yield portfolio and much more.

Historical Chart Book: Volume VII

Martin J. Pring, Editor
Fraser Publishing
P.O. Box 494
Burlington, VT 05402

PH: (802) 658-0322
Published 1989
Cost: $65.00

Historical charts on financial markets and economic indicators, ranging from 1800 to 1991. Relies primarily on technical indicators, but also includes fundamental relationships with good forecasting record. Fascinating and valuable aid for detecting and predicting business cycles in U.S. economic history. Oversize format.

How & When to Buy Stocks
How & When to Sell Stocks
Investing to Win
How to Make Money in Stocks

Investors Daily Library
P.O. Box 24018
Los Angeles, CA 90024

PH: (800) 733-8900
(213) 826-9601
Published 1989
Cost: $29.95 (all 4); 9.95 (each)

CASSETTES
Subjects addressed: investing theories, stock analysis. Over 40 minutes of advice on how to buy stocks and how to protect your profits so you can avoid heavy losses. Listen and learn from the 'best'. These are also available as books by William O'Neill.

How I Find Stocks that Double in a Year with the Scott Pricing Formula

Michael R. Scott
Windsor Books
P.O. Box 280
Brightwaters, NY 11718

Published 1973
Cost: $19.95

The result of years of serious study, research, and practical application, this book is written for both the neophyte and the sophisticated investor. Begins where other books leave off with a fresh perspective on a market profile. Examines market tools, discusses what to buy, and tells how to apply the Scott Pricing Formula.

How I Made One Million Dollars Last Year Trading Commodities

Larry R. Williams
Windsor Books
P.O. Box 280
Brightwaters, NY 11718

ISBN: 0-685-94276-7
Published 1979
Cost: $50.00

Provides the tools to find trades that can lead to gains of over 1000%. Based on the theory that future price direction is pretty well known by the large commercial users, producers, and consumers, who must have commodities to stay in business. The secret is to track these big guys. Refined with a unique technical timing system.

How the Average Investor Can Use Technical Analysis for Stock Profits

James Dines
Available through Fraser Publishing
P.O. Box 494
Burlington, VT 05402

PH: (802) 658-0322
Published 1972
Cost: $50.00

An in-depth work based on the philosophy that all stock market phenomena must be viewed from the psychological, technical, and fundamental aspects. Drawing on years of research, the subject is presented with greatest emphasis on technical analysis. Written for beginners and professionals; organized from least to most complex.

How The Bond Market Works

New York Institute of Finance - (written by staff)
70 Pine Street
New York, NY 10270-0003

PH: (212) 344-2900
FAX: (212) 514-8423
Published May 1988
Cost: $14.95

Subjects addressed: bond analysis. Details the workings of the bond market.

How the Foreign Exchange Market Works

Rudi Weisweiller
New York Institute of Finance
2 Broadway, 5th floor
New York, NY 10004

Published 1984, 1990 (update)
Cost: $19.95

Subjects addressed: market analysis. Clearly demonstrates the growth of international business and the spread of multi-national corporations have made the dynamic foreign exchange market a major concern for business in the 90s. Helps the individual investor analyze main factors and choices in this market.

How the Stock Market Works

John M. Dalton
New York Institute of Finance
70 Pine Street
New York, NY 10270-0003

PH: (212) 344-2900
Published 1988
Cost: $14.95

Subjects addressed: investing theories, market analysis. General overview of the workings if the market from IPOs to theories and operations.

How to Beat Wall Street

Harold B. Wilson
Liberty Hall Press
11 W. 19th Street, 3rd floor
New York, NY 10011

PH: (212) 337-6014
Published 1991
Cost: $18.95

Subjects addressed: investing theories, stock analysis, market analysis, commodities trading, fundamental analysis, technical analysis. Uses charts. Find out how the pros determine what stocks to buy, when to buy them and when to sell them.

How to Buy: An Insider's Guide to Making Money in the Stock Market

Justin Mamis
Farrar, Strauss & Giroux, Inc.
19 Union Square West
New York, NY 10003

PH: (212) 741-6900
ISBN: 0-374-17334-6
Published 1982
Cost: $11.95

Tells when and whether to buy what. Includes invaluable insider's tips such as: the only safe times in the market's cycle to buy stocks, how to pick a stock that is just starting to climb, which indicators identify a true bottom, the "magic twenty minutes" to make your move, plus many more strategies for successful investing.

How to Buy Foreign Stocks & Bonds

Gerald Warfield
Harper & Row
10 E. 53rd Street
New York, NY 10022

Published 1985
Cost: $18.95

Subjects addressed: bond analysis, stock analysis, market analysis. Nuts and bolts book about how and why to invest in foreign stocks and bonds. Explains risk, taxation, withholding, dividends, etc. and includes profiles of 10 major international exchanges.

How to Buy Stocks

Louis Engel and Brendan Boyd
Little Brown & Co.
34 Beacon Street
Boston, MA 02106

Published 1953, 1983 (7th edition)
Cost: $4.95

Subjects addressed: stock analysis, market analysis, bond analysis, commodities trading, mutual funds. The most reliable guide to money making market strategies. Fundamentals of investing in stocks and bonds for the beginner.

How to Forecast Interest Rates: A Guide to Profits for Consumers, Managers, and Investors

Martin J. Pring
Available through McGraw-Hill Publishing Company
1221 Avenue of the Americas
New York, NY 10020

PH: (800) 262-4729
ISBN: 0-07-050865-8
Published 1981
Cost $24.95

Also available in paperback
ISBN: 0-07-050917-4
Published 1986
Cost: $11.50

Protect capital and profit from interest-rate swings with this forecasting guide. A full-length treatment of interest rate changes, historical examples as well as strategies to take advantage of upswings and downturns. A fingertip reference for anyone with a financial interest in the bond, mortgage, or money markets.

How to Forecast Interest Rates

Martin J. Pring
International Institute for Economic Research
P.O. Box 329
Blackville Road
Washington Depot, CT 06794

PH: (800) 221-7514
Cost: Video and free 50 page booklet $95.00

VIDEO
Subjects addressed: interest rate forecasting. A complete description of the concepts and construction of models and their components used to identify various stages in the business cycle, including barometers for interest rates, equities, and commodities.

How to Invest in Bonds

Hugh C. Sherwood
McGraw-Hill Publishing Company
1221 Avenue of the Americas
New York, NY 10020

PH: (800) 262-4729
ISBN: 0-8027-0732-7
Published 1983
Cost: $13.95

Presents the many different facets of bonds in plain language for the average investor. Provides an overview of today's bond market, explains how bonds are rated, describes basic investment goals, details the pros and cons of various types of bonds, and includes important pointers that every investor should keep in mind.

How to Invest in Municipal Bonds

Franklin Watts - Robert Lam (Author)
387 Park Avenue South
Manhattan, NY
ISBN 0-531-09573-8

PH: (212) 686-7070
(800) 672-6672
Published 1984
Cost: $15.95

Subjects addressed:bond analysis. The rewards of tax exempt municipal securities. How to buy, strategies, risks, swaps, the bond markets.

How to Make Money in Commodities: The Successful Method for Today's Markets

Bruce G. Gould
Bruce Gould Publications
P.O. Box 16
Seattle, WA 98111

ISBN: 0-918706-05-9
Published 1982
Cost: $10.95

A respected authority on commodity trading reveals his single most rewarding technique. Concise handbook presents a case-by-case review of actual price moves that offered stunning profits when traded with this remarkable method. Once you've mastered the technique on paper, you are ready to join the ranks of winning speculators.

How to Make Money in Penny Stocks: The Ultimate Solution for the Small Investor

Jim Scott
Marathon International Book Company
P.O. Box 33008
Louisville, KY 40232

PH: (812) 284-4163
ISBN: 0-915216-84-1
Published 1982
Cost: $6.95

Examines the author's actual trading successes and failures. Explains in easy-to-understand and no-nonsense language how to make money trading in penny energy stocks. In addition to revealing his proven methods, also describes where a penny stock comes from, how and when to open an account, rules to trade by, and much more.

How to Make Money In Stock Index Futures

C. D. Smith
McGraw Hill, Inc.
11 West 19th Street
New York, NY 10011

PH: (800) 722-4726
(212) 512-4100
Published 1989
Cost: $13.95

Subjects addressed: index futures trading. "A clear, concise introduction to the subject for both private and professional investors." Shows how to hedge portfolios, save money on transaction costs, reduce losses and more.

How to Make Money in Stocks

By: William J. O'Neil
McGraw-Hill
1221 Avenue of the Americas
New York, NY 10020

PH: (800) 2- MCGRAW
(212) 512-2000
Published 1991 (2nd edition)
Cost: $26.25

Offers a simple, easy-to-use plan for making money in stocks. Drawing on a detailed study of the greatest money-making stocks in the last 33 years, the author gives well-documented guidance in making smart investments. O'Neil's system C.A.N.S.L.I.M. - gives investors an almost foolproof method for evaluating the potential success of a stock.

How to Make Money Trading Stocks & Commodities

George R. Sranko
Available through Gordon Soules Book Publishers, Ltd.
1916 Pike Place
Suite 620
Seattle, WA 98101

PH: (604) 922-6588
ISBN: 0-921110-00-6
Published 1987
Cost: $14.95

A simple, yet brilliant, strategy for those who have the time, the energy, and the inclination to make real money on the stock and commodity markets. Learn methods for selecting the most profitable trades used mainly by professional traders, detailed entry and exit techniques, and how to minimize risk and maximize profits.

How to Make Profits Trading in Commodities

William D. Gann
Lambert Gann Publishing Company
P.O. Box O
Pomeroy, WA 99347

PH: (800) 228-0324
ISBN: 0-939093-02-2
Published 1942, 1976 (reprint)
Cost: $35.00

A study of the commodity market, with charts and rules for successful trading and investing based on actual market highs and lows. Developed over forty years of experience, Gann's time-tested, practical, mathematical rules continue to be valuable indicators of market trends. Learn how to protect capital and make profits.

How to Pick the Best No-Load Mutual Fund for Solid Growth and Safety

Sheldon Jacobs
Business One Irwin
1818 Ridge Road
Homewood, IL 60430

PH: (708) 206-2700
(800) 634-3966
FAX: (708) 798-1490
ISBN: 1-55623-574-7
Published 1991
Cost: $12.95

This introduction to the opportunities and potential pitfalls of mutual fund investing gives readers practical advice on how to build and manage a portfolio of funds. Topics include: how to select funds appropriate for meeting or possibly exceeding investment goals, how to evaluate different types of funds, offers model portfolio recommendations for different life cycles, saves readers money by showing them how to manage no-load funds themselves.

How to Profit from the Money Revolution: The Insider's Guide to Financial Supermarkets, Their Super Products, and Super Brokers

Wayne F. Nelson
McGraw-Hill Publishing Company
1221 Avenue of the Americas
New York, NY 10020

PH: (800) 262-4729
ISBN: 0-07-046217-8
Published 1983
Cost: $12.95

With an accountant and tax advisor for support, helps you get solid advice from one organization on: getting money to buy a house, creative financing for other real estate, reducing your taxes, profiting from the stock market boom, buying life insurance, maximizing you IRS and avoiding the pitfalls of non-traditional financing.

How to Read the Financial Pages

Peter Passell
Warner Books
66 5th Avenue
New York, NY 10103

Covers: market analysis. Everything you need to master the vital yet often mystifying information published in the financial pages of newspapers and business publications.

Published February 1986
Cost $4.50

How to Read a Financial Report: Wringing Cash Flow and Other Vital Signs Out of the Numbers

John A. Tracy
Available through John Wiley and Sons, Inc.
605 Third Avenue
New York, NY 10158-0012

PH: (212) 850-6000
ISBN: 0-471-88859-1
Published 1983 (2nd edition)
Cost $27.95

Also available: Third text edition
ISBN: 0-471-50745-8
Published 1989
Cost: $27.95

This short, non-technical guide is designed to help non-financial people cut through the maze of accounting information and find out what those numbers really mean. Explains the basics of the three key statements in financial reports - balance sheet, income statement, and cash flow statement - and the relationship between them.

How to Triple Your Money Every Year with Stock Index Futures: An Insider's Strategy to Tap the Riches of Wall Street

George Angell
Windsor Books
P.O. Box 280
Brightwaters, NY 11718

ISBN: 0-930233-03-4
Published 1984
Cost: $39.95

How to trade and develop winning strategies in stock index futures. Presents the basics and explores the more advanced aspects of professional trading. Covers hedging, index options, market timing, cyclic models, and proven systems for consistent profits. Learn from a pro exactly when to plunge in and when to walk away.

How Wall Street Works: The Basics & Beyond

David L. Scott
Probus Publishing Co.
1925 North Clybourn Avenue
Chicago, IL 60614

PH: (800) PROBUS-1
FAX: (312) 868-6250
ISBN: 1-55738-267-0
Published 1991
Cost: $19.95

Contains all the essential information needed to "make sense" out of Wall Street and owning stock in today's markets, including: who should buy stocks and why, creating an investment plan, strategies to minimize risk, how stock is bought and sold and traded over-the-counter.

How Young Millionaires Trade Commodities

Futures Discount Group/Zaner & Company
600 W. Jackson
Chicago, IL 60606

PH: (800) USA-MORE
Cost: FREE

CASSETTE
Subject(s) addressed: investing theories, commodities trading, trading analysis, fundamental analysis, technical analysis and futures. Strategies that helped traders make $1,000,000 each in trading profits. Listen and learn 25 amazing secrets.

The Income Investor

Donald R. Nichols
Longman Financial Services Publishing
520 N. Dearborn Street
Chicago, IL 60610-4975

ISBN: 0-88462-738-1
Published 1988
Cost: $23.50

Subjects addressed: bond analysis, income investments. Covers bonds, CDs, options, precious metals, mutual funds, stocks, risks and rewards of each. Choosing investments that pay cash today and tomorrow. Nichols explains what income investments are, how they work, and how they can be used to best advantage during both inflation and economic downswings. He also explains why changing tax laws and uncertain equity markets make income investments attractive.

The Individual Investor's Guide to Computerized Investing

American Association on Individual Investors
International Publishing Company
625 N. Michigan Avenue
Suite 1920
Chicago, IL 60611

ISBN: 0-942641-22-1
Published 1990 (7th edition)
Cost: $19.95

Here's a primary source of information for individual investors. Features detailed descriptions of more than 380 software products and 90 database services. "The best comprehensive source of information on all aspects of computerized investing," says Black Enterprise.

The Individual Investors Guide to Program Trading

Jeffrey D. Madler/Prentice Hall - JK Lasser Institute
One Gulf + Western Plaza
New York, NY 10023

Subjects addressed: market analysis. How to invest safely in the post-crash stock market.

Published 1989
Cost: $14.95

Inflation: Causes and Effects

Robert E. Hall, Editor
University of Chicago Press
5801 Ellis Avenue
4th Floor
Chicago, IL 60637

PH: (312)702-7700
ISBN: 0-226-31323-9
Published 1982
Cost: $33.00

Also available in paperback
ISBN: 0-226-31324-7
Published 1984
Cost: $10.95

Assembled by the National Bureau of Economic Research, the contributors diagnose the problems and describe the events that economists most thoroughly understand. Reflecting a dozen diverse views - many of which challenge established orthodoxy - they illuminate the economic and political processes involved in this important issue.

The Informed Investor

Ray Vicker
Probus Publishing Co.
1925 North Clybourn Avenue
Chicago, IL 60614

PH: (800) PROBUS-1
FAX: (312) 868-6250
ISBN: 1-55738-134-8
Published
Cost: $21.95

Subjects addressed: investment.

The author surveys the financial media to show investors how to profit in the markets from readily-available information by examining all the major sources of financial news and by discussing when to use this information for personal financial decisions. The book examines the many sources of investment information, including brokers, mutual funds, federal and local governments, foreign press, seminars, newspapers, magazines, radio and television and investment and financial newsletters.

Ins and Outs of Institutional Investing

Dean LeBaron
Nelson-Hall, Inc.
111 N. Canal Street
Chicago, IL 60606

PH: (312)930-9446
ISBN: 0-88229-343-5
Published 1976
Cost: $21.95

Reveals the real workings of the institutional investment community as it is today - and takes a look into the future. Discusses how to construct a portfolio, how to select securities, how to achieve diversification, and how to deal with fluctuating market forces. Gives a real-life account of institutional investors in action.

Inside Investment Banking

Ernest Bloch
Business One Irwin
1818 Ridge Road
Homewood, IL 60430

PH: (708) 206-2700
(800) 634-3966
FAX: (708)798-1490
ISBN: 1-55623-128-8
Published 1986
Cost $42.50

Also available: second edition
ISBN: 1-55623-128-8
Published 1988
Cost: $45.00

An illuminating account of the dynamics of investment banking. Explores the market-making activities that differentiate investment banking firms from other financial institutions, and provides in-depth information in the new issues and process. Addresses the public policy implications of the recent changes in the financial markets.

Inside the Fed: Making Monetary Policy

William C. Melton
Business One Irwin
1818 Ridge Road
Homewood, IL 60430

PH: (708) 206-2700
(800) 634-3966
FAX: (708)798-1490
ISBN: 0-87094-544-0
Published 1985
Cost: $29.00

As lender of last resort, the Fed backstops all U.S. fianancial market participants - their objectives, uncertainties, mistakes, and triumphs. Learn the story of this unique institution, at once good and evil.

Inside the Financial Futures Markets

Mark J. Powers
John Wiley and Sons, Inc.
605 Third Avenue
New York, NY 10158-0012

PH: (212) 850-6000
ISBN: 0-471-89071-5
Published 1984
Cost: $34.95

A guide to financial futures contracts and corporate hedging strategies. Revised edition features comprehensive coverage of options contracts on financial instruments and stock index futures. Also examines such established contracts as mortgage certificates, Treasury bills, bonds, notes, Eurodollars, and foreign currencies.

Inside the Yield Book: New Tools for Bond Market Strategy

Sidney Homer & Martin L. Leibowitz, Ph.D.
Prentice-Hall
Route 9W
Englewood Cliffs, NJ 07632

PH: (201) 592-2000
ISBN: 0-13-467548-7
Published 1972
Cost $26.50

Takes the bond investor behind the scenes and reveals, in non-technical terms, the true nature of bond yields and the ways in which they are often misused. Corrects misconceptions as to bond prices and yields as calculated in the standard Yield Book, and provides a whole new set of tools to aid in bond investment strategy.

The Insider's Automatic Options Strategy: How to Win on Better than 9 Out of 10 Trades with Extremely Low Risk

Jon Schiller
Probus Publishing Co.
1925 North Clybourn Avenue
Chicago, IL 60614

PH: (800) PROBUS-1
FAX: (312) 868-6250
ISBN: 0-930233-49-2
Published 1992
Cost: $32.50

This book explains in understandable terms how to make money each month safely and how to make capital grow by trading in the options markets, specifically: stock index options, common stock options, foreign currency options, precious metal options, commodity futures options, treasury futures options. For each market covered, "The Insider's Automatic Options Strategy" provides step-by-step details, including: terms and concepts, trading models and strategies, how to get started trading, statistical analysis to reduce risk, using computer programs and PC spreadsheets as trading tools.

The Insider's Guide to the Financial Services Revolution

Alan Gart
McGraw-Hill Publishing Company
1221 Avenue of the Americas
New York, NY 10020

PH: (800) 262-4729
ISBN: 0-07-022891-4
Published 1984
Cost: $33.95

The entire financial industry is reeling from the impact of changing technology, volatile interest rates, inflation, brutal competition, and a fluctuating regulatory climate. This unique analysis of developing trends explores the implications of the revolution and provides solid advice to prepare for the coming shock waves.

Inside Wall Street

Robert Sobel
W. W. Norton & Company, Inc.
500 5th Avenue
New York, NY 10110

PH: (800) 223-2584
ISBN: 0-393-00030-3
Published 1982
Cost: $7.95

Learn how the greatest financial district operates from one who knows the world of finance inside and out. This highly readable account captures the atmosphere, excitement, and personalities of Wall Street. A good guide for both amateurs and professionals.

Instincts of the Herd in Peace and War

Wilfred Trotter
Omnigraphics, Inc.
2400 Penobscot Building
Detroit, MI 48226

PH: (800) 234-1340
ISBN: 0-8103-4090-9
Published 1923 (2nd edition), 1975 (reprint)
Cost: $34.00

Written at the time of WWI, this fascinating treatise is still remarkably relevant to the modern human instinct. Essays include "Herd Instinct and its Bearing on the Psychology of Civilized Man," "Sociological Applications of the Psychology of Herd Instinct," "Speculations upon the Human Mind in 1915," and "Postscript of 1919."

The Institutional Investor Focus on Investment Management

Frank J. Fabozzi, Editor
Harper-Collins Publishers, Inc.
10 E. 53rd Street
New York, NY 10022

PH: (800) 242-7737
ISBN: 0-88730-275-0
Published 1989
Cost: $69.95

Forty-five separate chapters with different authors combine to give the reader new rather than familiar information on a host of investment topics, especially equity management, fixed income management and asset allocation. Designed to help the reader understand and profit from recent innovations in investment management.

Insurance as an Investment: Getting the Most for Your Money

Ben G. Baldwin and Maureen M. Baldwin
Probus Publishing Co.
1925 North Clybourn Avenue
Chicago, IL 60614

PH: (800) PROBUS-1
FAX: (312) 868-6250
ISBN: 1-55738-238-7
Published 1992
Cost: $22.95

The complete book of life insurance and annuities - how to understand them, manage them and, most importantly, how to use them profitably as investment vehicles. Topics include: retail term life insurance, whole life insurance, universal life insurance, variable life insurance, managing your insurance investment portfolio, annuity products, taxation, insurance product investment strategies.

The Intelligent Investor

Benjamin Graham
Harper & Row
10 E. 53rd Street
New York, NY 10022

ISBN: 0-06-015547-7
Published 1973
Cost: $27.50

Subjects addressed: stock analysis, market analysis, earnings analysis, fundamental analysis. Guide to sound investing. Main objective is to guide the reader against areas of possible substantial error and to develop policies with which he will be comfortable.

Interest Rate Futures: A Market Guide for Hedgers and Speculators

Allan M. Loosigian
Available through Fraser Publishing
P.O. Box 494
Burlington, VT 05402

PH: (802) 658-0322
ISBN: 0-87128-579-7
Published 1980
Cost: $35.00

An indispensable guide to the interest rate futures market. Bankers, portfolio managers, and corporate financial officers will appreciate the sections on hedging against interest rate risks. Individual investors will find alternate strategies for both conservative and speculative objectives. Enhance your chance of success!

Interest Rate Spreads Analysis: Managing and Reducing Rate Exposure, Fourth Edition

Citicorp
Probus Publishing Co.
1925 North Clybourn Avenue
Chicago, IL 60614

PH: (800) PROBUS-1
FAX: (312) 868-6250
ISBN: 1-55738-180-1
Published 1992
Cost: $65.00

Provides readers with a thorough understanding of how rates react in different economic environments. This book traces the historical movements of key interest rates from 1981 to 1990, including spreads summary statistics for each year during the period as well as for the period as a whole. It also covers: instrument description, computation methodology, absolute rate levels, LIBOR based spreads, treasury based spreads, other money market indices.

Interest Rates, the Markets, and the New Financial World

Henry Kaufman
Random House, Inc.
201 E. 50th Street
New York, NY 10022

PH: (800) 733-3000
ISBN: 0-8129-1333-7
Published 1986
Cost: $22.50

One of the world's most respected financial analysts offers essential information on evaluating the markets and the new financial world. Provides an intimate analysis of the worldwide financial state of affairs, and allows you to identify the emerging financial trends and their implications. Counters dogma with fresh advice.

International Financial Management - Theory & Application

Donald R. Lessard
John Wiley & Sons
605 Third Avenue
New York, NY 10158-0012

PH: (212) 850-6418 orders
(212) 850-6233 info
Published 1979, 1985 (2nd edition)
Cost: $51.95

Subjects addressed: investing theories. TEXTBOOK. Discussion of positive theory of international investing and valuation, normative models and approaches to scientific international financial decisions.

International Investing Made Easy: Proven Money-Making Strategies with as Little as $5000

Martin J. Pring
McGraw-Hill Publishing Company
1221 Avenue of the Americas
New York, NY 10020

PH: (800) 262-4729
ISBN: 0-07-050872-0
Published 1981
Cost: $26.50

Explains why long-term growth is more easily and profitably achieved through international investments rather that domestic options. Points out many promising markets around the globe - including foreign stock markets, bond markets, currencies, gold, and financial futures markets - and demonstrates exactly how to invest them.

The International Money Markets: Overview, Analysis and Structure

Frank J. Fabozzi, Editor
Probus Publishing Co.
1925 North Clybourn Avenue
Chicago, IL 60614

PH: (800) PROBUS-1
FAX: (312) 868-6250
ISBN: 1-55738-251-4
Published 1991
Cost: $65.00

Subjects addressed: non-U.S. market analysis. This is an invaluable guide to non-U.S. markets, including: Japan, France, Germany, Italy, United Kingdom, Spain, Canada, Singapore, Australia, New Zealand. The important facets of each market covered are addressed in detail, including: money market instruments traded; tax considerations; futures and options markets; market participants; regulations and regulatory agencies; yield conventions and outlooks for the future. Also provides coverage of the Eurocurrencies market.

The Interpretation of Financial Statements

Benjamin Graham and Charles McGolrick
Harper-Collins Publishers, Inc
10 E. 53rd Street
New York, NY 10022

PH: (800)242-7737
ISBN: 0-06-0111566-1
Published 1975 (3rd edition)
Cost: $13.95

First published in 1937, this highly praised manual has become standard work for all who want to understand corporation balance sheets and income statements. Provides many valuable insights, all written in simple language. Authoritative and comprehensive enough to serve private investors and professionals alike.

In the Shadows of Wall Street: A Guide to Investing in Neglected Stocks

Peter Strebell & Steven Carvell
Prentice-Hall
Route 9W
Englewood Cliffs, NY 07632

PH: (201) 592-2000
ISBN: 0-13-455999-1
Published 1988
Cost: $26.95

The authors show the individual investor, the portfolio manager, and the seasoned professional how to maximize gains from security research. Pointer on how to identify neglected stocks and what kind of research to use in selecting these high-performing shadow stocks.

Introduction to Investments

Giorgio A. Christy and John C. Clendenin
McGraw Hill
1221 Avenue of the Americas
New York, MY 10020

PH: (800) 2-MCGRAW
(212) 512-2000
Published 1982
Cost: $49.45

Subjects addressed: investing theories and market analysis. Textbook on theory and practice of investments. Covers corporate securities and the securities markets, investment analysis, other investments (life insurance, real estate, etc.) and investment administration.

Introduction to Risk and Return from Common Stocks

Richard A. Brealey
MIT Press
55 Hayward Street
Cambridge, MA 02142

PH: (800) 356-0343
ISBN: 0-262-52116-4
Published 1986 (2nd edition)
Cost: $8.95

A brief, non-technical review of current research in investment management as well as its implications. Revised, second edition explains the new, unified theory of investment management and presents empirical research to test it. Divided into three parts dealing with market efficiency, valuation, and modern portfolio theory.

Invest Japan: The Structure, Performance and Opportunities of Japan's Stock, Bond and Fund Markets

William T. Ziemba & Sandra L. Schwartz
Probus Publishing
1925 North Clybourn Avenue
Chicago, IL 60614

PH: (800) PROBUS-1
FAX: (312) 868-6250
ISBN: 1-55738-234-4
Published 1991
Cost: $65.00

Subjects addressed: Japanese stock, bond, and fund markets. "Invest Japan" explores all the "ins and outs" of the structure, performance and wealth of opportunities to be found in Japan's markets. Topics in this detailed guide include: how the stock markets operate; the nikkei stock average and TOPIX indices; day of the week effects in Japanese stocks; monthly, turn of the month and year, holidays and the golden week effects; valuation and market timing techniques, market risks and protection strategies; mutual funds for investment in Japan by Japanese and by foreigners.

Investing for a Lifetime: Paul Merriman's Guide to Mutual Fund Strategies

Paul Merriman
Business One Irwin
1818 Ridge Road
Homewood, IL 60430

PH: (708) 206-2700
(800) 634-3966
FAX: (708) 798-1490
ISBN: 1-55623-485-6
Published 1991
Cost: $24.95

Subjects addressed: investing theories. Offers the one thing that nearly every investor wants to learn from a book on investing - how to make successful investment decisions in healthy or weak financial markets. While the book concentrates on mutual fund investing, several different strategies are outlined. Readers will find: ten rules for successful investing; how to distinguish good versus bad advice from brokers, advisors, and newsletters; how to maximize performance from a mutual fund; how to invest for specific purposes, such as retirement or a college fund; how to beat the market using Merriman's own timing techniques.

Investing Fundamentals Videocourse

American Association of Individual Investors
625 N. Michigan Avenue
Chicago, IL

PH: (312) 280-0170
Cost: $129.00
$98.00 for AAII members

VIDEO
Subjects addressed: bond analysis, stock analysis, earnings analysis, fundamental analysis, trading analysis, technical analysis. A 6 hour tape focusing on the fundamentals of investing: Basic Investment Concepts; The Language of Investments, Investment Choices, Stock Analysis and Research, Pooled Investment Products, Developing Your Financial Plan.

Investing in and Profiting from Legal Insider Transactions

Edwin A. Buck
New York Institute of Finance
2 Broadway 5th Floor
New York, NY 10004

Published 1990
Cost: $11.95

Subjects addressed: investing theories, market analysis, technical analysis. Minimal use of charts. Shows how to legally tap into valuable buying and selling signals from insiders, (corporate officers, e.g. stockholders). How to know when to buy, sell, or hold based in insider activity.

Investing in Call Options: An Alternative to Common Stocks and Real Estate

James A. Willson
Greenwood Publishing Group, Inc.
88 Post Road, W, Box 5007
Westport, CT 06881

PH: (203) 226-3571
ISBN: 0-03-059453-7
Published 1982
Cost: $35.00

Presents a convincing case for selling covered call options instead of investing in realty income property. Illustrates the basic ideas, the opportunities, and the possible pitfalls. Expert information on financing, expenses, tax shelter potential, return on investment, and the ease of dealing with common stock call options.

Investing in Convertible Securities

John P. Calamos
Longman Financial Services Publishing
520 N. Dearborn
Chicago, IL 60610

PH: (800) 621-9621
ISBN: 0-88462-736-5
Published 1988
Cost: $31.50

Subjects: convertible securities. Written for both investors and professional money managers, the book gives an overview of the various investment strategies and explains how to evaluate the risks and rewards.

Investing in Convertible Securities

Wayne F. Nelson
Business One Irwin
1818 Ridge Road
Homewood, IL 60430

PH: (800) 634-3966
Published 1991
Cost: $27.95

Investors of all sorts are discovering how to minimize investment risks while maximizing return by using convertible securities. The average convertible security yields three times more than common stocks and is less volatile. Wayne Nelson details the advantages and disadvantages of these investment vehicles. He shows how to: spot potential investment bargains and land mines, know an issue is fairly priced, time the sale of the convertible to maximize your profits, and use convertibles to make your current investment strategies more balanced.

Investing in Emerging Growth Stocks

J.W. Broadfoot
John Wiley & Sons
605 Third Avenue
New York, NY 10158-0012

PH: (212) 850-6418 orders
(212) 850-6233 info
Published c. 1989
Cost: $32.95

Covers: stock analysis. A book about making money in the stock market by investing in emerging growth stocks - small, fast-growing companies. Gives guidance on how to pick stocks that will outperform the market and how to avoid those that will fail. Includes what to look for in small companies, how to analyze them, and how to diversify among them. Shows you how to analyze profitability, competition, and management, with an eye toward when to buy, when to sell, and when to sit on the sidelines.

Investing in High-Yield Stocks

Peter D. Heerwagen
Probus Publishing Co.
1925 North Clybourn Avenue
Chicago, IL 60614

PH: (800) PROBUS-1
FAX: (312) 868-6250
ISBN: 1-55738-055-4
Published 1989
Cost: $24.95

Subjects addressed: investment. Provides the essentials of using high-yield stocks by discussing how to identify and analyze high-yield stocks, combine them into a portfolio, where to find information on high-yield stocks, how to use cash flow analysis, and further discusses risks and returns from high-yield stocks, common stock dividends, selecting high-yield stocks, blue chip stocks, public utility stocks and financial stocks.

Investing in Money Market Securities

Jeffery H. Katz
Probus Publishing Co.
1925 North Clybourn Avenue
Chicago, IL 60614

PH: (800) PROBUS-1
FAX: (312) 868-6250
ISBN: 1-55738-147-X
Published
Cost: $19.95

Subjects addressed: investment. Explains money market instruments, how money is invested, how the money markets work, how rates of return are calculated and how levels of safety are determined with information on U.S. Treasury Bills, U.S. Government Agency Discount Notes, Bank Negotiable Certificates of Deposit, Bank Euro Certificates of Deposit, Bank Euro Time Deposits, Bankers' Acceptances, Commercial Paper and Repurchase Agreements. Included are charts, graphs, case studies, definitions and exercises.

Investing in Tax-Saving Municipal Bonds

David L. Scott
Probus Publishing Co.
1925 North Clybourn Avenue
Chicago, IL 60614

PH: (800) PROBUS-1
FAX: (312) 868-6250
ISBN: 1-55738-182-8
Published 1991
Cost: $24.95

Subjects addressed: investment.
Shows how to use municipal bonds to save pre-tax dollars. Explains the specifics of municipal bonds such as interest payments, principal maturities, types of yields, individual bonds, mutual funds and trusts. Also included are a treatment of the Alternative Minimum Tax, a guide to the taxation of municipal bonds in each of the fifty states and an explanation of the bond ratings.

Investing in Uncertain Times

Donald R. Nichols
Longman Financial Services Publishers
520 N. Dearborn
Chicago, IL 60610

PH: (800)621-9621
ISBN: 0-8462-057-3
Published 1988
Cost: $19.95

Presents step-by-step information on what the economic cycles are, what the indicators mean, and which investments are most likely to prosper under different "tough times" scenarios. Sensible and refreshing perspective shows how to use publicly available information to evaluate the economy and choose your own investments wisely.

Investing in Utilities - A Comprehensive, Industry-by Industry Guide for Investors and Money Managers

Daniel D. Singer
Probus Publishing Co.,
1925 North Clybourn Avenue
Chicago, IL 60614

PH: (800) PROBUS-1
FAX: (312) 868-6250
ISBN: 1-55738-125-9
Published 1990
Cost: $42.50

Subjects: utility investing and utility stock analysis. Over the years, because of the unique and attractive combination of safety and returns that they offer, public utility stocks have always been popular investments with both individuals and institutions. However utility stocks may have performed in the past, as a group, they are certain to perform differently in the future. These changes will bring the investor opportunities in the 90s.

Investing Smart from the Start

Dick Goldberg
Longman Financial Services Publishing
520 N. Dearborn Street
Chicago, IL 60610

Published 1988
Cost: $14.95

Subjects addressed: stock analysis, market analysis, bond analysis, commodities trading, mutual funds. Tips for understanding and profiting from various investment vehicles, including stocks, bonds, mutual funds, commodities, real estate, retirement accounts and more.

Investing: The Collected Works of Martin L. Leibowitz

Frank J. Fabozzi, Editor
Probus Publishing Co.
1925 North Clybourn Avenue
Chicago, IL 60614

PH: (800) PROBUS-1
FAX: (312) 868-6250
ISBN: 1-55738-198-4
Published 1992
Cost: $75.00

Subjects addressed: investment.
Contains the writings of Liebowitz and his associates at Salomon Brothers who contributed to the development of many of the new concepts for the analytical basis of bonds. Included are bond investment theories and strategies, total return concept, horizon analysis, baseline portfolios, capitalization-weighted and specialized indexes, Macaulay's duration, bond and contingent immunizations, financial futures, dedicated portfolios, quality spread management and fixed-income roles.

Investing with the Best: What to Look For, What to Look Out For in Your Search for a Superior Investment Manager

Claude N. Rosenberg
John Wiley and Sons, Inc.
605 Third Avenue
New York, NY 10158-0012

PH: (212) 850-6000
ISBN: 0-471-83798-9
Published 1986
Cost: $24.95

Helps you cut through the confusing hype, marketplace jargon, and misleading claims about performance to find an investment manager who's not only savvy, but also trustworthy. Shows how to evaluate the risks a manager is taking with your money and how to interpret your fees to make sure they're reasonable.

Investment Policy: How to Win the Loser's Game

Charles D. Ellis
Business One Irwin
1818 Ridge Road
Homewood, IL 60430

PH: (708) 206-2700
(800)634-3966
FAX: (708)798-1490
ISBN: 0-87094-713-3
Published 1985
Cost: $27.50

A fresh approach to professional investment management that involves active client participation. Enables clients to understand the basic nature of institutional investing, formulate specific policies to reach long-term investment goals and objectives, and manage their investment managers in order to achieve their real goals.

Investment Fundamentals

Lawrence J. Getmar and Michael D. Joehnk
Harper & Row
10 E. 53rd Street
New York, NY 10022

Published 1988
Cost: $24.95

Subjects addressed: stock analysis, market analysis, bond analysis, trading analysis, commodities trading, technical analysis. A primer for all investors and essential reading for the novice who aims to become knowledgeable about the ways of the investing marketplace.

Investment Markets

Roger C. Ibbotson & G.P. Brinson
McGraw-Hill
1221 Avenue of the Americas
New York, NY 10020

PH: (800) 262-4729
ISBN: 0-07-031673-2
Published 1987
Cost: $36.50

Subject: market analysis; uses charts. Shows where and how money has been made in stocks, bonds, cash and cash equivalents, real estate, gold and silver, tangibles, options and futures, and more. Contains more than 80 graphs, charts, and tables containing extensive data and analysis are provided as an invaluable reference aid for both individual and institutional investors. This book provides groundwork for diversifying and structuring a portfolio, choosing asset classes, reducing transaction costs, and cracking the evolving multi-asset global capital market.

Investments

William F. Sharpe
Prentice-Hall
Route 9W
Englewood Cliffs, NJ 07632

PH: (201) 592-2000
ISBN: 0-13-504697-1
Published 1985 (3rd edition
Cost $48.00

Also available: Fourth text edition, casebound
ISBN: 0-13-504382-4
Published 1989
Cost: $49.20

Comprehensive text provides an overall framework of the subject, discusses taxes and inflation, describes and analyzes various instruments. Covers financial analysis, investment management, performance measurement, and extended diversification. Encyclopedic without excessive detail; rigorous without needless analytic apparatus.

Investment Strategy

C. Robert Coates
McGraw-Hill Publishing Company
1221 Avenue of the Americas
New York, NY 10020

PH: (800) 262-4729
ISBN: 0-07-011471-4
Published 1978
Cost: $40.95

Integrates modern investment theory with practical concepts to provide all the tools necessary for making wise investments. Helps form a consistent investment philosophy by exploring the efficient market concept. Written in an easy-to-read style; cleverly eliminates mathematics from investment theory, and uses many examples.

Investments

Zvi Bodie, Alex Lane, Alan J. Marcus
Business One Irwin
1818 Ridge Road
Homewood, IL 60430

PH: (800) 634-3966
(708) 206-2700
FAX: (708) 798-1490
Published 1989
Cost: $47.95

Subjects addressed: bond analysis, stock analysis, market analysis, earnings analysis, commodities trading, fundamental analysis. Textbook overview of different types of security market operations, portfolio theories, fundamental analysis, security valuation, options and futures, portfolio management and evaluation.

Investments: Analysis and Management

J.C. Francis
McGraw Hill, Inc.
1221 Avenue of the Americas
New York, NY 10020

Published 1972 /1991 - 5th edition
Cost: $55.79

Subjects addressed: investing theories, stock analysis, market analysis, bond analysis, earnings analysis, trading analysis, commodities trading, fundamental analysis, technical analysis. Includes minimal use of charts. Textbook covering a wide variety of investments and securities, the market itself, arbitrage, securities, and much more.

Investments: Analysis and Management

J. C. Francis
McGraw Hill, Inc.
11 West 19th Street
New York, NY 10011

PH: (800) 722-4726
 (212) 512-4100
Published 1991
Cost: $54.95

Subjects addressed: investing theories. "Comprehensive treatment of investments and facilitates the learning of both the traditional institutional material and the newer, more abstract risk-return theories."

The Investments Reader

Edited by Jay Wilbanks
Business One Irwin
1818 Ridge Road
Homewood, IL 60430

PH: (708) 206-2700
(800) 634-3966
FAX: (708)798-1490
ISBN: 1-55623-237-3
Published 1989
Cost: $22.95

A collection of ideas and viewpoints about investments, portfolios and markets. Get the answers to how interest rate changes affect bond prices, how single premium deferred annuities stack up, how the Securities and Exchange Commission works and much more. Filled with practical knowledge about investing.

The Investors Guide to Economic Indicators

Charles R. Nelson
John Wiley & Sons
605 Third Avenue
New York, NY 10158-0012

PH: (212) 850-6418 orders
(212) 850-6233 info
Published 1987
Cost: $12.95

Subjects addressed: market analysis, trading analysis; uses charts. Guide to reading, interpreting, and using economic and financial news reports to make better investment decisions. Shown in plain language and simple charts.

Investor's Guide to Online Databases

Kenneth M. Landis & J. Thomas Monk
Business One Irwin
1818 Ridge Road
Homewood, IL 60430

PH: (800) 634-3966
ISBN: 0-87094-751-6
Published 1988
Cost: $60.50

Subjects: online investment information services. This book established guidelines for determining what information is needed, how to get it, and how to use it. The book takes a detailed look at online investment information services and focuses on the information needs of investors.

The Investors Guide to Stock Quotations

Gerald Warfield
Harper & Row
10 E. 53rd Street
New York, NY 10022

Published 1990 (3rd edition)
Cost: $10.95

Subjects addressed: bond analysis and commodities trading. Clear explanations of how to identify, read, and interpret data pertaining to common and preferred bonds, corporate and municipal bonds, government securities, mutual funds, money market funds, options, commodity and financial futures.

The Investor's Quotient: The Psychology of Successful Investing in Commodities & Stocks

Jacob Bernstein
John Wiley and Sons, Inc.
605 Third Avenue
New York, NY 10158-0012

PH: (212)850-6000
ISBN: 0-471-07849-2
Published 1980
Cost: $27.50

An experienced commodity trader and former clinical psychologist helps you understand how your attitudes and emotional makeup can either contribute to or limit success. Oriented toward the individual investor, shows how to identify, analyze, and correct many of the personal emotional limitations to profitable investing.

It's Not What Stocks You Buy, It's When You Sell that Counts

Donald L. Cassidy
Probus Publishing Co.
1925 North Clybourn Avenue
Chicago, IL 60614

PH: (800) PROBUS-1
FAX: (312) 868-6250
ISBN: 1-55738-178-X
Published 1991
Cost: $22.95

Subjects addressed: investing theories.
Discusses when to sell, how identify trouble early to cut losses, earn maximum profit through strategic selling, how to avoid investment pitfalls, how to sell successfully in changing market conditions and includes a checklist to aid in the decision-making process of selling.

Jake Bernstein's Seasonal Futures Spreads

Jake Bernstein
John Wiley & Sons
605 Third Avenue
New York, NY 10158-0012

PH: (212) 850-6418 orders
(212) 850-6233 info.
Published July, 1990
Cost: $70.00

Subjects addressed: commodities trading. Uses charts. One of America's leading experts on seasonal futures tendencies explains the seasonal characteristics of commodity spreads and shows you how to use them to tilt the trading odds in your favor.

Japan Inc.: Global Strategies of Japanese Trading Corporations

Max Eli
Probus Publishing Co.
1925 North Clybourn Avenue
Chicago, IL 60614

PH: (800) PROBUS-1
FAX: (312) 868-6250
ISBN: 1-55738-223-9
Published 1991
Cost: $27.50

Subjects addressed: finance.
Examines Japan's rise to power, the powerful alliances and cliques within Japan's industrial, financial and trading sectors. All major industrial groupings are discussed such as Mitsubishi, Mitsui, Sumitomo, Fuyo, DKB Group, Sanwa, Tokai and IBJ. Considers the competitive atmosphere and explains how the kigyo keiretsu were formed, their purpose, and the types and extent of the power they have accumulated along with the changing directions and decisions within Japan.

Japanese Bond Markets

Frank J. Fabozzi, Editor
Probus Publishing Co.
1925 North Clybourn Avenue
Chicago, IL 60614

PH: (800) PROBUS-1
FAX: (312) 868-6250
ISBN: 1-55738-112-7
Published 1990
Cost: $65.00

Frank J. Fabozzi draws upon an elite group of international bond experts to present a richly detailed and comprehensive picture of all facets of the Japanese fixed income markets, including the various securities issued: Japanese government bonds, Japanese government-related organization bonds, local government bonds, repo debentures, corporate bonds, convertible bonds, commercial paper, foreign bonds (including Samurai, Daimyo, Shibosai, Shogun and Geisha Bonds), Euroyen Bonds. It also provides information on yield calculation conventions, volatility measures, tax treatment, the role of Ministry of Finance and the investment behavior of major institutional investors.

Japanese Stocks: Make Money on the Tokyo Stock Exchange

T. Matsumoto
McGraw Hill, Inc.
11 West 19th Street
New York, NY 10011

PH: (800) 722-4726
(212) 512-4100
Published 1990
Cost: $12.60

Explains to the reader what makes Japanese stocks such a hot commodity and "outlines strategies for anticipating trends and locating the best reasonably-priced stocks on the Japanese exchange."

Jesse Livermore's Methods in Trading Stocks

Richard D. Wyckoff
Windsor Books
P.O. Box 280
Brightwaters, NY 11718

Published 1984
Cost: $5.00

Active trading was not his game, but a careful study of the market was. Meet the market's greatest trader, Jesse Livermore, someone who earned his first thousand a mere boy, someone who made it, lost it, and gained it all over again. Learn his trading techniques as he goes through a normal business day.

Jesse Livermore: Speculator-King

Paul Sarnoff
Traders Press
P.O. Box 6206
Greenville, SC 2960

PH: (803) 288-3900
ISBN: 0-9343800-10-4
Published 1967
Cost: $18.00

Here is the true story of a man once blamed for causing the 1929 crash, a man blamed for every market break from 1917 to 1940. Here are his trials and triumphs, told with empathy and forthrightness. Here is one of the most legendary figures ever to haunt the annals of the stock market - Livermore brought startlingly to life.

Kroll on Futures Trading Strategy

Stanley Kroll
Business One Irwin
1818 Ridge Road
Homewood, IL 60430

PH: (800) 634-3966
FAX: (708) 798-1490
ISBN: 1-55623-033-8
Published 1988
Cost: $32.50

Covers commodities and trading analysis. An inside look at the strategies and tactics of a legendary futures trader Stan Kroll. Use his proven trading strategies and tactics to make more money. Reveals how to time trades more accurately, analyze and project price trends and conduct a trading campaign that consistently brings in profits.

Leading Indicators for the 1990s

Geoffrey H. Moore
Business One Irwin
1818 Ridge Road
Homewood, IL 60430

PH: (708) 206-2700
(800)634-3966
FAX: (708) 798-1490
ISBN: 1-55623-258-6
Published 1990
Cost: $25.00

Enables the reader to identify trends in the economy at an early stage. Suggests expanding the leading indicators from 11 to 15 and recommends a whole new set of leading indicators that will provide earlier clues to swings that the present set. The essential reference for anyone making investment decisions.

Lennox System of Market Forecasting

Radius Press Publisher
217 E. 85th Street
New York, NY 10028

PH: (212) 988-4715
Cost: $89.95

VIDEO
A one hour video-tape of the Lennox System tutorial seminar. Learn to compute daily buy and sell market signals based on the principles of pattern recognition, fractal geometry, probability and statistics. This system was developed by Sam Kash Kachigan a veteran options trader and author of one of the nations leading college statistics textbooks.

The Life Insurance Investment Advisor

Ben G. Baldwin and William G. Droms
Probus Publishing Co.
1925 North Clybourn Avenue
Chicago, IL 60614

PH: (800) PROBUS-1
FAX: (312) 868-6250
ISBN: 1-55738-110-0
Published 1990
Cost: $22.95

Subjects addressed: insurance.
Focuses on life insurance products with sections on how to understand, analyze and select appropriate insurance products with a complete discussion of term, whole, universal, variable life and hybrid policies and annuities. Also discusses how to analyze an insurance investment portfolio, how taxation affects insurance decisions, how to develop an investment strategy and more.

The Lifetime Book of Money Management

Grace W. Weinstein
New American Library
1633 Broadway
New York, NY 10019

PH: (800)526-0275
ISBN: 0-452-25893-6
Published 1987
Cost: $12.95

Designed to meet the challenge of your individual financial needs, to find answers to all your questions, and to help plan your financial future. Tells you how to save, spend, borrow, and invest your money - and where to go for expert advice. Learn how to protect and make the most of your money, without confusion and without risk.

Long Wave Economic Cycles

Jake Bernstein
Probus Publishing Co.
1925 North Clybourn Avenue
Chicago, IL 60614

PH: (800) PROBUS-1
FAX: (312) 868-6250
Published:
Cost: $150.00

AUDIO TAPES
Subjects addressed: market analysis. "Audio tapes that map out our economic future from one of the world's foremost cyclical analysts. These tapes will help you understand how history repeats itself in all world economics and how you can use these well-established patterns for survival and profit."

The Longman Investment Companion: A Comparative Guide to Market Performance

Gordon K. Williamson
Longman Financial Services
520 N. Dearborn
Chicago, IL 60610

PH: (800)621-9621
ISBN: 0-88462-832-9
Published 1989
Cost: $19.95

Prepare yourself against making poor investment choices or missing prime investment opportunities. A convenient, easy-to-use resource that provides a performance overview of a wide variety of stocks, bonds, currencies, mutual funds, interest rates, and more from a well-known financial planning expert.

The Lore and Legends of Wall Street

Robert M. Sharp
Business One Irwin
1818 Ridge Road
Homewood, IL 60430

PH: (708) 206-2700   (800) 634-3966
FAX: (708) 798-1490
ISBN: 1-55623-151-2
Published 1989
Cost: $18.95

Sharp presents in a lighthearted vein more than 50 information-filled vignettes of market history. Presented here are the colorful origins of many Wall Street institutions and practices and clear explanations of current "street" terms and practices. Glossary and Bibliography.

Low-Risk, High-Reward Technical Trading Strategies

Glen Ring
Commodities Educational Institute
219 Parkade
Cedar Falls, IA 50613

PH: (800) 635-3936
FAX: (319) 277-7982
Published 1991
Cost: $233.00 (complete set notebook included); $55.00 (individual tapes - 5 total)

VIDEO
Subjects addressed: trading analysis, technical analysis. Uses charts. A wide range of useful, profit making ideas to help you pinpoint trades with the greatest potential return for the least possible risk. Coverage includes: Personal trading management, Ancient Japanese charting techniques, Time-Based Trading, Stochastics and Directional Movement Indicator and other directional studies.

The Major Works of R.N. Elliott, Expanded Edition

Robert R. Prechter, Jr. editor
New Classics Library, Inc.
P.O. Box 1618
Gainesville, GA 30503

The three ground-breaking works by R.N. Elliott - "The Wave Principle" 1938, The Financial World articles - 1939, and "The Secret of the Universe" - 1946. Uses charts.

Published 1980, 1990 (2nd edition)
Cost: $34.00

Making Money

Ian Andersen
Simon and Schuster, Inc.
1230 Avenue of the Americas
New York, NY 10020

Presents a coherent, logical, and basically conservative method of making money, and making it work for the individual. Leads you through the complex maze of financial investments - real estate, stocks and bonds, and many other areas - and tells how to protect your earnings. Learn to gamble only when the odds are in your favor.

PH: (800) 223-2336
ISBN: 0-8149-0797-0
Published 1978
Cost $10.00

Making Money: Winning the Battle for Middle-Class Financial Success

Howard Ruff
Simon and Schuster, Inc.
1230 Avenue of the Americas
New York, NY 10020

The latest financial wisdom from the investment advisor to the middle class, completely updated and revised to reflect current trends. Details an innovative, high-profit investment strategy that tracks our economy's flip-flop "chill" and "fever" cycles and reviews your best tactics for taking financial advantage of these shifts.

PH: (800) 223-2336
ISBN: 0-671-61441-X
Published 1986 (revised edition)
Cost $8.95

Making Money with Mutual Funds

Werner Renberg and Jeremiah Blitzer
John Wiley & Sons, Inc.
605 Third Avenue
New York, NY 10158-0012

PH: (212) 850-6418 orders
Other: (212) 850-6233 info.
Published 1988
Cost: $23.95

Subjects addressed: mutual funds. How to pick funds to fit changing investment needs. A comprehensive portfolio strategy that helps you identify superior funds and control risk at low cost. Allows you to choose your own balance between risk and profitability.

Management and Control of Currency and Interest Rate Risk

Barry Howcroft and Cristopher Storey
Probus Publishing Co.
1925 North Clybourn Avenue
Chicago, IL 60614

PH: (800) PROBUS-1
FAX: (312) 868-6250
Published 1990
Cost: $55.00

Provides an introduction to the financial instruments designed to assist corporate managers and treasurers in controlling risk and minimizing the effects of uncertain cash flows, promoting a practical understanding of their applications, subsequent development and relative merits and disadvantages. The authors concentrate on the many instruments and principles of hedging currency and rate risk, from forward exchange through forward options and second and third generation hedging instruments. Specific topics include: currency options, currency futures, interest rate futures, interest rate options, forward rate agreements, gilt futures, U.S. Treasury bond futures.

Management of Investments

J. C. Francis
McGraw Hill, Inc.
11 West 19th Street
New York, NY 10011

PH: (800) 722-4726
 (212) 512-4100
Published 1988
Cost: $52.75

Subjects addressed: investing theories, bond analysis, commodities trading, stock analysis, earnings analysis, fundamental analysis, market analysis, technical analysis. Textbook for a financial undergraduate investment course. It combines theories with descriptions of various investments.

Managing Foreign Exchange Risk

David DeRosa
Probus Publishing Co.
1925 North Clybourn Avenue
Chicago, IL 60614

PH: (800) PROBUS-1
FAX: (312) 868-6250
ISBN: 1-55738-164-X
Published 1991
Cost: $55.00

An analytical treatment of the use of innovative and complex financial instruments and hedging strategies by banking and investment professionals to control the foreign exchange rate risks associated with institutional portfolios. This book contains introductory material about foreign exchange and its peculiar risks as well as descriptions and historical analyses of the major currencies. It also covers the Interest Parity Theorem, the linkages between the currency and debt markets, the valuation of currency forward and futures markets and currency option pricing, as well as extensive coverage of various hedging techniques.

Managing Your Investment Manager: The Complete Guide to Selection, Measurement, and Control

Arthur Williams III
Business One Irwin
1818 Ridge Road
Homewood, IL 60430

PH: (708) 206-2700
(800) 634-3966
FAX: (708) 798-1490
ISBN: 0-87094-723-0
Published 1986
Cost: $42.50

Shows plan sponsors how to establish a management system for investment capital. Covers how to build a framework for setting goals, how to train managers for achieving goals, and how to set up an information system to provide necessary feedback. Helps Build a communications bridge between fund sponsors and investment managers.

Marcia Stigum's The Money Market

Marcia Stigum
Business One Irwin
1818 Ridge Road
Homewood, IL 60430

PH: (708) 206-2700
(800) 634-3966
FAX: (708) 798-1490
ISBN: 1-55623-122-9
Published 1990 (3rd edition)
Cost: $67.50

Subjects addressed: market analysis. An in-depth look at the money markets. Chapters include: Interest Rate Swaps, T-Bonds and Note Futures, Euros, Options in the Fixed Income World, Government and Federal Agency Securities, The Federal Funds Market, Money Market Funds, The Treasury and Federal Agencies and much more.

Markets & Market Logic: Trading & Investing with a Sound Understanding and Approach

J. Peter Steidlmayer & Kevin Koy
Porcupine Press
401 S. LaSalle
Suite 1101
Chicago, IL 60605

ISBN: 0-941275-00-0
Published 1986
Cost: $39.00

Lets you translate chaotic price action into market-generated information through an easy to understand step-by-step process. Shows how the market determines and indicates value - and how to respond. The Market Logic approach applies to any market, whether you're trading or investing, running a company, or even buying a used car.

Market Psychology and Discipline

Commodities Education Institute
219 Parkade
Cedar Falls, IA 50613

PH: (800) 635-3936
(319) 277-6341
FAX: (319) 277-7982
Published 1990
Cost: $55.00

VIDEO
Subjects addressed: market analysis, technical analysis. Glen Ring will help you understand the psychology of the market place and of the trader and how this can affect your trading profits. Set of 5 tapes in this series available for $233.00

Markets 101-Insights into Understanding the Inner Working of Financial Markets

Kevin Koy
MLS Publishing
401 S. LaSalle Street, Suite 1101
Chicago, IL 60605

Published 1989
Cost: $35.00

Subjects addressed: market analysis and technical analysis. Learn how to spot prices below value, improve trade location, minimize losing trades while maximizing profitable ones, better monitor and manage positions.

Markets - Who Pays, Who Risks, Who Gains, Who Loses

Martin Mayer
W.W. Norton & Co., Inc.
500 5th Avenue
New York, NY 10110

PH: (800) 223-2584
ISBN: 0-393-02602-7
Published 1988

Subjects addressed: market analysis. Sophisticated analysis of the workings and history of the leading securities and common markets of the world.

Market Wizards: Interviews with Top Traders

Jack D. Schwager
New York Institute of Finance
2 Broadway
New York, NY 10004

PH: (212) 344-2900
ISBN: 0-13-556093-4
Published 1989
Cost $19.95

After interviewing top traders in a variety of markets, the author concludes that while method undoubtedly accounts largely for trading success, no one approach is used by all, or even most of the traders interviewed. Some are technicians, others are fundamentalists, some act on personal initiative and intuition, and others rely on automated systems. Glossary.

A Master Plan for Winning in Wall Street

Gene Brady
Windsor Books
P.O. Box 280
Brightwaters, NY 11718

ISBN: 0-685-61028-4
Published 1976
Cost: $39.95

Discusses a coherent investment strategy, investment analysis for selecting and evaluating stocks, market psychology and timing, economic considerations, stock market pitfalls to avoid, how to work with your broker, and a step-by-step description of how to incorporate this investment approach into your pattern of daily living.

The McGraw-Hill Handbook of Commodities and Futures

Martin J. Pring
1221 Avenue of the Americas
new York, NY 10020

PH: (800) 262-4729
Published 1985
ISBN: 0-07-050915-8
Cost: $62.50

Subjects: commodities trading. This handbook is a practical and comprehensive reference covering all aspects of commodity futures trading and hedging. It is filled with expert advice and valuable guidelines for professional investors, financial managers and novices in the field.

The Midas Touch: The Strategies that Have Made Warren Buffet America's Pre-eminent Investor

John Train
Harper & Row Publishers, Inc.
10 E. 53rd Street
New York, NY 10022

PH: (800) 242-7737
Published 1990
ISBN: 0-06-091500-5
Published 1987
Cost: $7.95

Analyzes the investment principles of Warren Buffet, the most successful investor alive- the only one of the Forbes 400 to have earned his fortune entirely through investing, in bull and bear markets. Buffet is a proponent of the value approach, a theory he learned early in his career and one that remains a powerful tool today.

The Mind of the Market: A Study of Stock Market Philosophies, Their Uses, and Their Implications

Charles W. Smith
Rowman & Littlefield Publishers, Inc.
4720 Boston Way
Lanham, MD 20706

PH: (301) 459-3366
ISBN: 0-8476-6983-1
Published 1981
Cost: $12.95

Penetrating view of the investor's mind. A leading sociologist and student of the stock market takes you behind the scenes of formal rules and regulations to reveal those intangible elements that make the market and move its players. A book for all who are fascinated by the world of money - and the mysteries of human behavior.

Mind Over Markets: Power Trading

James F. Dalton, Eric T. Jones, Robert B. Dalton
Probus Publishing Co.
1925 North Clybourn Avenue
Chicago, IL 60614

PH: (800) PROBUS-1
FAX: (312) 868-6250
ISBN: 1-55738-113-5
Published 1990
Cost: $45.00

Subjects addressed: options; uses charts.
Power trading with market generated information. Discusses integrative and intuitive capacity, organizing price activity according to time with helpful sections on how to read the market, market implications, timing and the dynamics of the markets through the organization of price, time, and volume. Also included is learning how to synthesize information with intuition.

Modern Commodity Futures Trading

Gerald Gold
Commodity Research Bureau
75 Wall Street
22nd Floor
New York, NY 10005

PH: (800) 446-4519
Published 1975 (7th edition)
Cost: $20.00

A practical explanation of the techniques and methods for successful trading in the commodity markets. Also presents the mechanics and background of the markets for those who are new to them. Written by an active commodity market expert and scholar, this book imparts technical knowledge in clear and comprehensible terms.

Modern Investment Theory

Robert A. Haugen
Prentice Hall
15 Columbus Circle
New York, NY 10023

Published 1986
Cost: $19.60

Subjects addressed: investing theories. Study Guide - question and answer - provides basics of securities and financial markets, a host of varied investment theories applicable to equities, options, and futures.

Money

Lawrence S. Ritter & William L. Silber
Basic Books, Inc.
10 E. 53rd Street
New York, NY 10022

PH: (800) 242-7737
ISBN: 0-465-04721-1
Published 1984 (5th edition)
Cost: $15.95

The most up-to-date, authoritative, and lively guide to money and monetary policy. Thoroughly revised fifth edition considers the financial gyrations that have recently shaken and continue to shake the United States. Provides a clear, complete, accurate, and even amusing analysis of the sphinx-like world of money.

Money Dynamics for the 1990s

Venita VanCaspel
S & S Trade
1230 Avenue of the Americas
New York, NY 10020

PH: (212) 698-7000
ISBN: 0-671-66158-2
Published 1988
Cost: $22.95

With the myriad of tax law changes in 1986 and the stock market collapse of 1987, financial planning, personal investing, and asset allocation became a whole new ball game. This dynamic directory to personal investing gives you all the strategies and techniques you'll need to achieve maximum financial gain in the decade ahead.

The Money Encyclopedia

Harvey Rachin, Editor
Available through Fraser Publishing
P.O. Box 494
Burlington, VT 05402

PH: (802) 658-0322
ISBN: 0-06-181711-2
Published 1984
Cost: $26.50

Comprehensive resource of information on personal finance, business practices, and the worldwide economic system. Hundreds of entries researched and written by dozens of experts in the field of finance. Explains not only how the financial system works, but also how you can apply this information to your financial circumstances.

The Money Game

Adam Smith
Random House, Inc.
201 E. 50th Street
31st Floor
New York, NY 10022

PH: (800) 733-3000
ISBN: 0-394-72013-9
Published 1976 (3rd edition)
Cost: $5.95

About image and reality and identity and anxiety and money, and in that order says the author. This veteran Wall Street observer informs with a thorough knowledge of financial affairs and delights with a keen sense of humor. "None of the solemn sacred cows of Wall Street escape debunking," says Library Journal.

The Money Manual

Peter Passell/Prentice Hall Press
15 Columbus Circle
New York, NY 10023

Published 1990
Cost: $5.95

Covers: investing theories. Classic guide for the individual investor. Complete up to the minute financial advice that works.

The Money Market

Marcia Stigum
Business One Irwin
1818 Ridge Road
Homewood, IL 60430

PH: (708) 206-2700
(800) 634-3966
FAX: (708) 798-1490
ISBN: 1-55623-122-9
Published 1989 (3rd edition)
Cost: $62.50

First published in 1978, The Money Market was received with respect and admiration by the financial, business, and investment communities. Having observed and carefully analyzed the recent changes thrust upon the market, Dr. Stigum has updated her book to cover the crucial developments that have accompanied explosive growth.

Money Market Calculations: Yields, Break-Evens, and Arbitrage

Marcia Stigum & John Mann
Business One Irwin
1818 Ridge Road
Homewood, IL 60430

PH: (708) 206-2700
(800) 634-3966
FAX: (708) 798-1490
ISBN: 0-87094-981-0
Published 1989 (2nd edition)
Cost: $45.00

Clearly explains important money market calculations - including those for computing yields to maturity, security prices, accrued interest, and break-even rates, as well as for directly comparing yields on instruments that differ by type and/or maturity. Unique notation system enables anyone to use all formulas and equations.

Money Matters

Charles S. Meek
Probus Publishing Co.
1925 North Clybourn Avenue
Chicago, IL 60614

PH: (800) PROBUS-1
FAX: (312) 868-6250
ISBN: 1-55738-136-4
Published 1991
Cost: $24.95

Subjects addressed: investing theories.
Focuses on investment and financial planning for the highly educated professional with a discussion of financial planning and types of and reasons for planning with information on retirement, estate and income tax planning and asset allocation. Also included are investment ideas, an examination of financial instruments with a question and answer section, simple forecasting models, organization and tips on choosing advisors.

The Moving Balance System . . . A New Technique for Stock and Option Trading

Humphrey Lloyd
Windsor Books
P.O. Box 280
Brightwaters, NY 11718

ISBN: 0-685-68982-4
Published 1976
Cost: $50.00

The author's moving balance indicator will assist the investor in meeting Wall Street's most demanding challenge - timing. It will allow you to gauge the technical strength or weakness of the market. A combination of self-disciplined suggestions and creative trading strategies.

Multifund Investing: How to Build a High Performance Portfolio of Mutual Funds

Michael Hirsch
Business One Irwin
1818 Ridge Road
Homewood, IL 60430

PH: (800) 634-3966
(708) 206-2700
FAX: (708) 798-1490
Published 1987
Cost: $37.50

Subjects addressed: mutual funds. How best to allocate assets in a 10-20 fund portfolio.

Municipal Bonds: The Comprehensive Review of Municipal Securities & Public Finance

Robert Lamb and Stephen P. Rappaport
McGraw-Hill Publishing Company
1221 Avenue of the Americas
New York, NY 10020

PH: (800) 262-4729
ISBN: 0-07-036084-7
Published 1987 (2nd edition)
Cost: $28.50

How municipal bonds originate and are marketed, their advantages and limitations, how to evaluate investment potential, and much more. Presents a clear picture of the market, accounting and legal issues, new bonds, and what the future holds for investors and issuing governments. Revised for the Tax Reform Act of 1986.

Municipal Bond Investment Advisor

Wilson White
Probus Publishing Co.
1925 North Clybourn Avenue
Chicago, IL 60614

PH: (800) PROBUS-1
FAX: (312) 868-6250
ISBN: 1-55738-190-9
Published 1991
Cost: $27.50

Subjects addressed: investing theories.
Explains tax-exempt investing in the municipal bond market with information on the basics of financial planning, personal income taxes, savings, municipals bonds and their markets and the four methods of investing in tax-exempts: unit investment trusts, managed funds, direct investing and delegated management.

The Mutual Fund Directory

Investment Company Institute
Probus Publishing Co.,
118 N. Clinton Street
Chicago, IL 60606

PH: (800) PROBUS-1
Published 1990
Cost: $18.95

Subjects addressed: mutual funds. Over 2500 identified, described, and categorized.

The Mutual Fund Encyclopedia

Gerald W. Perritt
Dearborn Financial Publishing, Inc.
520 N. Dearborn Street
Chicago, IL 60610

Published 1990
Cost: $27.95

Profiles 1100 mutual funds detailing objectives and strategies, financial statistics, current yields, portfolio turnover rate, year by year and 5 year average returns and more.

Mutual Fund Fact Book

Investment Company Institute
1600 M Street
Washington, D.C. 20036

PH: (202) 293-7700
(202) 955-3536
Published every May for the previous year.
Cost: $9.95

Covers: mutual funds. The book includes: facts and figures on mutual fund investing, information on the assets of mutual funds, the sales redemption value, a historical background on mutual funds and recent trends affecting various funds.

Mutual Fund Switch Strategies & Timing Tactics

Warren Boroson
Probus Publishing Co.
1925 North Clybourn Avenue
Chicago, IL 60614

PH: (800) PROBUS-1
FAX: (312) 868-6250
ISBN: 1-55738-184-4
Published 1991
Cost: $22.95

Subjects addressed: investing theories. This reference answers who prepares the financial statements and what is the relationship between the different elements with in-depth analysis on the balance sheet, the income statement, the statement of cash flows, the statement of changes in stockholder's equity and more. Also included is a glossary of financial terminology and sample financial statements.

Mutual Funds Explained: The Basics and Beyond

Robert C. Upton, Jr.
Probus Publishing Co.
1925 North Clybourn Avenue
Chicago, IL 60614

PH: (800) PROBUS-1
FAX: (312) 868-6250
ISBN: 1-55738-211-5
Published 1991
Cost: $14.95

Subjects addressed: investing theories. This book is a primer for the beginning investor and a refresher for the more experienced individual. Covers: goal setting, choosing a money manager, selecting a mutual fund, special funds, managing your mutual funds, mutual fund costs. Glossary of terms is included.

Mutual Funds - How to Invest with the Pros

Kurt Brouwer
John Wiley & Sons, Inc.
605 3rd Avenue
New York, NY 10158-0012

PH: (212) 850-6418 orders
Other: (212) 850-6233 info.
Published 1988
Cost: $19.95

Subjects addressed: mutual funds. Advice from nine investment pros on how to achieve your investment goals.

Mutual Funds - Taking the Worry Out of Investing

Joel Ross
Prentice Hall
Route 9W
Englewood Cliffs, NJ 07632

Published 1988
Cost: $14.95

Subjects addressed: mutual funds. Benefits both novice and experienced investors. Serves as a source of information for making rational decision, and presents criteria for reviewing and evaluating resent holdings.

Mutual Funds Videocourse

American Association of Individual Investors
625 Michigan Avenue
Chicago, IL

PH: (312) 280-0170
Published 1991 (last update)
Cost: $129.00, $98.00 for AAII members

VIDEO
A 4 hour video with workbook. Topics include: costs, fees, loads, redemption charges, taxation, cost basis, performance evaluation, risk/return, how to select mutual funds and much, much more.

Nelson's Directory of Investment Managers

Nelson Publications
1 Gateway Plaza
Port Chester, NY 10573

PH: (800) 333-6357
FAX: (914) 937-8908
Published 1991
Cost: $325.00

Subjects addressed: investment managers. In depth profiles of over 2000 money management firms... including 1, 3, 5 and 10 year performance results. Six fact filled sections: Section 1 - In-depth profiles of each money manager; Section 2 - Geographic listing of manager arranged by state; Section 3 - Rankings of all firms by asset size; Section 4 - Listing of firms by type of organization; Section 5 - Index of firms by specialized investment services offered; Section 6 - 1, 3, 5 and 10 year performance rankings of all firms by asset class.

Nelson's Directory of Investment Research

Nelson Publications
1 Gateway Plaza
Port Chester, NY 10573

PH: (800) 333-6357
FAX: (914) 937-8908
Published 1991
Cost: $450.00

Subjects addressed: stock analysis. Nelson's Directory is published in two volumes. Volume #1 contains expanded research and financial information on over 5,000 U.S. public companies. Volume #2 contains comprehensive information on over 4000 foreign-based public companies. And, of course analyst coverage of all 9000 companies, important stock data and research reports on each company.

Never Make a Rich Man Poor

Rand Management Corporation - Victor Sperandeo
1 Chapel Hill Road
Short Hills, NJ 07078

PH: (800) 842-RAND
Published 1990
Cost: $95.00

VIDEO
Victor Sperandeo, a 25 year Wall Street veteran will tell you how to preserve the profits you made in the 1980s and prosper in the 90s, as well as how his exceptional method of managing money has created a 35% plus average annual rate of return for 8 years or more.

The New Commodity Trading Systems and Methods

Perry J. Kaufman
John Wiley and Sons, Inc.
605 Third Avenue
New York, NY 10158-0012

PH: (212) 850-6000
ISBN: 0-471-878790-0
Published 1987 (2nd edition)
Cost: $49.95

Comprehensive guide critically examines the most commonly used technical trading techniques for determining price movement in today's agricultural, financial and stock market index markets. You'll learn what systems are most profitable under what conditions, why, and how. New edition reflects dramatic changes in the markets.

The New Complete Investor

Geoffrey A. Hirt and Stanley B. Block
Business One Irwin
1818 Ridge Road
Homewood, IL 60430

PH: (800) 634-3966
FAX: (708) 798-1490
ISBN: 1-55623-367-1
Published 1990
Cost: $44.50

Covers: investing theories, bond analysis, stock analysis, and fundamental analysis. Your guide for locating, analyzing, and choosing personal investments that are money makers. Shows you how to use classic investment strategies to improve you chances of making money in the stock, bond, and real asset markets, and how to pick winners for your portfolio by analyzing the long-term trends in stock market value... and avoid investment 'dogs' by finding the true value of a company before you invest your money.

New Concepts in Technical Trading Systems

J. Welles Wilder, Jr. author
Trend Research, Ltd.
P.O. Box 128
McLeansville, MC 27301

PH: (919) 698-0500
Published 1978
Cost: $65.00

Subjects addressed: trading analysis, commodities trading, technical analysis; uses charts. Presents 7 trading system concepts; directional movement index, volatility index, commodity selection index, relative strength index, swing index, parabolic time/price system, and Trend Balance Point concept.

The New Contrarian Investment Strategy: The Psychology of Stock Market Success

David Dreman
Random House, Inc.
201 E 50th Street
31st Floor
New York, NY 10022

PH: (800) 733-3000
ISBN: 0-394-52364-4
Published 1982
Cost: $21.45

Thoroughly updated revision of the highly successful and influential work analyzes the investment climate of the 1980s. Shows how the investor can take advantage of market fluctuations, and gives a personal contrarian assessment of current trends. Demonstrates where the opportunity lies - contrary to the opinion of most experts.

The New Corporate Bond Market

Richard S. Wilson and Frank J. Fabozzi
Probus Publishing Co.
1925 North Clybourn Avenue
Chicago, IL 60614

PH: (800) PROBUS-1
FAX: (312) 868-6250
ISBN: 1-55738-128-3
Published 1990
Cost: $55.00

Subjects addressed: bond analysis. "The New Corporate Bond Market" is designed to help investors of all levels, professional and individual, to better understand the increased complexity of the world of bonds. Reviewing the fundamentals of corporates, form the qualitative to the quantitative, the authors explore: bond indentures, interest payments, debt retirement, convertible bonds, speculative-grade bonds, yield measures and limitations, total return measures and applications, duration and convexity, option-adjusted valuation approach, option-adjust spread approach.

The New Dow Jones Irwin Guide to Zero Coupon Investments

Donald R. Nichols
Business One Irwin
1818 Ridge Road
Homewood, IL 60430
ISBN: 1-55623-213-6

PH: (708) 206-2700
(800) 634-3966
FAX: (708) 798-1490
Published 1989
Cost: $32.50

Subjects addressed: bond analysis. What they are, how they work, how to use and manage them. Full range of coverage of zero coupon investments from T-bills to commodity funds.

The New Encyclopedia of Stock Market Techniques

Michael L. Burke, Editor
Available through Fraser Publishing
P.O. Box 494
Burlington, VT 05402

PH: (802) 658-0322
ISBN: 0-936176-02-4
Published 1985 (4th supplement)
Cost: $60.00

Comprehensive survey of investing and trading methods developed over the years, all within a single column. The only source that cuts across the entire field: charting, fundamental, technical, and specialized approaches. Provides the necessary background for diversified operations. Loose-leaf format permits periodic updates.

The New Money Masters: Winning Investment Strategies of: Soros, Lynch, Steinhardt, Rogers, Neff, Wanger, Michaelis, and Carret

John Train
Harper-Collins Publishers
10 E. 53rd Street
New York, NY 10022

PH: (800) 242-7737
Published 1989
ISBN: 0-06-015966-9
Cost: $22.50

In this new revised edition, Train describes the techniques of today's investment wizards. Some of the useful ideas that emerge are the advantages of over-the-counter issues, the best ways to invest in foreign stocks and in newly industrializing countries, how to lay out the facts about a company in order to understand it most easily. Appendix, index.

The New Mutual Fund Investment Advisor

Richard C. Dorf
Probus Publishing Co.
1925 North Clybourn Avenue
Chicago, IL 60614

PH: (800) PROBUS-1
FAX: (312) 868-6250
ISBN: 1-55738-157-7
Published 1991
Cost: $24.95

Subjects addressed: investing theories.
Explanations of the principal measurements of investment risk with a practical system for evaluating fund pearformance, matching a fund's risk/reward characteristics with the investor's personal investment objectives and risk tolerance, building a portolio of mutual funds while protecting against losses and more. Included are charts, graphs, actual industry data and actual examples of mutual funds.

The New Options Market

Max G. Ansbacher
Walker & Company
720 Fifth Avenue
New York, NY 10019

PH: (212) 265-3632
ISBN: 0-8027-7308-7
Published 1987 (2nd edition)
Cost: $16.95

Updated and enlarged guide to the options market reveals strategies for profit by trading puts and calls. Describes the advantages and disadvantages of every strategy in easy-to-understand language. Leads you through sample trades and presents everything you need to know to invest and speculate successfully with options.

New Stock Market

Diana R. Harrington, H. Russell Fogler, and Frank J. Fabozzi
Probus Publishing Co.
1925 North Clybourn Avenue
Chicago, IL 60614

PH: (800) PROBUS-1
FAX: (312) 868-6250
ISBN: 1-55738-056-2
Published 1990
Cost: $40.00

Subjects addressed: investing theories.
Topics covered. Investing in equities, equity derivatives—options and futures; cycle theory, technical and fundamental analysis.

New Strategies for Mutual Fund Investing

Donald Rugg
Business One Irwin
1818 Ridge Road
Homewood, IL 60430

PH: (708) 206-2700   (800) 634-3966
FAX: (708) 798-1490
ISBN: 1-55623-045-1
Published 1989
Cost: $27.50

Subjects addressed: mutual funds. A strategy for selecting and managing a fund portfolio using current data available by personal computer.

The New World of Gold: The Inside Story of the Mines, the Markets, the Politics, the Investors

Timothy Green
Walker & Company
720 Fifth Avenue
New York, NY 10019

PH: (212) 265-3632
ISBN: 0-8027-7261-7
Published 1984 (Revised Edition)
Cost: $12.95

A skilled author and gold authority guides you from the depths of a South African gold mine to the back rooms of the great London banking houses. Illustrates the history and legends, outlines the facts and figures, and provides insightful forecasts into the precarious future of gold. Brings the world of gold to life.

The New York Times Complete Guide to Personal Investing

Gary L. Klott
Random House, Inc.
201 E 50th Street
31st Floor
New York, NY 10022

PH: (800) 733-3000
ISBN: 0-8129-1235-7
Published 1987
Cost: $22.50

A thorough, straightforward compendium of over 70 of today's most popular personal investment options, their pros and cons, costs, risks, and potential profits. Entries grouped according to investment objective, and extensively indexed for easy cross-reference and comparison. Considers the effects of the Tax Reform Act of 1986.

1991 Mutual Funds Almanac

Babson - United Investment Advisors, Inc.
101 Prescott Street
Wellesley Hills, MA 02181

PH: (617) 235-0900
FAX: (617) 235-9450
Cost: $32.00
Date of first publication: 1991

Covers: mutual funds. An indispensable reference book of concise, accurate mutual funds information. Includes performance statistics for the past 10 years on 2100 funds, fund objectives, total assets, net asset value, sales charges, expense ratios, minimum investments, addresses and straight talk about the mutual funds industry.

No Loads - Mutual Fund Profits Using Technical Analysis

James E. Keares
Liberty House/TAB Books, Inc.
Blue Ridge Summit, PA 17294-0214

Subjects addressed: market analysis, technical analysis, mutual funds. "A simple, effective system that any investor can use to achieve high profits."

Published 1989
Cost: $19.95

Oh Yeah?

Edward Angly
Fraser Publishing Company
P.O. Box 494
Burlington, VT 05402

PH: (802) 658-0322
ISBN: 0-87034-088-3
Cost: $8.00

This is a classic compilation from the newspapers and public records published in 1931 regarding the Great Crash. Quotations, cartoons, and tables which illustrate the propensity for leading politicians, economists, and business types to continually tell us how wonderful the future will be as prosperity continues to evade the bearers of good news.

The 100 Best Mutual Funds You Can Buy

Gordon K. Williamson
Bob Adams, Inc.
260 Center Street
Holbrook, MA 02343

PH: (617) 767-8100
ISBN: 1-55850-856-2
Published 1990
Cost: $12.95

Subjects addressed: mutual funds. Rated for performance over the long term, stability of management, and risk sensitivity. Covers: municipal bonds, government bonds, international bonds and equity, corporate bonds, growth and income, and metal funds.

The 100 Best Stocks to Own in America

Gene Walden
Longman Financial Services Publishers
520 N. Dearborn
Chicago, IL 60610

PH: (800) 621-9621
ISBN: 0-88462-831-0
Published 1989
Cost: $19.95

Did you know that the single best stock to own in America in Anhueser-Busch, or that 11 million cases of California Cooler were sold in 1987? Here's the Hall of Fame of companies whose stocks have been the best performers year-in and year-out.

The 100 Best Stocks You Can Own In The World

Gene Walden
Dearborn Financial Publishing, Inc.
520 N. Dearborn Street
Chicago, IL 60610-4354

Published 1991
Cost: $24.95

Subjects addressed: stock analysis. Rates these 100 companies according to earnings growth, stock growth, dividend yield, dividend growth, consistency, and momentum.

100 to 1 in the Stock Market

Thomas W. Phelps
Available through Fraser Publishing
P.O. Box 494
Burlington, VT 05402

PH: (802) 658-0322
ISBN: 0-07-049772-9
Published 1972
Cost: $25.00

A distinguished security analyst tells how to make the most of your investment opportunities. Illustrates a philosophy of "buy right and hold on" with more than 350 stocks that have returned 100 to 1. Explains the theory of money, interest, inflation, the relative value of stocks and bonds, the technician's approach, and more.

One Up on Wall Street: How to Use What You Already Know to Make Money in the Market

Peter Lynch
Simon and Schuster, Inc.
1230 Avenue of the Americas
New York, NY 10020

PH: (800) 223-2336
FAX: (212) 698-7007
ISBN: 0671661035
Published: 1989
Cost: $19.95

Subjects addressed: investing theories, fundamental analysis. The philosophy behind Peter Lynch's Stellar investing record. He shows how to research stocks and analyze financial statements and ignore every influence except the fundamentals of the company you're investing in.

The Only Money Book for the Middle Class

Don & Joan German
Available through Fraser Publishing
P.O. Box 494
Burlington, VT 05402

PH: (802) 658-0322
ISBN: 0-688-01567-0
Published 1983
Cost: $13.95

This practical and easy-to-live-with "Economics of Enough" plan is based on years of practical experience in retail banking, and related fields. Learn how to get the loan you want, achieve maximum safe earnings on your savings, save on insurance, put your kids through college, use tax shelters, and realize the American Dream.

Opening Price Statistical Data on the Futures Markets

R. Earl Hadady
Key Books Press
1111 S. Arroyo Parkway
Suite 410
Pasadena, CA 91105

PH: (818) 441-3863
ISBN: 0-9611390-1-3
Published 1984
Cost: $87.50

Qualifies and quantifies opening prices in order to help formulate profitable trading strategies. Identifies commodities that are most likely to open at the extremes of their trading range - which enables a trader to enter and exit the market with greater precision. Also reveals many other valuable trading applications.

The Option Player's Advanced Guidebook

Kenneth R. Trester
Investrek
419 Main Street, No 160
Huntington Beach, CA 92649

PH: (800) 334-0854
Published: 1980
Cost: $38.59

Subjects: options; uses pricing tables. An option book which displays when to buy or write specific options and exactly when to take profits. The many pricing tables wills tack the odds in your favor - you will never pay too much for an option again.

Option Pricing

Robert A. Jarrow and Andrew Rudd
Business One Irwin
1818 Ridge Road
Homewood, IL 60430

PH: (708) 206-2700
(800) 634-3966
FAX: (708) 798-1490
ISBN: 0-256-02947-4
Published 1983
Cost: $24.95

A masterly synthesis of mathematics and finance. Presents a comprehensive overview of the options market and winning strategies, plus valuable discussion on the theory of option pricing. Examines today's most important option pricing models, the influence of dividends on option valuation, premature exercise, and more.

Option Pricing and Investment Strategies

Richard M. Bookstaber
Probus Publishing Co.
1925 North Clybourn Avenue
Chicago, IL 60614

PH: (800) PROBUS-1
FAX: (312) 868-6250
Published 1991
Cost: $40.00

This third edition provides professional investors, traders and portfolio managers with insightful explanations of state-of-the-art options pricing theory and technology and shows how both theory and technique can be applied to real world investment and financial strategies. It clearly illustrates how options are used for speculation, hedging and arbitrage of equity, fixed income and futures positions. Subjects covered include: the theory and properties of options, how options are created and priced, measuring exposure to option positions, how to find and exploit mis-priced options, creating options through dynamic trading strategies, examining option pricing models, understanding how embedded options work, options in mortgaged-backed securities, portfolio insurance and option strategies and risk exposure measures (delta and gamma) .

Option Strategies -- Profit Making Techniques for Stock, Stock-Index and Commodity Options

Courtney Smith
John Wiley & Sons Publishing
605 Third Avenue
new York, NY 10158-0012

PH: (212) 850-6000
Published 1987
ISBN: 0-471-84367-9
Cost: $35.95

Subjects: options analysis. This book covers all types of options: stock index, stock, and commodity. Bullish and bearish strategies are covered equally. It will be useful to all options traders and hedgers, from novices to professionals.

Option Valuation: Analyzing and Pricing Standardized Contracts

R. Gibson
McGraw Hill, Inc.
11 West 19th Street
New York, NY 10011

PH: (800) 722-4726
(212) 512-4100
Published 1991
Cost: $40.65

Subjects addressed: options trading and analysis. "This book presents the option pricing theory not only as a rather complex set of valuation formulas, and as a powerful instrument to help readers understand the basic mechanisms tradeoff."

Option Volatility and Pricing Strategies

Sheldon Natenberg
Probus Publishing Co.
1925 North Clybourn Avenue
Chicago, IL 60614

PH: (800) PROBUS-1
FAX: (312) 868-6250
ISBN: 1-55738-009-0
Published 1988
Cost: $47.50

Subjects addressed: technical analysis. Combines the latest and most advanced option pricing theories with insights produced by Mr. Natenberg's many years as a professional trader to give prospective traders a richer and more comprehensive understanding of the behavior and applications of options.

The Options Advantage: Gaining a Trading Edge Over the Markets

David L. Caplan
Probus Publishing Co.
1925 North Clybourn Avenue
Chicago, IL 60614

PH: (800) PROBUS-1
FAX: (312) 868-6250
Published 1991
Cost: $40.00

Subjects addressed: trading analysis, options trading. "Illustrates trading methods that can be successful and profitable in flat or choppy markets, even when markets are poor. 'It' carefully shows traders a no-loss, cost-free hedging method to protect profits."

Options As a Strategic Investment (2nd edition)

Lawrence G. McMillan
New York Institute of Finance
2 Broadway
New York, NY 10004

PH: (212) 344-2900
Published 1986 (2nd edition)
ISBN: 0-13-638347-5
Cost: $48.25

Subjects: options. Written for investors who have some familiarity with the option market, this comprehensive reference explains both concept and applications of various option strategies - how they work, in which situations, and why. Examples make clear the power of each strategy under carefully described market conditions.

Options - Essential Concepts and Trading Strategies

The Educational Division of the Chicago Board
Options Exchange
Business One Irwin
1818 Ridge Road
Homewood, IL 60430

PH: (800) 634-3966
FAX: (708) 798-1490
ISBN: 1-55623-102-4
Published August 1990
Cost: $47.50

Covers investing theories and trading analysis. Describes the different trading strategies individuals, institutions and floor traders can use to close the deal. Demonstrates proven options pricing and forecasting theories. Individuals, institutions, and floor traders alike can use these comprehensive trading strategies to work faster and more accurately, predict the winners and avoid the losers and discover practical user-oriented issues and applications for options trading.

Options Hedging and Arbitrage: Pricing, Volatility and Valuation Models

Simon Eades
Probus Publishing Co.
1925 North Clybourn Avenue
Chicago, IL 60614

PH: (800) PROBUS-1
FAX: (312) 868-6250
ISBN: 1-55738-256-5
Published 1992
Cost: $55.00

This title conveys a clear grasp of the principles from which option theory derives and a clear sense of the importance of those principles in other areas of financial valuation and decision making. Topics in this groundbreaking work include: time value of money and discounted cash flow analysis; arbitrage pricing methods; do-it-yourself option pricing model; continuous-time option pricing model and annual standard deviation as measures of volatility; valuation of warrants, convertible bonds, derivative products and junk bonds using option pricing methodology; option theory in the valuation of common stocks; use of regression analysis for deriving probability distributions for future commodity prices.

The Options Manual

Gary L. Gastineau
McGraw Hill, Inc.
1221 Avenue of the Americas
New York, NY 10020

PH: (212) 512-2000
(800) 2-MCGRAW
Published 1975, 1988 (3rd edition)
Cost: $42.50

Subjects addressed: investing theories, market analysis, trading analysis, technical analysis. Find out exactly how the options market works and explore a wide variety of options products available. Get solid, proven help on how to use options to make your portfolio grow. COMMENTS: Author is a VP with Solomon Brothers.

Options on Foreign Exchange

David F. DeRosa
Probus Publishing Co.
1925 North Clybourn Avenue
Chicago, IL 60614

PH: (800) PROBUS-1
FAX: (312) 868-6250
ISBN: 1-55738-249-2
Published 1992
Cost: $65.00

Covers: currencies. State-of-the-art theories and strategies for the institutional investor. Aimed specifically at the needs of institutional/bank foreign exchange traders and hedgers who use options strategies and related synthetics. Topics include: currency futures options, mechanics of currency options markets, parity theorems, valuation of European and American currency options, listed currency warrants, OTC options and exotic currency options. Also includes an extensive and useful glossary of related terms.

The Options Strategy Spectrum

James Yates
Business One Irwin
1818 Ridge Road
Homewood, IL 60430

PH: (800) 634-3966
FAX: (708) 798-1490
ISBN:1-87094-961-6
Published 1987
Cost: $47.50

Covers: options analysis. An insider's book about how options can be used to manage the short-term risk equity investment. Shows you how to estimate the implied risk of individual stocks and the market as a whole.

Outperforming Wall Street: Stock Market Profits Through Patience and Discipline

Daniel Alan Seiver
Prentice-Hall
Route 9W
Englewood Cliffs, NJ 07632

Designed to help the serious investor earn higher profits. Shows how to acquire good growth stocks at reasonable prices. Makes clear recommendations on discount brokers. Explains the effects of fiscal and monetary policy on the stock market and much more.

PH: (201) 592-2000
ISBN: 0-13-645219-1
Published 1987
Cost: $33.75

The Pacific Rim Futures & Options Markets

Keith K. H. Park and Steven A. Schoenfeld
Probus Publishing Co.
1925 North Clybourn Avenue
Chicago, IL 60614

Subjects addressed: investing theories.
Covers the rapidly maturing financial derivative markets of Japan, Australia, Singapore, Hong Kong, New Zealand, Malaysia, Taiwan, Korea, the Philippines, Thailand, China and Indonesia. Uses a country-by-country breakdown and includes a detailed and comprehensive examination of each exchange including market structure, contract specifications, liquidity, trading volume and major participants.

PH: (800) PROBUS-1
FAX: (312) 868-6250
ISBN: 1-55738-207-7
Published 1992
Cost: $65.00

The PaineWebber Handbook of Stock and Bond Analysis

Kiril Sokoloff, Editor
Available through Fraser Publishing
P.O. Box 494
Burlington, VT 05402

Expert advise on when to buy or sell stocks on a unique industry-by-industry basis. Bonds analyzed by type; all information arranged in a quick reference format. The nation's foremost analysts reveal for the first time their own proprietary formulas - in a simple, easy-to-follow style for even beginning investors.

PH: (802) 658-0322
ISBN: 0-07-059576-3
Published 1979 (5th edition)
Cost: $58.50

Paper Money

Adam Smith
Summit Books
1230 Avenue of the Americas
New York, NY 10020

Having interpreted the prosperous '60s and the stressful 70s, Smith now tells what has happened since and what to expect next. How the age of paper money has arrived, what it means, and how it has changed our lives. Can there be a real estate crash? Is the stock market safe? Answers to these and many other important questions.

PH: (800) 223-2336
ISBN: 0-671-44825-0
Published 1981
Cost: $14.95

Passport to Profits: Opportunities in International Investing

John P. Dessauer
Dearborn Financial Publications, Inc.
520 N. Dearborn
Chicago, IL 60610

PH: (312) 836-4400
(800) 272-7550
Published 1990
Cost: $27.95

Subjects addressed: international markets, fundamental analysis, currencies, gold, precious metals. Shows investors and money managers how they can enter international markets and play them successfully. Dessauer shows that the years ahead stock market profits are most likely to be found outside the United States.

Penny Stocks: How to Profit With Low-Priced Stocks

Penny Stock News
McGraw Hill, Inc.
11 West 19th Street
New York, NY 10011

PH: (800) 722-4726
(212) 512-4100
Published 1986
Cost: $8.70

A basic how-to guide for investors interested in low-priced stocks and maximum profits.

Pension Fund Investment Management

Frank J. Fabozzi, Editor
Probus Publishing Co.
1925 North Clybourn Avenue
Chicago, IL 60614

PH: (800) PROBUS-1
FAX: (312) 868-6250
Published 1990
Cost: $69.95

Addresses all the important elements of pension fund management from the sponsor's perspective. Among the many topics discussed are: the sponsor's view of risk, managing the asset mix, benchmark portfolios, money manager fees and transactions cost, manager selection, attributing performance to sponsors and managers, accounting standards, public versus private pension funds.

The Pension Plan Investor

Daniel Kehrer
Probus Publishing Co.
1925 North Clybourn Avenue
Chicago, IL 60614

PH: (800) PROBUS-1
FAX: (312) 868-6250
ISBN: 1-55738-187-9
Published 1991
Cost: $32.50

Subjects addressed: investing theories.
A compendium of essential pension investment information on key subjects on asset allocation, zero coupon bonds, goals and strategies, manager selection, performance evaluation, pension rules and regulations, fixed-income investments, high-yield bonds, common stocks, foreign equities, picking GICs, real estate, venture capital, mutual funds, and more.

Personal Financial Planning

G. Victor Hallman & Jerry S. Rosenbloom
McGraw-Hill Publishing Company
1221 Avenue of the Americas
New York, NY 10020

PH: (800) 262-4729
ISBN: 0-07-025650-0
Published 1987 (4th edition)
Cost: $36.50

Reflecting the Tax Reform Act of 1986, shows how to set up a coordinated plan for your financial future. Covers every aspect of tax planning, taking advantage of market cycles, selecting and buying the right insurance, planning for retirement, and estate planning. Outlines a simple and practical financial panning process.

Personal Investing

Wilbur W. Widicus & Thomas E. Stitzel
Business One Irwin
1818 Ridge Road
Homewood, IL 60430

PH: (708) 206-2700
(800) 634-3966
FAX: (708) 798-1490
ISBN: 0-256-06797-X
Published 1988 (5th edition)
Cost: $40.95

The world of investments from the viewpoint of the individual investor. Examines the risks associated with different types of investments and the returns to be expected. After mastering the "basics," you'll learn to plan and investment program designed to use available financial resources to attain specific financial goals.

The Personal Investors Complete Book of Bonds

Donald R. Nichols
Longman Financial Services
520 N. Dearborn Street
Chicago, IL 60610

PH: (800) 621-9621
ISBN: 0-88462-627-X
Published 1989
Cost: $26.95

Subjects addressed: bond analysis. This book gives comprehensive, up-to-date and clearly written explanations of many investments, including CDs, treasury securities, municipals, zero coupon certificates, corporate convertible bonds and more. Its spells out specific features, advantages and disadvantages of each bond type. Details all types of bonds, assesses risks, and potential yields. Suggests plans for bond use in saving for retirement, college, etc. Beneficial for beginner or sophisticated investor.

The Plunderers

Edwin Lefevre
Fraser Publishing Company
P.O. Box 494
Burlington, VT 05401

ISBN: 0-87034-067-0
Published 1983
Cost: $17.50

Written in 1912, this novel is by the author of the bestseller, "Reminiscences of a Stock Operator". The book covers 4 tales of how the Plunder Recovery Syndicate, a group of intelligent men who deprecate alike violence and the immoderate accumulation of wealth, go about relieving malefactors of great abundance. Remarkable stories to be enjoyed before the next day of your own speculation.

The Plungers and the Peacocks: An Update of the Classic History of the Stock Market

Dana L. Thomas
William Morrow & Company, Inc.
105 Madison Avenue
New York, NY 10016

PH: (800) 843-9389
ISBN: 0-688-08136-3
Published 1989
Cost: $22.95

One hundred and seventy years of Wall Street history told through the anecdotes of the men and women who worked there, plus a data-packed manual of up-to-the-minute strategy for today's investor. Also, prophecies about the Wall Street of tomorrow. Provides an invaluable blueprint for predicting the future of the stock market.

Point & Figure Constructions and Formations

Michael Burke
Chartcraft, Inc.
1 West Avenue
Larchmont, NY 10538

PH: (914) 834-5181
Published 1990 (revised)
Cost: $9.95

Subject: point & figure charting; uses charts. This all new book modernizes the original P&F methodology first published in 1948 by A.W. Cohen. Concepts on constructing P&F charts remain unchanged, but emphasis is placed on relative strength analysis, use of trendlines and support and resistance areas. Several new formations are discussed along with new terminology. This book is designed to be a complete, updated guide to Point & Figure Charting.

The Point and Figure Method of Anticipating Stock Price Movements: Complete Theory & Practice

Victor deVilliers
Windsor Books
P.O. Box 280
Brightwaters, NY 11718

ISBN: 0-685-42039-6
Published 1933 (1973 reprint)
Cost: $15.00

Reprint of deVilliers' 1933 masterpiece on Point and Figure, including a chart on the 1929 crash. This system, according to the author's lucid analysis, gives the individual investor the advantages of the insider merely by recording and interpreting the full figures on all transactions. A respected classic of market literature.

Portfolio & Investment Management: State-of-the-Art Research, Analysis and Strategies

Frank J. Fabozzi, Editor
Probus Publishing Co.
1925 North Clybourn Avenue
Chicago, IL 60614

PH: (800) PROBUS-1
FAX: (312) 868-6250
Published 1989
Cost: $69.95

Containing chapters by 21 preeminent authorities in the field, this resourceful guide has been assembled to meet the informational needs of portfolio managers and other investment professionals who require the latest methodologies and strategies for staying competitive. This text reviews the investment management process, the foundations of capital markets, and the role of options and futures.

Power Cycles: A Strategy for Business and Investing Excellence in the 1980s and Beyond

William & Douglas Kirkland
Professional Communications
P.O. Box 7585
Phoenix, AR 85011

PH: (602) 274-2128
ISBN: 0-9614654-0-9
Published 1986 (2nd edition)
Cost: $19.95

The Power Cycle is a natural phenomenon - a recurring cycle of prosperity and depression, unaffected by human intervention of any kind. A knowledge of its characteristics allows investors a critically important opportunity to protect their capital during the powerful downswing that it now predicts - and to profit on the rebound.

The Power of Oscillator / Cycles Combinations

Walt Bressert - Publisher
6987 N. Oracle
Tucson, AZ 85704

PH: (800) 677-0120
Published 1991
Cost: $145.00

Subjects addressed: market analysis, trading analysis, technical analysis. Uses charts. "Trading legend Walter Bressert unveils his 'Secret Weapon' strategy for anticipating, identifying and confirming turning points."

PowerTiming: Using the Elliott Wave System to Anticipate and Time Market Turns

Robert C. Beckman
Probus Publishing Co.
1925 North Clybourn Avenue
Chicago, IL 60614

PH: (800) PROBUS-1
FAX: (312) 868-6250
ISBN: 1-55738-273-5
Published 1991
Cost: $35.00

Subjects addressed: investing theories. This new edition of "PowerTiming" includes: the origins of the wave principle, the cyclical nature of the market, applications to investment strategy, applying the Fibonacci series, the trend channel, Elliott and inflation, corrective wave formations.

Practical Asset Allocation and the Business Cycle

Martin J. Pring
International Institute for Economic Research
P.O. Box 329
Blackville Road
Washington Depot, CT 06794

PH: (800) 221-7514
Cost: Video and free 80 page booklet $95.00

VIDEO
Subjects addressed: Asset Allocation; uses charts. During a typical business cycle, the financial markets progress through six stages for which a different portfolio mix of stocks, bonds and inflation - hedge assets is appropriate. With animated diagrams and charts, the course explains when these stages occur, how you can identify them and which asset classes are likely to do best.

Pring Market Review Historical Chartbook (VII Edition)

Martin J. Pring
McGraw-Hill
1221 Avenue of the Americas
New York, NY 10020

PH: (800) 262-4729
Published 1991
Cost: $68.25

Subjects: market analysis; uses charts. Quarterly, monthly and weekly charts of the U.S. debt, equity and commodity markets together with key relative strength, momentum, and selected U.S. economic indicators going back to the 19th century. Coverage includes S&P stock groups, individual commodities, stock market volume, breadth and sentiment measures, foreign countries' stock markets, industrial production and CPI.

Profitable Grain Trading

Ralph M. Ainsworth
Traders Press
P.O. Box 6206
Greenville, SC 29606

PH: (803) 288-3900
ISBN: 0-934380-04-X
Published in 1933 (1980 reprint)
Cost: $25.00

This classic book on grain speculation was first published in 1933 by the respected grain trader, real estate speculator, and pioneer in the seed industry. Much of his trading philosophy and accumulated market wisdom are revealed in this volume, along with many of the most effective technical trading systems that he discovered.

Profitable Trading with Charts and Technicals

Commodities Education Institute
219 Parkade
Cedar Falls, IA 50613

PH: (800) 635-3936
(319) 277-6341
FAX: (319) 277-7982
Published 1990
Cost: $55.00

VIDEO
Subjects addressed: investing theories, trading analysis, technical analysis. Glen Ring, editor of Commodity Closeup shows you how to build your own "tool-box" of practical technical analysis techniques. Topics include: market psychology, bar charts, trend spotting, support and resistance, terminal areas, congestion patterns, Elliott Wave applications, Fibonacci numbers, introduction to Gann and RSI, using computerized technical tools, order placement and working with your broker.

Profitable Trading with Gann and Directional Indicators

Glen Ring
Commodities Educational Institute
219 Parkade
Cedar Falls, IA 50613

PH: (319) 277-6341
(800) 635-3936
FAX: (319) 277-7982
Published 3/90 re-done in March 91
Cost: $233.00/5 tapes and notebook

VIDEO
Subjects addressed: commodities trading, technical analysis. Coverage includes market psychology and discipline, how to improve performance, basic Gann techniques, relative strength index, stochastics, directional movement indicator and specific techniques for combining Gann and directional indicators into a disciplined, profitable, trading plan. COMMENTS: led in front of a live audience.

The Profit Magic of Stock Transaction Timing

J.M. Hurst
Prentice-Hall
Route 9W
Englewood Cliffs, NJ 07632

PH: (201) 592-2000
Published 1970
Cost: $8.95

Subjects addressed: investing theories, market analysis, trading analysis, fundamental analysis, technical analysis; uses charts. "A price forecasting technique that predicts price turns with 90% accuracy. Produces an average net profit of 10% per month and proves your stock market fortune can be built like clockwork."

The Prospect for Gold: The View to the Year 2000

Timothy Green
Walker & Company
720 Fifth Avenue
New York, NY 10019

PH: (212) 265-3632
ISBN: 0-8027-10026
Published 1987
Cost: $29.95

Who will buy all the new gold on the market? Get the answers from one with 20 years of experience in the gold market. An authoritative book on gold's role for the rest of the century.

The Prudent Investor: The Definitive Guide to Professional Investment Management

James P. Owen
Probus Publishing Co.
1925 North Clybourn Avenue
Chicago, IL 60614

PH: (800) PROBUS-1
FAX: (312) 868-6250
ISBN: 1-55738-106-2
Published 1990
Cost: $32.50

Subjects addressed: taking stock—developing an investment policy, allocating assets, understanding manager styles and selecting the right manager, monitoring performance, venturing beyond stocks and bonds. Offering a thorough description and analysis of all the variables that go into managing an investment portfolio successfully. *The Prudent Investor* uses easy-to-understand language and everyday examples to explain how and why the best money managers make the investment decisions they do. Geared toward the "middle market investor," the book is organized as a series of "steps," from taking stock of the situation and allocating financial assets to hiring the right investment advisor for a particular investment program.

The Prudent Speculator

Al Frank Asset Management, Inc.
P.O. Box 1767
Santa Monica, CA 90406-1767

PH: (800) 258-7786
Published 1990
Cost: $27.95

Subjects addressed: investing theories, fundamental analysis, trading analysis. Details the basics of stock investing and shows you how to develop a long term strategy. By using a combination of investment measurements, Frank shows you how to place your money in the right place at the right time so that it earns the best return for you.

Quality of Earnings: The Investor's Guide to How Much Money a Company Is Really Making

Thornton L. O'Glove
Free Press
866 Third Avenue
New York, NY 10022

PH: (800)257-5755
Published 1987
ISBN: 0-02-922630-9
Cost: $18.95

A long-awaited guide to maximum-return investment. Learn to spot trouble before the market catches wind of it and recognize the important differences between a corporation's shareholder books and its tax books. Gives the reader the meaningful edge over other investors.

Quantitative International Investing

Brian R. Bruce, Editor
Probus Publishing Co.
1925 North Clybourn Avenue
Chicago, IL 60614

PH: (800) PROBUS-1
FAX: (312) 868-6250
ISBN: 1-55738-121-6
Published 1990
Cost: $69.95

This book combines the work of experts from the most prestigious and advanced money management firms in the world to create a book that focuses on the foundation needed to manage international funds successfully.

Questions and Answers About Today's Securities Market

Dr. Nachman Bench
Prentice-Hall
200 Old Tappan Road
Old Tappan, NJ 07675

PH: (800) 922-0579
Published 1986
ISBN: 0-13-749227-8
Cost: $20.50

Subjects: bond analysis, options, stock analysis, options, and mutual funds. A unique investment guide that not only contains everything you need to plan and maximize a personal investment strategy, but also includes tested techniques for preserving your capital as well as your return on investment. Covering all types of investments including stocks, bonds, options, mutual funds, and tangible investments such as gold and other precious metals.

Raging Bull: How to Invest in the Growth Stocks of the '90s

David Alger
Business One Irwin
1818 Ridge Road
Homewood, IL 60430

PH: (708) 206-2700
 (800) 634-3966
FAX: (708) 798-1490
ISBN: 1-55623-462-7
Published 1991
Cost: $24.95

Subjects addressed: stock analysis. It is widely believed that the 89% of individual investors who own stocks will move from glass ceilinged blue chips to stocks that promise higher growth. David Alger shows investors how to discover the next Apple Computer, Cellular One, or Nike. This book gives readers: strategies for achieving high returns on growth stocks, guidelines for prudent stock analysis that safeguard against risky investments, details on several target industries with an important growth evaluation formula for finding the winning companies within each industry.

The Random Walk and Beyond: An Inside Guide to the Stock Market

Mark A. Johnson
John Wiley and Sons, Inc.
605 Third Avenue
New York, NY 10158-0012

PH: (212) 850-6000
ISBN: 0-471-63223-6
Published 1988
Cost: $22.95

Learn how the stock market really works. Learn how to evaluate workable and effective investment strategies. Learn why investments are not as risky as they seem. "Johnson's bibliography alone should be required reading for those seeking broker's licenses. I'm impressed." says Forbes columnist Kenneth L. Fisher.

A Random Walk Down Wall Street

Burton G. Malkiel
W.W. Norton & Co., Inc.
500 5th Avenue
New York, NY 10110

ISBN: 0-393-02793-7
Published 1973, 1990 (5th edition)
Cost: $22.95

Subjects addressed: investing theories, stock analysis, bond analysis, fundamental analysis, technical analysis. Beat the pros at their own game and learn a user friendly long range investing strategy that really works.

The Rational Investor: Common Sense Advice for Winning in the Stock Market

Edward F. Mrkvicka, Jr.
Probus Publishing Co.
1925 North Clybourn Avenue
Chicago, IL 60614

PH: (800) PROBUS-1
FAX: (312) 868-6250
ISBN: 1-55738-194-1
Published 1991
Cost: $22.95

Subjects addressed: investing theories.
A solid technical approach with a step-by-step plan for control of investments. Includes initial investment assessment, kinds of investment, choosing investment vehicles, flexibility, diversification, the ten commandments of stock market success, selecting mutual funds, the 12-percent investment rule, market benchmarks, devising an overall investment strategy, brokers and the role of savings in the investment plan.

Reminiscences of a Stock Operator

Edwin Lefevre
Fraser Publishing Company
P.O. Box 494
Burlington, VT 05402

PH: (802) 658-0322
Published 1923 (1980 reprint)
ISBN: 0-87034-065-4 (hardcover) $20.00
ISBN: 0-87034-058-1 (paperback) $12.00

First published 1923, tells the story of Jesse Livermore, one of the great speculators in the first half of the 20th century. Though the actions take place during an economic time far removed from our age, the human emotions and reactions remain the same. One classic that every marketeer should read before investing a cent.

Reuters Glossary: International Economic & Financial Terms

Reuters
Longman Financial Services Publishers
520 N. Dearborn
Chicago, IL 60610

PH: (800) 621-9621
ISBN: 0-582-04286-0
Published 1989
Cost: $12.95

More than 2,000 entries. Concepts such as accelerated depreciation and "zero coupons" explained in full. Originally used as a working tool for Reuters' staff worldwide, it's been expanded and brought up to date. Fully indexed and extensively cross-referenced.

Risk Based Capital Charges for Municipal Bonds

Robert Godfrey
JAI Press, Inc.
55 Old Post Road - 2
P.O. Box 1678
Greenwich, CT 06835-1678

PH: (203) 661-7602
Cost: $35.10 + 2.50 postage and handling

Subject addressed: bond analysis. Written by MBIA executive VP Robert Godfrey, chronicles nation's economic and bond default history from 1869 to present. Offers modern day stress test for bonds to determine whether or not they're likely to default.

The RSL Market Timing System

Humphrey E. D. Lloyd
Windsor Books
P.O. Box 280
Brightwaters, NY 11718

Published 1991
Cost: $50.00

Subjects addressed: market timing, mutual funds, futures and options. Uses charts. Shows how to use Humphrey Lloyd's personal market timing system to "Win on 4 of Every 5 Trades."

Scientific Interpretation of Bar Charts

John R. Hill
Available through Fraser Publishing
P.O. Box 494
Burlington, VT 05402

PH: (802) 658-0322
Published 1979
Cost: $40.00

Deciphers every possible market shift as reflected in the charts, and presents trading recommendations for each scenario. Discusses daily bar chart analysis, and teaches the law of supply and demand by exploring 82 examples of isolated chart sections. Trendline Theory, Daily Overlap Theory, Two-Day Intersection Theory, and more.

Seasonal Charts for Futures Traders: A Sourcebook

Courtney Smith
John Wiley and Sons, Inc.
605 Third Avenue
New York, NY 10158-0012

PH: (212) 850-6000
ISBN: 0-471-84888-3
Published 1987
Cost: $65.00

Easy-to-use guide to seasonal price movements provides the statistics you need to time entry and exit points, set stop-loss orders, and establish realistic goals. Offers insight into the profit potential and risk involved at any given time of the year. Charts and tables supply the odds for profit before you put in the trade.

The Secret of Finding Big Winners in the Stock Market

F. R. Margolius
Probus Publishing Co.
1925 North Clybourn Avenue
Chicago, IL 60614

PH: (800) PROBUS-1
FAX: (312) 868-6250
ISBN: 1-55738-281-6
Published 1991
Cost: $16.95

Subjects addressed: investing theories. This book provides everything needed to follow its proven techniques, including long- and short-range plans and step-by-step worksheets that keep the investor "honest" - that is, free of costly emotions like fear, greed and stubbornness. This book charts a steady course that will enable the investor to: increase not just dollars, but real wealth, protect investments from market declines, identify future "winners," eliminate expensive advisory fees, and remove the temptation to fall back on costly "hot tips."

The Secret of Selecting Stocks for Immediate and Substantial Gains

Larry R. Williams
Windsor Books
P.O. Box 280
Brightwaters, NY 11718

ISBN: 0-930233-05-0
Published 1986 (2nd edition)
Cost: $25.00

Presents a technique for selecting stocks based on identifying which ones are under professional buying and selling. Explains how to successfully forecast the market's short, intermediate, and long term trends. Finally, you'll learn how to combine stock selection and market timing for maximum profits. Many insights and pointers.

Secrets of the Temple: How the Federal Reserve Runs the Country

William Greider
S & S Trade
1230 Avenue of the Americas
New York, NY 10020

PH: (212) 698-7000
ISBN: 0-671-67556-7
Published 1987
Cost: $12.95

Chronicles the unseen political struggles that led to financial crisis and the stock market collapse of October 1987. The inside story of how the Federal Reserve, remote and mysterious to most Americans, actually ran things in the 1980s. Explains why politicians of both parties acquiesce to the power of the Federal Reserve.

Securitization

Christine Pavel
Probus Publishing Co.
1925 North Clybourn Avenue
Chicago, IL 60614

PH: (800) PROBUS-1
FAX: (312) 868-6250
Published:
Cost: $42.50

This book provides an in-depth study of the structures, key sectors, and innovations in the mortgage-backed markets. A significant portion of the book details new developments in the growing markets for securities backed by consumer installment loans, and other non-mortgage-related assets, including lease receivables and commercial loans. These new issues often provide tremendous value to investors, offering high yields with relative safety.

Security Analysis and Portfolio Management

Donald E. Fischer and Ronald J. Jordan
Prentice Hall
Route 9W
Englewood Cliffs, NJ 07632

PH: (201) 592-2000
Published 1975, 1991 (5th edition)
Cost: $58.92

Subjects addressed: investing theories, stock analysis, market analysis, bond analysis, earnings analysis, trading analysis, commodities trading, fundamental analysis, technical analysis. Uses charts. Includes the following; investing environment, risk/return analysis, common stock analysis, bond analysis, options, technical analysis, the efficient market theory, portfolio analysis, selection and management.

Selling Covered Calls: The Safest Game on the Option Market

C. J. Caes
McGraw Hill, Inc.
11 West 19th Street
New York, NY 10011

PH: (800) 722-4726
(212) 512-4100
Published 1990
Cost: $24.60

Subjects addressed: options trading. Uses charts. The author shows why covered calls are a good bet in both bull and bear markets. He reviews the entire options market and gives a clear explanation of how this complicated system works.

Short-Term Trading in Futures

Jacob Bernstein
Probus Publishing Co.
1925 North Clybourn Avenue
Chicago, IL 60614

PH: (800) PROBUS-1
FAX: (312) 868-6250
ISBN: 0-917253-66-3
Published:
Cost: $125.00

Subjects addressed: Futures.
The author illustrates how to profit from historically volitle price movements in a number of active futures markets, including the interest rate and stock index futures markets.

Simulation, Optimization and Expert Systems: How Technology is Revolutionizing the Way Securities Are Underwritten, Analyzed and Traded

Dimitris N. Chorafas
Probus Publishing Co.
1925 North Clybourn Avenue
Chicago, IL 60614

PH: (800) PROBUS-1
FAX: (312) 868-6250
ISBN: 1-55738-231-X
Published 1991
Cost: $65.00

Subjects addressed: technical analysis. This groundbreaking book, complete with case studies, contains all of the latest information on this technological revolution. Topics include: quantitative approaches to money management, simulations and optimization in securities decisions, preparing for supercomputer usage, expert systems in trust management, computer-based trading, statistically valid portfolio diversification, networks, databases, and supercomputers.

Smart Money: How to Be Your Own Financial Advisor

Ken Dolan & Daria Dolan
Random House, Inc.
201 E. 50th Street
31st Floor
New York, NY 10022

PH: (800) 733-3000
ISBN: 0-394-56516-9
Published 1988
Cost: $19.95

In question-and-answer form, provides the tools to help you become your own financial manager. Covers the basics, then gives you specific, dow-to-earth recommendations - the whys and wherefores you need in order to make sensible decisions for yourself and your family. Recommends a sample investment portfolio for each stage of life.

Smarter Money: An Investment Game Plan for Those Who Made It and Want to Keep It

Frank J. Fabozzi & Stephen Feldman
Available through Fraser Publishing
P.O. Box 494
Burlington, VT 05402

PH: (802) 658-0322
ISBN: 0-917253-16-7
Published 1985 (2nd edition)
Cost: $18.95

Build a financial plan and investment portfolio that will allow you to achieve your long-term goals. Whether you're a novice or an experienced investor, you are sure to profit from these straightforward descriptions of and gimmick-free strategies for stocks, bonds, mutual funds, real estate, and mortgage-backed securities.

Sooner Than You Think: Mapping a Course for a Comfortable Retirement

Gordon K. Williamson
Business One Irwin
1818 Ridge Road
Homewood, IL 60430

PH: (708) 206-2700
(800) 634-3966
FAX: (708) 798-1490
ISBN: 1-55623-541-0
Published 1991
Cost: $24.95

Uses charts. Shows readers how to determine a financial plan that will meet their retirement goals. Chock-full of charts, checklists, warnings, pro and con checklists, fill-in timelines, information sources, and a unique tickler system that alerts future retirees of important decisions to be made, this unique and lively book removes the mystique of retirement planning. Williamson shows readers how to: organize and begin planning for a comfortable retirement, prepare for the shortcomings in social security and medical coverage upon retirement, plan for post-retirement expenses, challenge professional sales pitches to ensure they are getting exactly what they need and want in insurance coverage, maximize the value of their estates.

Soybean Price Action

William A. Brown
Available through Fraser Publishing
P.O. Box 494
Burlington, VT 05402

PH: (802) 658-0322
Published 1976
Cost: $15.00

Learn to understand seasonal price action, an essential element for the producer, purchaser, or speculator in the commodities markets. Get a good idea of both the direction and probability of seasonal price change by using both the seasonal price charts and probability tables.

Speculation in Commodity Contracts and Options

L. Dee Belveal
Business One Irwin
1818 Ridge Road
Homewood, IL 60430

PH: (800) 634-3966
FAX: (708) 798-1490
ISBN:1-87094-672-2
Published 1985
Cost: $40.00

Shows you the smart way to profitable trading...by "reading" trade behavior and "anticipating" price behavior.

The Speculator's Edge - Strategies for Profit in the Futures Markets

Albert Peter Pacelli
John Wiley & Sons
605 Third Avenue
New York, NY 10158-0012

PH: (800) 526-5368 Orders (212) 850-6418 Info
Published March, 1989
Cost: $29.95

Subjects addressed: investing theories, market analysis, trading analysis, commodities trading, technical analysis; uses charts. Covers how to get started in futures trading, market timing, understanding cyclical trends. Shows how to be a profitable futures trader under the basic role of speculator.

Stan Weinstein's Secrets for Profiting in Bull and Bear Markets

Stan Weinstein
Business One Irwin
1818 Ridge Road
Homewood, IL 60430

PH: (800) 634-3966 (708) 206-2700
FAX: (708) 798-1490
Published 1988
Cost: $27.50

Subjects addressed: technical analysis; uses charts. Shows you how to identify predictable patterns in market trends as well as stock and mutual fund movements using techniques developed over the last 20 years.

Starting Small, Investing Smart - What to do With $5 - $5000

Donald R. Nichols
Business One Irwin
1818 Ridge Road
Homewood, IL 60430

PH: (800) 634-3966
(708) 206-2700
FAX: (708)798-1490
Published 1984, 1988-2nd edition
Cost: $24.95

Subjects addressed: stock analysis, bond analysis, precious metals. For beginning investors, outlines the features, advantages, disadvantages, and returns offered by bank deposits, stocks, bonds, mutual funds, precious metals, and other investments accessible for $5-$5000.

Steidlmayer on Markets ... New Approach to Trading

J. Peter Steidlmayer
John Wiley and Sons, Inc.
605 Third Avenue
New York, NY 10158-0012

PH: (212) 850-6000
ISBN: 0-471-62115-3
Published 1989
Cost: $34.95

Slow down. Avoid the "kill quick" approach, warns this author, whom Forbes calls "the revolutionary in the pit." Learn to read data from the futures market, and to detect patterns. An inside account based on 25 years of trading on the floor of the Chicago Board of Trade.

Still More Words of Wall Street

Allan H. Pessin and Joseph A. Ross
Business One Irwin
1818 Ridge Road
Homewood, IL 60430

PH: (800) 634-3966
FAX: (708) 798-1490
ISBN: 1-55623-329.9
Published September 1990
Cost: $17.95

Get the up-to-date current lingo to help you communicate on Wall Street. More than a mere glossary, this handy reference includes specific industry examples and mathematical formulas.

Stochastics

Commodities Education Institute
219 Parkade
Cedar Falls, IA 50613

PH: (800) 635-3936
(319) 277-6341
FAX: (319) 277-7982
Published 1990
Cost: $55.00

VIDEO
Subjects addressed: investing theories, technical analysis. Glen Ring shows you how to use this oscillator as an overbought/oversold and divergent indicator. He also shows how to use stochastics for entry buy and sell signals. Part of a series of 5 tapes available for $233.00

Stock & Commodity Market Trend Trading by Advanced Technical Analysis

John R. Hill
Available through Fraser Publishing
P.O. Box 494
Burlington, VT 05402

PH: (802) 658-0322
Published 1977
Cost: $50.00

Strictly technical; no fundamentals - except those revealed through chart interpretation. Examines technical tools that can be used to analyze supply and demand trends in order to properly time commodity and stock market trading. Includes Pivot Point Analysis, the Elliott Wave Theory, plus many new and unique technical tools.

Stock Index Futures

Frank J. Fabozzi and Gregory M. Kipnis, Editors
Available through Fraser Publishing
P.O. Box 494
Burlington, VT 05402

PH: (802) 658-0322
ISBN: 0-87094-424-X
Published 1984
Cost: $57.50

Experts from investment, law, and accounting firms as well as exchanges and the academic world explain how to compare and select, and price contract and how to use them for investing, hedging, and arbitrage. Also examines options on stock index futures and the cash index, and how they can best be used in portfolio management.

Stock Index Futures: Buying and Selling the Market Averages

Allan M. Loosigian
Available through Fraser Publishing
P.O. Box 494
Burlington, VT 05402

PH: (802) 658-0322
ISBN: 0-201-10267-6
Published 1985
Cost: $29.95

Provides a complete understanding of stock index futures contracts: how they began, how they work, how they can fulfill specific investment needs. Examines today's sophisticated strategies for professional portfolio management. Practical advice to minimize the risks and maximize the benefits of trading in the market indexes.

Stock Index Options, Revised Edition

Donald T. Mesler and Scot G. Barenblat
Probus Publishing Co.
1925 North Clybourn Avenue
Chicago, IL 60614

PH: (800) PROBUS-1
FAX: (312) 868-6250
ISBN: 1-55738-181-X
Published 1992
Cost: $29.95

Subjects: stock index options - definitions. Mesler's work is guide to the definitions and characteristics of stock index options. Revised Edition.

The Stock Market

Richard J. Teweles and Edward S. Bradley
John Wiley & Sons
605 Third Avenue
New York, NY 10158-0012

PH: (212) 850-6418 (orders)
(212) 850-6233 (info)
Published 1951, 1987 (5th edition)
Cost: $29.95

Subjects addressed: investing theories, stock analysis, market analysis, bond analysis, fundamental analysis, technical analysis. Definitive guide to the institutions, principles, and practices of today's market. Covers history, products, and operation of the market to the practical techniques used by seasonal shareholders and traders.

Stock Market Blueprints

Edward S. Jensen
Available through Fraser Publishing
P.O. Box 494
Burlington, VT 05402

PH: (802) 658-0322
Published 1983 (5th edition)
Cost: $18.00

For those who realize that successful investing, like any other venture, requires careful planning. Discusses the factors that are most likely to lead to success, and puts forth five detailed plans - the Blueprints - tailored to the temperament and goals of different individuals. Considers both emotional and empirical factors.

The Stock Market Investor's Computer Guide

Michael Gianturco
McGraw-Hill
1221 Avenue of the Americas
New York, NY 10020

PH: (800) 262-4729
ISBN: 0-07-023186-9
Published 1987
Cost: $36.50

Buyer's handbook cuts through the advertising claims to explain what combinations of hardware and software will automate your investing with the smallest outlay of time, effort, and money. Detailed information on software for both technical and fundamental analysis, portfolio management, all related hardware components, and more.

Stock Market Logic

Norman G. Fosbach
The Institute for Econometric Research
3471 N. Federal Highway
Ft. Lauderdale, FL 33306

PH: (800) 327-6700
(305) 563-9000
Published 1971
Cost: $40.00

Subjects addressed: investing theories, stock analysis, market analysis, earnings analysis, trading analysis, fundamental analysis, technical analysis; uses charts. Should be read by everyone interested in the market. Investors seeking a rational and sophisticated approach to profits on Wall Street will find the answers in this book. Revealed for the first time, all the complete results of a 5 year investigation of stock market behavior conducted at the Institute for Econometric Research.

Stock Market Primer

Claude N. Rosenberg, Jr.
Warner Books, Inc.
666 5th Avenue
New York, NY 10103

Published 1962, 1987 (last update)
Cost: $18.95

Subjects addressed: investing theories, stock analysis, market analysis, trading analysis. Classic guide to investment success for the novice and the expert. Tells you what to buy, when to buy, what to pay, and when to sell to get maximum return on investments.

Stock Market Rules

Michael D. Sheimo
Probus Publishing Co.
1925 North Clybourn Avenue
Chicago, IL 60614

PH: (800) PROBUS-1
FAX: (312) 868-6250
ISBN: 1-55738-150-X
Published 1991
Cost: $21.95

Subjects addressed: investing theories.
Fifty of the most widely held investment axioms explained. Uses an analytical approach to go beyond the generalities to the practical specifics of these maxims. Included are facts, figures, sample trades, historical data, charts, graphs, and more. The rules are demonstrated and explained which will and will not work.

The Stock Options Manual

Gary L. Gastineau
McGraw Hill
1221 Avenue of the Americas
New York, NY 10020

PH: (800) 2-MCGRAW
(212) 512-2000
Published 1979, 1988 (3rd edition)
Cost: $44.95

Subjects addressed: options. For the intelligent investor. Provides background of options markets, information on uses of options, strategies, tax treatments, regulations and evaluation techniques.

Strategic Investment Timing in the '90s, Revised Edition

Dick A. Stoken
Probus Publishing Co.
1925 North Clybourn Avenue
Chicago, IL 60614

PH: (800) PROBUS-1
FAX: (312) 868-6250
ISBN: 1-55738-103-8
Published 1990
Cost: $19.95

Subject: economic cycle. This book shows how investors can use changes in the economic cycle to enhance profits in the stock, bond, metals, and futures markets. The author has devised a formula that has retroactively accounted for every major turn in the economy since 1920. Stoken states that the direction of the economy can be determined by following four simple, accessible and fundamental indicators: the DJIA, the rate of inflation, short and long-term interest rates, and the four year presidential election cycle. Revised.

Strategies for the Options Trader

Claud E. Cleeton
John Wiley and Sons, Inc.
605 Third Avenue
New York, NY 10158-0012

PH: (212) 850-6000
ISBN: 0-471-04973-5
Published 1979
Cost: $49.95

An option's trader's sourcebook. Formulas for normal values of puts and calls cover all market conditions. Develops the concept of options volatility for price evaluation of individual options. Analyzes the various option strategies, and examines timing techniques. Includes universal option tables as an alternative to calculators.

Success in Commodities: The Congestion Phase System

Eugene Nofri & Jeanette Nofri Steinberg
Available through Fraser Publishing
P.O. Box 494
Burlington, VT 05402

PH: (802) 658-0322
Published 1980 (2nd edition)
Cost: $75.00

Reported to be close to 75 percent effective as a guide in market timing, the Congestion Phase System is made up of 32 short-term patterns which appear in a commodity chart, along with trading instructions. When the patterns match those on your charts, just follow the instructions to become a successful commodities trader.

Successful Investing: A Complete Guide to Your Financial Future

United Business Service
S & S Trade
1230 Avenue of the Americas
New York, NY 10020

PH: (212) 698-7000
ISBN: 0-671-46734-4
Published 1983
Cost: $12.95

Also available in paperback
ISBN: 0-671-64762-8, Fireside
Published 1987
Cost: $12.95

An authoritative financial self-help reference on the stock market. Sections include: the Art of Prudent Investing, Your Various Alternatives, How to Make Your Choices, Mastering the Strategies and Tactics, Taking Care of the Housekeeping, Investments and Your Financial Plan, and Speaking the Language of the Bulls and Bears.

SuperHedging

Thomas C. Noddings
Available through Fraser Publishing
P.O. Box 494
Burlington, VT 05402

PH: (802) 658-0322
ISBN: 0-917253-21-3
Published 1986
Cost: $35.00

The serious investor's guide to stock market hedging strategies for higher risk-adjusted returns. Traditional tactics are not enough. Explains each of over forty-different innovative hedging techniques, compares its risk/reward characteristics to the other strategies, and shows under what market conditions each performs best.

Super Investment Trends: Cashing in on the Dynamic '90s

James B. Powell
Business One Irwin
1818 Ridge Road
Homewood, IL 60430

PH: (708) 206-2700 (800) 634-3966
FAX: (708) 798-1490
ISBN: 1-55623-500-3
Published 1991
Cost: $24.95

Shows readers how to identify and capitalize on the investment opportunities of the '90s. Powell offers practical strategies and guidelines so readers can: identify the trends behind investment opportunities early enough to maximize their profits, pick companies prepared to meet trends as they materialize, find industries capable of making the necessary changes to take advantage of trends, fully understand new financial products and services that cater to the anticipated trends of the '90s.

The Super Saver: Fundamental Strategies for Building Wealth

Janet Lowe
Longman Financial Services Publishers
520 N. Dearborn
Chicago, IL 60610

PH: (800) 621-9621
ISBN: 0-88462-915-5
Published 1990
Cost: $19.95

Learn to create a flexible savings plan to fit your needs. Learn to take the best advantage of tax-free and tax-deferred savings opportunities. Be in charge of your finances, and reap the rewards down the road. A step-by-step guide on how and why to save.

Super Stocks

Kenneth L. Fisher
Business One Irwin
1818 Ridge Road
Homewood, IL 60430

PH: (800) 634-3966
(708) 206-2700
FAX: (708) 798-1490
Published 1984
Cost: $31.00

Subjects addressed: stock analysis, market analysis, earnings analysis, trading analysis, fundamental analysis; uses charts. Introduces unique and powerful, yet easily understood new methods for valuing stocks, analyzing and predicting future profit margins. Super Stocks shows how to use price/sales ratios and price/research ratios in conjunction with fundamental business analysis to spot the bargains on Wall Street.

Superstocks: A New Method to Uncover Rapid Appreciation Stocks

Hugh Ferguson
Windsor Books
P.O. Box 280
Brightwaters, NY 11718

Published 1979
ISBN: 0-685-49183-8
Cost $25.00

An infinitely readable guide to making it big on the stock market. Blends the whimsical with the empirical while teaching you exactly how to identify and invest in stocks that are on the verge of a major surge. Tells when to buy and sell each growth stock. Includes worksheets and figures to help you go figure for yourself.

The Super Traders: Secrets and Successes of Wall Street's Best and Brightest

Alan Rubenfeld
Probus Publishing Co.
1925 North Clybourn Avenue
Chicago, IL 60614

PH: (800) PROBUS-1
FAX: (312) 868-6250
ISBN: 1-55738-284-0
Published 1993
Cost: $24.95

This behind-the-scenes look at Wall Street contains personal and candid accounts of big-name traders like Bob Scavone, Steve Bodurtha, James Mangan, Joe Apisa, Frank Baxter, Jon Najarian, Denny Engleman, and Victor "Trader Vic" Sperandeo. In this provocative text, the traders disclose how they got started on Wall Street as well as their personal trading secrets and philosophies. The unadultterated insights presented here make this a one- of-a-kind book written by, for and about traders.

Sure Thing Commodity Trading: How Seasonal Factors Influence Commodity Prices

Larry R. Williams & Michelle L. Noseworthy
Windsor Books
P.O. Box 280
Brightwaters, NY 11718

ISBN: 0-930233-04-2
Published 1977
Cost: $50.00

Over 50 empirically derived trades based in extensively researched seasonal tendencies of virtually all major commodities as far back as 1955. Each trade is accompanied by clear commentary and simple rules showing when to get in and when to get out of each trade. Documented with results that would have been obtained each year.

Sure-Thing Options Trading: A Money-making Guide to the New Listed Stock and Commodity Options Markets

George Angell
New American Library
1633 Broadway
New York, NY 10019

PH: (800) 526-0275
Published 1983
Cost: $34.95
Also available in paperback
ISBN: 0-452-26110-4, Plume
Cost: $9.95

Join the boom in options trading and play the market to your advantage. Learn how to size up an options trade, what to pay, what to select, the advantages of options over stocks, how to trade the new stock index markets, and much more. Straightforward strategies for getting into the hottest investor area today.

Susan Lee's ABZ's of Money and Finance: from Annuities to Zero Coupon Bonds

Susan Lee
Poseidon Press
1230 Avenue of the Americas
New York, NY 10020

PH: (212) 698-7000
ISBN: 0-671-55712-2
Published 1988
Cost: $16.95

Called "A financial Berlitz course" by Vogue, it's everything one needs to know about saving, investing, and borrowing from annuities to zero coupon bonds. Straightforward information on CDs, Treasury notes, municipal bonds and much more, it's Wall Street jargon demystified.

The Takeover Game

John Brooks
Dutton—Orders toNew American Library
P.O. Box 120
Bergenfield, NJ 07621

PH: (800) 526-0275
ISBN: 0-525-48440-X
Published 1988
Cost: $9.95

The people, the power, and the Wall Street money behind today's nationwide merger wars. This wide-ranging and timely book starts at the beginning and takes you everywhere, including deep inside the game itself with its patchwork parade of white knights , greenmail, golden parachutes, leveraged buyouts, junk bonds, and more.

Technical Analysis & Options Strategies

Kenneth H. Shaleen
Probus Publishing Co.
1925 North Clybourn Avenue
Chicago, IL 60614

PH: (800) PROBUS-1
FAX: (312) 868-6250
ISBN: 1-55738-407-X
Published 1992
Cost: $55.00

A one-of-a-kind book that will be on the desk of every trader. *Technical Analysis & Options Strategies* takes seventeen of the most popular options strategies and shows how and when to use them depending upon market conditions. The author even goes a step further and shows traders the particular options position to take given a specific technical situation. More than just knowledge, this book imparts a *system*, providing traders with the means by which they can understand and apply each of the srtrategies cdiscussed. Furthermore, actual market conditions are used to demonstrate strategies, not "after-the-fact" examples. In addition, this title offers analyses and detailed charts for each of the strategies, as well as discussions of how and when to adjust them.

The Technical Analysis Course

Thomas A. Meyers
Probus Publishing Co.,
1925 North Clybourn Avenue
Chicago, IL 60614

PH: (800) PROBUS-1
Published 1989
Cost: $47.50

Subjects addressed: investing theories, stock analysis, market analysis, commodities trading, technical analysis; uses charts. Course study on technical analysis techniques that provide the critical tools, materials, and plans necessary to buy, sell, and trade more profitably.

Technical Analysis Explained

Martin J. Pring
International Institute for Technical Research
P.O. Box 338
Washington Depot, CT 06794

PH: (800) 221-7514
Cost: $395.00 (complete video with textbook); $375.00 (complete video without textbook); $95.00 (each, lessons 1,2,3,5); $115.00 (lesson 4)

VIDEO
Subjects addressed: technical analysis; uses charts. The video course on Technical Analysis contains 5 tapes, each lasting about 40 minutes. Lesson I - Basic Principles, Lesson II - Price Patterns, Lesson III - Support and Resistance, Trendlines and Moving Averages, Lesson IV - Momentum, Relative Strength and Volume, Lesson V - Mechanical trading Systems and Correct Attitudes. COMMENTS: Technical Analysis Explained (textbook) may be purchased separately $44.95

Technical Analysis Explained: An Illustrated Guide for the Investor (2nd Edition) The Successful Investor's Guide to Spotting Investment Trends and Turning Points

Martin J. Pring - author
McGraw- Hill
1221 Avenue of the Americas
New York, NY 10020
ISBN: 0-07-050885-2

PH: (800) 2-MCGRAW
(212) 512-2000
Publication Date: c. 1985 (2nd edition)
Cost: $53.00

Subjects addressed: technical analysis. Covered in detail are such topics as Dow Theory, price patterns, trendlines, moving averages, momentum, cycles, sentiment, speculation, interest rates and the stock market, breadth, volume and technical analysis of international stock markets. This unique guide also features over 130 historical charts, many previously unpublished and an extensive statistical section.

Technical Analysis in Commodities

Perry J. Kaufman, Editor
John Wiley and Sons, Inc.
605 Third Avenue
New York, NY 10158-0012

PH: (212) 850-6000
ISBN: 0-471-05627-8
Published 1980
Cost: $55.00

A collection of articles on technical analysis in futures markets, based on the proceedings of a 1978 symposium and supplemented with new, original research papers. Contributions range from the non-mathematical to the highly mathematical, from historical background to the most advanced developments in price analysis and modeling.

Technical Analysis of the Futures Markets: A Comprehensive Guide to Trading Methods and Applications

John J. Murphy
Prentice-Hall
Route 9W
Englewood Cliffs, NJ 07632

ISBN: 0-13-898008-X
Published 1986
Cost: $49.95

Logical, sequential reference describes - for beginners and more experienced traders alike - the concepts of technical analysis and their applications. Interprets the role of technical forecasters and explains how they apply their techniques to the futures markets. Includes 400 charts showing how time cycles enhance effectiveness.

Technical Analysis of Stock Options and Futures - Advanced Trading Systems and Techniques

William F. Eng - author
Probus Publishing Co.,
1925 North Clybourn Avenue
Chicago, IL 60614

PH: (800) PROBUS-1
(312) 868-1100
Published 1988
Cost: $60.00

Mr. Eng presents the latest technical analysis systems that are currently being used in the major exchanges around the world. This book includes, among others, the following trading systems: Williams ./.R, Wilder's Relative Strength Index, Lane's Stochastics, Elliott Wave Analysis, plus others.

Technical Analysis of Stock Trends

Robert D. Edwards and John Magee
John Magee, Inc.
65 Broad Street
Boston, MA 20109

PH: (617) 695-9292
Published 1983
Cost: $75.00

Subjects addressed: investing theories, trading analysis, technical analysis; uses charts. Written for informed layman and Wall Street professional in 2 parts: technical theory and trading tactics. The most definitive description of Dow Jones averages and pattern analysis of stocks using Applied Statistical analysis. Considered the trader's 'Bible'.

Technical Indicator Analysis by Point and Figure Technique

A.W. Cohen
Chartcraft, Inc.
1 West Avenue
Larchmont, NY 10538

PH: (914) 834-5181
Cost: $15.00

Subject: Point and Figure charts and technical analysis. This book takes 29 of the most widely followed technical indicators, tells us how each is compiled and how to analyze what a point and figure chart of each indicator tells us about a market trend.

Technical Traders Guide to Computer Analysis of the Futures Market

Charles LeBeau and David W. Lucas
Business One Irwin
1818 Ridge Road
Homewood, IL 60430

PH: (708) 206-2700
(800) 634-3966
FAX: (708) 798-1490
ISBN: 1-55623-468-6
Published 1991
Cost: $65.00

Subjects addressed: technical analysis. This book bridges the gap between the basic instruction that comes with software programs and what a trader actually needs to know to develop and test profitable futures trading systems. With specific information on how to set up and use computer-generated technical studies of the most popular indicators, the book includes: how to build a trading system tailored to the reader's specific needs, practical instruction on how to display and analyze technical information, advice for developing well disciplined money management and risk control strategies, techniques for monitoring a trading system to detect if something has gone wrong before major losses occur.

Techniques of Financial Analysis

Erich A. Helfert
Business One Irwin
1818 Ridge Road
Homewood, IL 60430

PH: (708) 206-2700
(800) 634-3966
FAX: (708) 798-1490
ISBN: 0-87094-944-6
Published 1987 (6th edition)
Cost: $39.95

Also available in paperback
ISBN: 0-256-03625-X
Cost: $23.95

The latest techniques and tools, including new material on inflation. Solve typical corporate financial problems by examining three basic financial concepts - operations, investment, and financing. Covers funds flow analysis, ratio analysis, cash budgets, proforma statements, breakeven analysis, and basic capital expenditure.

Techniques of a Professional Commodity Chart Analyst

Arthur Sklarew
Commodity Research Bureau
75 Wall Street
22nd Floor
New York, NY 10005

PH: (800) 446-4519
ISBN: 0-317-03272-0
Published 1980
Cost: $24.95

Success in commodity trading depends on good price forecasting. Learn to use commodity price chart and other simple technical indicators to time your trades better, spot price trends, estimate the distance a new price thrust will travel, and identify potential trend reversal points. Clear style; practical, original material.

The Theory and Practice of Futures Markets

Raymond M. Leuthold, Joan C. Junkus and Jean E. Cordier
Lexington, Books
125 Spring Street
Lexington, MA 02173

PH: (800) 235-3565
ISBN: 0-669-16260-4
Published 1989
Cost: $39.95

An introductory text about commodity and financial futures and options markets. Covers commodity, interest rate, stock index and currency future contracts along with options on these contracts. Many examples on how to use the market for hedging and arbitraging.

There's Always a Bull Market - Conservative Investing in Stocks, Bonds, and Gold

Robert Kinsman
Business One Irwin
1818 Ridge Road
Homewood, IL 60430

PH: (800) 634-3966
FAX: (708) 798-1490
ISBN: 1-55623-102-4
Published 1989
Cost: $27.50

Covers investing theories and market analysis. Learn how to identify when a bull market begins and ends, and allocate your assets into stocks, bonds, or gold.

The Thinking Investor's Guide to the Stock Market (revised edition)

Kiril Sokoloff
Available through Fraser Publishing
P.O. Box 494
Burlington, VT 05402

PH: (802) 658-0322
ISBN: 0-07-059616-6
Published 1984
Cost: $13.95

"The author has done his homework. He has taken pains to pick the brains of some of Wall Street's top market timers, letter writers, and investment counselors," says Barron's of the first edition. Study the methods the most astute stock market professionals have developed over time.

Tight Money Timing: The Impact of Interest Rates and the Federal Reserve on the Stock Market

Wilfred R. George
Greenwood Publishing Group, Inc.
88 Post Road, W, Box 5007
Westport, CT 06881

PH: (203) 226-3571
ISBN: 0-275-91708-8
Published 1982
Cost: $35.00

Provides the knowledge needed to make money grow in any money climate - tight or easy. Explicit advice in how to recognize tight and easy money signals, draw the appropriate conclusions, and take the correct action to maximize profits in rising and declining markets. A vital asset in today's treacherous investment waters.

A Time to Be Rich: Winning on Wall Street in the New Economy

Lacy H. Hunt
Rawson Associates
866 Third Avenue
New York, NY 10022

PH: (212) 702-3436
ISBN: 0-89256-325-7
Published 1987
Cost: $19.95

Provides a flexible system for investing that you can use over and over, no matter where the economy is or what your investment preferences. Enables you to determine economic trends, decide what to do at each point, sift through key economic indicators, and size up global events to ride the wave to wealth even in down times.

The Trader's & Investor's Guide to Commodity Trading Systems, Software and Databases

William T. Taylor
Available through Fraser Publishing
P.O. Box 494
Burlington, VT 05402

PH: (802) 658-0322
ISBN: 0-917253-41-8
Published 1986
Cost: $27.50

Learn how to use your computer to trade with the pros. Gives a complete picture of the trading opportunities made possible by the microcomputer. A practical introduction and reliable reference to all aspects of microcomputer-aided futures trading.

Trading in Commodity Futures

Frederick F. Horb and Robert E. Link
New York Institute of Finance
2 Broadway
New York, NY 10004

PH: (212) 344-2900
ISBN: 0-13-925991-0
Published 1984 (2nd edition)
Cost: $27.95

Revised and updated edition of the universally accepted standard work on commodities futures. Outstanding treatment of such subjects as fundamental and technical analysis techniques, investment objectives, hedging and speculating principles, and cash and futures market relationships. Plus new chapters on recent developments.

Trading Tactics - Livestock Futures

Edited by Todd Lofton
John Wiley & Sons
605 Third Avenue
New York, NY 10158-0012

PH: (212) 850-6418 orders
(212) 850-6233 info.
Published 1989
ISBN: 0-471-61492-0
Cost: $30.95

Subjects: trading analysis. Trading tactics is a whole bookshelf of the best known stock trading systems in a single book. All the classics are here: Elliott Wave forecasting, Point-and Figure charting, Moving Averages and more. These are not academic or theoretical descriptions. They are real-world tactics from real world traders.

Trading With the Elliott Wave Principle: A Practical Guide

David H. Weis
Tape Readers Press
P.O. Box 12267
Memphis, TN 38182

PH: (901) 276-0155
Published October 1988
Cost: $65.00

Subjects addressed: investing theories, trading analysis, technical analysis; uses charts. The bulk of this book is devoted to an extensive trading exercise. Shows how to analyze and trade a market day by day, using Elliott Wave. Weis explains Elliott's system of notation or symbols for labeling waves of different degrees, gives "Guideline for Wave Counting" formulas for projecting tops and bottoms. He also discusses many practical topics including when and how to enter market positions, where to place stops, when to move them and so on.

The Treasury Bond Basis

Galen Burghardt, Morton Lane and John Papa
Probus Publishing Co.
1925 North Clybourn Avenue
Chicago, IL 60614

PH: (800) PROBUS-1
FAX: (312) 868-6250
ISBN: 1-55738-050-3
Published 1989
Cost: $57.50

Subjects addressed: U.S. Treasury bond market analysis. Written for financial professionals seeking in-depth knowledge about the price relationship between the cash and futures treasury bond markets. Presents the financial professional with details on the current nature and behavior of the treasury basis, but also reviews its fascinating past and performance throughout the various stages of the interest rate cycle. This longer term perspective allows readers to see how the basis may behave in the future in response to similar circumstances and what the impact will be on market participants.

Trendiness in the Futures Markets

Bruce Babcock, Jr.
1731 Howe Ave, Suite 149
Sacramento, CA 95825

PH: (916) 677-7562
Cost :$95.00

Subjects addressed: trading analysis, futures; uses charts. How to choose the best markets to trade and the best time frames to trade them. Learn how to set trend indicators and oscillators for optimum results based on historical performance.

Trident: A Trading Strategy

Charles L. Lindsay
Probus Publishing Co.
1925 North Clybourn Avenue
Chicago, IL 60614

PH: (800) PROBUS-1
FAX: (312) 868-6250
ISBN: 0-930233-48-4
Published 1991
Cost: $50.00

How to contend with market rumors and greed. "Trident: A Trading Strategy" details the rules and applications of proven strategies that allow the trader to pinpoint future highs and lows in the market. Topics include: the history of Trident, price action theory, the Trident model, Trident market applications and trade criteria, Trident market analysis, creating a Trident strategy.

Truth of Stock Tape

William D. Gann
Available through Fraser Publishing
P.O. Box 494
Burlington, VT 05402

PH: (802) 658-0322
Published 1923 (1976 reprint)
Cost: $35.00

A Study of the Stock and Commodity Markets with Charts and Rules for Successful Trading and Investing. "I do not offer you a beautiful theory which will not work in practice," Gann wrote, "but give you invaluable advice which will insure success in practical everyday Wall Street speculations and other fields of investment."

A Turn in the Tidal Wave (Part I: The Stock Market; Part II: Implications)

Robert R. Prechter, Jr.
New Classics Library
P.O. Box 1618
Gainesville, GA 30503

PH: (800) 333-1618
(404) 536-0309
ISBN: 0-932750-12-5
Published 1989
Cost: $75.00

An analysis of the predictions made by the author and A.J. Frost in Elliott Wave Principle. "Now, over ten years later, the markets have progressed to a point at which it is prudent, if not crucial, to examine closely our original analysis," says the author.

24 Hour Trading - The Global Network of Futures and Options Markets

Barbara B. Diamond, Mark P. Kollar
John Wiley & Sons
605 Third Avenue
New York, NY 10158-0012

PH: (800) 526-5368 (orders)
(212) 850-6418 (info)
Published February, 1989
Cost: $29.95

Subjects addressed: futures and options, market strategies, technical analysis; uses charts. A dynamic overview of various futures markets, clearinghouse, and their regulations around the world.

Understanding and Managing Investment Risk and Return

David L. Scott
Probus Publishing Co.
1925 North Clybourn Avenue
Chicago, IL 60614

PH: (800) PROBUS-1
FAX: (312) 868-6250
ISBN: 1-55738-105-4
Published 1990
Cost: $21.95

Subjects addressed: investing theories.
Illustrates the various kinds of risk commonly encountered by investors, including purchasing-power risk, interest rate risk, reinvestment risk, market risk, financial risk, liquidity risk and more. Risks particular to each investment vehicle available to the individual investor are also examined, covering equities, stocks, fixed income securities and tangible assets. Also included are different methods available to analyze and measure risk and to control risk in an investment program.

Understanding and Trading Futures

Carl F. Luft
Probus Publishing Co.
1925 North Clybourn Avenue
Chicago, IL 60614

PH: (800) PROBUS-1
FAX: (312) 868-6250
ISBN: 1-55738-151-8
Published 1991
Cost: $22.95

Subjects addressed: investing theories.
Provides a precise description of the dynamics involved in the day-to-day trading of futures, including fundamental relationships and processes for risk management or speculative investment strategies. Shows how futures trading can be used by any investor to reduce investment risks and stabilize returns. Contains extensive glossary and annotated bibliography.

Understanding Fibonacci Numbers

Edward D. Dobson
Traders Press
P.O. Box 6206
Greenville, SC 29606

PH: (803) 288-3900
Published 1984
ISBN: 0-934380-08-2
Cost: $7.25

Subject: Fibonacci number sequence and trading analysis. Primer booklet which explains and describes the Fibonacci sequence and how it is utilized by traders to forecast and interpret price action.

Understanding Corporate Bonds

H. Kerzner
McGraw Hill, Inc.
11 West 19th Street
New York, NY 10011

PH: (800) 722-4726
 (212) 512-4100
Published 1990
Cost: $24.60

Subjects addressed: bond analysis. Advice for building and preserving wealth by investing in corporate bonds. Shows how to identify high-risk bonds, how to select quality junk bonds, use margin buying to your benefit, how to select a good broker and much more.

Understanding the Stock Market

David Sutton
Probus Publishing Co.
1925 North Clybourn Avenue
Chicago, IL 60614

PH: (800) PROBUS-1
FAX: (312) 868-6250
ISBN: 1-55738-035-X
Published 1989
Cost: $22.95

Subjects addressed: investing theories.

Understanding Wall Street

Jeffrey B. Little & Lucien Rhodes
Liberty Hall Press
11 W. 19th Street
3rd floor
New York, NY 10011

Published 1978, 1987 (2nd edition)
Cost: $9.95

Subjects addressed: investing theories, stock analysis, market analysis, bond analysis, earnings analysis, fundamental analysis, technical analysis, options. Very basic book for beginners. Begins with "What is a share of stock?" Covers history of Wall Street, reading the financial pages, security analysis, growth stocks, and options.

Up On The Market With Carter Randall: Wisdom, Insights and Advice from a Lifetime on Wall Street

Carter Randall with William Gianopulos
Probus Publishing Co.
1925 North Clybourn Avenue
Chicago, IL 60614

PH: (800) PROBUS-1
FAX: (312) 868-6250
ISBN: 1-55738-263-8
Published 1992
Cost: $21.95

Subjects addressed: investing theories. This common sense and back-to-the-basics approach is applied to all key investment areas, including: developing investment goals, stock investments, risk management techniques, structuring and managing a portfolio, tax considerations, mutual funds vs. individual stocks, selecting a money manager, the invertor's psyche, common misconceptions and pitfalls. This book includes a discussion of "Wall Street Week," including its panelists and how the show is produced.

Using the Relative Strength Indicator (RSI) and High/Low Moving Average Channel

Commodities Education Institute
219 Parkade
Cedar Falls, IA 50613

PH: (800) 635-3936
(319) 277-6341
FAX: (319) 277-7982
Published 1990
Cost: $55.00

VIDEO
Subjects addressed: investing theories, technical analysis. You'll learn how to use RSI as a directional indicator in conjunction with the High/Low Moving average channel as a market timing aid. Part of a series of 5 tapes available for $233.00

Using Technical Analysis

Clifford Pistolese
Probus Publishing Co.
1925 North Clybourn Avenue
Chicago, IL 60614

PH: (800) PROBUS-1
FAX: (312) 868-6250
ISBN: 1-55738-076-7
Published 1990
Cost: $22.95

Subjects addressed: How to use technical analysis. This approach utilizes self-teaching materials.

Value Investing: New Strategies for Stock Market Success

Lawrence M. Stein
John Wiley & Sons
605 Third Street
New York, NY 10158-0012

PH: (800) 526-5368
(212) 850-6000
ISBN: 0-471-62875-1
Published: 1988
Cost: $31.95

Subjects addressed: stock analysis and market timing. This book offers an honest appraisal of the stock market and shows how individual investors can earn consistently superior profits in both bull and bear markets. Stein explains how to value stocks and the stock market as a hole, use value as a basis for market timing, and implement value into a workable investment, strategy that has statistically proven itself in long-term computer simulations.

Value Investing Today

Charles H. Brandis
Business One Irwin
1818 Ridge Road
Homewood, IL 60430

PH: (800) 634-3966
FAX: (708) 798-1490
ISBN: 1-55623-102-4
Published 1989
Cost: $29.95

Covers investing theories, stock analysis, and fundamental analysis. Stresses the fundamentals of profit-making investing and concentrates on what to buy, what prices to pay, when to buy and sell and why. Alerts you to possible errors, and provides ways to select stocks successfully.

Valuing a Business: The Analysis of Closely Held Companies

Business One Irwin
1818 Ridge Road
Homewood, IL 60430

PH: (708) 206-2700
(800) 634-3966
FAX: (708) 798-1490
ISBN: 0-55623-127-X
Published 1988 (2nd edition)
Cost: $62.50

The first complete reference for determining the worth of closely held corporations or un-incorporated businesses - as opposed to publicly traded corporations. Describes the mechanics of a valuation in terms of data to be assembled, the analysis of financial statements, the presentation of the valuation report, and much more.

Volume and Open Interest: Cutting Edge Strategies in the Futures Markets

Ken Shaleen
Probus Publishing Co.
1925 North Clybourn Avenue
Chicago, IL 60614

PH: (800) PROBUS-1
FAX: (312) 868-6250
ISBN: 1-55738-114-3
Published 1991
Cost: $45.00

Subjects addressed: market analysis. "The definitive source for understanding how current market sentiment is reflected through volume and open interest indicators. Take advantage of this, the only book of its kind on the market and let internationally known futures, trader, educator and market advisor, Ken Shaleen, be your guide to this classic method of tracking market sentiment."

Volume Cycles in the Stock Market: Market Timing Through Equivolume Charting

Richard W. Arms, Jr.
Business One Irwin
1818 Ridge Road
Homewood, IL 60430

PH: (708) 206-2700
(800) 634-3966
FAX: (708) 798-1490
ISBN: 0-87094-405-3
Published 1983
Cost: $52.95

In discovering that stock price changes are governed by volume, not time, Arms revolutionized technical analysis. This work introduces two new concepts - volume cyclicality and ease of movement - and integrates all into a market trading technique for daily and long-range forecasting of individual issues as well as market indexes.

The Wall Street Dictionary

R.J. & Robert L. Shook
New York Institute of Finance
2 Broadway
New York, NY 10004

Published 1990
Cost: $14.95

Complete source of the language of finance and investment for the novice and seasoned professionals. Over 5000 entries.

The Wall Street Journal on Management: The Best of the Manager's Journal

David Asman & Adam Meyerson, editors
New American Library
1633 Broadway
New York, NY 10019

PH: (800) 526-0275
ISBN: 0-87094-685-4
Published 1985
Cost: $19.95

A treasury of advice from The Wall Street Journal, filled with solutions to the dilemmas that every manager must face. Draws on the wisdom of talented managers and advisors from around the worlds to answer the questions that can make or break you. Sixty clear, concise, and captivating articles on specific management problems.

The Wall Street Journal's Guide to Understanding Money and Markets

R. Wurman, A. Siegel and K. Morris
Prentice Hall Press
15 Columbus Circle
New York, NY 10023

PH: (800) 445-8000
(212)373-8500
Published 1989
Cost: $12.95

Subjects addressed: investing theories, bond analysis, commodities trading, stock analysis. Covers stocks, bonds, mutual funds, futures, money. A beginner's guide to the financial pages and investing. Covers everything from a cusip number to the futures exchanges.

Wall Street on $20 a Month: How to Profit from an Investment Club

Phyllis Humphrey
John Wiley and Sons, Inc.
605 Third Avenue
New York, NY 10158-0012

PH: (212) 850-6000
ISBN: 0-471-84038-6
Published 1986
Cost: $12.95

Shows how anyone can pool his or financial resources in an investment club with a few friends - and turn as little as $20.00 a month into a tidy profit. Solid advice and guidelines for setting up and operating an investment club, including how to screen potential members and find a "sponsoring" broker to execute your trades.

Wall Street Talk: How to Understand Your Broker

Barbara Gilder Quint
Walker and Company
720 Fifth Avenue
New York, NY 10019

PH: (212) 265-3632
ISBN: 0-8027-0754-8
Published 1983
Cost: $11.95

Also available in paperback
ISBN: 0-8027-7232-3
Cost: $5.95

Written for the millions who are confused about the terms they hear bandied about in the financial world. In her down-to-earth, often funny, eminently comprehensible style, the author defines and explains over 250 of Wall Street's most used and useful terms to help you be the master of your own financial future.

The Wall Street Waltz - 90 Visual Perspectives: Illustrated Lessons from Financial Cycles and Trends

Kenneth L. Fisher
Contemporary Books
180 N. Michigan Avenue
Chicago, IL 60601

PH: (312) 782-9181
ISBN: 0-8092-4797-6
Published 1987
Cost: $30.00

One of America's leading investment managers and financial columnists interprets 90 of the most revealing and provocative financial charts ever assembled. In each case, he provides a visualization that analyzes each chart according to its origin, historical significance, and most importantly, its relevance to today's market.

Wall Street Words: The Basics and Beyond

Richard J. Maturi
Probus Publishing Co.
1925 North Clybourn Avenue
Chicago, IL 60614

PH: (800) PROBUS-1
FAX: (312) 868-6250
ISBN: 1-55738-195-X
Published 1991
Cost: $14.95

Subjects addressed: investing theories.
Takes the terms and definitions of Wall Street and puts it into one easy reference. Examples are provided as is a 100-page glossary. Discussion of the understanding of various investment strategies with determinations made of the appropriateness of the investment vehicle. Rewards and risks of different investment paths are examined.

The W.D. Gann Method of Trading a Simplified, Clear Approach

Windsor Books
P.O. Box 280
Brightwaters, NY 11718

Subjects addressed: trading analysis. Gerald Marison has applied common sense and intuitive analysis strategy to uncover a profitable method in Gann's work.

Published 1990
Cost: $50.00

WealthBuilder by Money Magazine

Don and Doris Woodwell
Business One Irwin
1818 Ridge Road
Homewood, IL 60430

PH: (800) 634-3966
FAX: (708) 798-1490
ISBN: 1-55623-102-4
Published January 1991.
Cost: $24.95

This book compliments the New WealthBuilder by Money Magazine financial planning, investment counseling software program. Shows how to draw upon all of the programs features to create a conservative, long-term investment plan. The authors show you how to do more in less time by helping you understand the program better, set and meet savings and investment plans using the software, and become financially secure by diversifying your holdings using WealthBuilder software allocation information.

West of Wall Street

George Angell and Barry Haigh
Longman Financial Services, publisher
520 N. Dearborn
Chicago, IL 60601

PH: (800) 621-9621
ISBN: 0-88462-623-7
Published 1987 c. 1988
Cost: $27.50

Subjects addressed - commodities. West of Wall Street, written by market insiders, tells what it takes to win the game in a way that both the general public and the sophisticated investor can understand. The authors offer a first-hand account of the futures trading system - its rules, customs, and risks - with special emphasis on getting started, developing successful market strategies and maintaining the winning attitudes and values necessary to triumph.

Wheat Price Action

William A. Brown
Available through Fraser Publishing
P.O. Box 494
Burlington, VT 05402

PH: (802) 658-0322
Published 1975 (paper)
Cost: $15.00

Covers both cash prices and futures prices through detailed, computer-generated probability tables and seasonal price charts. Tracks short-term, intermediate and log-term trends. The valuable information can be used as a marketing and purchasing guide, as well as a guide in formulating speculative strategy.

Why Most Investors Are Mostly Wrong Most of the Time

William X. Scheinman
Fraser Publishing Company
309 S. Willard Street
Burlington, VT 05401

PH: (802) 658-0322
Published 1991
Cost: $17.00

Subjects addressed: bond analysis, stock analysis, trading analysis, and currencies; uses charts. Shows you what data to focus on where to get it and how to evaluate investment information for yourself. Includes an 11 point checklist to evaluate buying and selling decisions with specific chart illustrated examples of how to apply it.

Why Stocks Go Up (and Down) : A Guide to Sound Investing

William H. Pike
Available through Fraser Publishing
P.O. Box 494
Burlington, VT 05402

PH: (802) 658-0322
ISBN: 0-87094-314-6
Published 1983
Cost: $22.50

Explains the major influences affecting stock prices, and imparts a feel for the market through an 18 year history of Polaroid's stock. Originating in the introductory investing course offered by the Boston Security Analyst's Society, teaches the basics of financial statements, public offerings, price/earnings ratios and more.

Why the Best-Laid Investment Plans Usually Go Wrong and How You Can Find Safety and Profit in an Uncertain World

Harry Browne
William Morrow and Company, Inc.
105 Madison Avenue
New York, NY 10016

PH: (800) 843-9389
ISBN: 0-688-05995-3
Published 1987
Cost: $19.95

Study investment techniques from one of America's best-known investment advisors. The author tells why many common techniques fail when they're needed most and how to find safety and profit in the market. Witty and forceful, it's got good tips for both the aggressive and passive investor.

Why Traders Lose, How Traders Win: Timing Futures Trades with Daily Market Sentiment

Jake Bernstein
Probus Publishing Co.
1925 North Clybourn Avenue
Chicago, IL 60614

PH: (800) PROBUS-1
FAX: (312) 868-6250
ISBN: 1-55738-252-2
Published 1991
Cost: $37.50

This book explores how market sentiment - how public opinion is related to market trends - affects the individual's perception of the market and, thus, the ability or inability to trade effectively. Topics include: a history of market sentiment, how to measure market sentiment, daily sentiment index theory, constructing the daily sentiment index, applications of DSI readings, weekly DSI readings, combining DSI with your trading system, practical applications.

William E. Donoghue's Guide to Finding Money to Invest: Building a Lifetime Savings Program with Your Hidden Cash Resources

William E. Donoghue
Harper- Collins Publisher, Inc
10 E. 53rd Street
New York, NY 10022

PH: (800) 242-7737
ISBN: 0-06-015393-8
Published 1985
Cost: $15.95

The nationally syndicated newspaper columnist and expert on do-it-yourself investing strategies provides a straightforward guide on how to free up your hidden resources, start and sustain a lifetime savings program, find sources of added earnings and tax savings, and keep all of your investment cash working for you at all times.

William E. Donoghue's Lifetime Financial Planner: Straight Talk about Your Money Decisions

William E. Donoghue & Dana Shilling
Available through Fraser Publishing
P.O. Box 494
Burlington, VT 05402

PH: (802) 658-0322
ISBN: 0-06-015616-3
Published 1987
Cost: $9.95

Guides you through the critical financial transitions of a lifetime: being single, getting married - and divorced, selecting insurance, buying a car or home, paying taxes, investing money, putting the kids through college, preparing for retirement, planning your estate, and learning how to confidently plan your financial future.

Winner Takes All: A Privateer's Guide to Commodity Trading

William R. Gallacher
Available through Fraser Publishing
P.O. Box 494
Burlington, VT 05402

PH: (802) 658-0322
ISBN: 0-9691323-0-1
Published 1983
Cost: $21.00

For those of independent mind. Defends fundamental trading as best route to becoming a winner in the market. An opinionated antidote to today's "mechanistic, robotic philosophies of trading." Full wit, humor, energy, and insight, this may be one of the most entertaining and valuable investment books ever written.

Winning in the Futures Markets

George Angell
Probus Publishing Co.
1925 North Clybourn Avenue
Chicago, IL 60614

PH: (800) PROBUS-1
FAX: (312) 868-6250
ISBN: 1-55738-146-1
Published 1990
Cost: $21.95

Subjects addressed: investing theories.
Provides the basic training, explaining the meaning of a futures contract, how margin works, dealing with brokers, how to place orders and more. Stresses access to reliable information. Shows insights on chart trading, Gann techniques, options on futures, and the LSS Day-Trading System for the S&P Stock Index Option market.

Winning Investment Strategies

Burton G. Malkiel
W.W. Norton and Company, Inc.
500 5th Avenue
New York, NY 10110

PH: (800) 223-2584
ISBN: 0-393-30031-5
Published 1982 (2nd edition)
Cost: $3.95

An updated edition of The Inflation-Beater's Investment Guide. Drawing on important new findings about inflation and corporate profits, on the revolution in investment technology, and on his own analysis of price levels in the stock market, the author shows why common stocks are the best possible hedge against inflation.

Winning Investment Strategies: Using Security Analysis to Build Wealth

J. B. Malloy
McGraw Hill, Inc.
11 West 19th Street
New York, NY 10011

PH: (800) 722-4726
(212) 512-4100
Published 1990
Cost: $22.60

Subjects addressed: investing theories. "A successful long-term investment program safe from fluctuations in taxes, inflation, and interest rates."

The Winning Investors

Charles Schwab
Business One Irwin
1818 Ridge Road
Homewood, IL 60430

PH: (708) 206-2700
(800) 634-3966
FAX: (708) 798-1490
ISBN: 1-55623-436-8
Published 1991
Cost: $24.95

This book gives readers an inside look at the wealth-building techniques of 15 Schwab clients. This case-study approach offers unique insight into the potential successes and possible pitfalls of various investment strategies. Readers will find several investment options they can choose from, based on the amount of risk they are willing to take. Topics include: the principles of lifelong investing, clearly illustrating the advantages of a long-term approach, 10 different strategies so readers can choose which option will best suit their investment needs, step-by-step methodology on how to implement financial strategies.

Winning on Wall Street

Martin Zweig
Warner Books, Inc.
666 5th Avenue
New York, NY 10103

Published 1986, 1990-update
Cost: $12.95 (paperback)

Subjects addressed: investing theories, stock analysis, market analysis, technical analysis. Uses charts. Zweig clearly explains his proven methods for avoiding the most common investment errors, preserving capital and increasing profits.

Winning the Investment Game - A Guide for All Seasons

James Gipson
McGraw-Hill
1221 Avenue of the Americas
New York, NY 10020

PH: (800) 262-4729
Published 1987
ISBN: 0-07-023296-2
Cost: $13.00

Subject: investing theories and strategies. The author identifies 3 different investment "games" and tells which investment strategies are appropriate (and which are not) for each game. He tells investors how to recognize when the game is starting to change so that they can shift strategies in time.

Winning Market Systems: 83 Ways to Beat the Market

Gerald Appel
Traders Pr.
P.O. Box 6206
Greenville, SC 29606

PH: (803) 288-3900
Published 1986 (revised from 1974 edition)
ISBN: 0-934380-12-0
Cost: $32.25

Encyclopedia of winning strategies and technical indicators. The system strategies and indicators of many well-know market analysts are detailed. You are also shown the inner workings of the Haurlan Index, the Haller Theory, and interpretation of the A/D line, the McClellan Oscillator as a short term indicator and many other tools. Other helpful strategies include the most bullish trendline formation, how to predict trendline violations, an early warning system, how to interpret the most active, the best hours and months to buy and more.

Winning with Mutual Funds

Money Magazine Editors
Oxmoor House Inc.
P.O. Box 2463
Birmingham, AL 35201

Everything you need to know to invest with success plus the impact of tax reform, performance data, yields, fees, and phone numbers for 738 mutual funds.

Published 1987
Cost: $12.95

Winning with New IRAs

Martin Zweig
Warner Books, Inc.
666 5th Avenue
New York, NY 10103

Subjects addressed: stock analysis, market analysis, bond analysis; uses charts. Stock & bond investment timing strategies that can make a $1,000,000 difference when you retire.

Published 1987
Cost: $20.00

Words of Wall Street: 2000 Investment Terms Defined

Allan H. Pessin & Joseph A. Ross
Business One Irwin
1818 Ridge Road
Homewood, IL 60430

PH: (708) 206-2700
(800) 634-3966
FAX: (708) 798-1490
ISBN: 0-87094-417-7
Published 1983
Cost: $11.95

Complete and up-to-date compilation of the words, phrases, and jargon used in the day-to-day dealings of the securities industry - selected and defined by two seasoned veterans of Wall Street. Also includes many helpful examples, illustrations, and mathematical formulas for all serious traders, brokers, bankers, and investors.

World Futures and Options Directory 1991-92

Nick Battley
McGraw Hill Book Co., UK
Shoppenhangers Road
Maidenhead, Berkshire
SL62QL, England

FAX 0628-770224
Special numbers 0628-23432
Published 1991
Cost: $95.00

A comprehensive and up-to-date reference to the futures and options exchanges. Includes details in 48 exchanges, over 350 contracts, in-depth contract specifications, 1989 turnover, and open interest statistics, membership listings of over 30 exchanges.

World Mutual Fund Survey

Gary Scott
International Service Center
3106 Tamiami Trail North
Suite 264P
Naples, FL 33940

PH: (813) 261-1222
FAX: (813) 261-2001
Published 1991
Cost: $79.00

Subjects addressed: mutual funds. Researches 3864 foreign mutual funds and explains the advantages of foreign funds. Also explains how to choose funds to best suit your needs. Covers tax, legal and asset protection angles and much more.

The Worldly Wise Investor International Opportunities in Today's Markets

David Smyth
Franklin Watts
387 Park Avenue South
Manhattan, NY

PH: (212) 686-7070
Published 1988
Cost: $18.95

Subjects addressed: market analysis. Explains how to's, risks and benefits of international investing. Gives address on international mutual fund, closed-end funds, foreign stocks and brokers, foreign banks, 300 most actively traded stocks on the world's 3 biggest stock markets outside the US and much more.

The World's Emerging Stock Markets: Structure, Development, Regulations and Opportunities

Keith K. H. Park and Antoine W. van Agtmael, Editors
Probus Publishing Co.
1925 North Clybourn Avenue
Chicago, IL 60614

PH: (800) PROBUS-1
FAX: (312) 868-6250
ISBN: 1-55738-240-9
Published 1993
Cost: $55.00

Covers all the important regions in the small but emerging and dynamic foreign stock markets, including: Asia, Europe, Latin America, South Africa. This comprehensive reference provides all the pertinent information for each country, including: market overview and structure, recent stock market performance, investors, international investor issues, tax and foreign exchange regulations, and much more.

The World's Most Valuable Investment Strategy

B. Buck Fisher, Jr.
Windsor Books
P.O. Box 280
Brightwater, NY 11718

Published 1990
Cost: $24.95

Subjects addressed: bond analysis, stock analysis, market analysis, mutual funds. Shows how to protect yourself from runaway inflation, stagnant and bear markets, the coming market crash, and the inevitable recession.

Worldwide Investor

William J. Corney and Leonard E. Goodall
Probus Publishing Co.
1925 North Clybourn Avenue
Chicago, IL 60614

PH: (800) PROBUS-1
FAX: (312) 868-6250
ISBN: 1-55738-205-0
Published 1991
Cost: $27.50

Subjects addressed: investing theories.
Includes discussion of tax-sheltered accounts, overseas banking, real estate, dollar averaging, asset allocation and market timing and analyzes the regions of North America, Greater Europe and the Asian Pacific Basin. Benefits from the international banking system are explored as well as the opportunities available through owning foreign real estate.

Your Inner Path To Investment Success: Insights into the Psychology of Investing

Albert Mehrabian
Probus Publishing Co.
1925 North Clybourn Avenue
Chicago, IL 60614

PH: (800) PROBUS-1
FAX: (312) 868-6250
ISBN: 1-55738-210-7
Published 1991
Cost: $22.95

Subjects addressed: investing theories.
Every investor has an investment temperament - this book help investors identify, direct and fine-tune their individual styles to achieve optimal investment results.

Your Money & Your Life: How to Plan Your Long-Range Financial Security

C. Colburn Hardy
Available through Fraser Publishing
P.O. Box 494
Burlington, VT 05402

PH: (802) 658-0322
ISBN: 0-8144-5529-8
Published 1979
Cost: $15.95

Examines prudent and proven steps to minimize the risk of financial problems and help you live comfortably during retirement. Considers the importance of net worth and personal budgeting, the mechanics of money, how you can cope with college costs and still plan your own future successfully, and many other crucial questions.

General Reference

For convenience, the following sources of authority and information are listed:

Exchanges
Government Agencies and Regulatory Bodies
Federal Reserve Banks
U.S. State Securities Regulators
Associations
Corporations
Reference Guides

Exchanges

New York Stock Exchange
NYSE
11 Wall Street
New York, NY 10005
PH: (212)623-3000
(800)692-6973

American Stock Exchange
AMEX
86 Trinity Place
New York, NY 10006
PH: (212)306-1000
(800)843-2639

NASDAQ, Inc.
National Association of Securities Dealers, Inc.
1735 K Street NW
Washington, DC 20006
PH: (202)728-8000
(800)243-4284

The Chicago Board of Trade
CBOT
141 West Jackson Boulevard
Chicago, IL 60604
PH: (312)435-3500

Chicago Mercantile Exchange
CME
30 South Walker Drive
Chicago, IL 60606
PH: (312)930-3457

Chicago Board of Options Exchange, Inc.
CBOE
400 South LaSalle Street
Chicago, IL 60605
PH: (312)786-5600

The Pacific Stock Exchange, Inc.
233 South Beaudry
Los Angeles, CA 90012
PH: (213)977-4500

or
301 Pine Street
San Francisco, CA 94104
PH: (415)393-4000

New York Mercantile Exchange
NYME
4 World Trade Center
New York, NY 10048
PH: (212)938-2222

Boston Stock Exchange, Inc.
One Boston Place
Boston, MA 02108
PH: (617)723-9500
(800)828-3545

Midwest Stock Exchange, Inc.
440 South LaSalle Street
Chicago, IL 60605
PH: (312)663-2209

The Philadelphia Stock Exchange, Inc.
1900 Market Street
Philadelphia, PA 19103
PH: (215)496-5000
(800)843-7459

Coffee, Sugar and Cocoa Exchange, Inc.
CSCE
4 World Trade Center
New York, NY 10048
PH: (212)938-2800

Commodity Exchange Center, Inc.
COMEX
4 World Trade Center
New York, NY 10048
PH: (212)938-2937
(212)938-9020 for prices 24 hours a day

Kansas City Board of Trade
KCBT
4800 Main Street
Suite 303

Kansas City, MO 64112
PH: (816)753-7500
(816)753-1101 daily closing prices

Mid America Commodity Exchange
MACE
444 West Jackson Boulevard
Chicago, IL 60606
PH: (312)341-3000
(800)572-3276

Governmental Agencies and Regulatory Bodies

Commodity Futures Trading Commission
CFTC
2033 K Street NW
Washington, DC 20581
PH: (202)254-6387

Department of the Treasury
13th and C Streets, SW
Washington, DC 20228
PH: (202)622-2000

Securities Industry Conference on Arbitration
SICA
New York Stock Exchange, Inc.
11 Wall Street
New York, NY 10005
PH: (212)656-2772

U.S. Securities and Exchange Commission
450 5th Street NW
Washington, DC 20549
PH: (202)272-7450

Government National Mortgage Association (GNMA)
451 7th Street S.W.
Room 6224
Washington, DC 20410
PH: (202)708-0926

Federal National Mortgage Association (FNMA)
3900 Wisconsin Avenue
Washington, DC 20016
PH: (202)752-7000

National Association of Securities Dealers, Inc.
NASD
District Office #12
1 World Trade Center
New York, NY 10048
PH: (212)839-6251

NASD
District Office #1
1 Union Square
Suite 1911
Seattle, WA 98101
PH: (206)624-0790

NASD
District Office #2
425 California Street
Room 1400
San Francisco, CA 94101
PH: (415)781-3434

NASD
District Office #2S
727 West 7th Street
Los Angeles, CA 90017
PH: (213)627-2122

NASD
District Office #3
1401 17th Street
Suite 700
Denver, CO 80202
PH: (303)298-7234

NASD
District Office #4
911 Main Street
Suite 2230
Kansas City, MO 64105
PH: (816)421-5700

NASD
District Office #5
1004 Richards Building
New Orleans, LA 70112
PH: (504)522-6527

NASD
District Office #6
1999 Bryan Street
14th Floor
Dallas, TX 75201
PH: (214)969-7050

NASD
District Office #7
250 Piedmont Avenue NE
Atlanta, GA 30308
PH: (404)239-6100

NASD
District Office #8
3 First National Plaza
Suite 1680
Chicago, IL 60602
PH: (312)236-7222

NASD
District Office #9
1940 East 6th Street
5th Floor
Cleveland, OH 44114
PH: (216)694-4545

NASD
District Office #10
1735 K Street NW
Washington, DC 20006
PH: (202)728-8400

NASD
District Office #11
1818 Market Street
12th Floor
Philadelphia, PA 19103
PH: (215)665-1180

NASD
District Office #13
50 Milk Street
Boston, MA 02109
PH: (617)439-4404

Federal Reserve Banks

Atlanta
Federal Reserve Bank of Atlanta
104 Marietta Street, N.W.
Atlanta, GA 30301
PH: (404)521-8500

Boston
Federal Reserve Bank of Boston
600 Atlantic Avenue
Boston, MA 02106
PH: (617)973-3000

Chicago
Federal Reserve Bank of Chicago
230 South LaSalle Street
Chicago, IL 60690
PH: (312)322-5322

Cleveland
Federal Reserve Bank of Cleveland
1455 East Sixth Street
Cleveland, OH 44101
PH: (216)579-2000

Dallas
Federal Reserve Bank of Dallas
400 South Akard Street
Dallas, TX 75222
PH: (214)651-6111

Kansas City
Federal Reserve Bank of Kansas City
925 Grand Avenue
Kansas City, MO 64198
PH: (816)881-2000

Minneapolis
Federal Reserve Bank of Minneapolis
250 Marquette Avenue
Minneapolis, MN 55480
PH: (612)340-2345

New York
Federal Reserve Bank of New York
33 Liberty Street
New York, NY 10045
PH: (212)791-6134

Philadelphia
Federal Reserve Bank of Philadelphia
100 North Sixth Street
Philadelphia, PA 19106
PH: (215)574-6000

Richmond
Federal Reserve Bank of Richmond
701 East Byrd Street
Richmond, VA 23261
PH: (804)643-1250

St. Louis
Federal Reserve Bank of St. Louis
411 Locust Street
St. Louis, MO 63166
PH: (314)444-8444

San Francisco
Federal Reserve Bank of San Francisco
101 Market Street
San Francisco, CA 94120
PH: (415)974-2000

U.S. State Securities Regulators

Alabama
Securities Commissioner
10th Floor
100 Commerce Street
Montgomery, AL 36130
PH: (205)261-2984

Alaska
Banking, Securities & Corporations Division
Commerce & Economic Development Department
Pouch D
Juneau, AK
PH: (907)465-2521

Arizona
Securities Division
Corporation Commission
1200 West Washington
Phoenix, AZ 85007
PH: (602)255-4242

Arkansas
Securities Commissioner
Suite 4B-206
#1 Capitol Mall
Little Rock, AR 72201
PH: (501)371-1011

California
Securities Commissioner
Department of Corporations
Suite 205
1025 P Street
Sacramento, CA 95814
PH: (916)445-8200

Colorado
Division of Securities
Department of Regulatory Agencies
1560 Broadway
Suite 1450
Denver, CO 80203
PH: (303)866-2607

Connecticut
Securities and Business Investments
Department of Banking
44 Capitol Avenue
Hartford, CT 06106
PH: (203)566-4560

Delaware
Secretary of State
Townsend Building
Dover, DE 19901
PH: (302)736-4111

District of Columbia
Deputy Mayor for Financial Management
Suite 423
1350 Pennsylvania Avenue, NW
Washington, DC 20004
PH: (202)727-2476

Florida
Securities Division
Department of Banking and Finance
The Capitol
Tallahassee, FL 32301
PH: (904)488-9805

Georgia
Securities Commissioner
Suite 802W
2 Martin Luther King Jr. Drive
Atlanta, GA 30334
PH: (404)656-2894

Hawaii
Business Registration Division
Commerce and Consumer Affairs Department
1010 Richards Street
Honolulu, HI 96813

IdahoDepartment of Finance
700 West State Street
Boise, ID
PH: (208)334-3313

Illinois
Secretary of State
213 State House
Springfield, IL 62706
PH: (217)782-2201

Indiana
Securities Commissioner
Suite 560
1 North Capitol Street
Indianapolis, IN 46204
PH: (317)232-6681

Iowa
Securities Division
Insurance Department
Lucas Stone Office Building
Des Moines, IA 50319
PH: (515)281-4441

Kansas
Securities Commissioner
Suite 501
109 West Ninth Street
Topeka, KS 66612
PH: (913)296-3307

Kentucky
Financial Institutions Department
Public Protection and Regulation Cabinet
911 Leawood Drive
Frankfort, KY 40601
PH: (502)564-3390

Louisiana
Department of the Treasury
P.O. Box 44154
Baton Rouge, LA 70804
PH: (514)342-0010

Maine
Bureau of Banking, Business,
Occupational and Professional Regulations Department
Suite 36
State House Station
Augusta, ME 04333
PH: (207)289-3231

Maryland
Division of Securities
Office of the Attorney General
3rd Floor
7 North Calvert Street
Baltimore, MD 21202
PH: (301)576-6360

Massachusetts
Securities Division
Office of Secretary of Commonwealth
Suite 1719
1 Ashburton Place
Boston, MA 02133
PH: (617)727-7190

Michigan
Securities Division
Department of Commerce
6546 Mercantile Way
Lansing, MI 48909
PH: (517)373-0485

Minnesota
Registration and Licensing Division
Department of Commerce
5th Floor
Metro Square Building
St. Paul, MN 55101
PH: (612)296-2594

Mississippi
Securities Division
Office of Secretary State
401 Mississippi Street
Jackson, MS 39201
PH: (601)359-1350

Missouri
Division of Securities
Office of Secretary of State
Truman Building
Box 778
Jefferson City, MO 65102
PH: (314)751-4136

Montana
Securities Division
Office of State Auditor
Capitol Station
Helena, MT 59620
PH: (406)444-2040

Nebraska
Department of Banking and Finance
P.O. Box 95006
301 Centennial Mall South
Lincoln, NE 68509
PH: (402)471-2171

Nevada
Securities and Fraud Division
Office of Secretary of State
State Capitol
Carson City, NV 89710
PH: (702)885-5203

New Hampshire
Division of Securities
Department of Insurance
169 Manchester Street
Concord, NH 03301
PH: (603)271-2261

New Jersey
Bureau of Securities
Department of Law and Public Safety
Suite 308
80 Mulberry Street
Newark, NJ 07102
PH: (201)648-2040

New Mexico
Securities Division
Regulation and Licensing Department
Lew Wallace Building
Santa Fe, NM 87503
PH: (505)827-7750

New York
Bureau of Investor Protection and Securities
2 World Trade Center
New York, NY 10047
PH: (212)488-5389

North Carolina
Division of Securities
Office of Secretary of State
Suite 302
300 North Salisbury Street
Raleigh, NC 27611
PH: (919)733-3924

North Dakota
Securities Commissioner's Office
9th Floor
State Capitol
Bismarck, ND 58505
PH: (701)224-2910

Ohio
Division of Securities
Department of Commerce
3rd Floor
2 Nationwide Plaza
Columbus, OH 43215
PH: (614)466-3440

Oklahoma
Securities Commissioner
2915 North Lincoln Boulevard
Oklahoma, OK 73105
PH: (405)521-2451

Oregon
Division of Securities
Department of Commerce
158 12th Street N.E.
Salem, OR 97310
PH: (503)378-4385

Pennsylvania
Securities Commissioner
14th Floor
333 Market Street
Harrisburg, PA 17120
PH: (717)787-6828

Puerto Rico
Securities Commissioner
Department of the Treasury
P.O. Box 3508
San Juan, PR 00904
PH: (809)723-1122

Rhode Island
Banking Division
100 North Main Street
Providence, RI 02903
PH: (401)277-2405

South Carolina
Secretary of State
P.O. Box 11350
Columbia, SC 29211
PH: (803)758-2744

South Dakota
Division of Securities
Commerce and Regulations Department
1st Floor
State Capitol
Pierre, SD 57501
PH: (605)773-3177

Tennessee
Securities Division
Department of Commerce and Insurance
614 Tennessee Building
Nashville, TN 37219
PH: (615)741-2947

Texas
Securities Board
P.O. Box 13167
Capitol Station
Austin, TX 78711
PH: (512)474-2233

Utah
Securities Commissioner's Office
Department of Business Regulation
160 East 300 South
Salt Lake City, UT 84110
PH: (801)530-6600

Vermont
Securities Commissioner
Department of Banking and Insurance
120 State Street
Montpelier, VT 05602
PH: (802)828-3301

Virginia
State Corporation Commissioner
13th Floor
Jefferson Building
Richmond, VA 23219
PH: (804)786-3601

Virgin Islands of the United States
Corporations and Trade Names Division
Office of the Lieutenant Governor
P.O. Box 450
St. Thomas, VI 00801
PH: (809)774-2991

Washington
Securities Division
Department of Licensing
Highways-Licensing Building
Olympia, WA 98504
PH: (206)753-6928

West Virginia
Securities Division
Office of State Auditor
W-100 State Capitol Complex
Charleston, WV 25305
PH: (304)348-2257

Wisconsin
Commissioner of Securities
P.O. Box 1768
111 West Wilson Street
Madison, WI 53701
PH: (608)266-3433

Wyoming
Secretary of State
State Capitol
Cheyenne, WY 82002
PH: (307)777-7378

Associations

AIMR
Association for Investment Management and Research
P.O. Box 7947
Chartollesville, VA 22906
PH: (804)977-5724

Seminars, books, journals, etc.

The Research Foundation of the Institute of Chartered
Financial   Analysts
P.O. Box 3668
Chartollesville, VA 22903
PH: (804)977-6600

Research, books, monographs.

AAII
American Association of Individual Investors
625 N. Michigan Avenue
Chicago, IL 60611
PH: (312)280-0170

Newsletters, books, seminars, tapes.

National Association of Investors Corporation
1515 E. Eleven Mile Road
Royal Oak, MI 48067
PH: (313)543-0612

Newsletters.

Commodities Educational Institute (CEI)
219 Parkade
Cedar Falls, IA 50613
PH: (800)221-4352
    (319)277-6341

Future Industry Association (FIA)
1825 Eye Street, N.W.
Suite 1040
Washington, DC 20006
PH: (202)466-5460

National Futures Association (NFA)
200 W. Madison Street
Suite 1600
Chicago, IL 60606
PH: (312)781-1300

Public Securities Association (PSA)
40 Broad Street
New York, NY 10004
PH: (212)809-7000

College for Financial Planning
9725 E. Hampden Avenue
Denver, CO 80231
PH: (303)755-7101

Financial Executives Institute
10 Madison Avenue
Morristown, NJ 07960
PH: (201)898-4600

International Association for Financial Planning
Two Concourse Parkway
Suite 800
Atlanta, GA 30328
PH: (404)395-1605

No-Load Mutual Fund Association
11 Penn Plaza
New York, NY 10001
PH: (212)563-4540

Securities Industry Association
120 Broadway
New York, NY 10271
PH: (212)608-1500

Corporations

Standard and Poors
25 Broadway
New York, NY 10004
PH: (800) 777-4858
(212) 208-8768

Research, rating services, on-line services.

Moody's Investor Service
99 Church Street
New York, NY 10007
PH: (800)342-5647
(212) 553-0300

Research, rating services, on-line services.

Value Line Publishing
711 Third Avenue
New York, NY 10017-4064
PH: (800)633-2252
(212) 687-3965

Research, performance rating services, on-line services.

Dow Jones and Company, Inc.
200 Liberty Street
World Financial Center
New York, NY 10281
PH: (800) 628-9320

On-line services, publications.

General Reference

Barron's Finance and Investment Handbook

John Downes and Jordan Elliot Goodman
Barron's (Publishing)
250 Wireless Boulevard
Hauppauge, NY 11788
PH: (516) 434-3311
Published 1990
Cost: $26.95

The Business One Irwin Business & Investment
Almanac, 1991

Sumner N. Levine
Business One Irwin
1818 Ridge Road
Homewood, IL 60430
PH: (800) 634-3966
(708) 206-2700
FAX: (708) 798-1490
Published 1991
Cost: $40.00

Dictionary of Finance and Investment Terms

John Downes & Jordan Elliot Goodman
Barron's Educational Series, Inc.
P.O. Box 8040
250 Wireless Blvd.
Hauppauge, NY 11788
PH: (800) 645-3476
Published 1987
Cost: $8.95

The Money Encyclopedia

Harvey Rachin, Editor
Available through Fraser Publishing
P.O. Box 494
Burlington, VT 05402
PH: (802)658-0322
Published 1984
Cost: $26.50

The Mutual Fund Encyclopedia

Gerald W. Perritt
Dearborn Financial Publishing, Inc.
520 N. Dearborn Street
Chicago, IL 60610
Published 1990
Cost: $27.95

The New Encyclopedia of Stock Market Techniques

Michael L. Burke, Editor
Available through Fraser Publishing
P.O. Box 494
Burlington, VT 05402
PH: (802)658-0322
Published 1985 (4th supplement)
Cost: $60.00

The Wall Street Dictionary

R. J. & Robert L. Shook
New York Institute of Finance
2 Broadway
New York, NY 10004
Published 1990
Cost: $14.95

Words of Wall Street: 2000 Investment Terms Defined

Allan H. Pessin & Joseph A. Ross
Business One Irwin
1818 Ridge Road
Homewood, IL 60430
PH: (800) 634-3966
(708) 206-2700
FAX: (708) 798-1490
Published 1983
Cost: $11.95

Cross Reference Index

OPTIONS

Newsletter and Chart Services

MUTUAL FUNDS

Newsletter and Chart Services

FUTURES AND COMMODITIES

Newsletter and Chart Services

Computer and Quote Services

INVESTMENT PLANNING

Newsletter and Chart Services

Computer and Quote Services

About the Author

Spencer D. McGowan is a financial advisor and Vice President with Rauscher Pierce Refsnes, Inc., a leading investment firm in Dallas. He has counseled thousands of investors.

Previously, he was an account executive with PaineWebber where he developed a computerized Account Review System for individual clients. He was the youngest advisor to earn a position in the PaineWebber Leadership Development Program.

Mr. McGowan wrote *The Do-It-Yourself Guide to Investment Information* in response to the need of individual investors for a comprehensive guide to financial information.

Note from the Author

I plan to update *The Do-It-Yourself Guide to Investment Information* every two years. Please contact me if you have new entries to add or changes to be made on existing entries: Spencer McGowan, (214) 788-3911.

About the Publisher

PROBUS PUBLISHING COMPANY

Probus Publishing Company fills the informational needs of today's business professional by publishing authoritative, quality books on timely and relevant topics, including:

- Investing
- Futures/Options Trading
- Banking
- Finance
- Marketing and Sales
- Manufacturing and Project Management
- Personal Finance, Real Estate, Insurance and Estate Planning
- Entrepreneurship
- Management

Probus books are available at quantity discounts when purchased for business, educational or sales promotional use. For more information, please call the Director, Corporate/Institutional Sales at 1-800-PROBUS-1, or write:

Director, Corporate/Institutional Sales
Probus Publishing Company
1925 N. Clybourn Avenue
Chicago, Illinois 60614
FAX (312) 868-6250